THE SQUATTER AND THE DON

This text was originally published in the US
in the year 1885. The text is in the public domain.
The edits and layout of this version are Copyright © 2023
By Bergenline Press. This publication has no affiliation with the
original Author or publication company. The publishers have made
all reasonable efforts to ensure this book is in the Public Domain in
any and all territories it has been published, and apologise for any
omissions or errors made. Corrections may be made to
future printings or electronic publications.

Printed or published to the highest ethical standard.

BERGENLINE
... PRESS ...

The Squatter and the Don

By María Amparo Ruiz de Burton

United States
1885

CONTENTS

CHAPTER I. 1
   Squatter Darrell Reviews the Past. 1

CHAPTER II. 8
   The Don's View of the Treaty of Guadalupe Hidalgo. 8

CHAPTER III. 15
   Pre-empting under the Law. 15

CHAPTER IV. 21
   Efforts to Right the Wrong. 21

CHAPTER V. 30
   The Don in his Broad Acres. 30

CHAPTER VI. 38
   Naughty Dog Milord an Important Factor. 38

CHAPTER VII. 45
   From Alameda to San Diego. 45

CHAPTER VIII. 51
   Victoriano and His Sister. 51

CHAPTER IX. 57
   Clarence is the Bearer of Joyful News. 57

CHAPTER X. 64
   But Clarence Must Not be Encouraged. 64

CHAPTER XI. 72
   George is a Christian Gentleman. 72

CHAPTER XII. 79
   Why the Appeal was Not Dismissed. 79

CHAPTER XIII. 85

 At San Francisco. 85

CHAPTER XIV. 92
 Of Miscellaneous Incidents. 92

CHAPTER XV. 98
 Journeying Overland. 98

CHAPTER XVI. 102
 Spanish Land Grants Viewed Retrospectively. 102

CHAPTER XVII. 110
 Doña Josefa at Home. 110

CHAPTER XVIII. 119
 At Newport. 119

CHAPTER XIX. 126
 In New York. 126

CHAPTER XX. 134
 At the Capitol. 134

CHAPTER XXI. 142
 Looking at the Receding Dome. 142

CHAPTER XXII. 148
 Perplexities at Alamar. 148

CHAPTER XXIII. 156
 Home Again. 156

CHAPTER XXIV. 162
 The Brewers of Mischief. 162

CHAPTER XXV. 169
 The Squatter and the Don. 169

CHAPTER XXVI. 177
 Mrs. Darrell's View of Our Land Laws. 177

CHAPTER XXVII. 185
 Darrell Astonishes Himself. 185

CHAPTER XXVIII.	193
Shall it be Forever?	193
CHAPTER XXIX.	200
Hasty Decisions Repented Leisurely.	200
CHAPTER XXX.	208
Effect of Bad Precept and Worse Example.	208
CHAPTER XXXI.	217
A Snow Storm.	217
CHAPTER XXXII.	224
A False Friend Sent to Deceive the Southerners.	224
CHAPTER XXXIII.	231
San Diego's Sentence is Irrevocable.	231
CHAPTER XXXIV.	239
The Sins of Our Legislators!	239
CHAPTER XXXV.	248
The Fashion of Justice in San Diego.	248
CHAPTER XXXVI.	258
Clarence and George with the Hod-carrier.	258
CHAPTER XXXVII	269
Reunited at Last.	269
CONCLUSION.	279
Out with the Invader.	279
DETAILED HISTORICAL CONTEXT	289

CHAPTER I.

Squatter Darrell Reviews the Past.

"To be guided by good advice, is to profit by the wisdom of others; to be guided by experience, is to profit by wisdom of our own," said Mrs. Darrell to her husband, in her own sweet, winning way, as they sat alone in the sitting room of their Alameda farm house, having their last talk that evening, while she darned his stockings and sewed buttons on his shirts. The children (so-called, though the majority were grown up) had all retired for the night. Mr. and Mrs. Darrell sat up later, having much to talk about, as he would leave next day for Southern California, intending to locate— somewhere in a desirable neighborhood— a homestead claim.

"Therefore," continued Mrs. Darrell, seeing that her husband smoked his pipe in silence, adding no observations to her own, "let us this time be guided by our own past history, William— our experience. In other words, let us be wise, my husband."

"By way of variety, you mean," said he smiling. "That is, as far as I am concerned, because I own, frankly, that had I been guided by your advice— your wisdom— we would be much better off to-day. You have a right to reproach me."

"I do not wish to do anything of the kind. I think reproaches seldom do good."

"No use in crying over spilt milk, eh?"

"That is not my idea, either. On the contrary, if by '*milk*' it is meant all or any earthly good whatever, it is the '*spilt milk*' that we should lament. There is no reason to cry for the milk that has not been wasted, the good that is not lost. So let us cry for the *spilt milk*, by all means, if by doing so we learn how to avoid spilling any more. Let us cry for the *spilt milk*, and remember how, and where, and when, and why, we spilt it. Much wisdom is learnt through tears, but none by forgetting our lessons."

"But how can a man learn when he is born a fool?"

"Only an idiot is, truly speaking, a born fool; a fool to such a degree that he cannot act wisely if he will. It is only when *perversity* is added to foolishness, that a being— not an idiot— is utterly a fool. To persist in acting wrongfully, that is the real folly. To reject good counsel, either of one's own good thoughts or the good thoughts of others. But to act foolishly by deciding hastily, by lack of mature reflection, that I should only call a foolish mistake. So, then, if we have been foolish, let us at least utilize our foolishness by drawing from it lessons of wisdom for the future. We cannot conscientiously plead that we are born fools when we see our errors."

Mr. Darrell smilingly bowed, and with a voice much softer than his usual stentorian tones, said:

"I understand, little wife, but I fear that my streak of perversity is a broad one, and has solely been the bane of my life; it has a fatality accompanying it. I have often seen the right way to act, and yet I have gone with my eyes wide open to do the wrong thing. And this, too, not meaning to do harm to any one, nor wishing to be malicious or mean. I don't know what power impelled me. But if you will forgive my past wickedness, I'll try to do better."

"Don't say that. Don't speak of your wickedness, for real wickedness is perversity. You have acted wrongly at times, when you have misapplied your rights and the rights of others, but you have not intentionally done wrong. You are not perverse; don't say that."

"In a few days it will be twenty-four years since we crossed the plains with our three babies, in our caravan of four wagons, followed by our fine horses and choice Durham cows. I firmly believed then, that with my fine stock and my good bank account, and broad government lands, free to all Americans, I should have given you a nice home before I was five years older; that I would have saved money and would be getting more to make us rich before I was old. But see, at the end of twenty-four years, where and how do I find myself? I am still poor, all I have earned is the name of '*Squatter.*' That pretty name (which I hate because you despise it) is what I have earned."

"Don't say that either, William. We will only recommence one of numerous fruitless discussions. We are not poor, because we have enough to live in comfort, and I do not despise the name of Squatter, for it is harmless enough, but I do certainly disapprove of acts done by men because they are squatters, or to become squatters. They have caused much trouble to people who never harmed them."

"They, too, the poor squatters, have suffered as much distress as they have caused, the poor hard-worked toilers."

"That is very true, but I am afraid I shall never be able to see the necessity of any one being a squatter in this blessed country of plentiful broad acres, which a most liberal government gives away for the asking."

"That's exactly it. We aren't squatters. We are '*settlers.*' We take up land that belongs to us, American citizens, by paying the government price for it."

"Whenever you take up government land, yes, you are 'settlers,' but not when you locate claims on land belonging to any one else. In that case, you must accept the epithet of '*Squatter.*'"

Darrell set his teeth so tightly, that he bit a little chip off his pipe. Mrs. Darrell went on as if she had not observed her husband's flash of irritation.

"But I hope we will never more deserve such name; I trust that before you locate any homestead claim in Southern California, you will first inform yourself, very carefully, whether any one has a previous claim. And more specially, I beg of you, do not go on a Mexican grant unless you buy the land from the owner. This I beg of you specially, and must *insist upon it.*"

"And how am I to know who is the owner of a rancho that has been rejected, for instance?"

"If the rancho is still in litigation, don't buy land in it, or if you do, buy title from the original grantee, on fair conditions and clear understanding."

"I don't know whether that can be done in the Alamar rancho, which I am going to see, and I know it has been rejected. But of one thing you can rest assured, that I shall not forget our sad experience in Napa and Sonoma valleys, where— after years of hard toil— I had to abandon our home and lose the earnings of years and years of hard work."

"That is all I ask, William. To remember our experience in Napa and Sonoma. To remember, also, that we are no longer young. We cannot afford to throw away another twenty years of our life; and really and truly, if you again go into a Mexican grant, William, I shall not follow you there willingly. Do not expect it of me; I shall only go if you compel me."

"Compel you!" he exclaimed, laughing. "Compel you, when you know I have obeyed you all my life."

"Oh! no, William, not all your life, for you were well grown before I ever saw you."

"I mean ever since I went to Washington with my mind made up to jump off the train coming back, if you didn't agree to come North to be my commandant."

"I don't think I have been a very strict disciplinarian," she said, smiling. "I think the subaltern has had pretty much his own way."

"Yes, when he thinks he might. But when the commandant pulls the string, by looking sad or offended, then good-by to the spirit and independence of the subaltern."

"One thing I must not forget to ask you;" she said, going back to the point of their digression, "and it is, not to believe what those men have been telling you about the Alamar rancho having been finally rejected. You know John Gasbang could never speak the truth, and years have not made him more reliable. As for Miller, Hughes and Mathews, they are dishonest enough, and though not so brazen as Gasbang, they will misrepresent facts to induce you to go with them, for they want you with them."

"I know they do; I see through all that. But I see, too, that San Diego is sure to have a railroad direct to the Eastern States. Lands will increase in value immediately; so I think, myself, I had better take time by the forelock and get a good lot of land in the Alamar grant, which is quite near town."

"But, are you sure it is finally rejected?"

"I saw the book, where the fact is recorded. Isn't that enough?"

"Yes, if there has been no error."

"Always the same cautious Mary Moreneau, who tortured me with her doubts and would not have me until Father White took compassion on me," said he, smiling, looking at her fondly, for his thoughts reverted back to those days when Miss Mary was *afraid* to marry him; but, after all, he won her and brought her all the way from Washington to his New England home.

William Darrell was already a well-to-do young farmer in those days, a bachelor twenty-eight to thirty years of age, sole heir to a flourishing New England farm, and with a good account in a Boston bank, when Miss Mary Moreneau came to New England from Washington to visit her aunt, Mrs. Newton. As Mrs. Newton's husband was William Darrell's uncle, nothing was more natural than for Mary to meet him at his uncle's house. Nobody expected that William would fall in love with her, as he seemed to be proof against Cupid's darts. The marriageable maidens of William's neighborhood had in vain tried to attract the obdurate young farmer, who seemed to enjoy no other society than that of his uncle Newton and his wife.

But Mary came and William surrendered at once. She, however, gave him no encouragement. Her coldness seemed only to inflame his love the more, until Miss Moreneau thought it was best to shorten her visit and return home about the middle of September.

"Why are you to return home so early?" Darrell asked Mary, after Mrs. Newton had informed him of Mary's intention of going.

"Because I think it is best," she answered.

"Why is it best?"

"For several reasons."

"May I be permitted to ask what are those reasons?"

"Certainly. One reason is, that as I came to see my aunt and at the same time to rest and improve my health, and all those objects have been accomplished, I might as well go home. Then, my other aunt, with whom I reside, is not feeling well. She went to spend the summer in Virginia, but writes that her health has not improved much, and she will soon come back to Washington. Then some of my pupils will want to recommence their lessons soon, and I want to have some little time to myself before I begin to work. You know, Mr. Darrell, I teach to support myself."

"Yes, only because you have a notion to do it."

"A notion! Do you think I am rich?"

"No, but there is no need of your working."

"It is a need to me to feel independent. I don't want to be supported by my aunts, while I know how to earn my own living."

"Miss Mary, please, I beg of you, let me have the happiness of taking care of you. Be my wife, I am not a rich man, but I have enough to provide for you."

"Mr. Darrell, you surprise me. I thank you for the compliment you pay me with your honorable offer, but I have no wish to get married."

"Do you reject me, Miss Mary? Tell me one thing; tell me truly, do you care for any one else?"

"No, I care for nobody. I don't want to marry."

"But you will marry some time. If you knew how very miserable you make me, I think you would not have the heart to refuse me."

"You will get over it. I am going soon. Forget me."

Darrell made no answer. He staggered out of the room and did not return until the following week, when Mary had left for Washington, accompanied by Letitia, her colored servant (called Tisha), who was devotedly attached to her.

Darrell had become rather taciturn and less sociable than ever, Mrs. Newton noticed, and since Mary left he seemed to lose flesh and all his spirits, and passed the winter as if life were a burden to him. But when spring came, he brightened up a little, though he felt far from happy. About that time Mrs. Newton had a letter from Mary, saying that she was going to spend vacation in Maryland with her other aunt, and Tisha for her escort.

"She don't come here, because she fears I shall pester her life with my visits. As she knows I can't keep away from her, she keeps away from you. She hates me. I suppose you, too, will take to hating me, by and by," said Darrell, when he heard that Mary was not coming that summer.

"No danger of that, William," Mrs. Newton replied.

"Yes, there is. You ought to hate me for driving her away. I hate myself worse than I hate the devil."

"William, you mustn't feel so. It isn't right."

"I know it. But when did I ever do anything right, I'd like to know? I wish I could hate her as I hate myself, or as she hates me."

"William, she does not hate you."

"How do you know she don't?"

"Because she would have told me. She is very truthful."

"I know it. She gave me my walking papers in a jiffy. I wish I could hate her."

"William, do you promise not to get angry, if I tell you why Mary declined your offer?"

"Say on. You couldn't well make a burning furnace any hotter. I am too mad already."

"Well, I'll tell you. She likes you, but is afraid of you."

"Afraid? afraid?" said he, aghast— "why! that is awful! I, an object of fear, when I worship the ground she treads on! But, how? What have I done? When did I frighten her?"

"At no particular time; but often you gave her the impression that you have a high temper, and she told me, 'If I loved Mr. Darrell better than my life, I wouldn't marry him, for I could never be happy with a man of a violent temper.' Then she spoke, too, of her being a Roman Catholic and you a Protestant."

"But you are a Catholic and uncle is Protestant."

"Certainly, I think the barrier is not insuperable."

"So, my temper frightened her! It is awful!" He mused in silence for a few minutes and then left the room.

About an hour after, he returned dressed for traveling, carrying a satchel in one hand and a tin box under his arm. He put the box on the table, saying:

"Aunt Newton, I am going away for a few days. Please take care of this box until I return or you hear from me. Good-by!" and he hurried away, for he had only barely time to catch the train going to New York.

Darrell was in New York for a few hours. He bought a finer suit of clothes, a very elegant light overcoat, hat and boots, and gloves to match, and thus equipped so elegantly that he hardly recognized himself, as he surveyed his figure in a large mirror of the furnishing store, where he was so metamorphosed, he took the night train for Washington.

It was early on a Sunday morning that Darrell arrived at Washington. He went to a hotel, entered his name, took a room, a bath and a breakfast, and then called a hack to go in search of Mary. He knew that was not an hour for calling, but he had *business* with Mary. His was no friendly visit; it was a matter of life and death with him.

He rang the bell, and presently he heard Tisha's flapping steps coming. "Lud a massa!" she exclaimed, stepping back. But recovering herself, said with true heartiness—

"Come in the parlor, please. It is true glad Miss Mary will be to see ye."

"Do you think so, Tisha?" he asked.

"I know it; no thinking about it, neither. She is going to mass; but she'll see you for a little while, anyway."

Opening the parlor door for Darrell to walk in, Tisha ran up stairs to Mary's room.

"Oh Miss Mary!" said she, "guess who is down stairs."

"I couldn't, Tish, being so early and on Sunday, but I heard a man's voice. Is it a gentleman?"

"You bet; ah! please excuse me, I mean sure as I live it is, and no other than Mr. Darrell, from New England."

"Ah!" said Miss Mary, affecting indifference, but her hands trembled as she tied her bonnet strings.

Darrell knew he must appear self-contained and not in the least impetuous, but when he saw those beautiful dark eyes of Mary's he forgot all his pretended calmness.

"Is my aunt well?" Mary began as she came in.

"Yes, yes, everybody is well; don't be alarmed at my coming, I know it must seem strange to you. Two days ago I had no idea of coming to Washington, but Miss Moreneau, your aunt told me you were not coming North this summer, and this news nearly drove me crazy."

"Oh, Mr. Darrell!"

"Wait, don't drive me off yet. Your aunt told me that you refused me because you believe I have a violent temper. Now, I am not going to deny that, but this I am going to say— That I have never violated my word, and never shall, and I make a most solemn oath to you, that if you will marry me you shall never have occasion to be made unhappy or displeased by my quick anger, because you will only have to remind me of this pledge, and I shall curb my temper, if it kills me."

"Mr. Darrell, I believe you are perfectly sincere in what you say, but a strong trait of character is not controlled easily. It is more apt to be uncontrollable."

"For God's sake don't refuse me, I feel I must kill myself if you spurn me. I don't want life without you."

"Don't say that," Mary said, trying to keep calm, but she felt as if being carried away in spite of herself, by the torrent of his impetuosity. She was afraid of him, but she liked him and she liked to be loved in that passionate rebellious way of his; she smiled, adding, "we must postpone this conversation for I must go to church, and it is quite a long walk there."

"The carriage that brought me is at the door, take it, and don't walk, it is quite warm out."

"Will you go with me to church? You see, that is another obstacle; the difference of religions."

"Indeed, that is no obstacle; your religion tells you to pity me."

"We will talk to Father White about that."

"Then Mary, my beloved, will you give me hope?"

"And will you really try to control your anger when you feel it is getting the mastery over you?"

"I will, so help me God," said he, lifting his hand.

"Take care, that is an oath."

"I know it, and mean it," said he, much moved.

They went to church together. After church, Mary had a few moments conversation with her pastor. She explained everything to him. "Do you love him, my child," asked the good father, knowing the human heart only too well. Mary blushed and said—

"Yes, father, I believe I do."

"Very well, send him to see me to-morrow morning."

Darrell had a long talk with Father White, and promised solemnly not to coerce or influence his wife to change her religion, and that should their union be blessed with children, they should be baptized and brought up Catholics.

And his union was blessed. Mary made his New England home a paradise, and eight children, sharing largely their mother's fine qualities, filled to overflowing his cup of happiness.

CHAPTER II.

THE DON'S VIEW OF THE TREATY OF GUADALUPE HIDALGO.

If there had been such a thing as communicating by telephone in the days of '72, and there had been those magic wires spanning the distance between William Darrell's house in Alameda County and that of Don Mariano Alamar in San Diego County, with power to transmit the human voice for five hundred miles, a listener at either end would have heard various discussions upon the same subject, differentiated only by circumstances. No magic wires crossed San Francisco bay to bring the sound of voices to San Diego, but the law of necessity made the Squatter and the Don, distant as they were— distant in every way, without reckoning the miles between them— talk quite warmly of the same matter. The point of view was of course different, for how could it be otherwise? Darrell thought himself justified, and *authorized*, to "take up lands," as he had done before. He had had more than half of California's population on his side, and though the "*Squatter's Sovereignty*" was now rather on the wane, and the "*squatter vote*" was no longer the power, still, the squatters would not abdicate, having yet much to say about election times.

But Darrell was no longer the active squatter that he had been. He controlled many votes yet, but in his heart he felt the weight which his wife's sad eyes invariably put there when the talk was of litigating against a Mexican land title.

This time, however, Darrell honestly meant to take no land but what belonged to the United States. His promise to his wife was sincere, yet his coming to Southern California had already brought trouble to the Alamar rancho.

Don Mariano Alamar was silently walking up and down the front piazza of his house at the rancho; his hands listlessly clasped behind and his head slightly bent forward in deep thought. He had pushed away to one side the many arm-chairs and wicker rockers with which the piazza was furnished. He wanted a long space to walk. That his meditations were far from agreeable, could easily be seen by the compressed lips, slight frown, and sad gaze of his mild and beautiful blue eyes. Sounds of laughter, music and dancing came from the parlor; the young people were entertaining friends from town with their usual gay hospitality, and enjoying themselves heartily. Don Mariano, though already in his fiftieth year, was as fond of dancing as his sons and daughters, and not to see him come in and join the quadrille was so singular that his wife thought she must come out and inquire what could detain him. He was so absorbed in his thoughts that he did not hear her voice calling him—

"What keeps you away? Lizzie has been looking for you; she wants you for a partner in the lancers," said Doña Josefa, putting her arm under that of her husband, bending her head forward and turning it up to look into his eyes.

"What is the matter?" she asked, stopping short, thus making her husband come to a sudden halt. "I am sure something has happened. Tell me."

"Nothing, dear wife. Nothing has happened. That is to say, nothing new."

"More squatters?" she asked. Señor Alamar bent his head slightly, in affirmative reply.

"More coming, you mean?"

"Yes, wife; more. Those two friends of squatters Mathews and Hager, who were here last year to locate claims and went away, did not abandon their claims, but only went away to bring proselytes and their families, and a large invoice of them will arrive on to-morrow's steamer. The worst of it all is, that among the new comers is that terrible and most dangerous squatter William Darrell, who some years ago gave so much trouble to the Spanish people in Napa and Sonoma Counties, by locating claims there. John Gasbang wrote to Hogsden that besides Darrell, there will be six or seven other men bringing their families, so that there will be more rifles for my cattle."

"But, didn't we hear that Darrell was no longer a squatter, that he is rich and living quietly in Alameda?"

"Yes, we heard that, and it is true. He is quite well off, but Gasbang and Miller and Mathews went and told him that my rancho had been rejected, and that it is near enough to town to become valuable, as soon as we have a railroad. Darrell believed it, and is coming to locate here."

"Strange that Darrell should believe such men; I suppose he does not know how low they are."

"He ought to know them, for they were his teamsters when he crossed the plains in '48. That is, Miller, Mathews, Hughes and Hager, were his teamsters, and Gasbang was their cook— the cook for the hired men. Mrs. Darrell had a colored woman who cooked for the Darrell family; she despised Gasbang's cooking as we despise his character, I suppose."

Doña Josefa was silent, and holding to her husband's arm, took a turn with him up and down the piazza.

"Is it possible that there is no law to protect us; to protect our property; what does your lawyer say about obtaining redress or protection; is there no hope?" she asked, with a sigh.

"Protection for our land, or for our cattle, you mean?"

"For both, as we get it for neither," she said.

"In the matter of our land, we have to await for the attorney general, at Washington, to decide."

"Lizzie was telling Elvira, yesterday, that her uncle Lawrence is a friend of several influential people in Washington, and that George can get him to interest himself in having your title decided."

"But, as George is to marry my daughter, he would be the last man from whom I would ask a favor."

"What is that I hear about not asking a favor from me?" said George Mechlin, coming out on the piazza with Elvira on his arm, having just finished a waltz— "I am interested to know why you would not ask it."

"You know why, my dear boy. It isn't exactly the thing to bother you with my disagreeable business."

"And why not? And who has a better right? And why should it be a bother to me to help you in any way I can? My father spoke to me about a dismissal of an appeal, and I made a note of it. Let me see, I think I have it in my pocket now,"— said George, feeling in his breast pocket for his memorandum book,— "yes, here it is,— 'For uncle to write to the attorney general about dismissing the appeal taken by the squatters in the Alamar grant, against Don Mariano's title, which was approved.' Is that the correct idea? I only made this note to ask you for further particulars."

"You have it exactly. When I give you the number of the case, it is all that you need say to your uncle. What I want is to have the appeal dismissed, of course, but if the attorney general does not see fit to do so, he can, at least, remand back the case for a new trial. Anything rather than this killing suspense. Killing literally, for while we are waiting to have my title settled, the *settlers* (I don't mean to make puns), are killing my cattle by the hundred head, and I cannot stop them."

"But are there no laws to protect property in California?" George asked.

"Yes, some sort of laws, which in my case seem more intended to help the law-breakers than to protect the law-abiding," Don Mariano replied.

"How so? Is there no law to punish the thieves who kill your cattle?"

"There are some enactments so obviously intended to favor one class of citizens against another class, that to call them laws is an insult to law, but such as they are, we must submit to them. By those laws any man can come to my land, for instance, plant ten acres of grain, without any fence, and then catch my cattle which, seeing the green grass without a fence, will go to eat it. Then he puts them in a '*corral*' and makes me pay damages and so much per head for keeping them, and costs of legal proceedings and many other trumped up expenses, until for such little fields of grain I may be obliged to pay thousands of dollars. Or, if the grain fields are large enough to bring more money by keeping the cattle away, then the settler shoots the cattle at any time without the least hesitation, only taking care that no one sees him in the act of firing upon the cattle. He might stand behind a bush or tree and fire, but then he is not seen. No one can swear that they saw him actually kill the cattle, and no jury can convict him, for although the dead animals may be there, lying on the ground shot, still no one saw the settler kill them. And so it is all the time. I must pay damages and expenses of litigation, or my cattle get killed almost every day."

"But this is infamous. Haven't you— the cattle owners— tried to have some law enacted that will protect your property?" George asked. "It seems to me that could be done."

"It could be done, perhaps, if our positions were reversed, and the Spanish people— *'the natives'*— were the planters of the grain fields, and the Americans were the owners of the cattle. But as we, the Spaniards, are the owners of the Spanish— or Mexican— land grants and also the owners of the cattle ranchos, our State legislators will not make any law to protect cattle. They make laws *'to protect agriculture'* (they say proudly), which means to drive to the wall all owners of cattle ranchos. I am told that at this session of the legislature a law more strict yet will be passed, which will be ostensibly 'to protect agriculture,' but in reality to destroy cattle and ruin the native Californians. The agriculture of this State does not require legislative protection. Such pretext is absurd."

"I thought that the rights of the Spanish people were protected by our treaty with Mexico," George said.

"Mexico did not pay much attention to the future welfare of the children she left to their fate in the hands of a nation which had no sympathies for us," said Doña Josefa, feelingly.

"I remember," calmly said Don Mariano, "that when I first read the text of the treaty of Guadalupe Hidalgo, I felt a bitter resentment against my people; against Mexico, the mother country, who abandoned us— her children— with so slight a provision of obligatory stipulations for protection. But afterwards, upon mature reflection, I saw that Mexico did as much as could have been reasonably expected at the time. In the very preamble of the treaty the spirit of peace and friendship, which animated both nations, was carefully made manifest. That spirit was to be the *foundation* of the relations between the conqueror and conquered. How could Mexico have foreseen then that when scarcely half a dozen years should have elapsed the trusted conquerors would, *'In Congress Assembled,'* pass laws which were to be retroactive upon the defenceless, helpless, conquered people, in order to despoil them? The treaty said that our rights would be the same as those enjoyed by all other American citizens. But, you see, Congress takes very good care not to enact retroactive laws for Americans; laws to take away from American citizens the property which they hold *now*, already, with a recognized legal title. No, indeed. But they do so quickly enough with us— with us, the Spano-Americans, who were to enjoy equal rights, mind you, according to the treaty of peace. This is what seems to me a breach of faith, which Mexico could neither presuppose nor prevent."

"It is nothing else, I am sorry and ashamed to say," George said. "I never knew much about the treaty with Mexico, but I never imagined we had acted so badly."

"I think but few Americans know or believe to what extent we have been wronged by Congressional action. And truly, I believe that Congress itself did not anticipate the effect of its laws upon us, and how we would be despoiled, we, the conquered people," said Don Mariano, sadly.

"It is the duty of law-givers to foresee the effect of the laws they impose upon people," said Doña Josefa.

"That I don't deny, but I fear that the conquered have always but a weak voice, which nobody hears," said Don Mariano. "We have had no one to speak for us. By the treaty of Guadalupe Hidalgo the American nation pledged its honor to respect our land titles just the same as Mexico would have done. Unfortunately, however, the discovery of gold brought to California the riff-raff of the world, and with it a horde of land-sharks, all possessing the privilege of voting, and most of them coveting our lands, for which they very quickly began to clamor. There was, and still is, plenty of good government land, which any one can take. But no. The forbidden fruit is the sweetest. They do not want government land. They want the land of the Spanish people, because we 'have too much,' they say. So, to win their votes, the votes of the squatters, our representatives in Congress helped to pass laws declaring all lands in California open to pre-emption, as in Louisiana, for instance. Then, as a coating of whitewash to the stain on the nation's honor, a 'land commission' was established to examine land titles. Because, having pledged the national word to respect our rights, it would be an act of despoliation, besides an open violation of pledged honor, to take the lands without some pretext of a legal process. So then, we became obliged to present our titles before the said land commission to be examined and approved or rejected. While these legal proceedings are going on, the squatters locate their claims and raise crops on our lands, which they convert into money to fight our titles. But don't let me, with my disagreeable subject spoil your dance. Go back to your lancers, and tell Lizzie to excuse me," said Don Mariano.

Lizzie would not excuse him. With the privilege of a future daughter-in-law, she insisted that Don Mariano should be her partner in the lancers, which would be a far pleasanter occupation than to be walking up and down the porch thinking about squatters.

Don Mariano therefore followed Lizzie to their place in the dance. Mercedes sat at the piano to play for them. The other couples took their respective positions.

The well-balanced mind and kindly spirit of Don Mariano soon yielded to the genial influences surrounding him. He would not bring his trouble to mar the pleasure of others. He danced with his children as gaily as the gayest. He insisted that Mr. Mechlin, too, should dance, and this gentleman graciously yielded and led Elvira through a quadrille, protesting that he had not danced for twenty years.

"You have not danced because you were sick, but now you are well. Don't be lazy," said Mrs. Mechlin.

"You would be paying to San Diego climate a very poor compliment by refusing to dance now," George added.

"That is so, papa. Show us how well you feel," Lizzie said.

"I shall have to dance a hornpipe to do that," Mr. Mechlin answered, laughing.

To understand this remark better, the reader must know that Mr. James Mechlin had come to San Diego, four years previously, a living skeleton, not expected to last another winter. He had lost his health by a too close application to business, and when he sought rest and relaxation his constitution seemed permanently undermined. He tried the climate of Florida. He spent several years in Italy and in the south of France, but he felt no better. At last, believing his malady incurable, he returned to his New York home to die. In New York a friend, who also had been an invalid, but whose health had been restored in Southern California, advised him to try the salubrious air of San Diego. With but little hope, and only to please his family, Mr. Mechlin came to San Diego, and his health improved so rapidly that he made up his mind to buy a country place and make San Diego his home. William Mathews heard of this, and offered to sell his place on what Mr. Mechlin thought very moderate terms. A lawyer was employed to pass upon the title, and on his recommendation the purchase was made. Mr. Mechlin had the Mathews house moved back near the barn, and a new and much larger one built. When this was finished the Mechlins moved into it, and Mr. Mechlin devoted himself to cultivating trees and flowers, and his health was bettered every day. This was the compensation to his wife and two daughters for exiling themselves from New York; for it was exile to Caroline and Lizzie to give up their fine house in New York City to come and live on a California rancho.

Soon, however, these two young ladies passed their time more pleasantly, after making the acquaintance of the Alamar family, and soon their acquaintance ripened into friendship, to be made closer by the intended marriage of Gabriel— Don Mariano's eldest son— to Lizzie. Shortly after, George— Mr. Mechlin's only son— came on a visit, and when he returned to New York he was already engaged to Elvira, third daughter of Señor Alamar.

Now, George Mechlin was making his second visit to his family. He had found New York so very dull and stupid on his return from California that when Christmas was approaching he told his uncle and aunt— with whom he lived— that he wanted to go and spend Christmas and New Year's Day with his family in California.

"Very well; I wish I could go with you. Give my love to James, and tell him I am delighted at his getting so well," Mr. Lawrence Mechlin said, and George had his leave of absence. Mr. Lawrence Mechlin was president of the bank of which George was cashier, so it was not difficult for him to get the assistant cashier to attend to his duties when he was away, particularly as the assistant cashier himself was George's most devoted friend. George could have only twelve days in California, but to see Elvira for even so short a time he would have traveled a much longer distance.

Mr. James Mechlin affirmed repeatedly that he owed his improved health to the genial society of the Alamar family as much as to the genial climate of San Diego County. Mr. Mechlin, however, was not the only one who had paid the same tribute to that most delightful family, the most charming of which— the majority vote said— was Don Mariano himself. His nobility of character and great kindness of heart were well known to everybody.

The Alamar family was quite patriarchal in size, if the collateral branches be taken into account, for there were many brothers, nephews and nieces. These, however, lived in the adjoining rancho, and yet another branch in Lower California, in Mexico. Don Mariano's own immediate family was composed of his wife and six children, two sons and four daughters.

All of these, as we have seen, were having a dance. The music was furnished by the young ladies themselves, taking their turn at the piano, assisted by Madam Halier (Mercedes' French governess), who was always ready to play for the girls to dance. Besides the Mechlins, there were three or four young gentlemen from town, but there were so many Alamares (brothers, nieces and nephews, besides) that the room seemed quite well filled. Such family gatherings were frequent, making the Alamar house very gay and pleasant.

George Mechlin would have liked to prolong his visit, but he could not. He consoled himself looking forward to the ninth of June, when he would come again to make a visit of two months' duration. On his return East, before renewing his duties at the bank, he went to Washington to see about the dismissal of the appeal. Unfortunately, the attorney general had to absent himself about that time, and the matter being left with the solicitor general, nothing was done. George explained to Don Mariano how the matter was delayed, and his case remained undecided yet for another year longer.

CHAPTER III.

Pre-empting under the Law.

"All aboard for San Diego!" shouted a voice from a wagon, as it rumbled past Darrell, who walked leisurely with a satchel in his hand, swinging it unconsciously, lost in thought. He looked up and saw that the wagon whence the voice came carried ten or twelve men, sitting on trunks and packages and carpet-bags. These men Mathews and Gasbang had presented to him, saying that they were settlers already residing at the Alamar rancho, and others who were going down to take up claims, at the same time that he would locate his. Darrell looked at his future neighbors with feelings of anything but pleasure. The broad, vulgar face of Gasbang, with its square jaws, gray beard, closely clipped, but never shaved, his compressed, thin, bloodless lips, his small, pale, restless eyes and flat nose, Darrell soon recognized, though the wagon was going rapidly. Mathews' visage was equally noticeable for its ugliness, though of a different type; for his face was long and shaved; his nose was pinched and peaked and red; his cheeks were flabby; and his long, oily, dusty, hair dragged over his neck in matted, meshy locks, while a constant frown settled on his brow. As he was broad-shouldered and rather tall, his face seemed made for some other man much weaker than himself. His face looked mean and discontented, while his body seemed strong and self-reliant.

The wagon had arrived and gone away, and the men had walked aboard the boat, when Darrell, still swinging his satchel abstractedly, stood on the wharf looking at the steamer as if not quite resolved to go. He felt no sympathy, no liking, for any of those men with whom he was now associated.

It was different to have Gasbang as his hired man, as before, but now he was not under orders, and was much older. Years, moreover, had not improved his low nature. Darrell had no higher opinion of the others. He was sure these were not the sort of people whom his wife would like to have for neighbors. He felt self-accused and irresolute. A shout from Gasbang, who was observing him from the steamer's deck, made Darrell look up quickly, ashamed of having betrayed his irresolution. "I can return immediately, if things don't suit me," he thought, walking towards the gang-plank.

"Come on. Your luggage is all aboard, I took care of it," Gasbang said, coming to meet him. He snatched Darrell's satchel, in friendly obsequiousness, to carry it for him. "Come along; you'll be left," said he, and Darrell followed him, half-disgusted at his vulgar officiousness. "I got your berth for you. The steamer is so crowded, that men have to be crammed into rooms by the bunch, so you and I and Mathews must room together."

"That is all right," said Darrell, with a shiver of disgust, and went to take a seat on deck where he could be alone.

The bustle and hurry of getting off was over at last, and the steamer was furrowing her way through the spacious bay of San Francisco towards the Golden Gate. Groups of passengers stood here and there, admiring the beautiful harbor and its surrounding country. Darrell sat alone, fixing his gaze upon the receding verdure of Alameda County. Above that green, undulating line of diminishing hills, which seemed to fly from him, Darrell could see plainly one face, one form, beautiful to him as none other could be, the face and form of his wife, his beloved Mary. This was the first time he had ever left her for any longer time than a two days' absence, since they were married. Now he might be absent several months, for if he decided to locate in San Diego County, he would first build a house before he sent for his family. He would first send for Clarence— his eldest son— and then, when a comfortable home was prepared, the family would come.

The voyage down the coast was made safely. Darrell had managed to keep away from his fellow-travelers, to think of home unmolested.

It was a bright morning of January, 1872, when he stood far forward, watching the course of the steamer Orizaba, as she made her way around Point Loma, then between Ballast Point and the sandy peninsula, and passing by La Playa, came in sight of San Diego city.

"Here we are," said John Gasbang; "how do you like the looks of our little city, Mr. Darrell?"

"Very well; it is larger than I supposed, and the site of it seems very pleasant."

"Pleasant! I should say it was. A perfect slope, sir, as gentle and regular as if made to order. The best drained city in the world, sir, when we put in sewers. Too poor for that, yet, sir, but we are coming to it, sir, growing, growing, sir."

"When we get the railroad," added Mathews, with a mouth full of tobacco, spitting profusely on the deck.

"Exactly, and we'll soon have that. Our news from Washington is very encouraging. Tom Scott will visit us this summer," Gasbang said.

"I like a town with plenty of trees," said Darrell, with his gaze fixed on the approaching panorama, thinking that his wife would be pleased with the place, she being so fond of trees. "I had no idea you had so many trees about you. Many are small, yet, but all seem healthy."

"And health-giving trees, they are, too. Most of them are eucalyptus and pepper trees, the healthiest in the world. You never hear of any malarial fevers in San Diego, sir, never. Our perfect climate, the fine sloping ground of our town site, our eucalyptus trees, sea breezes and mountain air, make San Diego a most healthy little city," said Gasbang.

"That is an excellent recommendation, as life is not worth having without health," Darrell observed.

"We have it here," Hughes said. "A man has to be very imprudent not to keep well in our climate, sir. All we want now is a little stimulus of business prosperity, and the railroad is sure to bring us that. Then San Diego will be the best place on the coast for a residence."

The loud report of a cannon, close by, made Darrell jump and look around quickly, not knowing what that explosion could mean.

"That is our visiting card to the people of San Diego, to announce our coming," said the captain, laughingly. "I am sorry it startled you."

"That is nothing. I didn't know I had nerves. I believe that is what women call it. I was not expecting such a military salute," Darrell said.

"O yes, we always give it. The San Diego people are very military. At least, I should say the settlers on Señor Alamar's rancho are, as I hear they practice rifle shooting there all the time," the captain said, looking at Mathews and Gasbang.

"That is a shot at us," Gasbang answered, laughing.

"But it is a blank cartridge, meant not to hurt," the captain replied.

"The rifle practice is in dark nights," said a young Spaniard, who had been listening at what was said by the others.

"Or in the daytime, if the cattle deserve it," Mathews said.

"That is very creditable and brave, to shoot tame cows," the Spaniard rejoined.

"Perhaps you had better come and try it," Mathews returned.

"Thank you. It is the mischievous brutes I would like to shoot, not the good, useful cattle;" so saying, the Spaniard walked away, followed by the scowls of the settlers.

"That is impudence for you," Gasbang exclaimed.

"Those greasers ain't half crushed yet. We have to tame them like they do their mustangs, or shoot them, as we shoot their cattle," said Mathews.

"O, no. No such violent means are necessary. All we have to do is to take their lands, and finish their cattle," said Hughes, sneeringly, looking at Darrell for approval. But he did not get it. Darrell did not care for the Spanish population of California, but he did not approve of shooting cattle in the way which the foregoing conversation indicated. To do this, was useless cruelty and useless waste of valuable property, no matter to whom it might belong. To destroy it was a loss to the State. It was folly.

"Why must cattle be shot? Can't they be kept off, away from your crops without shooting them?" he asked.

"Not always. At first, that is, for the first three years after we located our claims," Gasbang said; "we had to shoot them all the time. Now the Don has sold a good many, or sent them to the mountains, so that few have been killed."

"I suppose fencing would be too expensive."

"Phew! It would be ruinous, impossible," Mathews said.

"Mr. Mechlin is the only one who has attempted to put up any fences," Romeo said, who had been listening in silence.

"He did so, because he is an old hypocrite," Mathews said.

"Because his daughter Lizzie is going to marry Gabriel Alamar, and of course, they have to be on friendly terms," said Hughes.

"That ain't the reason. He fenced a hundred acres the first year, and he never sows outside, so that he's not at all troubled by the Don's cattle," said Romeo.

"But Gabriel is going to marry Lizzie all the same, and the two families are as thick as can be. Old Mechlin has gone back on us. I wish he would go away," Mathews said.

"Why should he go? He paid a very good price for his farm, and has made many improvements," said Romeo.

"Who did he buy from?" asked Darrell.

"From me. I sold him that claim, and took up another a mile up the valley," said Mathews.

"And a good bargain it was, too," Romeo observed.

Mathews gave him a black look, but made no answer.

The steamer had now reached the wharf. The deck was filled with passengers and their baggage ready for shore. Pittikin, with wife and daughters blonde and freckled, and Hughes, with his wife and daughters dark and gypsy-looking, were all there, ready for their drive to Alamar.

There were several wagons, light and heavy, waiting to convey the newly-arrived and their luggage to the Alamar rancho. Darrell, having his choice of conveyances, preferred to go in a light wagon with Romeo Hancock, but Gasbang and Mathews joined him. Miller and Hager had come to meet their prodigal sons, who had been in San Francisco for several months, when they had permission to remain only a few weeks. But they had fallen into Peter Roper's company, and that individual had represented the fascinations of whiskey most alluringly to them, advising them to have a good time now that they had the opportunity. They yielded to the tempter, and now had returned home like repentant prodigals.

In a few hours Darrell was driving by Don Mariano Alamar's house, a one-story mansion on a low hill, with a broad piazza in front, and in the interior a court formed by two wings, and a row of rooms variously occupied at its back. That the house was commodious, Darrell could see. There was a flower garden in front. At the back there were several "*corrales*" for cattle and horses. At the foot of the hill, on the left, there was an orchard, and some grain fields enclosed with good fences.

Darrell took notice of all these particulars. He also noticed that there were females on the front piazza. He was taken to see the best unoccupied lands to make his selection. He ran his practiced eye over the valley from the highest point on the hill. He then came to the next bench; he stopped there, also, and finally came to the broad slope of the foothills.

"I think I'll locate here," said he, "if no one else has already filed a claim to this land."

This he said to his fellow-settlers, all being present, addressing all.

"I am sure I have no objection," said Hughes.

"Nor I, neither," said Gasbang. "What do you say, Pittikin and Mathews? Do you know *if* this land is located, or who done it?"

Mathews shook his head in the negative, and kept on chewing his tobacco in silence.

Pittikin said, "I reckon nobody is located here, and if they *done it*, why don't they leave stakes? They leave no stakes, no notice to settlers; they can't make any row if somebody else takes the land."

"Well, I want to respect everybody's right; so I want you all to bear witness, that I found no stakes or notices of anybody. I don't want to jump anybody's claim; I want a fair deal. I shall locate two claims here— one in my own name and one for my oldest son, Clarence," said Darrell.

"You'll take 320 acres?" asked Hughes.

"Yes, 320 acres,— according to law," replied Darrell.

"All right. Let us measure them now," said Gasbang. "We have time to mark the limits and put the corner stakes. I have a cord here in my wagon, which is a chain's length. That will do the business."

"That will do temporarily, I suppose; but I'll have the two claims properly surveyed afterwards according to law," Darrell said.

"Of course, you will. We all know you will do the fair thing by everybody, and follow the law strictly," said Hughes. In which opinion all concurred.

"Have you all made your selections?" Darrell asked Hughes.

"Yes; Pittikin and I will locate near Hancock. We like that valley; it is further off, but better soil," said Hughes. "My oldest boy will put a claim near me, and Miller's two boys have staked theirs also. I think we'll like that location better."

"I am glad you like it. I think this is good enough soil for me," Darrell said.

"It is good enough for anybody. The whole rancho is all good soil. Let us put the stakes now," said Gasbang; and assisted by Mathews, Romeo Hancock and Sumner Pittikin, Darrell proceeded by making a rough guess to measure 320 acres (more or less), and put the corner stakes.

"This is what I call business," said Gasbang, carrying cheerfully one end of the rope used for measurement; "and all inside of the law. That is the beauty of it— all perfectly lawful."

And so it was.

The stakes having been placed, Darrell felt satisfied. Next day he would have the claim properly filed, and in due time a surveyor would measure them. All would be done "according to law," and in this easy way more land was taken from its legitimate owner.

This certainly was a more simple way of appropriating the property of "*the conquered*" than in the days of Alaric or Hannibal.

There would have been bloodshed then. Now tears only flowed; silent tears of helpless discouragement; of a presentiment of impending desolation.

Sadly Doña Josefa and her daughters had witnessed from the half-closed shutters of their bedroom windows Mr. Darrell's performance, and fully anticipated serious trouble therefrom.

Don Mariano Alamar, Gabriel and Victoriano— his two sons— had also silently witnessed Mr. Darrell's *lawful* appropriation of their own property. Gabriel was pale and calm. Victoriano was biting his lips, and his face was flushed.

"The government has for sale hundreds of millions of acres, but yet these men must come and take my land, as if there was no other," said Don Mariano, sadly.

"And as we pay the taxes on the land that they will cultivate, our taxes will double next year," Gabriel added.

"Undoubtedly. That climax to injustice has been the most fatal of all the hardships imposed upon us. George could not believe me when I told him that we (the land-owners) have to pay the taxes on the land cultivated by the pre-emptors, and upon all the improvements they make and enjoy. When he at last understood that such unfair laws did exist, he was amazed, but understood then why the settlers wished to prolong litigation, since it is '*the natives*' who must bear the burden of taxation, while the titles are in the courts, and thus the pre-emptors hold the land free."

"I wish we were squatters," Victoriano remarked.

"During litigation, yes; but there have been cases where honest men have, in good faith, taken lands as squatters, and after all, had to give them up. No, I don't blame the squatters; they are at times like ourselves, victims of a wrong legislation, which unintentionally cuts both ways. They were set loose upon us, but a law without equity recoils upon them more cruelly. Then we are all sufferers, all victims of a defective legislation and subverted moral principles."

CHAPTER IV.

Efforts to Right the Wrong.

Darrell was not the man to make any delay in putting into practice a project, when once adopted. He therefore immediately wrote home saying that he "had located," and wished Clarence to come down as soon as home matters permitted it. All the crops must be in first, so that Everett and Webster could take care of the farm when Clarence left. They had two good farm hands and a man to take care of the dairy, but still, Darrell made his boys give their personal attention to all the work on the farm. He wrote to Clarence that he would build a small house quickly, which afterwards could be used for the hired men, and would wait until he came down to begin building their dwelling house. That he would level the ground for the house, sink a couple of wells and put up two windmills, the running stream not being sufficient.

"I think I had better buy the lumber for the house up here and charter a schooner to send it down," Clarence said to his mother, after reading his father's letter.

"Did he say anything to you about the condition of the title?" Mrs. Darrell asked.

"Not a word. I suppose the land is vacant," Clarence replied. Mrs. Darrell shook her head, as if in doubt.

"I want you to see to that, before there is any house built in which I shall be expected to reside," she said. "The first thing you do when you get there is to inquire whether the land has been finally rejected and there is no litigation for it. If there is, I want you to pay for it to the owner. And if he will not or cannot sell, write to me at once."

"Very well, mother, I shall do as you say, and I assure you I do not wish father to take up any land claimed by any one under a Mexican title. I think those Spanish people ought to be allowed to keep the land that their government gave them. We ought not to have made any laws that would place their titles in a bad light and be questioned. We should have accepted the legality they had before their own Mexican government, without making some other legality requisite, to please ourselves," Clarence said.

"That has always been my opinion, but I have failed to convince your father. However, with our combined efforts, we might dissuade him from his present way of thinking," said Mrs. Darrell.

Clarence would not be able to leave home for a few weeks yet. In the meantime, his father had not been idle, he had lost no time in carrying out his plans, and shortly after making his "location" in the manner described, he had several men engaged in different employments at his place. When he had already begun building the small house, of which he spoke in his letter to

Clarence, Don Mariano, accompanied by his two sons, rode up to the place where he was then superintending his workmen.

"Good morning, Mr. Darrell," said Don Mariano.

"Good morning," Darrell answered, laconically.

"Can I speak a few words with you?"

"Certainly," he said, going a few steps nearer.

"I see you have taken up some land here, and I suppose you think it is government land, but if so, you are misinformed. This land belongs to me," Don Mariano said.

"Why is it reported rejected then? I have seen the law report, stating that your title was rejected."

"Yes, I know that such is the case. For some mistake or other the entry was made placing my title in the list of those rejected, but I assure you that it is a mistake. My title is now before the attorney general in Washington, because, having been approved, the settlers took an appeal. If the attorney general sustains the appeal, I suppose he will remand the case for a new trial, but I have reasons to suppose he will dismiss the appeal and affirm the decision of the District Court in my favor."

"We will see about that," Darrell said.

"Undoubtedly we will; meantime I thought it was best to undeceive you, and give you warning that you are building on my land."

"Your land if you get it," was the answer.

"If you knew the condition of my title I don't think that you would doubt that this land is mine. However, all I wish to do is to prevent you from spending money here and then naturally get into litigation with me to defend your property," said Don Mariano.

Darrell thought of his wife, and her earnest injunctions. He wished to keep his promise to her. He said:

"If the courts say that this land rightfully belongs to you, I shall pay you for your land or vacate."

"But, Mr. Darrell, you will get me into litigation with you, and I wish to avoid that."

"No, I shall not get you into any law suit with me. I shall buy your land or leave."

"Very well, Mr. Darrell, I shall rely on your word. I shall remember what you say; please do the same."

"I am not in the habit of forgetting what I say."

Don Mariano and his two sons lifted their hats, bowed slightly, turned their horses' heads and moved off.

Darrell returned their bow, muttering to himself, "They take off their hats and bow like gentlemen, anyway."

While he was talking with Don Mariano, Mathews, Hughes, Gasbang, Miller and Pittikin had come. They heard all that was said and looked disappointed. They evidently had counted upon Darrell to help them to fight the rightful owner.

"Did I understand you to say to the Don that you will not maintain your claim, if the attorney general dismisses our appeal?" asked Gasbang.

"I don't know what you understood, or what you did not understand. What I said was that if the Don's title is decided to be right and legal, I shall not contest it. Why should I, if the land is his? I came here to take up government land, believing his title was rejected. He says it is not."

"He lies; it was rejected," Gasbang said.

"That is why we appealed," Mathews added.

"Very well; we will wait. For my part, I think that if his title was rejected he will find it hard to get it back," said Darrell.

The fact of his going on with his building ought to have been sufficient proof to the other settlers that he had cast his lot with them. But it was not. They feared that at any time he might pay the Don for his land, and cease to be one of them; cease to be a "*squatter*." These doubts, these fears, were the perennial theme of endless discussion with the settlers of Alamar.

With date of February 14, 1872, the Honorable Legislature of California passed a law "*To protect agriculture, and to prevent the trespassing of animals upon private property in the County of Los Angeles, and the County of San Diego, and parts of Monterey County.*"

In the very first section it recited, that "every owner *or occupant* of land, *whether it is enclosed or not*," could take up cattle found in said land, etc., etc. It was not stated to be necessary that the *occupant* should have a good title. All that was required seemed to be that he should *claim to be an occupant* of land, no matter who was the owner.

Before this law came out, Don Mariano had already had a great deal of trouble with the squatters, who kept killing his cattle by the hundred head at times. After this law passed, he had the additional annoyance of having to pay money for the release of cattle taken up by *occupants* who would not fence their ten-acre crops. Thus, the alternative was, that if cattle were not taken up, he was sure to find them shot dead by some invisible hand. He had hoped that the Legislature would pass a law saying that "unless *occupants* of land put fences around their fields, they would not be authorized to take up cattle." But, instead of this, the above-mentioned law was enacted.

This was, of course, ruinous to Don Mariano, as well as to all owners of cattle ranchos where settlers had seen fit to locate homesteads. Now any one man, by planting *one acre* of grain to attract cattle to it, could make useless thousands of acres around it of excellent grazing, because it became necessary to drive cattle away from the vicinity of these unfenced fields.

In view of all this, and seeing that the new law would confirm the right to plant fields without fencing, and take up cattle, horses or any other animals found therein, Don Mariano thought he would call together all the settlers in his rancho, and make some proposition to them that would be fair to everybody, and by which he would save his cattle from getting killed or captured (when he must ransom them) all the time.

He told his idea to Mr. Mechlin, who thought it was a good plan, and volunteered to see some of the settlers with whom he was acquainted, thinking that these could see others, and in this manner a meeting be arranged. He started in the morning on his errand, and in the evening Don Mariano called to learn the result.

"These men are meaner and lower than I had supposed," said Mr. Mechlin, whose very fine nervous organization ill-fitted him for the rough contact of Gasbangs. "Would you believe it, they suspected I wanted to lay a trap in which the innocent lambs would fall, and you— the wolf— catch them. If it had not been that I saw Darrell, I would have been utterly discouraged. And I suspect he would not have been half so polite and considerate but for the influence of his son, who has just arrived."

"I heard he had. You saw him?"

"Yes; and a very gentlemanly, handsome young fellow he is. He made his father promise to go with him to see the settlers in person, and arrange for you to meet them; he will report to me in the evening the result of their embassy."

Clarence kept his word to Mr. Mechlin, and immediately after breakfast he had his buggy and horses (a fine turnout he had brought from San Francisco) at the door. Darrell smiled, and good-naturedly took his seat beside his son, saying it would be best to begin by seeing Gasbang and Mathews. Fortunately they met these men, who were driving to see him, to ask his opinion about agreeing to meet Don Mariano. Darrell promptly told them that he thought no one of the settlers should refuse a request so easy to grant.

"But don't you think there is a trap in it?" Mathews asked.

"None whatever. We are not children," Darrell replied.

"But suppose he makes us promise something?" Mathews argued.

"How can he coerce any one against his will," said Darrell.

"No one will be obliged to accede unwillingly," said Clarence. "Let us at least be courteous."

"Certainly. Have you any idea what it is that he wants to say?" asked Gasbang.

"He wants to make some proposition to the settlers, by which he hopes that the interests of all concerned will be subserved," said Clarence.

"Visionary!" exclaimed Gasbang, tapping his forehead with his forefinger; "not practical."

"But his intentions are perfectly kind and fair," Clarence said.

"That is to say, Mr. Mechlin thinks they are."

"Why shouldn't they be? He certainly can't coerce anybody. Here we are on what he believes to be his land, and we don't think it is. Well, what of that?"

"He certainly won't propose to fight us single-handed. We are the majority," said Darrell.

"All right. We'll see Hager and Miller, and the other fellows in that valley. But we think Mr. Clarence will do better with Hancock, Pittikin and Hughes. The female element is strong there, but it will weaken in his hands, and in that malleable condition, he can shape it to suit himself, with one look out of his eyes at the whole troop of girls," said Gasbang.

"Goodness! You don't suppose I would go to play the sweet fellow to those ugly old girls, and make a fool of myself," said Clarence, with so genuine a look of thorough disgust, that it made John Gasbang indulge in one of his loudest fits of hilarity. "Don't be alarmed, my young friend. There is no harm for you there. I could turn you loose among those girls and you would be as safe as Daniel among 'lions' or in 'fiery furnace.' You would not get a single scratch, or feel any flames at all," said he.

"What a low, vulgar fellow this is, even too low for a squatter," said Clarence, driving off.

"Phew!" ejaculated the elder Darrell, "you speak like *a Don*. Your idea of *a squatter* is not flattering."

"It is flattering thus far, that I think Gasbang is too low for the settler, who means no wrong-doing,— the average squatter. As for Mathews, I am sure he is a cut-throat by instinct."

"That may be; but I think their idea of your seeing Pittikin and Hughes is good. You can have more effect on them than Gasbang or Mathews."

"O, I am willing to go to speak to the old men, but why should I see the girls?"

"You manage that part to suit yourself. And now stop. I'll drop here; you needn't go out of your way. I'll walk home. I want to see this piece of land near by. It has not been located. I might put a claim there for Everett and another for Webster."

Clarence sighed, and silently drove on. He had passed by the Pittikin and Hughes farms the day he arrived, as his father had taken him to see how nicely the settlers were doing in Southern California; all expecting their prosperity to increase by the building of the railroad. Clarence saw the two houses and began to feel like a mariner of old between Scylla and Charybdis. There might be a troop of ugly old girls in each house. If he could only see some men out in the fields. But the fields looked deserted. Where could the men be— this being no Sunday nor Fourth of July, that they should leave off work? On looking about for some human being to guide him, he saw in the distance, under a clump of dark trees, several wagons, and horses unhitched, standing harnessed near them.

He was about to turn to the left, to take the road between two fields, when he heard voices, shouting loudly. He supposed they were calling some one. The shouts were followed by a man on horseback galloping towards him. Clarence stopped and waited. The rider was no other than Mr. Pittikin, who came in person to invite him to join their picnic, in honor of his daughter's wedding. The opportunity to see *the men* together would be excellent, but the *girls* would be there, too, thought Clarence, not over pleased.

"Please excuse me, I am not dressed to appear in company. I came to see you on business," said he.

"The girls said I must bring you." Clarence felt a qualm. "And even if I have to fight you I must obey; obey the ladies, you know. There ain't many there. Only our two families— Hughes and mine, and neighbor Hancock's and a few friends. Indeed, we will feel slighted if you don't join us. We will feel you think us too humble a class for you to associate with."

"Nothing of the kind. If I thought so, I would not hesitate to present myself before the ladies in this dress."

"Come along, anyhow. We'll make all the allowance you want. But you see, this is my daughter Fanny's birthday and her wedding day. She was married to Romeo Hancock this morning. So we wanted a room as big as all out doors to celebrate the occasion. We thought the best thing would be to have a picnic under those beautiful trees. Come, please. If you ain't with us, you are against us."

"I'll go home and put on other dress and come back immediately," said Clarence.

Pittikin laughed. "Just what Fanny said. I tell you she is an awfully smart girl. She said, 'He'll tell you he is going home to change his clothes, but don't you let him, because he'll only give us the slip.' So you see, I can't let you go. Besides, they are setting the table,— I mean to say, spreading the eatables,— so you have no time to go home now."

"But, look here, Mr. Pittikin, what is to become of my mission? I came to see you and Mr. Hughes on business, and not on a picnic."

"Can't the business wait till to-morrow?"

"Not very well, as I promised Mr. Mechlin."

"Oh! I know; Hughes told me," interrupted Pittikin. "The Don wants to make speeches to the settlers to fool us into a— into— some terms of his, so that we'll kick ourselves out of our farms."

"Nothing of the kind. He is not going to make any foolish propositions, but even if he were, you can lose nothing by being polite and listening to him."

"I don't know but what you are right. I like always to be polite; and as for Hughes, he is the politest man going, and no mistake. He never speaks loud, and he always listens to you. I think it will be the best thing, perhaps, to see Hughes, now. Then there is neighbor Hancock, and neighbor Miller and Jackson, and the boys. Come along, we'll collar them in a bunch."

"Then, I can count upon your help?"

"Certainly you can; for when it is a question of politeness, I won't be left behind, and if I give you my word, you can bet on me."

Clarence was received with loud demonstrations of pleasure.

"Here he is," said Pittikin, on arriving at the picnic ground; "I got him; but as he has some business to talk to us about, I promised him we would attend to that too, and mix business with pleasure, as it were. So, you talk to them girls, Mr. Darrell, while we old men see what can be done and how, and we'll let you know."

Clarence was presented by Mr. Pittikin to Mrs. Pittikin, and this lady presented him to the company, saying that he must make himself at home, which Clarence did not see well how he could do.

But the young ladies could not boast of having often the good fortune to entertain a young gentleman as elegant, handsome and rich as Clarence, and they made good use of their golden opportunity. Sweet glances and complimentary expressions of pleasure, because the Darrell family were to be their neighbors, showered upon him, until he was ready to laugh outright. But he was too kind to have done anything so discourteous, and took it all in good part, thinking it was all meant in kindness.

"Come, let us show to Mr. Darrell our ice fountain; it is, I think, a great natural curiosity," said Mrs. Romeo Hancock, the heroine of the day, being the lady in whose honor the hymeneal festivities took place. "Come girls and boys," said she, and accompanied by Clarence, and followed by eight or ten others, she guided them to a little cave under a large oak, from which a muffled sound of tiny bells that seemed to tinkle and sigh and whisper, came forth. It seemed to Clarence as if the little fountain was in sympathy with the dispossessed owners, but did not dare to raise its timid voice in behalf of the vanquished, who no longer had rights in their patrimony, and must henceforth wander off disinherited, despoiled, forgotten.

"This is a lovely place," said Clarence.

"Yes, and Mathews wanted to kill me for it," said Romeo.

"Why so?" asked Clarence.

"Because he had just sold his place to Mr. Mechlin, intending to locate here. So when he went to town to sign his conveyance, I put some boards in a wagon and came here, and in two hours my father and myself had put up my cabin. Then we put up this fence around one acre, and by nightfall we had placed my boundary stakes. That night I brought my blankets and my rifle, to sleep in my cabin. Mother sent father to keep me company, and we slept soundly, in splendid style. I wasn't afraid of Mathews. Next morning, at daybreak, we heard the rumbling of a wagon, and soon after we spied old Mathews sitting on the top of his boards. He came smack against my fence.

"What the devil is this?" said he, and began to swear a perfect blue streak. Then he took a hammer from his wagon, and began hammering.

I jumped up, took my rifle and hallooed to him, as if I didn't know him, "Who is there, hammering my fence?"

"Your fence?" said he; "your fence?"

"Yes, sir, mine. I located here yesterday."

"You! you! Get a beard first," said he, and with another streak of oaths, began hammering again.

I came up nearer, holding my rifle in good position. I said, "Look here, Mr. Mathews, leave my fence alone, or you will get into trouble." I leveled my rifle at him. "Will you stop? I give you just two minutes."

He stopped.

"You have no right to locate— you are a minor," said he, livid with rage.

"You just inform yourself better, by asking a polite question or two of my parents. They will tell you that I am just twenty-one years and two days old, and I can prove it by our family Bible and certificate of baptism. I am a Christian, I am, though you don't seem to be, judging by your cursing,— and as for my beard, you be patient, and you'll see it, for it is coming as fast as your gray hairs."

"Why didn't you say you wanted this place?" he growled.

"What a question!" I answered. "You ask it because you don't see my beard, but I feel it pushing ahead with all its might. I didn't tell you, because we ain't exactly bosom friends, and because that is not the style in which we settlers do business. I kept dark, hoping that you would hold on a while longer, trying to get a bigger price for your place from Mr. Mechlin. I watched you, and when you let Saturday pass I knew this sweet little spot was mine,— for on Saturday I was twenty-one, and you couldn't sign your conveyance to Mr. Mechlin until Monday. To-day is Tuesday, Mr. Mathews, I shall be twenty-one years and three days old at 11 o'clock A.M. this day, if I live five hours longer."

"I don't believe a word. You ain't twenty-one. 'Tis a lie!"

"No, it ain't," my father said, coming from the cabin.

"Then he is a jumper. He's jumped my claim."

"No, he ain't. Look here, Mathews," said father, dragging his rifle along as if it was a dead cat, "you know well it is yourself who is lying when you say that. You had no right to this claim while you held the other."

"But I put up my notice that I was going to locate here."

"Now, don't be silly," said father, leaning on his rifle. "It is painful to my feelings to hear a grey-headed man talk like a child. You might have put twenty notices— what of that? The law don't allow any circus performances like that, and if it did, you ain't a good enough performer to ride two horses at once."

"I think it is a mean performance on your part, too, coming here to steal a march on me."

"A mean performance, you say? Do you remember how I had my notices up and my stakes on the ground, six years ago, and when I went to town to bring my lumber, you jumped my claim? My boy has just barely returned the compliment."

"I'll be even with you yet," said he, climbing into his wagon, and beginning to whip his horses, and swear at us worse than ever.

"The same to you; the same to you," father would say, as if answering prayers, and then we both laughed heartily.

"That is not the worst, but that you jumped the claim of his affections," said Tom, whereupon all laughed, and Fanny bashfully hung down her head.

Voices calling them to dinner were now heard, and they returned to the picnic grounds.

No banquet of the Iliad warriors surpassed this, showing that the settlers of Alamar had found the Don's land and the laws of Congress very good.

The elder Mrs. Hancock and Mrs. Pittikin were proud of having given a banquet which no other settler would dare surpass in Alamar.

When the dessert was being served, Clarence said, "We must drink to the bride and groom." All agreed that it should be done.

He arose and made a neat little speech, which was so "*sweetly pretty*," Mr. P. said, that it brought tears to the eyes of Mrs. Pittikin and Mrs. Hancock, the elder.

This put Clarence's popularity beyond doubt.

"Fill your glasses, for I have something to say to Mr. Clarence Darrell, but we must first drink his health," said Mr. Pittikin.

"Here is to our friends, the Darrell family, but more particularly to Mr. Clarence. We respect him, we like him, we are proud of him;"— all drank— "and I now take the occasion to say to Mr. Darrell, in the presence of our friends here, that I fulfilled my promise to him, and have spoken to our friends here, the heads of families, and they will speak to those who are not present, and we will meet to hear what the Don has to say."

"But we don't promise to accept any proposition, if it don't suit each one, no matter what anybody votes," said old Hughes.

"That is understood; we want to be polite, that's all," explained Mr. Pittikin.

"And that is all I have requested," Clarence said. "I do not ask any one to accept any proposition against his will."

"That is fair enough," said old Hancock.

"And little enough, considering we are in possession of land that the Don believes to be his own," said Romeo.

"But it ain't," said old Hager.

"It has been for more than fifty years," Romeo asserted.

"But he lost it by not complying with the law," said Hughes.

"Yes, if he had not neglected his rights, his title would not have been rejected; he went to sleep for eight years, and his right was outlawed," said Miller.

"That was the fault of his lawyers, perhaps," Clarence said.

"Of course it was, but he should have watched his lawyers. The trouble is, that you can't teach 'an old dog new tricks.' Those old Spaniards never will be business men," said Pittikin, sententiously.

It was finally agreed that Clarence would call on Mr. Mechlin that evening, to notify him that the settlers would meet the Don on Monday afternoon at 2 o'clock on the porch of Gasbang's house.

CHAPTER V.

THE DON IN HIS BROAD ACRES.

"The one great principle of English law,"— Charles Dickens says, "is to make business for itself. There is no other principle distinctly, certainly and consistently maintained through all its narrow turnings. Viewed by this light, it becomes a coherent scheme, and not the monstrous maze the laity are apt to think it. Let them but once clearly perceive that its grand principle is to make business for itself at their expense, and surely they will cease to grumble."

The one great principle of American law is very much the same; our lawgivers keep giving us laws and then enacting others to explain them. The lawyers find plenty of occupation, but what becomes of the laity?

"No. 189. *An Act to ascertain and settle the private land claims in the State of California,*" says the book.

And by a sad subversion of purposes, all the private land titles became *unsettled*. It ought to have been said, "An Act to *unsettle* land titles, and to upset the rights of the Spanish population of the State of California."

It thus became not only necessary for the Spanish people to present their titles for revision, and litigate to maintain them (in case of any one contesting their validity, should the least irregularity be discovered, and others covet their possession), but to maintain them against the government before several tribunals; for the government, besides making its own laws, *appeals to itself* as against the land-owners, after their titles might have been *approved*. But this benign Act says (in "Sec. 11"), "That the Commissioners, the District and Supreme Courts, in deciding on the validity of any claim, shall be governed by the treaty of Guadalupe Hidalgo; the law of nations; the laws, usages, and customs of the government *from which the claim is derived*; the principles of equity, and the decisions of the Supreme Court of the United States, etc., etc."

Thus the government washes its hands clean, liberally providing plenty of tribunals, plenty of crooked turnings through which to scourge the wretched land-owners.

Don Mariano had been for some years under the lash of the maternal government, whom he had found a cruel stepmother, indeed.

As it was arranged with Clarence, the meeting would take place that day on the broad piazza of John Gasbang's house, this being the most central point in the rancho.

The heads of families all came— the male heads, be it understood— as the squatters did not make any pretence to regard female opinion, with any more respect than other men.

All the benches and chairs that the house contained, with the exception of

Mrs. Gasbang's sewing rocker, had been brought to the porch, which was quite roomy and airy.

At ten minutes before two, all the settlers were there, that is to say, all the old men, with their elder sons.

Clarence, Romeo, Tom and Jack, sat together in a corner, conversing in low tones, while Gasbang was entertaining his guests with some broad anecdotes, which brought forth peals of laughter.

At five minutes to two, Señor Alamar, accompanied by Mr. Mechlin, arrived in a buggy; his two sons followed on horseback.

Clarence had time to look at them leisurely, while they dismounted, and tied their horses to a hitching post.

"They are gentlemen, no doubt," observed Clarence.

"You bet they are," Romeo coincided. Evidently he admired and liked them.

"How much the boys look like the old man," Tom said.

"They look like Englishmen," was Clarence's next observation.

"Yes, particularly Victoriano; he is so light he looks more like a German, I think," said Romeo.

"I think Gabriel is very handsome," Tom said, "only of late he seems always so sad or thoughtful."

"That won't do for a man who is to marry soon," said Romeo. "I think he has always been rather reserved. He has only a cold salutation to give, while Victoriano will be laughing and talking to everybody. But, perhaps, you are right, and he is changed. I think he is less reconciled than the others, to have us, settlers, helping ourselves to what they consider their land. He certainly was far more talkative four or five years ago. I used to work with them in ploughing and harvesting time, and both boys, and the Don, were always very kind to me, and I can't help liking them."

"The ladies, though, ain't so affable. They are very proud," said Tom; "they walk like queens."

"They didn't seem proud to me, but I never spoke to them," said Romeo.

Gasbang went forward to meet his guests, and all came into the porch.

"Good afternoon, gentlemen," said Don Mariano to the settlers, lifting his hat and bowing. His sons and Mr. Mechlin did the same. Clarence arose, and so did the other young men with him, returning their salutation. The elder Darrell, Pittikin and Hughes followed this example; the other settlers nodded only, and remained sitting with their hats on, looking with affected indifference at the trees beyond.

"I thank you for your courtesy in complying with my request to have this meeting," he said. Some nodded, others grinned and winked, others smiled silently.

"Take this chair, Señor, and you, Mr. Mechlin, take this one. They are the best in my establishment," said Gasbang. "The young gentlemen will find seats somewhere on the benches."

Clarence came forward and offered three chairs. Mr. Mechlin took his arm and presented him to the Alamars.

"I take pleasure in making your acquaintance, and I hope to have the opportunity to thank you for your kind co-operation more appropriately afterward," said Don Mariano. His sons shook hands with Clarence cordially, and accepted the proffered chairs.

Don Mariano excused himself for not speaking English more fluently.

"If you don't understand me I will repeat my words until I make my meaning clear, but I hope you will ask me to repeat them; or, perhaps, some one of these young gentlemen will do me the kindness to be my interpreter," said he.

"Romeo talks Spanish; he can interpret for you," said Victoriano.

"You talk English better," Romeo proudly replied, thinking he could tell his wife that the Don had asked him to be his interpreter.

"Perhaps Mr. Clarence Darrell would do me the favor," said Don Mariano.

"You speak very good English, señor. We understand you perfectly. You do not require an interpreter," Clarence said.

"That is so; you speak very well," said Mr. Mechlin.

Gasbang and Pittikin added: "Certainly, we understand him very well."

"Of course we do," said Darrell and others.

"You are very kind," said the Don, smiling, "and I will try to be brief, and not detain you long."

"We have all the afternoon," said Hughes.

"That's so, we ain't in a hurry," said several.

"Only let us out in time to bring the milch cows home, before night comes on," said old Miller, dryly.

"Exactly, we want to look after our cows, too," said the Don, laughing.

All saw the fine irony of the rejoinder, and laughed heartily. Miller scratched his ear, as if he had felt the retort there, knowing well, that with the exception of Mathews and Gasbang, he had killed and "*corraled*" more of the Don's cattle than any other settler.

"Speaking about cows, brings us at once to the object of this meeting,"— Don Mariano, still smiling, went on, saying: "You know that I have lost many, and that it is natural I should wish to save those I have left. To do this, and yet not ask that you give up your claims, I have one or two propositions to make to you. The reason why you have taken up land here is because you want homes. You want to make money. Isn't that the reason? Money! money!"

"That's it, exactly," said many voices, and all laughed.

"Well, I can show you how you may keep your homes and make more money than you can by your present methods, while at the same time, I also save my cattle. That little point, you know, I must keep in view."

All laughed again.

"To fence your fields, you have said, is too expensive, particularly as the rainy seasons are too uncertain to base upon them any calculations for getting crops to pay for fencing. I believe this is what most of you say; is it not?"

"We could have raised better crops if your cattle hadn't damaged them," said Mathews.

"I beg to differ; but supposing that you are right, do you think you could be sure of good crops if you killed all my stock, or if I took them all away to the mountains? No, most assuredly. The rainy season would still be irregular and unreliable, I think. Yes, I may say, I feel sure, it is a mistake to try to make San Diego County a grain-producing county. It is not so, and I feel certain it never will be, to any great extent. This county is, and has been, and will be always, a good grazing county— one of the best counties for cattle-raising on this coast, and the very best for fruit-raising on the face of the earth. God intended it should be. Why, then, not devote your time, your labor and your money to raising vineyards, fruits and cattle, instead of trusting to the uncertain rains to give you grain crops?"

"It takes a long time to get fruit trees to bearing. What are we to do for a living in the meantime?" asked Miller.

"Begin raising cattle— that will support you," the Don replied.

"Where is the capital to buy cattle with?" Gasbang asked.

"You don't require any more capital than you already have. I can let each of you have a number of cows to begin with, and give you four or five years' time to pay me. So you see, it will be with the increase of these cattle you will pay, for I shall charge you no interest."

"What do you expect us to do in return? To give back to you our homesteads?" asked Hughes.

"No, sir; I have said, and repeat again, you will retain your homesteads."

"And will you stop contesting our claims?" asked Mathews.

"I will, and will give each one a quit-claim deed."

"You will not fight our claims, but you don't want us to plant grain on our land," said Gasbang.

"You can plant grain, if you like, but to do so you must fence your land; so, as you all say, that fencing is expensive, I suggest your fencing orchards and vineyards only, but not grain fields— I mean large fields."

"Pshaw! I knew there was to be something behind all that display of generosity," muttered Mathews.

Don Mariano reddened with a thrill of annoyance, but quietly answered:

"You are too good business men to suppose that I should not reserve some slight advantage for myself, when I am willing you should have many more yourselves. All I want to do is to save the few cattle I have left. I am willing to quit-claim to you the land you have taken, and give you cattle to begin the stock business, and all I ask you in return is to put a fence around whatever land you wish to cultivate, so that my cattle cannot go in there. So I say, plant vineyards, plant olives, figs, oranges; makes wines and oil and raisins; export olives and dried and canned fruits. I had some very fine California canned fruit sent to me from San Francisco. Why could we not can fruits as well, or better? Our olives are splendid— the same our figs, oranges, apricots, and truly all semi-tropical fruits are of a superior quality. When this fact becomes generally known, I feel very sure that San Diego County will be selected for fruit and grape-growing. In two years grape vines begin to bear; the same with figs, peaches and other fruits. At three years old they bear quite well, and all without irrigation. So you would not have to wait so very long to begin getting a return from your labor and capital. Moreover, an orchard of forty acres or vineyard of twenty will pay better after three years' growth than one hundred and sixty acres of wheat or barley in good seasons, and more than three hundred acres of any grain in moderately good seasons, or one thousand acres in bad seasons. You can easily fence twenty or forty or sixty acres for a vineyard or orchard, but not so easily fence a field of one hundred and sixty, and the grain crop would be uncertain, depending on the rains, but not so the trees, for you can irrigate them, and after the trees are rooted that is not required."

"Where is the water to irrigate?" asked Miller.

"The water is in the sea now, for there we let it go every year; but if we were sensible, judicious men, we would not let it go to waste— we would save it. This rancho has many deep ravines which bring water from hills and sierras. These ravines all open into the valleys, and run like so many little rivers in the rainy season. By converting these ravines into reservoirs we could have more water than would be needed for irrigating the fruit trees on the foothills. In the low valleys no irrigation would be needed. If we all join forces to put up dams across the most convenient of these ravines, we will have splendid reservoirs. I will defray half the expense if you will get together and stand the other half. Believe me, it will be a great God-send to have a thriving, fruit-growing business in our county. To have the cultivated land well fenced, and the remainder left out for grazing. Then there would not be so many thousands upon thousands of useless acres as now have to be. For every ten acres of cultivated land (not fenced) there are ten thousand, yes, twenty thousand, entirely idle, useless. Why? Because those ten acres of growing grain must be protected, and the cattle which don't know the '*no fence*' law, follow their inclination to go and eat the green grass. Then they are '*corralled*' or killed. Is it not a pity to kill the poor dumb brutes, because we can't make them understand the law, and see the wisdom of our Sacramento legislators who enacted it? And is it not a pity to impoverish our county by making the bulk of its land useless? The foolishness of letting all of the rainfall go to waste, is an old time folly with us. Still, in old times, we had, at least, the good excuse that we raised all the fruits we needed for our use, and there was no market for any more. But we were not then, as now, guilty of the folly of making the land useless. We raised cattle and sold hides and tallow every year, and made money. When gold was discovered, we drove our stock north, got a good price for it, and made money. But now no money will be made by anybody out of cattle, if they are to be destroyed, and no money made out of land, for the grazing will be useless, when there will be no stock left to eat it. Thus, the county will have no cattle, and the crops be always uncertain. Believe me, in years to come, you will see that the county was impoverished by the 'no fence law,' unless we try to save our county, in spite of foolish legislation. If our wise legislators could enact a law obliging rain to come, so that we could have better chances to raise grain, then there would be some show of excuse for the *'no fence law,' perhaps*. I say PERHAPS, because, in my humble opinion, we ought to prefer cattle raising and fruit growing for our county. We should make these our specialty."

"I think it would be much more foolish to trust to a few cows to make out a living while trees grow," said Miller, "than to the seasons to give us grain crops."

"No, sir; because cattle are sure to increase, if they are not killed, and you could make cheese and butter, and sell your steers every year, while trees grow. You have been seven years a settler on this rancho. In these seven years you have raised two good crops; three poor, or only middling, and two, no crops at all."

"Yes, because your cattle destroyed them," said Mathews.

"No, sir; my cattle were not all over California; but the bad seasons were, and only in few places, moderately good crops were harvested; in the southern counties none at all. We had rains enough to get sufficiently good grazing, but not to raise grain."

"I think you are right about the uncertainty of our seasons, and I think a good dairy always pays well, also a good orchard and vineyard," said Darrell. "But the question is, whether we can adopt some feasible plan to put your idea into practice."

"Yes, how many cows will you let us have?" asked Hager.

"I will divide with you. Next week I shall have my '*rodeo*.' We can see then the number of cattle I have left. We shall count them. I shall take half, the other half you divide pro rata; each head of a family taking a proportionate number of cattle."

"That is fair," Darrell said.

"I don't want any cattle. I ain't no '*vaquero*' to go '*busquering*' around and *lassoing* cattle. I'll lasso myself; what do I know about whirling a *lariat*?" said Mathews.

"Then, don't take cattle. You can raise fruit trees and vineyards," said Darrell.

"Yes, and starve meantime," Mathews replied.

"You will not have to be a vaquero. I don't go '*busquering*' around *lassooing*, unless I wish to do so," said the Don. "You can hire an Indian boy to do that part. They know how to handle *la reata* and *echar el lazo* to perfection. You will not starve, either, for if you wish, you can make butter and cheese enough to help to pay expenses. I think this State ought to make and export as good cheese as it now imports, and some day people will see it, and do it, too. Thus, with the produce of your dairies, at first, and afterward with your fruits, you will do far better than with grain crops, and not work as hard. Let the northern counties raise grain, while we raise fruits and make wine, butter and cheese. You must not forget, either, that every year you can sell a number of cattle, besides keeping as many milch cows as you need."

"Where can we sell our cattle?" asked Hancock.

"Cattle-buyers will come to buy from you. But if you prefer it, you can drive your stock north yourselves, and make a good profit. Since 1850, I have sent nine times droves of cattle to the northern counties, and made a handsome profit every time. The first time we took stock north, was in '50; I took nearly six thousand head— three thousand were mine— and the others belonged to my brothers. We lost very few, and sold at a good price— all the way from eighteen to twenty-five dollars per head. About five hundred of mine I sold as high as thirty dollars per head. I made sixty thousand dollars by this operation. Then out of the next lot I made twenty-seven thousand dollars. Then I made twenty-two thousand, and so on, until my tame cows began to disappear, as you all know. In four years after my cows began to get shot, my cattle decreased more than half. Now I don't think I have many more than three thousand head. So you cannot blame me for wishing to save these few. But believe me, the plan I propose will be as beneficial to you as to me, and also to the entire county, for as soon as it is shown that we can make a success of the industries I propose, others will follow our example."

"If you have only three thousand head, you can't spare many to us, and it will hardly be worth while to stop planting crops to get a few cows," said Gasbang.

"I think I will be able to spare five or six hundred cows. I don't know how many I have left."

"We will buy from somebody else, if we want more," said Darrell. "We won't want many to begin with; it will be something of an experiment for some of us."

"For all of us here. Perhaps you understand *vaquering*; we don't," said Hancock; all laughed.

"Then fence your claim and plant grain," Darrell retorted.

"I am not so big a fool as to spend money in fences. The '*no fence*' law is better than all the best fences," Mathews said.

"But what if you make more money by following other laws that are more just, more rational?" said the Don.

"The 'no fence' law is rational enough for me," said Miller.

"And so say I," said Mathews.

"And I," said Gasbang.

Hughes nodded approvingly, but he was too much of a hypocrite to commit himself in words.

"We did not come to discuss the 'no fence' law, but only to propose something that will put more money in your pockets than killing dumb beasts," said Mr. Mechlin.

"Then propose something practicable," said Mathews.

"I think what has been proposed is practicable enough," Darrell said.

"Certainly it is," Mr. Mechlin added.

"I don't see it," said Mathews.

"Nor I, either," added Gasbang.

"Nor I, neither," said Hughes.

"Well, gentlemen," said Don Mariano, rising, "I shall leave you now; you know my views, and you perhaps prefer to discuss them, and discuss your own among yourselves, and not in my presence. Take your time, and when you come to a final decision let me know. Perhaps I can advance the money to those of you who do not have it ready to purchase fencing lumber. I shall charge no interest, and give you plenty of time to pay."

"I will do that, Señor Alamar," Clarence said; "if the settlers agree to fence their lands, I will advance the money to them to put up their fences."

"Yes, and if our crops fail, we will be in debt to the ears, with a chain around our necks," Mathews growled.

"I thought you said that if it were not for my cattle, your crops would not have failed," said Don Mariano, smiling.

"I said so, and it is so. But you see, that was before we had the '*no fence*' law," answered he, grinning.

Don Mariano shook hands with Clarence, whom he invited to call at his house— this invitation Clarence accepted with warm thanks— and followed by his sons and his friend Mr. Mechlin, Don Mariano took his leave, bowing to the settlers, who nodded and grinned in return.

"I suppose you, too, think the '*no fence*' law iniquitous, as you appear to favor the aristocracy," said Gasbang to Clarence.

"It is worse than that, it is stupid. Now it kills the cattle, afterwards it will kill the county," Clarence answered.

"Shall we plant no wheat, because the Spaniards want to raise cattle?" Mathews asked.

"Plant wheat, if you can do so without killing cattle. But do not destroy the larger industry with the smaller. If, as the Don very properly says, this is a grazing county, no legislation can change it. So it would be wiser to make laws to suit the county, and not expect that the county will change its character to suit absurd laws," Clarence replied.

CHAPTER VI.

Naughty Dog Milord an Important Factor.

Three large wagons, each drawn by six horses, were hauling the lumber for Mr. Darrell's house, which was already commenced.

Victoriano, riding across the valley, had to stop to let the heavily loaded wagons pass. This gave Clarence time to overtake him.

"Good morning," said he, "I am glad to catch up with you, Don Victoriano. I have been wanting to speak to you."

Victoriano bowed, saying, "Will you go to my house?"

"No, I'd rather not. I am not dressed to be seen by ladies. I would rather speak to you here."

"You are going to build a large house, Mr. Darrell?" said Victoriano, turning his horse so as to ride beside Clarence; "judging by the amount of lumber being hauled."

"Yes; rather. We are a large family, and require a good deal of room. But before we do any more work I want to speak with your father. I want to ask him— ask him as a favor— and yet, as a business proposition"— he hesitated; he was evidently embarrassed; but Victoriano, not guessing the drift of his words, remained waiting silently, offering no assistance. "Well," he continued, "I mean this: I don't like this fashion of taking people's lands, and I would like to pay to Señor Alamar for what has been located by us, but at the same time I do not wish my father to know that I have paid for the land, as I am sure he would take my action as a reproach— as a disclaimer of his own action, and I don't wish to hurt his feelings, or seem to be disrespectful or censorious."

"I understand, and I think my father will be willing to sell the land. He is at home now. Let us go up to see him."

"Had you not better speak to him, and make an appointment for me to see him to-morrow, or some other time? I'd rather not risk being seen by the ladies in this blue flannel shirt and heavy boots. I look too rough— like a smuggler or a squatter, sure."

"I can call my father to speak to you outside, so that the ladies need not see you. But if they should, that needn't disturb you. They have too much sense not to know that you would not be working in white kid gloves. Come on. The front veranda is empty. Mother and three of my sisters are at the Mechlin's. Mercedes is the only one at home, and she is too busy with her embroidery in Madam Halier's room to come near you. I'll bring father to the front veranda."

Clarence and Victoriano tied their horses by the garden gate and walked to the piazza. The hall door was ajar. Clarence saw no ladies about and felt reassured.

There were three steps leading from the walk through the garden up to the front veranda. These steps were exactly opposite to the hall door.

Victoriano took the path to the right, saying: "Go up and sit down. I'll bring my father here."

"Do not disturb him if he is taking his *siesta*."

"The *siesta* hour is past, I'll find him at the office," said he, going round the corner, leaving Clarence to walk up the front step. As he did so, he heard a tinkling of little bells and rushing of feet, as if somebody was running. Then a laughing voice, the timbre of which was sweetly pleasing, saying:

"Stop, Milord! you bad dog! Milord! Milord!"

At the same moment, through the narrow opening of the door, out darted a little white dog, dragging after him a large and much entangled skein of bright-colored silk. Clarence was nearly stepping on the little runaway, when the door was flung open, and a girl rushed out, coming against him before she could check herself. In her effort to do so she turned her foot and staggered forward, but before she realized she was in any one's presence, she felt two strong arms holding her.

"Oh!" she exclaimed, as a sharp, hot pain darted through her ankle. She saw that the two arms which held her were none of her father or brothers', and that they were covered with blue flannel.

Looking up to see the face above them, their eyes met. Hers expressed surprise, his merriment. But a change in their expression flashed instantaneously, and both felt each other tremble, thrilled with the bliss of their proximity. Her face was suffused with burning blushes. She was bewildered, and without daring to meet his eyes again, stammered an apology; extending her hand, to reach some chair or table to hold herself, but they all were crowded at both ends of the piazza.

"You are hurt. I am afraid you are hurt," said he, with pale lips, reflecting the pallor he saw come to her face, succeeding her crimson blush. "I know you are suffering. What can I do? I am so sorry!"

"O no, I only turned my foot a little," she answered, venturing to look at him for an instant. "I shall be all right in a minute."

"If you turned your foot, don't put any weight upon it. Do not try to walk, let me carry you to a chair."

"O no, no! I am not so much hurt as to require giving all that trouble."

"*Please* let me. It will be no trouble; only a great pleasure." He was in earnest and spoke quite seriously. "Are you afraid I could not carry you?"

"No, not that, but it is not necessary," and she tried to walk. A quick, sharp, burning pain through her ankle admonished her that she was more hurt than she had believed. A slight contraction of her brows betrayed her pain.

"There! You will hurt yourself worse," said he, and before she knew what he was going to do, he stooped a little and lifted her as easily as if she had been a little child. She had no time to think whether to be grateful or offended, for he quickly walked to the further end of the piazza and carefully placed her in a roomy arm chair. Then bending a knee before her, said:

"Forgive my lifting you without your permission. I knew you would not give it, and I knew also that you were suffering. Will you forgive me?" His voice was soft, caressing, pleading, but his eyes seemed to her to emit rays full of attractive, earnest force which she felt had great power. They dazzled her, and yet those eyes were so mild, so kind. She looked down, making no answer. "When Don Victoriano comes he can carry you to bed, and— please— take my advice, stay there until the pain has entirely left your foot."

She ventured to look at his eyes again. Who could this strong young man be, so bold, and yet so gentle, so courteous and yet waiting for no permission to take so positively hold of her, to carry her bodily half the length of the piazza. And now so respectfully asking on his knees to be forgiven? Asking with tones of tender humility in his voice, while his eyes she knew could emanate subduing magnetic beams.

"How do you know Victoriano is coming? He went out riding," she said, evading the question of forgiveness, and for the sake of making some reply that would hide her confusion.

"Yes, but I met him and he returned with me. He has gone to look for Señor Alamar, I came to see him on business," said the respectful young man, still on his knees.

"Do you know my father?"

"Only very slightly." They were silent. He added: "I met him a few days ago when he had that meeting with the squatters."

"Were you at the meeting?" said she, avoiding his gaze.

"Yes," he said, watching her beautiful face. What would she think of him, believing him a *Squatter*, one who came to take land that did not belong to him? How he wished that she would look up, that he might see her lovely eyes again, for if to her his eyes seemed so glorious, to him hers fascinated, conquered, with a power that he never thought could exist in any human being. Trembling, he felt that he was madly in love with her. Yes, already in love. Love at first sight, surely. But if it killed him, no matter, he would love her to the last instant of his life.

Voices were heard approaching through the hall. He stood up and walked towards the door. Señor Alamar came forward and shook hands with him. Victoriano explained the reason of his delay being, that he had to look for his father all over the house, and at last found him in the furthest "*corral*" looking at some new colts just brought in.

"I am glad that Mercedes came to converse with you," said Victoriano.

"I did not come to converse. I did not know that the gentleman was here. I came by accident," she hastened to reply. "I was trying to catch Milord when I stumbled and would have fallen, had not this gentleman prevented it." So saying, she blushed anew; her blushes being immediately reflected on Clarence's forehead, made them both look like a couple of culprits.

"I fear the lady's foot is hurt," said he.

"Is it?" exclaimed Don Mariano, going towards Mercedes. "Does it pain you baby?"

"Yes papa, a little. It burns me. Do you think it would be bad for me to walk to my room?"

"Of course it would," Clarence said, and blushed redder yet at his temerity.

"Can you stand on your foot?" Victoriano asked.

"I don't know."

"Don't try. I'll carry you to your room," said her father.

"Women have no business to have such small feet. They are always stumbling and can't walk worth a cent," said Victoriano, going to look at his sister's foot. "See here. No wonder they stumble. Look at the little slipper. Why don't they wear good broad boots?" So saying he took off the little slipper, which seemed made for a Cinderella.

"You are too absurd," said Mercedes, blushing again, to see her slipper brandished aloft, in the face of a stranger.

"I ain't. It's women's feet that are absurd."

"When we want the ladies to be infantry soldiers, then we will ask them to cultivate big feet," said Don Mariano, laughing.

"But not until then, please," said Clarence, smiling.

"Aha! I see you cherish the general male weakness," said Victoriano, kneeling before his sister to put on the little slipper. "I am the only strong-minded man, I know. Come, pussy, I'll carry you to your room."

"No, no. You take me, papa, Tano might drop me."

"Nonsense; as if I couldn't carry a kitten like you."

"Papa, you take me, but not to bed. Put me on the lounge in mamma's room, and call Madam Halier to me."

"All right; anything to please the children," said Don Mariano, stooping to lift her.

She put her arms around his neck, and whispered: "Papa, who is this young man? I never saw him."

"That is a fact," said Don Mariano, taking her up, and turning toward Clarence, said: "Mr. Darrell, permit me to present you to my daughter, Mercedes, 'our baby.'" So saying, he dandled her a little in his arms.

"Oh, papa, you make me ridiculous! How can I bow like a lady, when you are rocking me like an infant!" she said, laughing, but blushing again like a rose.

"Shake hands with the gentleman, that's a dear," said Victoriano, talking baby talk to her.

"Oh, papa, make Tano hush. Mr. Darrell, I am afraid that I shall always seem ridiculous to you."

"Not at all; I don't see why," Clarence replied, "but I fear that your hurt might be serious."

"That's it. You might be ridiculous, but your hurt might be serious," said Victoriano.

It was Clarence's turn to blush now, but he smiled good naturedly.

"You won't be serious, though. I wish you were, and polite, too," said Mercedes. "I don't know what Mr. Darrell will think of us."

"Mr. Darrell will see us often, I hope, and think better of Tano," said Don Mariano, carrying away his precious burden.

"My opinion is all that you could wish, Miss Mercedes," said Clarence, and their eyes met, transmitting that strange thrill to both.

Don Mariano placed Mercedes tenderly on her mamma's lounge, called Madam Halier to attend to the sprained ankle, and returned to the veranda.

Clarence made no delay in stating the object of his visit. He said:

"Since the meeting I have had several talks with the settlers, and the result has been my conviction, that they will not accept your generous offer. They, no doubt, wish to take up more land, and think it cannot be done if they bind themselves to put up fences by accepting your proposition. How short-sighted they are time alone will show, for at present they will not listen to reason."

"I am very sorry. There is no alternative for me but to sell all my cattle as soon as possible, and in the meantime drive all I can to the mountains."

"But that will be ruinous, father. How can we herd them in the mountains? They will all become wild and run away," said Victoriano.

"I am afraid they will. I am sure of it, in fact. But there is no other way to save any at all."

"I think this 'no fence' law the most scandalous, bare-faced outrage upon the rights of citizens that I ever heard of," said Clarence, warmly. "It is like setting irresponsible trespassers loose upon a peaceable people, and then rewarding their outrage. To let any one take up your lands right before your eyes is outrage enough, but to cap the climax by authorizing people to plant crops without fences and then *corral* your cattle, which must be attracted to the green grass, I call positively disgraceful, in a community which is not of vandals. It is shameful to the American name. I am utterly disgusted with the whole business, and the only thing that will make matters a little tolerable to me will be for you to do me the favor of permitting me to pay for the land we have located."

"Does your father wish to pay?"

"I do not know whether he would or not. I fear he would not. My father is a blind worshiper of the Congress of these United States, and consequently it is difficult to persuade him that our legislators might possibly do wrong. He believes that Congress has the right to declare *all* California open to pre-emption, and all American citizens free to choose any land not already patented. Thus, he thinks he has the right to locate on your land (according to law, mind you), because he believes your title has been rejected. But as my faith in our law-givers is not so blind, my belief is that Congress had no more right to pass any law which could give an excuse to trespass upon your property, than to pass a law inviting people to your table. I feel a sort of impatience to think that in our country could exist a law which is so outrageously unjust. My pride as an American is somewhat different from that of my father. He thinks it is a want of patriotism to criticise our legislation. Whereas, I think our theory of government is so lofty, so grand and exalted, that we must watch jealously that Congress may not misinterpret it; misrepresent the sentiments, the aspirations of the American people, and thus make a caricature of our beautiful ideal. It is our duty and privilege to criticise our laws, and criticise severely. As long as you, the native Californians, were to be despoiled of your lands, I think it would have been better to have passed a law of confiscation. Then we would have stood before the world with the responsibility of that barbarous act upon own shoulders. That would have been a national shame, but not so great as that of guaranteeing, by treaty, a protection which was not only withheld, but which was denied,— snatched away, treacherously,— making its denial legal by enactments of retroactive laws. This I call disgraceful to the American name. Therefore, in my humble way and limited sphere, if I cannot repeal, I will at least evade such unjust laws to the best of my ability, and make them ineffective as far as I am individually concerned. I only wish I could wipe out those stains on our national honor, by repealing at once laws so discreditable to us. Yes, the more so, as they bear directly upon the most defenseless, the most powerless of our citizens— the orphaned Spano-Americans. So, then, I hope you will help me to avoid this American shame, by permitting me to pay for our land whatever price you think just."

"Very well," said Don Mariano, pleased with Clarence's honest warmth, and to hear him express opinions and sentiments so very similar to his own. "You can pay whatever you wish, or we can make an agreement that I will sell to you when I get my patent. Such is my understanding with Mr. Mechlin and also with your father."

"That is rather vague. I would prefer to pay to you now so much per acre. With the understanding that my father (or any one else) is not to know I have made this purchase. I mean not for the present."

"Would your father object to it?"

"Perhaps not. And yet he might see in it a disclaimer from my part— a criticism. He is a settler— a *'Squatter'*— you know, and consequently very sensitive about (what they call) *'rights of settlers under the law.'* He knows my sentiments, but one thing is my expressing them to him, and another is to pay money for land he thinks he has lawfully appropriated. It might seem to him, I imply that his locating perhaps was not altogether as honorable a transaction in my eyes, as it may be lawful in the eyes of the lawmakers."

"You are certainly very honorable, and I am willing to abide by your wishes in the matter," said Don Mariano. "You view this question exactly as I do."

Clarence blushed with pleasure and bowed, saying:

"You are very kind, and that you, who are so generous, should be made to suffer as you have, it is, I assure you, so revolting to me (as an American and a civilized being) that I have felt great desire to go away rather than to live among these short-sighted and unappreciative people that have unfortunately fallen upon you."

Don Mariano laughed and said, "No don't go away. Let me have one friend at least, among so many opponents. Pay whatever you wish, and take as much land as you desire to have, but don't go."

"I thank you, indeed, but will you not name the price? I don't think it is right for me to put a price upon your property."

"My dear sir, that would be so if my property was not going into— smoke of sulphur— but as it is, and growing fast so 'beautifully less' that I suppose even the $1.25 of government price ought to be a handsome figure to my weary eyes. So name any price you wish."

It was agreed that Clarence would pay $10.00 per acre, and take up 640 acres where his father had already located. It was also understood that the purchase should not be mentioned to any one. Don Mariano excepted only his son Gabriel. Clarence said he would except his mother, inasmuch as she had told him to pay for the land or else she would not come to reside upon it.

Don Mariano said that he would like to mention it to his family and the Mechlins, but feared that if only some allusion was overheard by the servants, it would be repeated.

"I have no objection to Mr. Mechlin knowing it," Clarence said.

"No, but they have for servants Hogsden and his wife, and they are very dishonorable. They would repeat it if by accident they heard it."

"It is a pity that Mrs. Mechlin don't send those two thieves away," Victoriano said.

"Yes, I hear that the woman Hogsden repeats things she hears at the Mechlins," Clarence said.

"Of course she does, and steals too, and yet Mrs. Mechlin keeps them," Victoriano said, impatiently.

"Perhaps it would be best to say nothing, and I will watch my chance to tell my father myself, that I paid for the land," Clarence said. He then rose to go.

As he went down the veranda steps he met Milord returning, still dragging the skein of silk. But this was no longer of bright variegated hues, it was black with mud and sadly masticated by Milord's sharp teeth, which proudly held it as if challenging any one to take it.

"You wicked Milord. See what you have done with your poor mistress' silk. She will be distressed," said Victoriano.

On hearing himself thus apostrophised, Milord ran off again with his plunder, and it was with difficulty that by the combined efforts of Victoriano and Clarence he was at last captured, but the bright colors of the silk had all disappeared, a blackened skein resembling a piece of wet rope was pulled from Milord's sharp teeth.

CHAPTER VII.

From Alameda to San Diego.

The Darrell house was now finished, the furniture had arrived, been unpacked and distributed in the rooms, but the house seemed to old Darrell entirely too sumptuous for the plain folks, that his family ought to be. That was a truth.

"Look here, Clarence, haven't you been too extravagant in buying such expensive carpets, such fine furniture? For gracious sake, how big is the bill for all this grandeur?"

"I don't know yet the price of every item, but don't be alarmed, I am sure they would not go beyond the limit I gave Hubert (Hubert made the purchases), and I assure you, it will all be paid with our volunteer crop."

"Don't be sure of that."

"O, but I am sure— only not too much so— which is the right way of being sure," he replied.

Clarence was now a regular caller at the Alamar and the Mechlin houses. He felt that in both places the welcome he received was sincere, for even the silent Gabriel was always ready to talk to him. As for Victoriano, his attachment to Clarence was now an acknowledged and accepted fact,— not rejected by Señor Alamar, to judge by appearances,— and certainly fully and sincerely reciprocated by Clarence. Both found great pleasure in each other's society, and saw each other every day.

It was now time for Clarence to go to Alameda to bring down the family. He and Victoriano talked about it walking towards the Alamar house from the Darrells, discussing the probable time of his return.

"Clarence has come to bid us good-by," said Victoriano, walking into the parlor, followed by Clarence.

"Why! Where is he going?" said Mercedes, rising, dropping the book she was reading.

"Don't be alarmed, he is only going to bring his mother and sisters down," added Victoriano, maliciously, causing the blood to rush to her forehead.

"Oh!" she exclaimed, sitting down, with a resentful look toward her brother, and a half appealing, half deprecating one to Clarence, who was contemplating her in ecstatic silence.

"I think the Holman girls will be coming about the same time. I was telling Clarence to look after them a little, if convenient, and if they are not sea-sick," said Victoriano.

"They will require my services more if they are sick," said Clarence, laughing.

"If you are a good nurse," Victoriano observed; adding, "Imagine Corina Holman nursed by a strange young gentleman; that would kill her sure."

"I would try and prevent that," said Clarence.

"Thank you, for my friends. I do not think they will be very ill; but I am sure it will be pleasant for them to have so good an escort," said Mercedes.

Clarence promised, therefore, to look after the Misses Holman, and let them know which steamer would be best to take coming to San Diego.

Mercedes said she would write notifying them of this arrangement.

There was a great *something* in Clarence's mind that he wished to say to Mercedes before leaving, but he had neither courage nor opportunity to say it, so he left, carrying with him the burden of his thoughts untold.

His voyage was accomplished in safety, the steamer arriving at San Francisco at the regular time. Hubert Haverly came to meet him, and together they went to a restaurant for breakfast.

"Give us the most secluded room and the nicest breakfast your establishment can produce, for this gentleman is very particular, and I am very hungry," said Hubert.

The waiter smiled, showed them to the best room in the house, and retired.

"Now let us talk," said Hubert, "I am dying to tell you how rich you are, and scold you for not letting me keep your stock longer and making you richer. Why were you so anxious to sell? The stock kept rising steadily. I was a 'bull' all the time. There was a slight break once— only once. Some fellows wanted to pull the stock down, and got a few 'bears' to work with them. It lowered a little, but only a few of the heavy holders had any fear, and it soon recovered, shooting up higher than ever. I got your order to sell about that time, and did so, but I assure you my heart ached when I did it."

"I wrote you immediately after that, it was only the first hundred shares I wanted sold."

"Yes, but that letter I got three days after I had sold all. I almost cried like a girl, with disappointment, when you wrote that I was to send you only $6000. Now, you could have made a whole million with your thousand shares."

"A whole million?"

"Most assuredly. Look at yesterday's quotations, and the stock is still rising."

"Truly," said Clarence, reading the stock report; "the last paper I saw was dated six days ago. But even then 'Crown Point' was still very high."

"And so it was, but it is very disappointing to get one-half of a million when you might as well get a whole million. I shall never cease scolding you for it."

"Well, I'll bear the scolding patiently, considering that it was to avoid scoldings that I gave you the order to sell."

"To avoid scolding? How so? From whom?"

"From my father. He is terribly down on mining stocks. He would consider me next to a thief if he thought I bought stocks."

"That is absurd. You needn't tell him how much money you have. Here is my statement of all I made; my commission and moneys paid for you. I sold your stock at a fraction over $800 per share. Oh, Clarence, why did you make me sell? Look at this. After buying the government bonds as ordered you have left $260,000, when you might have had half a million over."

"Never mind. I made enough. I'd rather let some one else make the balance than to sell when things begin to tumble down. Did you say $260,000?"

"Yes, $260,000, when it ought to be $400,000 at least."

Clarence laughed at Hubert's rueful face.

The waiter brought in their breakfast.

"Broiled oysters on toast! Oysters baked in the shell! Broiled chicken. Let us discuss them in preference to stock," said Clarence.

Having helped his friend and then himself, Hubert said:

"What are you going to do with your $260,000 now since you are not to buy stock?"

"I have not thought about it, but I guess the best thing would be to invest all in government bonds."

"Which is the same as burying your cash."

"I'll tell you what I'd like to do. I would like to make a safe investment that would give me about $30,000 a year, and then I could afford to let you gamble with the balance, if there was any balance left," Clarence said.

"I'll see to-day what government bonds are selling for, and report to you this evening."

"That can't be, as I am to take the two o'clock boat for Alameda."

"When will you be back?"

"To-morrow evening if you want me, but if not I shall wait until the family comes down."

"What a lucky fellow he is," said Hubert, walking towards the Stock Exchange, after promising Clarence to see him to the boat at two o'clock. "In two years he has made a fortune with a capital of $2000."

Hubert was right. Clarence had been a lucky investor. With the sum of $2000 bequeathed to him by Mrs. Darrell's Aunt Newton, when he was only five years old, and which sum she ordered should be put at interest until he was twenty-one years of age, Clarence speculated, and now he was worth close on to a million dollars.

Everything was ready for the journey when Clarence arrived at his Alameda home.

"Don't you know that it pulls my heart string to tear you away from this place?" Clarence said, looking towards the nice orchard and field beyond.

"You'll make us cry if you talk like that," said Mrs. Darrell. "Alice has nearly cried her eyes out already."

"Never mind, our lease of this place won't be out for two years yet, and we can come back if the other don't suit," said Clarence encouragingly.

Two days after, the Darrells left Alameda on their way to San Diego, stopping for a couple of days only at San Francisco. On board the steamer

Clarence met Mr. Alfred Holman, who had accompanied his daughters and now placed them under Clarence's care— "According to instructions from Miss Mercedes"— Mr. Holman added, making Clarence's blood rush to his head, as it always did whenever that sweetest of all names was mentioned in his presence. "Tell the Alamares I shall be down soon. I am only waiting for Tom Scott to escort me." So saying, Mr. Holman laughed and hurriedly kissing his daughters, ran down the gang plank.

Clarence lost no time in presenting the Misses Holman to his mother, sisters and brothers, all of whom received them with politeness, though with different degrees of warmth, according to the natural share of affability or that diffidence which half of Darrell's children inherited from him, especially the two eldest daughters. The amiability of Alice and her mother's gentle, winning ways, however, soon dispelled the damp chill that Jane and Lucy's reserve generally managed to throw over strangers, thus before the steamer got under way, all were conversing and laughing like old friends, discussing things in general and people in particular.

"I think you have made a conquest," said Amelia Holman to Alice. "Or perhaps two, for I saw a little yellow haired man with a very red neck, come this way and look at you. Then a loose jointed fellow who walks as if his feet are too heavy to lift and just drags them, follows, and he too looks at you beseechingly."

"Mercy! I don't want to be so fascinating as all that might indicate," said Alice, laughing, and a little man gesticulating, and a big man with shuffling gait and hands in the pockets of his pantaloons, listening wearily, were seen coming.

"I know who they are," said Clarence. "The little one is married, so Alice can rest her hopes on the big footed one only."

"Gracious, how very repulsive the small one is," Corina exclaimed.

"Who are they?" Mrs. Darrell asked when they had turned to go back.

"The large fellow is Dick Mason, brother-in-law of the little red-skinned one, who told me his name is Peter Roper, and he is a lawyer bound for San Diego to practice law there (no matter by what means), he says. He gave me this information himself when I went to check our baggage. He introduced himself and his brother Dick on the strength of his being acquainted with father. He also asked permission to present his wife, to my mother and sisters."

"Did you give that permission?" asked Jane, sternly.

"I did, of course; but if his skin is not so thick as it is red he will never avail himself of it. I noticed he had been drinking, so I told him that at present my mother and sisters wished to converse alone with the Misses Holman, of whom we are the escort, but that before we reached San Diego I thought there might be an opportunity to present his wife, perhaps."

"What did he say to that?" Alice asked.

"He grinned and said: 'Pretty large escort, ain't it? About a dozen people.'

Yes, I said, but the young ladies are very nice, and require a great deal of attention. 'Do they?' said he, and his yellow eyes leered, and sticking his tongue to one side of his mouth, made his cheek bulge out; he then raised his shoulders and lifted his elbows, as if he would have flown aloft had his arms been wings."

"How impertinent and vulgar," Jane exclaimed.

"He is of the genus *hoodlum*. A bird aboriginal of the San Francisco sand dunes, resembling the peacock," said Corina Holman.

"What did you do when he made those grimaces?" Alice asked.

"Nothing. I looked at him as if I expected nothing else, considering that it must be natural to him to act like a monkey. My impassibility rather disconcerted him, as evidently he expected me to consider him very funny, and laugh at his droll antics. He added, 'Any time will do, as my wife is not over-anxious to make acquaintances generally.' So saying, he threw back the lappels of his coat, putting his thumbs in the arm-holes of his vest, and strutted off, leaving me to guess whether he was making fun of his wife's exclusiveness or ours. He turned back soon, though, and said, 'We'll call it square, if you come and take a drink.' When I declined that also, he went off again, and this time angry in good earnest."

"I hope he will remain so, and not come near you again," said Jane.

Vain wish! When the boat stopped at Santa Barbara, Roper took that opportunity to present his wife to Mrs. Darrell on the strength of his acquaintance with her husband. He grinned and suppressed a giggle, thinking it was very funny to claim friendly relations with Darrell, whom he had never seen. It was a matter of perfect indifference to him that Mrs. Darrell would find out his falsehood afterward. All that he wanted now was to become acquainted with the Darrell and Holman ladies. In this he succeeded, and what is more, succeeded according to his principles, in utter disregard of truth or self-respect. He trusted to his inventive genius to explain how he came to imagine he was acquainted with Mr. Darrell.

When the boat arrived at San Diego, Gabriel and Elvira came to the wharf to meet the Misses Holman. They thanked Clarence for the excellent care he had taken of them, and Elvira asked him to present her to his mother and sisters. This was done with pleasure, and he was glad to see that Elvira and Gabriel seemed pleased with his family.

The Holmans would remain in town for a couple of days at a friend's house, after that they would go to the Alamar rancho to make their visit there. Elvira and Gabriel would remain with them to be their escort. Such was Elvira's message home sent with Clarence.

Mr. Darrell came on board to meet his family, but Mr. Peter Roper was too intently occupied with his baggage to renew his acquaintance; in fact, he rather hurried off the boat to avoid him.

The Darrells arrived at the hotel about the same time, but Peter was then particularly engaged making important inquiries from one of the hotel clerks.

He was saying: "So, you think there is no lawyer of any prominence; not one that might be called a leading lawyer?"

"I didn't say that; I only said I don't know of any."

"Exactly. You hear, though, who has the largest practice?"

"If you call a large practice to get people into trouble by spying about people's business and getting commercial agencies (I believe that is what he calls to spy and pry into people's affairs), then old Hornblower is the leading lawyer, for he leads people into long law suits always, and bleeds them and makes money."

"That's the man for me," said Roper, showing his purple gums in a broad grin, and the orange and green of his eyes expanding with feline instincts.

Romeo Hancock had been engaged by Clarence before leaving, to take charge of hauling their effects to the rancho. Romeo, therefore, was there with three large wagons, and two vaqueros to convey Mrs. Darrell's pretty Jersey cows. But Clarence had to see that everything started in good order before he joined his family at the hotel.

"I brought the Concord wagon for the women folks and the light spring wagon for the boys and Tisha," said Mr. Darrell. "The Concord holds six people well, and at a pinch, eight. The light wagon the same; so you don't have to have any extra conveyances."

"No, father, I have not hired any," Clarence replied, and exchanging a look with his brothers, said that everything was ready to start, and all walked down stairs.

In front of the ladies' entrance was a very handsome carriage which Mrs. Darrell and her daughters had admired very much on board the steamer; next to it was a pretty phæton which they also had admired, and behind the phæton was Mr. Darrell's Concord. He frowned and said:

"There was no use in hiring those carriages, Clarence."

"Count noses, father," said Clarence, going about busily carrying parcels to the carriages assisted by his brothers, allowing no time for discussion—"Let us see. Mother and father in the back seat; Jane and Lucy in the front, Clementina with Everett, the driver. In the phæton I will take Alice, her lap dog and our two satchels, and last but not least, Webster will take 'the Concord' with Willie in the front seat and Tisha in the back in state, with the cockatoos and canaries and parcels," said Clarence, patting Tisha on the back.

All laughed, approving the disposition of forces.

"Are these carriages ours, Clary?" asked Clementine.

"It looks like it," said Clarence, lifting her to her place, "and you shall see how soon the phæton distances the big carriage."

CHAPTER VIII.

Victoriano and His Sister.

The golden rays of a setting sun were vanishing in the west, and a silvered moon was rising serenely over the eastern hills, when the phæton, having distanced the other carriages by a full half hour, reached the foot of the low hill where the Alamar house stood. The French windows opening upon the front veranda, sent broad streams of light across the garden and far over the hill. Sounds of music greeted Alice and Clarence on their arrival. He checked his horses saying:

"You see there are two roads here; one goes directly to our house, while the upper one passes close to the gate of the Alamares. I can take the upper road if you would like to hear the music."

"I would, indeed, unless it might seem intrusive."

"They are too kind hearted to think that, besides, I have a message of Doña Elvira to deliver," he said, guiding his horses to the left, slowly climbing the hill to approach the gate silently. The phæton stood in the penumbra between the lights of two windows, and it had not been heard. The singing had ceased, the prelude of a Spanish song was begun and interrupted. The lady at the piano arose and selected another piece of music, and began the accompaniment of the old and well known "Don't you Remember Sweet Alice, Ben Bolt?"

"Who is that lady?" asked Alice in a whisper.

"She is Miss Mercedes," whispered Clarence, glad of the excuse to whisper, and with a preparatory checking of breath and swallowing of something that seemed to fill his throat always, when her name was mentioned.

"I hope she will sing," said Alice.

"Perhaps," was the laconic reply, and both waited in silence. Clarence could distinctly hear his heart throbs.

A man's voice, a fine tenor, began the song. He sang the first stanza so correctly and with so much feeling that it seemed to Clarence that he could not have listened to the simple melody before now attentively enough to appreciate its pathos, for it sounded most sweetly touching to him. Only one verse was sung.

"I never thought that song capable of so much expression, or Tano capable of giving it so well."

The reason why Victoriano interrupted this song was because Mercedes had said, "Sing something else, Tano, that song is too sad. It will give me the blues."

"Me too. Those American songs always speak of death or dying. Ugh! You sing something lively." Then he added, "I wonder why the Darrells haven't come? I suppose they are going to remain in town until to-morrow." So saying he walked to the window. His eyes were too well trained to distinguish objects in the darkness not to have quickly perceived the phæton, though it could not be seen very distinctly. He saw it, but thought it must be Gabriel and Elvira returning unexpectedly. He ran to the gate, exclaiming:

"Hallo! What made you return? Didn't the Holmans come? What has happened?"

"Nothing," Clarence answered. "The Holmans came all safe and sound, and I delivered them into the hands of Don Gabriel, who, accompanied by Doña Elvira, came to meet them. Doña Elvira requested me to say that they will remain in town a couple of days and then come home."

"And where is your family?" asked Tano, coming to the phæton.

"They are coming, and here is a small part and parcel of the same— called our sister Alice. Don Victoriano permit me to present Miss Alice Darrell."

"Miss Alice, your humble servant," said Victoriano, bowing. "Allow me to go to the other side of the phæton to try a more graceful bow a little nearer, and the honor of shaking hands, *a la Americana*".

Mercedes came now, tripping down in the path, also thinking that their carriage had returned, because some accident had happened to somebody.

"Is that you, Gabriel?" said she.

"You come and see," said Victoriano.

She came close to the phæton, right between the wheels, but still thinking she saw Gabriel, said: "What has happened? Ah! it is Mr. Darrell," she added, with a tremor in her voice, that made Clarence think she was alarmed.

He hastened to reply: "Nothing has happened. Your friends are all safe and well."

"This is Miss Alice Darrell. Can you bow to her in the dark, and shake hands?" asked Victoriano.

"I think I can, but she might not see my bow," said Mercedes, laughing, and extended her hand, saying: "I am glad to make your acquaintance, Miss Darrell."

Clarence took her hand, as Alice had not seen it.

"See here, that hand was for me," Alice said, laughing.

"Certainly," said Clarence, putting Mercedes' hand in hers.

"Will you not shake hands with Clarence?" said Victoriano. "I declare, solemnly, girls are very ungrateful. Here Clarence has been so sorry, because you hurt your foot, and you have never thanked him for his kind sympathy."

"Mr. Darrell has never expressed his kind sympathy to me, how was I to presume he felt it?"

"The presumption would have been mine had I expressed all I felt," said he, taking off his glove, which action she rightly understood to mean that he wished to shake hands with her.

She extended her hand, and he clasped it in his. That ineffable thrill which he felt for the first time in his life when he lifted her in his arms was now felt again. It coursed through his veins with the warm blood that rushed to his heart.

Neither one took any notice of what Victoriano and Alice were saying until they heard him say:

"That's all right. He is going to be married soon, then he'll be on the shelf. That's a comfort."

"Who will be on the shelf?" Mercedes asked.

"Gabriel, of course; and I am glad of it, as Miss Alice has just coolly told me that he is the handsomest man she ever saw, forgetting that Clarence is here, and poor me, too."

"Present company is always excepted," Alice argued; "and the rule, I suppose, applies now, though I cannot well see whether it does or not, you being in the dark."

"That is so. Come out of the shadow." Clarence suggested.

"I can't now. I feel too abashed," Victoriano replied.

"He will soon recover. His fits of diffidence don't last long," said Mercedes.

"So he is diffident now?" asked Alice, laughing.

"Yes; that is why I don't want you to tell me that Gabriel is handsome; it abashes me too much."

"He is a good reasoner, too, you see that, Miss Darrell; though by moonlight his logic shines but dimly. Come, we must not keep Miss Darrell longer, since they will not come in," said Mercedes.

"I think you might stop and take supper with us," said Victoriano.

"O, no, thank you," Clarence answered. "We came in advance to light the lamps, and attracted by the music, took the liberty of coming over the road."

"I am sorry. Then you must have heard me sing. Bah! Mercedes, it is your fault," said Victoriano.

"Don't say that. You sing very well, only the song is very plaintive, and the better it is sung, the sadder is its melody," Clarence said.

"It must have seemed like a lugubrious welcome to Miss Alice. I shall never sing that song again," said Victoriano, emphatically. "See if I do."

"I am glad to hear you say that, for you are constantly singing it," Mercedes said.

"I hope it will not be a prophetic coincidence that you should sing it as I came," said Alice, and as she spoke the supper bell rang.

"That is the prophecy I meant," said Victoriano, and all laughed, glad of the timely turn thus given to the conversation.

"With this assurance we must go home comforted," said Clarence, and all bade each other good night.

The lamps were lighted, and the windows and doors opened. The Darrell house looked as if there was an illumination for a national celebration.

"Let us go and see how the house looks from the front outside, all lighted up," said Clarence.

They went out to look at it from the garden.

"How could you build such a nice house, Clary, and how could papa allow it?" Alice said.

"Hush! You must never speak about the cost of this house or its furniture. I have made lots of money in stocks, and can afford it, but father thinks stock gambling is next to robbery."

Mercedes and Victoriano remained for a few moments standing by the gate, watching the phæton.

"By Jove! but isn't she sweet! She has just left me deaf and dumb!" said Victoriano, as the phæton disappeared down the hill.

"Perhaps you are deaf, since you don't hear the supper bell ringing again, but as for being dumb I am sure the greatest beauty on earth couldn't produce that effect."

"But I tell you I am, and I will go to see her and tell her so to-morrow," said he, following his sister to the supper room.

"You will do nothing of the kind. The idea!"

"Why not, pray? Clarence told me to call soon."

"Yes, but he supposed you would have the good taste to wait at least two or three days."

"Three days! Three days! Not if I am alive!"

"What is that about being alive?" asked Rosario.

"Let him tell you," Mercedes replied.

"That I am going to see that sweet little Alice Darrell to-morrow, dead or alive," explained Victoriano.

"Who will be dead or alive?" asked Carlota.

"I, of course! What a question?" Victoriano exclaimed.

"As you could not go there if you were dead, I thought you meant that you were to go and see her in that insensible state," said Carlota.

Victoriano looked at his sister reproachfully, saying:

"How mean to talk so about that sweet girl."

"It was to correct you from expressing yourself in that style of yours, mixing up things and ideas so incongruously. You ought to take care not to confuse things so absurdly," Doña Josefa said.

"Why don't you talk like Gabriel? He always uses good language— in Spanish or in English," Carlota added.

"Bother Gabriel, and Gabriel, and Gabriel! Everybody throws him at my teeth," said Victoriano, beginning to eat with very good appetite.

"The operation don't hurt your teeth, though," said Rosario, "to judge by the very effective manner in which you use them."

"Of course, I do, because I am an amiable good fellow, who bears nobody ill-will, even towards his harassing sisters, and much praised elder brother, who is hoisted up to the skies a million times a day for my special edification and good example. It is a good thing, I tell you, ladies and gentlemen, a very fortunate thing, that I am so amiable, and Gabriel so good a fellow, or else I would have punched his head into calf's head-jelly, twice a day, many times."

"There is your confusion of ideas again. You are thinking that yours might have been the calf's head made into jelly," said Rosario.

"No, miss. I meant what I said."

"Gabriel is very strong and a good boxer," Don Mariano said.

"There it is again! Sweet Alice says he is the handsomest man she ever saw; Lote says he uses beautiful language, and now father implies that the fellow could whip me! Give me some more of that chicken *pipian* to console myself with. Say, mother, why is this delicious chicken stew called '*pipian*?' Because it makes a fellow '*pio*' '*pio*' for more? or because the chicken themselves would cry '*pio*,' '*pio*', if they were to see their persons cooked in this way?" Without waiting for an answer to his question, he added: "I say, mother, arn't you and the girls going to call on the Darrells?"

"No," laconically answered Doña Josefa.

"Why should we?" queried Carlota.

"Because they are neighbors like the Mechlins," Victoriano replied.

"Old Mathews is our neighbor, too," said Rosario.

"But he is a thief," replied Victoriano.

"Isn't to steal land robbery?" asked Carlota.

"The Darrells occupy the land they selected, with my consent, so I hope no one in my family will do them the injustice to say that they have stolen our land, or that they are squatters," said Don Mariano firmly. Then added: "But I do not desire any one of you to speak of this matter with anybody. Only remember, the Darrells are not squatters."

"What shall we say, for instance, if the Holmans should notice that we are very friendly to the Darrells, but not so towards the squatters?" Rosario asked.

"I think the Holmans will be too well-bred to ask questions," said Doña Josefa.

"They are well-bred, but they are very intimate friends," Rosario said

"And very inquisitive ones, too," added Victoriano.

"Refer them to me," Don Mariano said; "I'll give them quite a satisfactory answer."

"Meantime, are we not to visit them?" Victoriano asked.

"Visit whom?" Carlota asked.

"The Darrells, of course," Victoriano answered.

"I thought you meant the Holmans, as we spoke of them last."

"Bother, with your grammar, you had better keep school," Victoriano said.

"You had better go to one," Carlota retorted.

"I have enough of it here. The question now is the visit to the Darrells. Is this family to visit them or not?"

"Why, you are to do so to-morrow, dead or alive," Rosario said.

"Bother! You will call, Mercita, won't you?"

"With pleasure, if mamma will permit me," Mercedes replied.

"You are a sweet pussy always, and the best of sisters. Can't she go,

- 55 -

mother?"

"Certainly, if her father does not object."

"I not only do not object, but I shall be pleased to have Mercedes and her mamma and sisters all call, for I think Clarence's mother must be a lady."

"Hurrah for father, he is a man after my own heart," said Victoriano, clapping his hands.

"Papa feels proud of your approval," Carlota said.

"I would suggest that Tano make a *reconnoitering* visit before Mercedes goes, as a leader of a forlorn hope," said Rosario.

"Goodness, how military your terms, but how little your courage," said Victoriano, derisively.

"I admit that I always dread to face squatters," said Rosario.

"I think I said that the Darrells are not to be considered squatters nor called so by any Alamar, and I repeat that such is my wish. Moreover, not every settler is necessarily a squatter," said Don Mariano.

"I beg pardon. I forgot that," said Rosario.

"Don't do it again, Rosy Posy, don't," said Victoriano, rising from the table, stroking his sister's back as if to pacify a fractious colt. Then going to a window, said: "Mercedes come here. Look at that; isn't that fountain lovely?"

In the front garden of the Darrell house, opposite to the front door and surrounded by flowers and choice plants, Clarence had erected a fountain which was to emit its numerous jets of chrystaline water for the first time, when his mother should drive up to the door. She had done so, and the fountain was sending upwards its jets of diamonds under the rays of the reflectors at the front door. The effect was pretty and brilliant. Clarence's filial love was sweetly expressed in the music of the fountain.

CHAPTER IX.

Clarence is the Bearer of Joyful News.

The Darrell family had been the happy dwellers of their fine house on the Alamar rancho for nearly two months, and the three Misses Holman had been the guests of the Alamar family for the same length of time, and now the month of September, 1872, had arrived.

The awnings at the east and south side of the front veranda were down, and in that deliciously cool place, the favorite resort of the Alamar ladies, they now sat with their guests— the Holmans— engaged in different kinds of fancy work, the greater portion of which was intended to be wedding presents for Elvira and Lizzie Mechlin, who were to be married in a few months.

Mercedes was the only one not at work. She was reclining on a hammock, reading.

"Arn't you going to work anything for the girls, Mercedes?" Rosario inquired.

"Which girls?" Mercedes asked, with her eyes fixed on her book.

"Lizzie and Elvira, of course," Rosario answered.

"I will when the wedding day is fixed."

"It will soon be, when George arrives," Doña Josefa said.

"That will be time enough for my work," said Mercedes, looking from her book down the valley, towards the Darrell house, as if casually observing from under the awning the green meadows below.

"What made you come here? The back veranda is entirely shaded, and much cooler. I have been waiting for you there. Pshaw!" said Victoriano, coming forward and stretching open a hammock to throw himself into it.

"Had we known that, we would all have rushed there," said Corina Holman.

"In a perfect stampede," added Rosario.

"I thought you had gone with your father," Doña Josefa said.

"No, he said he might stay to lunch at aunt's. It is too hot a day to be riding about in the sun."

"Certainly, after having been in the moon for two months the change of temperature might hurt you," said Amelia Holman.

"That's a fact; I have been in the moon ever since *you* came," assented Victoriano.

"Your moon stays in the valley, it doesn't rise to this level," said Amelia.

"It is a lovely moon wherever it may shine. I say, Baby, won't you go with me to the Darrells this evening?" asked he, addressing Mercedes, who had made no reply, for the reason that she had just seen Clarence coming on horseback, and, as usual, when any one spoke of him, or she unexpectedly saw him, she found it necessary to take a little time, in order to steady her voice, which otherwise might betray her heart's tumult.

"Mercedes' French novel must be very interesting," Carlota said.

"It is not a novel— it is French History," said Madam Halier.

"Mercedes, Tano wants you to escort him this evening," said Rosario. "Will you take him?"

"Where?" Mercedes asked, without moving.

"To the moon," said Corina.

"She means to the third heaven," rejoined Victoriano.

"I declare, the God of Love is truly miraculous. I think it could even poetize the Pittikin girls, or the Hughes, in Tano's opinion," said Carlota.

"Talk of the angels, and you hear the clatter of their hoofs," said Rosario; "there he is at the gate."

"This awning is too low— we don't see people until they are upon us," said Carlota.

"I am off. I suppose he will stay to lunch, that will give me all I want of his charming society," said Rosario, rising to go as Clarence dismounted at the gate.

"Stay, he has seen us all; it would be discourteous to leave now," said Doña Josefa, and Rosario remained.

Victoriano jumped out of the hammock to meet Clarence.

"Hallo, yourself and welcome! Any news?"

"Yes, *big* news," Clarence replied, blushing crimson,— not at the news he brought, as one might have supposed,— but because he had just seen two little feet, in a tiny pair of slippers, with blue rosettes, which he well knew. These little blue rosettes had set his heart to beating, sending more than the normal amount of blood to his head.

On leaving her hammock to take a chair Mercedes had shown those tantalizing tip ends of her slippers, half hidden in a mass of lace ruffles. That was all, and yet poor Clarence was disconcerted, and became more and more so, on perceiving that there were not less than nine ladies on that veranda; nine pairs of eyes which had undoubtedly observed his own, devouring the blue rosettes.

"What is the news, pray? Don't kill us with suspense," pleaded Miss Corina Holman.

"The news is that Colonel Scott has arrived at San Francisco, and will be in San Diego next week."

"Hurrah," shouted Victoriano, "now we'll all be rich."

"How do you make that out?" Rosario asked.

"Never mind how, we'll not go into particulars."

"No, better not," Rosario advised.

"Papa will be so glad to hear this news," said Mercedes, "and Mr. Holman, also. He'll come down now, will he not?"

"Yes, father will come down with Col. Scott, and may be build us a house right away," said Amelia.

"There is papa now; I am so glad," Mercedes exclaimed.

"I must run with the news to him," said Victoriano, rushing madly through the hall, to the *patio*, or court, where Don Mariano had just dismounted.

The news was so gladdening to Don Mariano, that he came immediately to propose to the young ladies to have a dance that evening.

"But where are the gentlemen? There are plenty of ladies, but unless you invite squatters"— Rosario began, but Doña Josefa stopped her with a look.

"Let us see," said Don Mariano, counting on his fingers, "there are three or four Darrells, and six or eight Alamares, if my brothers and half of my nephews come. That ought to be enough, I think."

"Plenty. I'll send a vaquero to aunt's to call the boys, and you bring your brothers and sisters, Clarence," said Victoriano.

"With pleasure," was Clarence's reply.

"There will surely be some fellows from town this evening, and we'll make them stay," added Victoriano.

The dance took place and was followed by many others. The Alamar family were very hospitable, and had many visitors, who were only too glad to spend their evenings, dancing with charming and refined young ladies, whose society was certainly most attractive.

There were several young gentlemen from the Eastern States stopping at the principal hotel in San Diego, and they came to Alamar almost daily, to have a dance, or picnic, or musicale, or a card party.

These gayeties were not confined to the Alamar and Mechlin and Darrell families, nor was the Alamar rancho only made happy because Tom Scott was coming. The entire county of San Diego was buoyed up with hopes of prosperity, which now seemed founded upon a solid basis.

As for the town of San Diego itself, the dwarfed and stunted little city, she went crazy with joy. Her joy, however, was not of the boisterous, uproarious kind, it was of a mild character, which smiles at everybody, and takes all that comes in good part, ready always to join in the laugh on herself, provided everybody enjoys it. She was happy, seeing a broad vista of coming prosperity in the near future. Why not? She had every reason and every right to expect that the Texas Pacific would be built.

At last, Col. Scott arrived, and drove to the principal hotel, where a deputation of the most prominent citizens immediately waited on him to pay their respects, and learn his wishes as to how his time should be occupied during his stay in San Diego. The city desired to honor the distinguished guest with liberal hospitality, but the business of the railroad was the main point in view. There were speeches to be made at "Armory Hall," with meetings and consultations to be had at nights, besides drives to examine the town site and surrounding country during the day. The ladies wished to give him a ball, but the business men said Tom Scott did not come to dance, he came to work. There was a banquet given to him, but no ladies were present, only men, and plenty of railroad speeches. The ladies could only meet him at private receptions in the evening, when he was tired out with driving. Yet, this was the best that could be done, as his time was limited. But he was amiable, the ladies were amiable, and the gentlemen were amiable. So the little city of San Diego gave all she had to give; all the lands that had belonged to the old "San Diego & Gila R. R. Co.," all that had been transferred to "The Memphis & El Paso R. R. Co.," all the town lands, water front and rights of way that could by any means be obtained, all was most generously proffered, adding more lands than those originally given to the road under the old names of "The San Diego & Gila Railroad" or "The Memphis & El Paso Railroad."

Col. Scott left well satisfied with the people of San Diego, and the people were charmed with Col. Scott. Speculation then ran wild. Town lots were bought and sold at fancy prices, but in the madness of the hour folly seemed wisdom.

Among the heaviest investors, Don Mariano Alamar, Mr. James Mechlin, and Mr. Alfred Holman were the most prominent. They bought block after block of building lots, and only stopped when their money was all invested. Clarence also bought a few blocks, and George and Gabriel risked all they dared. Many other people followed this (which proved to be disastrous) example, and then all sat down to wait for the railroad to bring population and prosperity.

The day of the double wedding which was to tie together (with a double loop) the Alamar and Mechlin families, was set for the 24th of May, 1873. On that day Gabriel and George would lead to the altar their respective sisters, Lizzie and Elvira.

Don Mariano wished to celebrate that double wedding in the same old-fashioned way in which his own had been solemnized. He wanted at least three days of good eating and drinking, and dancing; to have noise and boat racing; to have a day's sailing on the bay, and a day's picnic in the woods, to which picnic even the stubborn, hostile squatters should be invited. But with the sole exception of Victoriano, no one of his family approved this programme.

"I'm afraid my dear husband that we are too closely surrounded by Americans for us to indulge in our old-fashioned rejoicings," Doña Josefa said.

"We would be laughed at," Carlota added.

"Who cares for that?" Victoriano asked, scornfully.

"I don't believe that the right thinking and kind-hearted Americans would say anything, except that such is customary among us. But if George and Gabriel desire to run off in the steamer, as though they were ashamed of matrimony, I say let them have their way. But they will have a wedding that will look like a funeral," said the disappointed Don Mariano.

"George and Gabriel are willing to have their wedding celebrated as you propose, but it is the girls that object; they wished to run off and hide for a month in a fashionable hotel in San Francisco; afterward they came to the conclusion that they didn't want to go to a hotel, so Gabriel proposed that they will take the steamer that goes to Mazatlan and Guaymas and La Paz, thus to visit all of those places on their wedding tour," Victoriano said. "As George had been wishing to see the Mexican coast, this plan suited all very well, and George has written to have the steamer stop for them on her way south," Victoriano explained, half apologetically, half resentfully.

"That is all right; if they are satisfied I am," said Don Mariano, philosophically, with characteristic amiability.

The steamer running between San Francisco and the Mexican ports on the Gulf of California stopped at San Diego to take the newly married couples; a large party of friends escorted them on board.

Don Mariano was kind and affable to all, but many days passed before he became reconciled to the fact that the marriage of his two children was not celebrated as his own had been, in the good old times of yore.

The brides and grooms had been gone for some time, and might now be coming back in a few days.

"I am glad we three are alone, for there is something of which I wish to speak with you two when no one of the family is with us," said Doña Josefa to Carlota and Rosario, as they sat in their favorite front veranda, sewing.

The girls looked up, and casting a quick glance to see whether any one was approaching, waited to hear what their mother had to say. The awnings being only half down no one could come from the outside unobserved.

"What is it, mamma?" Carlota asked, seeing that her mother seemed to hesitate; "anything unpleasant?"

"Well, no— yes. That is to say, to me it is, very. Have you noticed Mercedes' manner lately? She seems absorbed, silent, thoughtful, sad, and— and— you know what I fear. She says she is not sick, then it is some mental trouble, I am sure. So, then, I have been thinking that she had better go with Elvira and visit New York for a while, the change will do her good. I do not approve of young girls going from home on visits, but as she will go with her married sister, and— and— I hope it will be for her good."

"And yet it may not," said Carlota.

"Perhaps, if it is as you— as we three— fear, absence might be worse for her," added Rosario; "Mercedes is very gentle, but she is very loving and constant, so it might do more harm than good to send her away now. Remember what the poet says about it:

> 'La ausencia es para el amor
> Lo que el aire para el fuego;
> Si es poco, lo apaga luego,
> Si es grande, lo hace mayor.'

and I fear that Mercedes is too deeply interested already."

"That is so. Have you spoken to papa about it?" Carlota asked.

"I mentioned it only once, knowing his partiality to Clarence," Doña Josefa replied.

"He might be partial, but when it comes to the danger of his daughter's marrying a *squatter* I should think there would be a limit to partiality," Carlota said, warmly.

"I fear your father views the matter differently. The one time I mentioned to him that Clarence seemed to be more and more in love with Mercedes, and my fear that she also liked him more than I care to believe. He said, 'Has he made love or proposed to her?' I told him I hoped he had not been so audacious as that. 'Audacious!' said he, and laughed. 'I tell you, wife, if all that is necessary for Clarence to propose be courage, neither you nor I can stop him, for the boy is no coward. I reckon that it is Mercedes herself who gives him no encouragement; that is what deters him, but none of our *sangre azul*,' and he laughed again. I said to him, you take very coolly a matter that might be a question of our child's fate for life, but he only appeared amused at my anxiety. He said: 'Don't borrow trouble; Clarence is a most excellent young fellow— bright, energetic and honorable. Don't bother them or yourself; if they feel true love they have a right to it. Trust him, he is all right.'"

"But a squatter! The idea of an Alamar marrying a squatter! For squatters they are, though we dance with them," Carlota said. "I am shocked at papa's partiality. I must say yes, mamma, send poor Mercita away."

"Yes; with all due respect to papa, I fear I will not be reconciled to the idea of Mercedes being a daughter-in-law of old Darrell," Rosario said, with a shudder.

"Neither could I," added Carlota.

And thus felt and thus reasoned these proud ladies *in those days*. For although the shadows of black clouds were falling all around, they had not observed them, or suspected their proximity; they held up their heads proudly.

"And has Clarence the means of supporting a wife?" Rosario asked. "That is another question to be considered."

"I don't know. I heard he had made money in stocks, but I don't know how much," Doña Josefa replied.

"I have no faith in stocks," said Carlota.

"Let us not mention this to Mercedes yet. When Elvira returns we will consult with her," Doña Josefa said.

Nothing was said to Mercedes about her journey, but she was never allowed to see Clarence alone.

Elvira returned, and the project mentioned to her. She, as a matter of course, was delighted at the prospect of having her favorite sister with her. The pain of leaving her home would be lessened in her company.

A day or two after, when Elvira was alone in her room, Mercedes came in, looking rather pale, and letting herself drop into the first chair she came to, said:

"What is this unexpected news about my going to New York with you?"

"Good news, I think. Don't you like it?"

"Certainly. But it is too sudden. Why hadn't mamma thought of it before?"

"Because she did not think your health required any change."

"I tell you what, mamma alarms herself unnecessarily, and puts but poor reliance on me. I understand it all, but as a trip to New York is a most delightful medicine, I am willing to take it, and that she should consider my health in a precarious state."

"But you *do* look pale and thin, Mercita."

"Nonsense!" Mercedes exclaimed. "I have been keeping late hours, and dancing too much. If I go to bed early I shall get back my good color and flesh again. However, I am glad to play the invalid until I get on board the cars."

"Very well. I'll be alarmed for you, too, until we get off."

Mercedes laughed, and went to her room singing, but once there her gayety vanished. She locked her door, and threw herself on the bed, burying her face in her pillow to stifle her sobs.

"Can anything tear his image from my heart? No. Nothing! nothing! They may send me away to the other end of the world, they shall not part us, for you will still fill my heart, my own darling, holding my very soul forever in full possession."

Mercedes, being not quite seventeen, her grief at parting from Clarence was wild, vehement and all-absorbing. But she had been trained to obedience, and her battles with the spirit always took place after she carefully locked her bedroom door. Then Clarence was wildly apostrophized, and a torrent of tears relieved the overcharged, aching heart.

The day of departure arrived, and she had not had one minute's conversation alone with Clarence.

CHAPTER X.

But Clarence Must Not be Encouraged.

The wharf was over-crowded. The steamer was about to leave. The last car-load of baggage had been quickly shipped, and Clarence had not been able to say a word to Mercedes which might not have been heard by the persons surrounding her. He was pale and desperate. He had gone on board the steamer just to ask her one question, but she had never been alone for an instant. And thus they must part,— for the embodied "*Fuerza del destino*" now came in the shape of a boy clanging in deafening clatter a most discordant bell, saying that those who were not going on the steamer must go ashore. A hurried hand-shaking, and the troop of friends marched down the gang-plank to turn round and look many more tender adieus from the wharf.

Don Mariano had observed Clarence's deathly pallor, and how faithfully it was reflected on Mercedes' face; he saw the unhappy young man standing aloof from the crowd on the extreme edge of the wharf. He went to him, and laying his hand gently on his shoulder, said:

"That position is dangerous— you might lose your balance," and he pulled him gently away. "You are very pale. I fear, my dear boy, that you are more troubled than you have admitted to any one. What is it? Tell me."

Clarence shook his head, but suppressing his emotion, said:

"I cannot express my misery. She is sent away that I may not even have the pleasure of seeing her. No one can love her as I do, impossible!"

"Why have you not spoken to me of this before?" asked Don Mariano, kindly.

"Because I did not dare. I thought of doing so a thousand times, but did not dare. I did not fear unkindness or rejection from *you*, but from Doña Josefa and the young ladies I did, and I have never had an opportunity to speak alone to Miss Mercedes."

"That was an additional reason for speaking to me. Cheer up. '*Faint heart never won fair lady.*'"

"Tell me that again. Say you do not reject me, and I'll jump aboard and follow her."

"I do not reject you, and I repeat what I said, follow her if you wish, and try your luck. I want to see you both happy, and both of you are very unhappy."

Clarence looked toward the boat. The gang-plank had been removed.

"What a happy girl you are, Mercedes, to visit New York. How I wish I, too, could go," he heard Corina Holman say.

"Come on, it is not too late yet," George replied.

Clarence looked up, and met Mercedes' eyes. It seemed as if George's words were intended for him.

He clasped Don Mariano's hand, saying hurriedly:

"If I understand you, I have your permission to go. May I? Tell me 'yes.'"

"'*Faint heart never won fair lady*,'" he repeated, smiling, and returning the warm pressure of his hand, added: "Yes, go and try your luck."

Clarence turned, and without another word quickly made his way through the crowd.

The steamer's wheels began to move; the captain was already on the bridge, over the starboard wheel, and had given the order to let go the hawsers. In another instant the steamer would leave the wharf.

Clarence felt himself pulled by the arm, he turned impatiently, and met Everett, who handed him two telegrams, saying:

"I have looked for you everywhere. These telegrams followed each other quickly."

"Yes, I know," Clarence said, taking them; adding, without stopping his hurried walking, "Retty, I am going. Tell them at home I got three telegrams calling me to San Francisco."

"But you haven't read them," urged Everett, trying to follow him.

"But I know what they are; I have another in my pocket."

Lifting his arm with the telegrams in his hand, he said to the captain:

"Captain, one moment. I must go north. Please take me."

The captain did not hear him, and at the same time called out:

"Let go that hawser! Do you want it to snap?"

The crowd ran off, giving a wide berth to the heavy rope, which now, by its own tension, made it impossible to be slipped off the pile, although many pairs of hands were tugging at it manfully.

The stern expression of the captain's face softened as he saw Clarence standing on the brink of the wharf.

"Step back, Mr. Darrell, quickly, the rope might part," said he; but noticing that Clarence desired to speak to him, motioned to the first officer to take his place, and ran down to hear what Clarence said.

A minute after the steamer stood still for an instant, then the wheels began to revolve in reversed motion.

"There she is, Mr. Darrell; she'll be alongside in a minute," the captain said, pleased with the opportunity to oblige Clarence.

And the steamer, propelled by one wheel, began to back as if with the sidelong motion of a highly intelligent crab who understood the situation.

"Read your telegrams," Everett repeated.

"All right— to please you," said Clarence, tearing them open. Adding, after reading a few words, "It is as I expected. I am wanted by Hubert. Send him a dispatch to-night saying I left, and to accept M.'s offer, and pay the money at once."

"Now, Mr. Darrell, come on," the captain said.

Hurriedly Clarence shook hands with Don Mariano, Gabriel, Everett and Victoriano.

"Take care, jump in on the downward swing, when about on a level with the wharf," said Gabriel.

Clarence nodded, gave him his hand, and planting his foot firmly on the wharf, gave one spring, and wiry as a cat, alighted on the steamer beside the captain, who hugged him, saying:

"Bravo, my boy, I could have done that twenty years ago."

Don Mariano and Gabriel lifted their hats in congratulatory salutation; Victoriano and Everett twirled theirs in the air hurrahing; the ladies waved their handkerchiefs, and the steamer giving a dip and a plunge— by way of a very low courtesy— bounded up and started onwards, as if satisfied she had been good natured long enough, and now must attend to business. In a few minutes she had made up for lost time, and was heading for Ballast Point, leaving San Diego's shore to be merged into the blue hills of Mexico beyond, as if obeying the immutable law which says that all things must revert to their original source.

Elvira's beautiful eyes were so filled with tears that she could see nothing. Still, she kept her gaze riveted upon that fast receding wharf. George stood a few feet apart, prudently thinking that the two sisters would perhaps prefer to be by themselves while taking their last look at the dear ones standing on the wharf. He, too, felt much moved; he would have preferred to remain with his family at Alamar. He would come next year— he thought— and perhaps remain in California permanently. With this thought in his mind, almost shaped into resolve, he came to Elvira's side, and quietly slipping his arm round her waist, said:

"Don't cry, sweetest, I will bring you back next year, and we will make our home near our parents. No matter if I make less money, we will have more happiness."

Elvira looked unutterable thanks.

"Do you hear him, Mercedes?" she said, and Mercedes nodded, but moved a little further off, not yet trusting her voice to make any reply.

"Look here, this won't do; this will spoil our blue eyes," said George, putting his other arm around Mercedes' pretty shoulders. "I insist upon you turning your thoughts toward New York, Long Branch, Newport and Washington; think of all the fun we will have visiting all those places. Then we will come back gay and happy, and our dear ones will be so glad to see us again. Think of all that," and thus George exerted his eloquence to administer consolation. "I am sure all at home will be thinking of our return by to-morrow morning," he added, by way of climax to his consoling rhetoric.

But George was mistaken. The Alamar ladies found it very hard and difficult to reconcile themselves to be separated from Elvira and Mercedes.

The fact that Clarence had gone in the same steamer, added much bitterness to Doña Josefa's sorrow at separating from both daughters. She did not even wish any one to mention Clarence's name in her presence. Don Mariano's arguments in favor of the bold young man were at first ineffectual, but after a while she began to think that she ought to trust more in Mercedes' pride and Elvira's vigilance.

In the meantime the travelers continued their voyage very happily. Clarence rightly conjectured that Mercedes would suppose he had followed her to declare his love, and this supposition would redouble her shyness. Her manner at first, fully confirmed this surmise, so, to put her at her ease, he was very kind and attentive, but never betrayed by word or look, his heart's devotion. His manner was exactly all that she could wish, the behavior of a devoted brother, and in consequence she began to be less shy. He spoke of having received three telegrams, calling him north; this surely was a good reason for his unexpected journey.

They visited Los Angeles, went ashore at Port Harford and Santa Barbara, and as George was naturally devoted to his bride, there seemed no alternative for Mercedes but to accept Clarence's escort, and lean on his arm whenever that operation became necessary.

The nights were lovely, with a full moon in the azure sky, and the sea air, neither cold nor warm, but of that California temperature, which seems to invite people to be happy, giving to all an idea of the perfect well-being we expect to find in the hereafter.

There was a great deal of freight to be landed at Santa Barbara. The passengers going to San Francisco were already on board. Still the steamer tarried. Some lady friends of Elvira, who were going north had come aboard, and as they had much to say, took her away to their staterooms.

"Wait for me here, I'll return in half an hour," said she to George; but he thought he knew how ladies measure time when engaged in talking, so he slowly arose and said he would go to play cribbage with the captain.

The steamer now shivered and trembled, as if awakening from a nice nap. The wheels revolved lazily and then she was off, dragging a luminous wake of myriads of evanescent diamonds.

"If you wish to go, Mr. Darrell, please do so; do not remain on my account," said Mercedes, when George rose to go.

"Not at all. I remain entirely on my own, as I do not particularly desire to play cut-throat cribbage, and as it is too early for you to retire, suppose you permit me to remain until your sister returns."

"Certainly, do so, else I'll stay," said George, going.

"Have I offended you in any way?" Clarence asked.

"No, of course not. What a question. What makes you ask that?"

"Because you must know it would be cruel punishment to send me off."

"I didn't think anything of the kind, only I didn't wish to be selfish and keep you from going if you wished it."

"How could I wish to go anywhere and leave you; I would not go to heaven, if to do so I would have to renounce you."

"Please do not talk like that, some one might hear you."

"There is not a soul within hearing. Our only witness is that lovely moon, and she will not betray."

"No matter, please do not speak like that."

"Like what? That I love you? I have never yet said it in words, but you know it."

"Oh! Mr. Darrell!"

"Yes, you know it, and to avoid me you are going away; going from me, no matter if it killed me."

"It is not my choice, I only obey," said she, clasping her trembling hands, now cold as ice.

"Is it so? Did you not wish to avoid me?"

"Please do not ask me, you'll make me very miserable."

"I would not cause you one single pang, if to avoid it I had to die. Believe me, all I wish to know is, whether I have been so blind as not to see your dislike; whether it was your own choice to go, or you were compelled to do so by your mother?"

"Please don't blame mamma."

"I do not blame her in the least. She has a perfect right to object to me if she wishes, but I too, have at least, the sad privilege of asking whether you also object to me?"

"I have nothing against you; I like you very much, as— as a friend," she said, trembling, painfully agitated.

Clarence laughed a hoarse, discordant laugh that made her feel miserable.

"I have been told that young ladies say that always, when they mean to let down easily a poor devil whom they pity and perhaps despise. Thanks, Miss Mercedes, for liking me 'as a friend,' thank you. Perhaps I am a presumptuous fool to love you, but love you I must, for I can not help it."

He stood up and looked down at the dark ocean in silence. She looked up to his face and her beautiful features looked so pleadingly sad, that he forgot his own misery and thought only of the pain those superb eyes revealed.

He seated himself very near her, and took both of her hands in his own. Surely there was something troubling her.

"How cold these dear little hands are. Have I caused you pain?" he asked. She nodded but did not speak.

"Yes, I have pained you, when I would give my heart's blood to make you happy. Oh! Mercedes, I cannot give you up, it is impossible while I live. Do you command me to do so? Do you wish it? You know that I have loved you from the first moment I saw you; when I lifted you in my arms. The exquisite pleasure I felt then, and the yearning I have felt ever since, to hold you in my arms again, as my own sweet wife, that longing tells me incessantly that I can never love any one else; that I must win you or renounce love forever on earth. Tell me, will you cruelly repel me?"

She was silent, listening with averted face, as if afraid to meet his gaze, but she did not withdraw her hands, which he still held in both his own, as if he would never willingly release them again.

"Mercedes, say that you reject me only to obey your mother, and I will not despair, for I know that your father does not object to me; on the contrary, he sanctions my love, he would accept me as his son-in-law."

She turned quickly, gazed at him with an eager, inquiring look.

"Yes, he gave me permission to follow you and ask you to be my wife."

"What? He? My papa did that?"

"Yes. When he saw me looking so wretched with the pain of parting from you, he said to me, 'Cheer up; faint heart never won fair lady.' I said to him, if you tell me that in earnest, I'll jump aboard the steamer and follow her. He repeated the quotation, adding: 'Go and try your luck.' Is not that sufficient?"

"Darling papa, he is so kind," she said, eluding Clarence's question, but her evident gratitude toward her father spoke volumes.

"Indeed he is. His heart is full of nobility. He does not permit unjust prejudices to influence him into dislikes."

"You must not blame my poor mamma. She thinks you did some wrong act, but she is not prejudiced against you, nor does she dislike you."

"I did some wrong act? What is it? When?"

"That I couldn't tell you, for I do not know, and perhaps I am wrong to have said so much. But I spoke because it was painful to me to think that you believe my own loving, lovely mamma prejudiced, for she is not. She might be mistaken, but she is kindness itself."

Clarence mentally demurred to this warm praise, but wisely held his peace.

"Promise me you will not think mamma is prejudiced," said she, without the least suspicion of the tyranny, the unreasonableness of such a request.

"I promise it, of course, if you desire it, but I would at the same time, like to know what is the *wrong* act of which I am accused, that has brought upon me her censure. I assure you I have not the slightest idea; I think my record as an honest man can well bear scrutiny. Can it be that I have made money in mining stocks?"

"Oh, no. She does not know that, and if she did, she would not think it wrong, for she knows nothing about stocks."

"Then I vow I have not the remotest idea of what it is."

"Think no more about it now, and when you return, you ask papa. He will soon find out the mistake and vindicate you."

"Yes, he will do so I am sure. I would blindly trust my life and honor in his hands," said he, warmly, and quick as a flash came his reward, for she pressed his hands most gratefully. "Ah! Mercedes why did you do that?" The poor young man was trying to make up his mind not to press his suit until he had been vindicated, and Doña Josefa had nothing against him. But that pressure made him ambitious, impatient; he wished to have some promise that she would not accept any one else's suit. She was going from him, out of his sight. He was certain that dozens, yes hundreds, would fall in love with her as soon as they saw her. Would she not love some one? It would be natural to prefer to him, some of those elegant New Yorkers, or some fascinating foreigner whom she might meet in Washington. This thought made him wretched.

"I'm so glad you appreciate papa," said she, withdrawing her hands, which she considered he had held long enough. Noticing that he looked troubled, and that his hand trembled, she added: "I fear I have been indiscreet, and have caused you pain by what I said; if so, I am very sorry. Have I pained you?"

"I have never done anything dishonorable. I can prove that to Doña Josefa at any time. But"— he broke off, and after a paused, added: "Oh! Mercedes! how wretched I shall be, thinking that you might love some one else. Is not your refusal to give me any encouragement a proof that you feel you never can care for me?"

"Please don't say that. I do care for you. That is, I mean, I ought not to tell you so, but— but"— she did not finish, for the rash young man had again seized her little hands, and was covering them with kisses, forgetting that any passenger had the right to come and sit there on the same bench to enjoy the silvery moonlight, sailing over the broad, sublime Pacific.

"Oh! Mr. Darrell! Don't do that. Please let us go now to call Elvira. She thinks George is with me," she said, rising.

"We don't want Elvira, we don't want George. Let them be. Why do you grudge me this happiness of being alone with you for the first and, perhaps, for the last time in my life? Please sit down. I will behave myself. I will not kiss your hands, I promise; but won't you reward my self-restraint by answering one question?"

"What is the question?" said she, sitting down again, only a little further off; "tell me, and then we must go to find Elvira."

"I want you to tell me— I mean, I beg and entreat you to tell me this— if I can prove that I have never done anything dishonorable, and your mother ceases to object to my marrying you, will you then consent to be my wife?"

The question gave Mercedes exquisite pleasure, for she loved him with all her heart. The word wife soundly so sweetly coming from his lips, but she had promised her mother "*not to encourage him.*" So she must not. It would be dishonorable to break her word. What could she say, not to make him unhappy, and yet not commit the sin of disobedience to her mother's command?

She looked down, and her expressive features again showed that she was troubled.

"Oh! I was mistaken. Your silence tells me I cannot hope."

"Do not be impatient, please. I was trying to think how I could explain to you my position."

"Your position?"

"Yes. How much what papa said to you might alter things. But I cannot see how I can say anything to you, except to be patient. Yes, let us both be patient."

"Patience and despair do not travel together."

"Discard despair, and trust to patience, and"— she was going to say, "trust me," but remembered her mother's commands, and that to say so much even would be *to encourage him*. She was silent. She could have rejected an offer of marriage easily without taking away all hope, but as she "*must not encourage him*," that was the most difficult dilemma for the poor girl. "Trust to papa, and— and do not be blaming me in your heart. I cannot bear that."

"I shall not blame you. I shall do whatever you order me. But at all times I do not understand you," said he, sadly.

"It is because my position is so— so difficult, so unnatural. I wish you could understand it without my explaining it. Can't you?"

"I'll try," said he, in most dejected tones, again thinking of the elegant New Yorkers, and fascinating Washingtonians, on their knees before her. "But I do not understand why you refuse me one word of encouragement."

"Oh! that is just *the word* I cannot give," she sighed.

"This is all the work of Doña Josefa," thought he, and the form of the handsome matron seemed to rise before him from the billows of the Pacific, and stand with Juno's lofty majesty in severe impassibility before his sad gaze.

Mercedes, too, was looking at the immense sea, as if trying to discover in that vast expanse some consoling words that a good, obedient daughter might speak on such an occasion.

CHAPTER XI.

George is a Christian Gentleman.

In vain did Mercedes scan the broad bosom of the Pacific Ocean in search of something to say that would be soothing to Clarence's feelings, very proper for her to utter, and very acceptable to her mamma's sentiments, had she been there to hear it. But that vast sea was dark and mute. It did not respond. It only made her shudder to think of its awful silence that was so solemn, but not in the least comforting. It was so dark, so limitless, so cold. She turned her eyes to the luminous wake trailed by the steamer where such wealth of diamonds was wasted. "Fitful scintillations and then all lost in gloom," she said, adding: "No, all is not wasted, those bright diamonds are not as evanescent as we, they will sink, but reappear again and remain there always to gladden or amuse poor travelers for ages to come; yes, when our two poor hearts have ceased forever to throb with joy or pain."

"Is it not, then, wrong when life is so flitting to refuse pure and holy happiness which God has permitted to the children of man?"

"We will be talking bookish, like Corina Holman, if we sit here alone with the silent Pacific. Let us go to find Elvira," said she, rising. "Ah, there she is now!"

Elvira was bidding good night to her two lady friends who stood at the door of their state-room, and (as all ladies must) had something very interesting to say at the last moment.

"And so I am to be patient whether there is hope or not," said Clarence.

"You said you would speak with papa. You forget how very kind he is to everybody in general, and how partial to you in particular."

"Yes, he is most generous, almost too noble for this world."

"I have often thought that, but as he is past fifty, I trust that a kind Providence will spare him to us for many years yet."

"Of course, he will be spared to you. If no good man could live, then the gift of life would be a brand upon man's forehead. But a character as his, is truly very rare. He comes nearer to my standard of excellence than any other man I ever saw, and I revere and love him for it."

"I shall treasure those words in my heart, believe me. Let them remain there forever," she said, her voice vibrating with emotion.

"Well, well, and where is George?" said Elvira, looking around for her missing husband.

"He went to the captain's room to play cribbage about two minutes after you left," said Mercedes.

"Good chaperone he is; and what have you been talking about here like two little owls who know they musn't jump into the water because they are not ducks?"

"One isn't, any way," Clarence said, smiling.

"As my married experience is yet fresh and limited, I don't know whether it would be proper or not for us three to take a turn on deck and see whether George is enjoying himself. What do you think, Mr. Darrell, would a husband object to that?"

"I should say not. Why should he? To my way of thinking no husband of ordinary good sense could object to his wife showing that interest in him. Mr. Mechlin will not, I am sure."

"Let Mr. Darrell take a look first," suggested Mercedes.

Clarence arose to go, Elvira said: "Only pass by, as if by accident, and we'll go or not, according to circumstances."

When Clarence had gone beyond hearing, Elvira said: "He looks pale again, have you made him unhappy?"

"I have not made him happy, that is sure, and I am miserable, but you know mamma's feelings, what can I do? Oh, what can I do?" said she, putting her arms around her sister and the hot tears she had been repressing flowed fast. "I am so sorry I have to make him so unhappy."

"I must say I feel sorry for him myself. I am not sure that mamma does him justice," Elvira observed reflectively.

"And to think that papa himself told him to follow me."

"Is that so?"

"Yes; and he is disappointed, but what can I do, dear, when mamma told me *not to encourage* him?"

"I certainly am under no pledge, and papa's authority is entitled to as much respect as mamma's," Elvira said significantly.

"That is true, but you see mamma made me promise not to *encourage* him," said Mercedes with sad insistence.

"Yes, and Rosa and Lota urged her to it. There is George now."

"I will go to my room; they will see by my red eyes that I cried."

"Go and bathe them. Drink some water, too, and come back."

"And I'll bring you some by way of an excuse."

"Why did Mercedes run off?" George asked.

"She will be back in a minute; she went to take a glass of water."

"Oh! why did she not tell me to bring it to her?" said Clarence regretfully. "I ought to have thought of bringing it. Wouldn't she rather have a glass of wine or lemonade? and you, too, Mrs. Mechlin? I shall take it as a favor if you will accept. A glass of champagne with ice I think would do very well for all of us; don't you think so Mr. Mechlin?"

"Yes, champagne with ice would be very nice, provided the champagne be good," George replied.

"Let us try any way," said Clarence, going to order the wine. George and Elvira watched him, and when out of hearing George said:

"Don't you know I like that young man very much. What is your mother's objection to him?"

"His family, I believe, or rather his father."

"Old Darrell looks like a decent, honorable sort of a man to me. Certainly Clarence is very gentlemanly, and (what is equally to be considered) Mercedes likes him more than is good for her peace of mind if she is not to have him."

"My poor little sister, she is so unhappy, and, just think of it, papa told Clarence to come, to follow Mercedes and propose to her."

"He did? That is just like him. Doubtless he thought of the times when he would ride eighty miles to go and serenade Doña Josefa, and his sympathies all went to Darrell. It is a pity your mother doesn't feel as kindly."

"And what makes me feel more for Mercedes is, that she loves Clarence dearly, but in obedience to mamma's wishes she will not even give him any encouragement at all."

"Then *we* must, that's all. Only let us first be sure that she loves him."

"Oh, as to that, if you had only seen her beautiful eyes filled with such sad tears because she cannot accept his love, you would have no doubts as to her feelings."

"Then my course is clear. I am a Christian gentleman and will not see savage torture inflicted on my blue-eyed *hermanita*. I think I know how to fix it up."

"What will you do?"

"*Quien sabe* just this minute, but it will be *something*, depend upon it. There he is now," and Clarence came, followed by a waiter bringing the champagne and ice. He looked disappointed at not finding Mercedes.

"That little sister of ours I fear has given us the slip. I think I'll go and fetch her bodily," George said, rising to go.

"No; let me go," said Elvira. When George was left alone with Clarence he said:

"I fear that Mercedes is very unhappy, she left when she saw us coming, Elvira says, because she feared her eyes showed traces of tears."

Clarence clenched his hands as if he would like to throttle all bad luck in general, and this one in particular, looked haggard, but remained silent. George continued:

"Spanish girls are trained to strict filial obedience, and it is a good thing when not carried too far. Now, Mercedes made to her mother some very foolish promise, and if her heart was to break into little pieces she would not swerve— not she— though she be fully aware that her happiness would be wrecked for ever, she would not disobey her mother."

"But is it alone her mother's wishes? In obeying her mother, does she not follow her own inclination?"

George laughed, saying: "She must be a strange girl, indeed, if she weeps so bitterly and is so unhappy to follow her inclination."

"Oh, if I only could think that! Are you sure?"

"Why did Doña Josefa wish to send her away? Only for the hope that she might get over her love for you. Mercedes is not yet eighteen, and, being so young, her mother thought that by sending her away from you and yours, she might forget you. Only such hope as that could have prevailed upon Doña Josefa to part with her baby. Spanish mothers will never let a daughter go out of the maternal sight until they are married; but for the fear that Mercita's attachment to you might become incurable if not effaced early, the mother was ready to sacrifice her feelings. For it was a terrible sacrifice, it was like pulling her heart strings to send her baby off."

"Oh, how she must hate me then to have such strong objections to me," said Clarence, sadly.

"No, she does not hate you"— and George hesitated.

"Yes, I know she thinks I have done something wrong or dishonorable, but what that is, I have not the slightest idea."

"Excuse me for saying so, but I think it was a mistake not to tell her— and Mercedes also— that you bought the land you occupy. Doña Josefa cannot think it is honorable to take up land as your father did. She cannot understand how any law of Congress can authorize a man to take the property of another against his will and without paying for it."

"And she is perfectly right. I see the mistake now, and I regret it more than words can tell. You knew why I asked Don Mariano not to mention that I had paid him."

"Yes, Gabriel told me first, and he, too, thinks it is a mistake to let the Alamar ladies have a wrong idea of you. He thinks you do an injustice to yourself. We were talking about it when Don Mariano joined us, and he agreed with Gabriel and said that he would speak to you about it very soon. Doesn't any of your family know about it?"

"Yes, Everett and mother do. She would not have come down if I had not told her I paid for the land. But she and I thought that for the present we had better say nothing about it to father, knowing how sensitive he is about his views of '*Squatter rights*?' He has had so much trouble about those same rights."

"I suppose you will have to tell him soon— I mean when the attorney general dismisses the appeal."

"When will that be, do you think?"

"Just as soon as the Supreme Court is in session. It would have been done last fall had not the solicitor general interfered in the most absurd and arbitrary manner."

"I heard he had, and I heard the settlers rejoicing about it, but I never knew how it happened— I would like to hear."

"Well, ladies and gentlemen," said Elvira, coming, "if my eloquence and persuasive powers were not of the unprecedented quality they really are, I would never have been able to persuade the señorita to come. Would you believe it? she was actually in bed for the night."

"Ah!" Clarence exclaimed, regretfully.

"Yes, I told her that if she didn't come, you would take the champagne to her room, and this so frightened her, that she began to dress herself immediately, but the poor little thing trembles as if she had the ague. I gave her a cashmere wrapper and soft shawl to wrap up and not take cold."

"Go and tell her we have good news for her," suggested George.

"She'll think you are jesting," Elvira answered.

"Not if you tell her that we know what it is that Doña Josefa has against Darrell, and we'll make it all right."

"Oh, don't deceive the poor little thing when she seems as if all her strength is already gone from her," Elvira said.

"But we are not deceiving her," George insisted.

"Hush! here she comes," Elvira said, and Mercedes slowly approached them. "Come, sweet Baby, these gentlemen say they have some awful nice news for you."

"News that the wine is good, I suppose, but I don't like wine," she said.

"No, it isn't the wine," George said, rising for Mercedes to take his place. "Sit down here between Darrell and myself and you shall hear all about it."

"What is it?" Mercedes asked, looking from one to the other.

"I can't tell you, little sister, for they haven't told me," Elvira said.

"Darrell, you fill the glasses now while I tell these señoritas what sort of a black sheep Doña Josefa thinks you are, and so thinking, objects to you." Clarence proceeded to put ice into the glasses, while George continued: "The objection is, that she believes the Darrells are '*squatters*,' like all the others at the rancho, whereas Clarence bought their land from Don Mariano and paid for it even before they built their house."

"Oh! I am so glad to hear that!" Elvira exclaimed with a sigh of relief. "But why don't papa tell it to mamma? It is an injustice to the Darrells to let her ignore it."

"It is my fault, Mrs. Mechlin," Clarence said; "my father holds the accepted but very erroneous popular opinions about '*squatter rights*,' and I, to avoid painful discussions with him, requested Señor Alamar not to say, for the present, that I had paid for the land."

"You see, little sister, how, after all, you have not been loving a squatter? What a pity," said George, putting his arm around Mercedes, who buried her face in the lappels of his coat. "It isn't half so romantic to love a plain gentleman as to love a brigand, or, at least, a squatter."

"Doña Josefa's objection to me is perfectly proper and correct. I would not let a daughter of mine marry a squatter no more than to marry a tramp. I shall, of course, request Don Mariano to put me right in her estimation, and tell her I do not feel authorized by Congress to steal land, though my father and many other honest men hold different opinions about it."

"There! Do you hear that? Let us have a bumper, and drown the squatter in champagne! Exit tramp! Enter gentleman! Here is to Baby's health," said George.

All emptied their glasses, except Mercedes, whose hand shook so violently that she spilled more wine than she drank.

"Don't lose your courage now," Elvira said to her.

"I believe pussy is regretting she lost her squatter. Isn't that so, pussy? You have not said one word. Are you regretting that, after all, you cannot sacrifice to love your patrician pride by marrying a land-shark, thus proving you are a heroine?"

"Oh, what a silly boy," she said, laughing.

"Really, I think our romance is spoiled. It would have been so fine— like a dime novel— to have carried you off bodily by order of infuriated, cruel parents, and on arriving at New York marry you, at the point of a loaded revolver, to a bald-headed, millionaire! Your midnight shrieks would have made the blood of the passers-by curdle! Then Clarence would have rushed in and stabbed the millionaire, and you, falling across his prostrate body, said: 'Tramp or not, I am thine!'"

"Oh, George, stop your nonsense," Elvira said.

"Whereas now," George went on, "the unpoetical fact comes out that Darrell is a decent sort of a fellow, and there is no reason why a proper girl shouldn't have him for her husband; and our romance is stripped of its thrilling features, as the hero will not steal, even when Congress tells him to. And that is the *dénouement*, with the addition only that I am hungry. What have you got to eat in those two little baskets that Tano brought on board, and which smell so nice?"

"Ah, yes, I had forgotten. Mamma put up a nice lunch, thinking we might want it if we felt sick, or didn't want to go to the table. I'll go and bring it," said Elvira, setting down her glass, and rising.

"Let me go," said George, "as I am the hungry one."

"Bring both baskets. Let us see what they have. Ah, I was forgetting, I have the three little silver plates in my satchel; we must have those," added Elvira, following her husband.

"Can you forgive my stupidity? See what a world of anxious thoughts we would have avoided by explaining to Doña Josefa everything," said Clarence to Mercedes.

"Yes, it was unfortunate. But you will return soon and ask papa to tell her all, will you not?"

"Indeed I will, by the next steamer; and will have better heart to await your return. My precious angel, don't ever forget how devotedly I idolize you! Will you let me send you a ring, if your mother allows me?"

"Couldn't you *bring* it yourself?"

"Oh, Mercedes, my beloved! how happy you make me!"

"Look here," said George, groping in the dark; "Where are the magic baskets? I don't smell them."

"I knew you wouldn't, that is why I came to find them."

"Look here! if you follow a fellow like that, you'll get kissed," said he, taking his wife in his arms, and covering her face with kisses.

"Stop, George, some one might pass who didn't know you are my husband."

"That's so," said he, desisting. "But the fact of the matter is, that I want to kiss you all the time, you are so pretty and such a sweet darling. Give me the basket, and let your hungry husband go before he eats you up."

"Here they are. I'll carry the plates and knives."

"Tano said something about boned turkey, *a la espanola*, stuffed with mashed almonds and '*ajonjoli*,'" said George, setting the baskets on a chair before Clarence; "and something about a '*tortita de aceituna*,' with sweet marjoram, and I think we got them, to judge by their fragrance."

"Shall I go and order more wine?" asked Clarence.

"Oh, no, no," said Elvira, "this is plenty."

"How strange it is that I haven't felt this wine at all," said Mercedes; "one-half glass only will make my face unpleasantly warm always, for that reason I dislike wines; but see, I drank this whole glassful, and I don't feel it any more than if it was water."

"But don't you feel warmer? You were shivering when you came from your room," George said.

"Yes, I feel better," she said, timidly.

"Now eat a little and you will sleep better. Take one of these '*empanaditas de pollo*,'" said Elvira, offering one.

"Give me one," George said. "I know them by experience, and the trouble about them is that you can never have enough, though you feel you have eaten too many. Try them, Darrell, and when you have filled our glasses I'll satisfy your curiosity, telling you why the Solicitor General would not dismiss the appeal of the squatters."

"Yes, I want to know all about that," said Clarence, filling the glasses.

CHAPTER XII.

Why the Appeal was Not Dismissed.

At the time when this moonlit picnic of four took place on the steamer's deck, as it glided northward over the glassy surface of the immense Pacific, the people of California had not yet heard about the disclosure of the famous *Colton suit*. This suit was hidden in the mists of a distant future, and therefore the famous "*Huntington Letters*" had not come forth to educate the American mind in the fascinating, meandering, shady ways of "*convincing*" or of "*bribery and corruption*," as the newspapers and committee reports have harshly stigmatized Mr. Huntington's diplomacy(!) At that time, 1872, people yet spoke of "*bribery*" with a degree of shamefacedness and timidity. It was reserved for Mr. Huntington to familiarize the American people with the fact that an American gentleman could go to Washington with the avowed purpose of influencing legislation by "*convincing*" people with money or other inducements, and yet no one lose caste, or lose his high social or public position, but on the contrary, the *convinced and the convincer* be treated with the most distinguished consideration. So after drinking half of his second glass, George said:

"I don't believe the stories about Washington being such a corrupt place, where people get everything by bribing. That is a shameful slander. I went there about that dismissal of the Squatters' Appeal, and was treated like a gentleman, even by the Solicitor General, who was outrageously unjust to us. After my uncle had sent to the Attorney General Don Mariano's letter explaining the case and stating how the transcript had been in Washington two years, I went as Don Mariano's attorney to look after the case. I saw the Attorney General immediately, and he told me to return at ten o'clock next morning. I did so, and was shown in at once. He said:

"'I looked at the case again last evening, and don't see where those settlers can find a hook on which to hang their appeal. There isn't any. It is very singular that this case has not been dismissed before by my predecessor. So I was just telling the Solicitor General, as you entered, to have it dismissed this morning. I have explained my opinion to him. He is going now to the Supreme Court and can make the motion and tell the clerk to enter the dismissal to-day. The United States have no case against Señor Alamar, his title is perfectly good,' said he, looking at the Solicitor, who stood by silent and motionless. 'You have only this one case to attend to this morning, besides the one I want continued until I return. The others, you understand, I leave you to manage as you think proper, and at such times as you think best.'

"I thanked the Attorney General, and as I took my leave I said I did not know he was going away.

"'Yes,' he said, 'I am going this evening to Oregon to see my constituents, but my absence will not affect your case, the Solicitor General takes my place during my absence, and he has only to say before the Supreme Court that I enter a dismissal, and that ends the matter.'

"As I went out I said to the Solicitor, 'I suppose then this business is finished now?'

"'Such is the supposition,' said he, and we went out together. I had a great mind to follow him to the Supreme Court and see what he was going to do, but I thought he might not like being watched. Well, sir, would you believe it? That man went to the Supreme Court and never said *boo* about our dismissal. Next morning I went to ask him if the dismissal was entered. He sent word he was engaged,— to call again. I called in the afternoon, and he had left the office. Next morning I called again, and he of course was engaged. I went to the clerk of the Supreme Court, and giving him the number of the case, asked if it had been dismissed. He said no, that the Solicitor General had been at the Supreme Court every day, but had entered no dismissal. I telegraphed to Uncle Lawrence to come, and as soon as he arrived we went to see the President about it. I laid the whole case before him. I told him how the squatters were destroying Don Mariano's cattle, and how by a law of the California legislature, any one could plant grain field without fencing, and take up cattle that went to those fields, no matter whether there was any title to the land or whether the field was no larger than one acre.

"'But the law does not open to settlers private property, private lands?'

"'Yes it does, because land is not considered *private property* until the title to it is confirmed and patented. As the proceedings to obtain a patent might consume years, almost a life time, the result is that the native Californians (of Spanish descent) who were the land owners when we took California, are virtually despoiled of their lands and their cattle and horses. Congress virtually took away their lands by putting them in litigation. And the California legislature takes away their cattle, decreeing that settlers need not fence their crops, but put in a *corral* the cattle that will surely come to graze in their fields. As the cattle don't know the law, they eat the crops and get killed.'

"'But that is very hard on those land owners.'

"'Certainly. They are being impoverished with frightful rapidity. In a few years the majority of them will have been totally ruined, socially obliterated. I doubt if a dozen families will escape ruin. There seems to be a settled purpose with our law-givers to drive the natives to poverty, and crowd them out of existence. If we don't turn them all into hardened and most desperate criminals, it will be because they are among the most incorruptible of the human race. But there is no denying that our laws are doing all that can be done to drive them into squalid hovels, and thence into the penitentiaries or the poor houses.'

"'This is certainly very sad,' said the President, with genuine sympathy, adding after a short pause:

"'Wait for me here. I'll run across the street to the Attorney General's office, and I'll ask the Solicitor what it all means in this Alamar case,' so saying he put on his hat and went out.

"'That is what endears General Grant to all his friends,' said my uncle; 'the idea of his going personally to see the Solicitor, he the President, and only because he wishes to do a kindness.'

"'I wish he had sent for the proud Solicitor to come here. This visit of the President will make him more over-bearing,' said I. 'I am disgusted at his most arbitrary conduct.' 'Wait,' said my uncle, 'let us hear first what he has to say to the President.'"

In a short time the President returned. He said: 'Well, gentlemen, I cannot make out why the Solicitor did not dismiss the case, as he was ordered. He says he found that the Attorney General had not looked into the record carefully, and so he did not think the case should be dismissed.'

"'But how could he have found out that the Attorney General had not looked into the case carefully only by riding from the office to the Supreme Court? He must have *disobeyed the instructions of the Attorney General first*, and then to justify his disobedience, trumps up the pretext that the case had not been examined,' said uncle.

"'The Attorney General did not tell him to look into the case and give his opinion. He was told that the case *had been examined*; that the pleadings and allegations were trivial; that the United States had *no case*, and the matter should be dismissed,' I said.

"'It is clear, that without authority he took upon himself to review and reverse the decision of the Attorney General,' said my uncle.

"'I don't understand his motive or object,' the President said. 'But I told him I presumed he could state his opinion in writing, and he said he would. Perhaps he will give a better reason for his action than he did verbally.'

"'No, sir,' uncle said, 'he will give no better reason, as he has none to give. He has some spite against the Attorney General, and is laying in wait to catch something to hurt him. Fortunately, he can't use this case for any such purpose, for it is a very clear one, and the hands of the Attorney General are very clean.'

"'Of course they are,' the President said.

"'And now, sir, what do you advise us to do?' asked uncle.

"The President smiled, mused a little, and said:

"'My advice would be to wait until the Attorney General returns from Oregon. I know it is a hardship for the rightful owner of the land to wait so long, but the question is, would it not be longer if the Solicitor finds other reasons to take this case into his own hands. Now he has promised me to let the matter rest until the Attorney General comes back.'

"'Yes,' my uncle said, 'I think what you advise is the best thing to do. Evidently the Solicitor is beating the bush to start some game, and will be satisfied with a 'mare's nest,' if he can only entangle the Attorney General in it. But this is a very paltry and picayunish business for a Solicitor General, Mr. President, and it is silly, too, because he has shown his hand to little purpose. He has plainly demonstrated how anxious he is to find something against the Attorney General, but that something he hasn't got yet.'

"The President laughed, and said: 'You mustn't be so hard on the Solicitor.'

"It was decided that my uncle would return to New York by the four o'clock train that afternoon, and I would remain to receive the opinion in writing which the Solicitor had promised the President he would give.

"I did not have to wait until next day for that profound opinion. As I was going to dinner at six o'clock, a messenger handed me a closed official envelope which felt quite heavy. But that was all the weight the thing possessed, for it was the lightest, most vapory composition that a grown-up man, long past boyhood, could evolve from a mature brain.

"It made me angry to read it. 'The man is evidently not a fool, but thinks we are,' I said to myself, and made up my mind I would go next morning and tell him to his face what I thought of his conduct and his document.

"Promptly at ten o'clock next morning I presented myself at the Attorney General's office, and was immediately ushered before the august presence of the great Solicitor, the mighty hunter of 'mare's nests.' He evidently thought I had come to thank him for his vapory effusion, for he received me quite smilingly, and without a trace of that hauteur which he had at first meant should be so crushing.

"Taking the chair he so graciously offered me, I said: 'Sir, without meaning any disrespect to the Solicitor General of the United States, I would like to inquire what is the meaning of the document I had the honor to receive from you yesterday?'

"He colored up, but still smiling, answered: 'Did you not understand it? I thought I wrote in very plain English.'

"'The English was plain enough, but I failed to catch your idea. Will you permit me to make a few enquiries?'

"'Certainly.'

"'You remember I was present when the Attorney General told you that he had examined the transcript carefully, and not finding that the government has any case at all, ordered you to dismiss it.'

"He bowed, but did not speak.

"I continued: 'The Attorney General did not request you or authorize you to review his opinion. He merely said you were to dismiss the appeal, and have the clerk of the court enter in the record the order of dismissal that same morning. Had you obeyed the Attorney General's order, you could not have had time to review his opinion, and find that it was incorrect. Has the Solicitor General the right, and is it incumbent upon him, to correct the Attorney General's acts and opinions?"

"'You evidently do not understand our relative positions, and I have not the time to instruct you.'

"'Whose positions do you mean?'

"'Ours— mine and the Attorney General's.'

"'Who is the head of the department— the Attorney General or the Solicitor?'

"'The Attorney General.'

"'Then he was your chief— your superior— when he gave the order to make the dismissal?'

"'But I was not his clerk. You do not know how far it was discretionary with me to execute the order that day or not.'

"'Ah, I see. The chief might issue an order, but the subaltern might only execute it if he deems it proper.'

"'I am not a subaltern— I have as much authority— '

"'Yes, in the absence of the Attorney General.'

"'Always— when absent or present'

"'Then the department has two heads. That is, I suppose, what confused things in my mind. The matter then is to rest as it now is until the Attorney General returns?'

"'Yes, I shall not remand the case, as I might have done; it will wait.'

"I took my leave then, having seen that he understood I saw through the contemptible impertinence of his conduct. That is all the satisfaction I could have then, but next winter, as soon as the Supreme Court convenes, the matter will be settled."

"And will the squatters have to go then?" Elvira asked.

"Not immediately, unless they were to be guided by honorable motives. The rancho will be surveyed first, and then the patent issued after the survey is approved by the Surveyor General," George replied.

"Ah! The endless red tape," said Elvira.

"Poor papa, he has so much trouble," Mercedes sighed. "In another year all the cattle will have been killed."

"And the squatters will be more murderous, when they learn that their appeal is dismissed," George said.

"Yes, I was thinking what will be the best to do to meet the emergency. I shall speak about that to Don Mariano on my return," said Clarence.

"Yes, you help him all you can," George said.

"Most undoubtedly. I will be able to do much more if I can persuade my father to take a correct view of the matter. But he might not, for as he has had so much trouble sustaining the rights of squatters, he has got to feel as if he were the champion of a misunderstood cause and much maligned people," Clarence said, smiling sadly.

"No doubt, if Mr. Darrell is to be unfriendly, papa will have much more trouble to manage the others," Elvira said.

"How singular that a man as bright and honorable as he is, can find any reason to justify '*squatterism*,'" said George.

- 83 -

"I think he began by being persuaded to take a claim in the Suscol rancho, honestly thinking it was government land. Afterwards the grant was confirmed, I think, but then he already felt compelled to maintain his position to justify his action, and so he began by a mistake which his pride will not let him acknowledge. I was a little child then, but I know he has had a great deal of trouble. For the last ten years we have been leasing land, but he had been wishing to have a farm of his own, so as not to be putting his labor and time and money to improve some one else's land. Thus he was induced to come south on the representations that there was plenty of vacant government land, and that the Texas Pacific railroad would soon be built and southern California be prosperous," said Clarence, anxious to extenuate his father's errors.

"I shall telegraph to Don Mariano when the appeal is dismissed, so you can prepare the ground the best way you can," said George. "And now young ladies it is near midnight, and is time for well regulated children to be asleep."

"The moon is so lovely I could sit here for hours, watching its flashes on the water," said Mercedes.

"So could I," Clarence exclaimed.

"But I could not allow it, and let you both run the risk of being considered moon struck," said George, laughing.

CHAPTER XIII.

At San Francisco.

The sun was quite high above the horizon when George joined Clarence on deck; and both began to promenade and talk while waiting for the ladies to come, that the four might go to breakfast together.

"My private opinion is that these young ladies are going to oversleep themselves," George said, as they passed the door of his room, after promenading for half an hour.

"No they are not," Elvira said, coming out as fresh and beautiful as a *rosa de castilla*. "Good morning, Mr. Darrell, I hope you are well."

"I thank you," replied Clarence, "I believe I never felt better. I am delighted to see you so bright and blooming; you are evidently an excellent sailor."

"Oh yes," Elvira answered, "I really enjoy it; but where is the Señorita Mercita; is she not yet up?"

"I think not. She has not come from her room," was Clarence's reply.

"I am going to peep through her window," said Elvira. She did so by turning the slats and pushing aside the curtain just a little. She then motioned to George to come and look.

"By jove, Darrell, you ought to see this picture."

"Hush! you will awake her by speaking so loud," Elvira said, still looking at her sister.

A tiny sunbeam played over Mercedes' forehead, making the little curls over it look like golden threads. Her head was thrown back a little and turned towards the window, displaying her white throat, partially covered by the lace frills of her night dress. Her left arm rested gracefully over her head, with the sleeve pushed off displaying part of the forearm and the perfect curve of her delicate wrist. The right hand rested over the coverlet, and it looked like a child's hand, so dimpled and white and soft. It was a perfect picture of a "sleeping beauty."

"Doesn't she look like a baby? My own sweet sister; I am so glad she is sleeping so sweetly. She has slept very poorly for months," whispered Elvira. "Come away, we mustn't talk near her window, she must have all the sleep she wants."

So saying, she pulled back the curtain, shut down the window slats, and all walked noiselessly away.

As they went down to breakfast, Elvira said:

"I hope no one will come smoking some nasty cigar by her window, poisoning the air and making her miserable, for she cannot bear tobacco smoke when the boat is in motion."

"I thought she was not subject to sea-sickness," George said.

"No, not at all, as long as there are no tobacco fumes near, but it seems that tobacco smoke, combined with the rocking of the sea, make her deathly sick, whereas the tobacco alone or the rocking by itself, will not affect her."

"I understand that well, for I don't like to smoke while sailing either, if there is much motion, and I think no one ought to be allowed to smoke on deck where ladies are," George said.

"I think so too. We have too many rights, and more than our share of privileges," Clarence added.

"Wait until we have woman suffrage. We will make things uncomfortable for inebriates and tobacco smokers," Elvira said, laughing.

Their pleasant voyage came to its end, as all things must in this fleeting life, and the names of Mr. George Mechlin and party, from San Diego, were duly entered in the hotel register.

"I put your name down, Darrell, for we want you with us while in the city," said George.

"I thank you sincerely; that is exactly what I wished."

"We will be ready for dinner at six."

"I shall be on hand promptly."

Clarence was anxious to see his broker and afraid he would leave the office before he got there, but it was more imperative yet to visit his tailor. He did so, and though in haste, selected with care the cut and style and color which he knew was most becoming. He left a list of all the articles of clothing he desired to be sent to his hotel by five o'clock, and then directed his driver to take him to his broker's office.

"Just in time," said Hubert Haverly, coming forward to meet him. "As soon as the steamer was signaled at the gate, I sent to look for our Arizona men. They are now at the back office waiting for you."

"Tell me something about the matter, to guide me. And tell me too, how poor or how rich I am, before I make any bargain to purchase mines."

"Well, on the whole, I guess I'll call you rich. I bought the farm as you— or rather as Everett— telegraphed. I paid— well, how much do you think I paid for it?"

"Hundred and forty thousand?"

Hubert shook his head, saying "Try again."

"Hundred and twenty?"

"Ninety thousand only, lucky fellow."

"What? You said he asked a hundred and fifty thousand."

"Yes, and you— or Everett— telegraphed to pay the money, but you see the poor fellow lost heavily in stocks that day, and as the bank was going to foreclose on the farm for a loan of forty thousand, he thought the best thing he could do was to sell out quick. He came to see me and said 'Do you think Clarence will buy for one hundred and twenty thousand?' I told him I had telegraphed to you and probably you would come up. He said 'If you pay me ninety thousand cash down *to-day*, Clarence can have the farm for that price.'

I told him to let me have the refusal for you, for that price, until the next morning. I got your telegram in the evening. Next morning he came looking very dejected, and asked if I had heard from you. 'Yes,' I said. He waited, but as I said no more, he added, 'I hope Clarence is not going to pinch me hard. The farm is worth two hundred thousand, but as the Darrells made all the improvements on it, I am willing he should have it cheaper than any one else. How much does he offer?' 'He left it to me to make the best bargain I can. I will let you have the ninety thousand, of course.' You never saw a man so relieved. He lifted his head and said, 'I will pay all my debts and have thirty thousand clear, anyway, to make a beginning,' and so the papers were drawn up and the farm is yours. I congratulate you."

"Thanks," Clarence said, squeezing Hubert's hand. "And now about the balance on hand and the Arizona mines."

"Well, you have about one hundred thousand dollars. If you sell all your stocks, you could have two hundred thousand," Hubert replied.

"Besides the interest on the bonds?"

"Certainly. I never figure on that."

"What about the Arizona mines?"

"Well, the men say they are yet '*a prospect*,' but a very good one. Their proposition is that you pay them five hundred dollars down if you accept their proposal. Then you are to send an expert to examine the mines. If on his report you conclude to buy them at once, you can have them for ten thousand dollars. If you prefer to bond them to prospect further before buying, then you can have six months to prospect; but then you must pay two thousand down, and at the end of the six months you must pay fifty thousand dollars if you want both mines, or twenty thousand if you only take one. The shaft they have sunk is the dividing line between the two mines."

"Between the two prospects," Clarence suggested.

"Yes, that is more proper, the shaft is only about one hundred feet deep. But you had better talk to them. They brought rock similar to that which they sent me last month."

Rather rough looking men were the three waiting, but all had good faces. After exchanging salutations with them, Clarence asked:

"Have you had any assays made?"

"Yes sir," said the oldest of the three handing to him three slips of paper. "Here are three certificates from assayers recommended to us as the best in San Francisco."

"What! One hundred silver and one hundred and fifty gold? And two hundred, and three hundred and fifty? But that is enormous for surface rock."

The miners laughed. The oldest said:

"And the ledge is so wide that it almost takes the half of the hill. We took two claims and put our prospect shaft in the middle."

"Did you make your locations in good legal form?" was the next question.

"Yes sir, we have our papers," said the spokesman, handing to Clarence some papers.

"I see you are four partners, where is the other?"

"He is at the mine, working at the shaft."

"Well gentlemen," Clarence said, "I have just come, an hour ago. I don't know how soon I will find an expert, but I think I will do so between now and to-morrow by mid-day. I will consult with him and see how soon he can go to look at your mines. Meantime I'll have some of the rock assayed. From what depth was the rock assayed taken?"

"From fifty, seventy and ninety feet. We have some few pieces from the last we took the day we left, at a depth of one hundred feet." So saying, he handed to Clarence other pieces of rock which looked much richer, adding, "This is the ore we have not had assayed yet. My opinion is that the rock hasn't changed much."

It was agreed that Clarence would meet them at eleven next morning and notify them if he had found an expert. When they had left the room Clarence asked Hubert where his brother Fred was.

"He is here, he came yesterday."

"And you did not mention that fact to me, when you know I want a good, reliable expert."

"I did not, because I wouldn't urge his services upon any one— even you— and then I think he might be already engaged to go to examine some mines in Nevada, as parties have been looking for him for that purpose."

"Please don't be so proud as to deprive me of the services of so good a man, but tell him to come to my hotel at once."

"Very well, I'll tell him, but he will not be here until five o'clock. Shall I tell him to call on you after dinner?"

"Yes, at half-past seven exactly, to send his card to me to any place I may be at the hotel. And now I'll go to have two or three assays more of this rock. Remember, I shall be looking for Fred at half-past seven."

"I'll remember. He will be there promptly."

It was very evident that the "party from San Diego" made an impression and quite a stir among the guests of the hotel, who were at dinner when they entered the dining-room. Preceded by the head waiter, they had to cross the entire length of the room, for the seats assigned to them were at the furthest corner from the door. Everybody turned to look, to see what everybody else was looking at, and all acknowledged that they had never seen handsomer or more graceful people than those two couples. Exclamations of surprise were uttered in suppressed tones, and unqualified praises were whispered everywhere. The head waiter was called here and there to say who these four people were, so very handsome and *distingué*.

"They are from Southern California, on their way east. Mr. George Mechlin and bride, her sister, and their friend Mr. Darrell, travelling with them," was the answer that the steward had to give twenty times.

"Which is the bride, the blonde or the brunette?"

"The brunette."

After dinner several young gentlemen remained in the corridors to see them pass, and some four eastern tourists who were dining at the next table, made a pretext of drinking more wine, to remain looking at the southern beauties. One of them especially looked at Mercedes so persistently that Clarence began to feel angry, and when they arose from the table he looked at the admirer with a bold stare of defiant reproval. But that in no way checked the admiration of the New Yorker, and he followed as near to Mercedes as he could, and when he saw her disappear into her parlor, he looked at the number on the door and went straight to the office to make all the enquiries he could concerning those two beautiful ladies. The clerk gave all the information he could, and added laughing:

"I have had to answer those questions a dozen times already."

Immediately after dinner a waiter came from the office and handed to Clarence a card, with "Fred Haverly" written on it.

"Say to the gentleman I shall be down immediately," Clarence said to the servant; and then to George, "This is the expert I want to send to Arizona. It is lucky for me to find him in town."

"I'll go down with you," George said. "One of the clerks promised to get me a box at the opera, or if that can't be had, to get the four best seats he could find disengaged. Do you think you will have finished with your expert in half an hour? I want the girls to see the opera bouffe; they have never seen it."

"I shall be with you in fifteen minutes," was the reply.

George was talking with the clerk about the seats at the opera, when he felt a hand laid softly on his shoulder. Looking back, he saw his friend, Charles Gunther, of New York, standing by him, and behind him the four gentlemen who had dined at the next table. After shaking hands most cordially, and congratulating him on being a married man, Gunther presented to George his four friends, and his brother Robert, who now came in; then he said:

"I heard you say you wanted a box at the opera, and that there are ladies with you. Permit me to offer you our box, we can take seats anywhere else. I shall be glad if you will accept."

"But there are no seats that you can have that I would offer you in exchange," was George's reply.

"Those I got for you are good seats for gentlemen," the clerk suggested, "and I think you can get two more."

Gunther was so urgent that George, only by being very rude, could have declined making the exchange. There was nothing else to do but accept, order a carriage for eight o'clock, and then go up stairs to tell the ladies that they were to get ready for the opera.

"The opera! Why didn't you tell us before?" was Elvira's exclamation.

"Because I was not sure I could get seats," was George's reply; and he then explained how he obtained their box by casually meeting Gunther, adding:

"By the by, he introduced me to his brother Robert and those four admirers of yours, Mercedes, who dined at the next table. They are all of the same party. The young fellow of the little saffron whiskers, who stared at you so persistently, making Clarence's ears red, is a Mr. Selden, of New York; he and Robert Gunther have been in Europe several years. His father I know is a millionaire, and he is the only son. So he considers himself a good catch, I suppose, Señorita Mercedes."

"Bah!" ejaculated Mercedes; "who cares!"

"Be ready with your hats and cloaks on at five minutes to eight. Clarence and I will come for you. I am going to look for him now, and see Gunther for a few moments," George said, leaving the two sisters to go to their bedrooms to delve for their opera cloaks and white hats in the deep recesses of their Saratoga trunks.

"It is a lucky thing for me that Lizzie's aunt sent this pretty cloak and bonnet to her. Poor Lizzie! I am to *splurge* in her fine Parisian things, while she remains at the *rancho*, buried alive," said Mercedes.

"She is perfectly willing to have that sort of burial as long as she has Gabriel near her."

Mrs. Lawrence Mechlin had sent to Elvira and Lizzie their wedding trousseau, which she ordered from Paris. To do this was a pleasure to Mrs. Mechlin, which she could well afford, being rich, and which she delighted in, being devoted to her sister's children.

The theatre was filled to its utmost capacity when our four *San Dieguinos* arrived and occupied their proscenium box, which was on the left of the auditorium, very roomy and elegantly furnished. Elvira's seat faced the stage, and Mercedes' faced the audience, so that the perfect contour of her features was clearly seen when she looked at the actors. Between the sisters sat their cavaliers. The curtain rose as they took their seats, so that not one of them gave a thought to the audience, until the curtain fell on the first act.

Then they all looked at the house which was filled with a brilliant audience. Immediately in front, in the first row of orchestra chairs, were Mr. Gunther and the party of New Yorkers. They were all looking at their box. Mercedes blushed when she met the steady gaze of Mr. Selden, and his face reproduced the blush, while his heart beat with wild throbs of delight. Clarence's face also flushed, and then turned pale. He had seen the two blush, and a cold feeling of undefinable fear and savageness seized him— a desire to go and choke Mr. Selden where he was— right there in his orchestra chair.

George by this time was exchanging bows with the New Yorkers. They spoke among themselves, and soon after all arose and left their seats.

"I think Gunther is bringing his brother and friends to present them to you, ladies," said George.

"Being your friends, we shall be pleased to see them," Elvira answered.

"I hope those gentlemen will cease to stare when they are acquainted. That young man of the red whiskers made me blush by looking at me so steadily. I hope that that is not the custom of New Yorkers," said Mercedes.

"I am afraid it is. You had better try to get used to it, and don't mind it," George replied.

Mr. Gunther now presented himself at the door, followed by his brother and the four others, already well known by sight, the ceremony of introduction being performed by George, with the ease and grace of one used to those society duties. All took seats, there being room enough for a dozen people in the spacious box.

George and Clarence had left their seats to receive the guests, so very naturally Mr. Selden slipped by and sat next to Mercedes.

CHAPTER XIV.

Of Miscellaneous Incidents.

"What do you think of the opera— are you enjoying it much?" asked Mr. Selden, by way of opening conversation, having turned his chair to face Mercedes.

"I am enjoying the novelty of the thing, but I don't know what I shall think of the opera. I suppose I shall like it better when I understand it. Thus far it is to me only a very puzzling maze of hastily uttered French, imperfectly heard and mixed with music, all of which is rather unintelligible to me, so unprepared to judge of it as I am," said Mercedes, smiling, watching to see the effect that her candid avowal of ignorance would have upon such a "*muscadin*" and well traveled young man.

"Ah! you never saw the opera before to-night!"

"Not the French opera. I was at two matinees of the Italian opera about five years ago, when I left my San Francisco school. Mamma thought I was too young to go out at night, and since then I have been living at the *rancho*."

"Yes, yes; Mr. Mechlin said you had not been in San Francisco since you were twelve months old."

"Twelve months?"

A laugh immediately behind him, made Mr. Selden turn quickly around. He met the eyes of Mr. Robert Gunther, who had taken the chair next to him, and made no secret of being amused at Mr. Selden's mistake.

"What are you laughing at?" Mr. Selden asked, sharply.

"I suppose Mr. Gunther thinks that girls must grow very quickly in California if I was twelve months old five years ago."

Mr. Selden could not escape now the raillery of his friends. Each one had something to say on the subject of Mr. Selden's ideas of the wonders of California, until the bell rung for the curtain to rise for the second act.

They all arose to go. George said: "Will not some of you remain? there is room for two or three more."

"If I am not going to crowd you, I shall accept your kind invitation and hide about here," said Robert Gunther, taking a chair behind Elvira.

"Bob Gunther is always such a good boy that I always like to follow his example; so, with your kind permission, Mr. Darrell, I shall sit here behind you. Keep your chair," said Mr. Selden, refusing to change seats with Clarence.

But Mercedes saw that this arrangement was not as satisfactory as might be, so she moved her chair, and making room for Clarence on her left, told Mr. Selden to push his chair further to the front, on her right. This was a more desirable distribution, and it pleased Clarence better, for she would turn her face to him on looking at the stage. Still, there was that odious little fellow with his red mutton chops sitting so near her, that he wanted to pitch him out of the box. Mercedes watched for an opportunity to say to him:

"You look unhappy; have I done anything to displease you?"

"No, never!" he quickly answered, but did not dare to look at her. Presently he added: "It is too painful to think that only for one day more I can see you, then we must part, and— and others will be with you."

"Could you not go with us as far as the Yosemite?"

Clarence turned quickly to look at her, and her eyes had that sweet, loving expression which, to him, was always irresistible, entrancing. He had never seen it in any other eyes, and in hers only very seldom.

"Oh! if you will only let me."

"Let you! Your pleasure is the only thing to consult."

"Then I know what I shall do."

───────────

Neither Mr. Selden nor Mr. Gunther could sleep that night. Those little golden curls over the blue eyes floated in a hazy mist and music in tantalizing recurrence until dawn.

"Did you make a satisfactory bargain?" George asked Clarence next morning, when the ladies had gone to church.

"Yes, as far as we can see at present. I am to send an expert to look at the mines to-morrow, and on his report will decide what to do. But I am in a quandary now about one thing. Have you positively decided to leave to-morrow at seven A.M.?"

"If we don't oversleep ourselves," was George's reply. "But that depends. Why do you ask? If by waiting a few days we can have your company further on, we will wait, of course. The girls are enjoying themselves very much, and will be glad to wait for you."

"Thanks, thanks," said Clarence, warmly. "Yes, I would like to go as far as the Yosemite with you; but as I would like to have one final talk with the miners to-morrow before I pay them any money, I would be much obliged if you could wait until Tuesday morning."

"Most willingly, my dear fellow, particularly as these señoritas are not in a hurry to leave fascinating San Francisco."

"We have not driven anywhere around the city, and Miss Mercedes wishes to see more of San Francisco," said Clarence, "as she has not seen it since she was *twelve months old*."

"Poor Selden; those fellows will never cease laughing at his mistake," George said.

After mass, our travelers went immediately to luncheon. At their table were already seated the six New Yorkers, but four chairs were carefully turned, in token of being reserved. Clarence sat next to Mercedes, but Selden was opposite, and anxiously expected the moment when she would lift her veil. He dreaded to be disenchanted by finding her to be less beautiful in daylight, but such was not the case. She appeared to him even prettier, seeing better the lovely dark blue of her eyes. He looked at her in silence, saying to himself mentally: "She is exquisite; am I going to love her hopelessly!" And he looked at Clarence with a pang of jealousy, for he could not deny to himself that he was handsome, yes, beautiful as an Apollo, and very manly.

Next to Selden sat Robert Gunther, making almost the same mental observations, and resolving to try and win her in spite of all obstacles.

Luncheon was much enjoyed by all excepting Mr. Selden, who seemed to get more and more nervous as he sat there trying not to look at Mercedes as much as he wished.

The Gunther brothers were very brilliant conversationalists, and so was George, who was in his element in the company of such polished gentlemen as were now before him. On leaving the table, Mr. Charles Gunther begged Elvira's permission to pay their respects, asking if it would suit her convenience for them to call that evening after dinner, to which she gracefully assented, and all walked towards the parlor.

"Shall we go to the Cliff House this afternoon?" George asked his wife.

"You may, but Mercedes and I are going to vespers," she replied, and soon after the two sisters retired to their rooms.

As all of the gentlemen walked down to the reading room, Selden said: "And how in thunder are we going to kill time this afternoon until dinner? It will be intensely stupid here."

"I thought we all were going to drive to the Cliff," Bob Gunther said, maliciously. "Perhaps you would rather go to church."

"You judge others by yourself," Selden retorted.

"I believe I do. But our sudden access of religion, I fear, would not be appreciated. My dear fellow, our piety, like that of his satanic majesty, would be distrusted. It would edify no one, only make us ridiculous. Let us go to the Cliff."

And to the Cliff all went, but the drive was not much enjoyed. Bob and Selden were quarrelsome, and all the others laughed at them, which ended by making them surly. Selden ridiculed the San Franciscans for their stupid Cliff House, while all sat in arm-chairs on the broad veranda and looked at the Pacific Ocean, and Pacific sea lions, and Pacific rocks, and thought them all equally monotonous. To watch the ugly sea beasts awkwardly dragging their unwieldly hulks up the rocks, there to spread themselves in the sun, was not a very exhilarating spectacle for young gentlemen who desired to see other kinds of lions. Sunday not being the fashionable day for San Franciscans to drive to the Cliff, the New Yorkers concluded that the elite would not be seen that afternoon and returned to the hotel.

After dinner several lady friends, who had received Elvira's wedding cards and had seen her and Mercedes at church that morning, called.

The cards of the New Yorkers, also, were brought, and they followed immediately. Elvira presented them very gracefully, while George watched with delighted attention the perfect ease and natural elegance with which she did the honors as hostess.

Robert Gunther and Arthur Selden seated themselves in a corner, on the right of Mercedes' chair, but Clarence held his place on the end of the sofa, very near her.

About ten o'clock, Mr. Charles Gunther said to them:

"Much as it pains me to tear myself away, young men, it must be done, for we have made *a first call* of nearly two hours' duration."

"It has not seemed to us nearly so long," Mercedes said.

"It was no more than two minutes," Bob Gunther added.

"How you exaggerate," Mr. Selden exclaimed.

"Ask him how long it has seemed to him," Bob suggested.

"I would not dare. He thinks you exaggerate, that is enough," replied Mercedes.

Selden gave her a look of tender reproach, and a savage one at Bob, as he bowed, leaving the room.

By nine o'clock Monday morning Clarence had received the certificates of assay he had ordered on Saturday afternoon. It seemed to him that there must be a mistake somewhere about the rock, for these assays gave even a higher percentage than those shown him by the miners. He went to Hubert's office and found Fred already there waiting for him.

"Look here, Hubert, are you sure that these men did not bring us this rich rock from some other mine? The assays are very high. One goes as high as $2000 per ton."

"They might have selected the specimens, but I can vouch for their being from the same ledge, for I know the rock. I can also vouch for the honesty of the men, for I know them well; besides, what would be the good of telling a falsehood that would be found out the minute the expert got there? Their reputation is worth more to them than the five hundred dollars that you will pay now," was Hubert's reply.

"They are good men. I have known them for years, and have had them working with me," Fred added.

"Then let us finish this business now, for I go out of town to-morrow morning," Clarence said, and in half an hour he had explained his views and wishes and made his contract with Fred Haverly, the terms of which had been already mentioned on Saturday night and Sunday morning. The miners now came and the contract with them, also, was made and acknowledged in due form.

By twelve o'clock that day Clarence had dispatched his business with the miners and with Fred Haverly, reserving until he returned instructions regarding his Alameda farm.

In the afternoon all drove to the Cliff House. The ugly sea lions did not seem so clumsy to Mr. Selden, as Mercedes laughed, amused to see their ungainly efforts at locomotion, and as she pronounced the Pacific Ocean to be grand and the wild surf dashing madly against the impassive rocks very impressive, Mr. Selden was of the same way of thinking, and found the sea lions rather graceful and dignified, the black rocks more interesting than they had been the day before.

The gayeties of San Francisco made time slip away magically, and a week passed in receptions, drives and yacht sailing, in honor of Elvira, seemed very short indeed. But now another week had begun, and the journey eastward must be resumed.

Our travelers took an early breakfast on Tuesday morning, and by seven o'clock they left the hotel. Half an hour later, they were on the Oakland boat, crossing San Francisco Bay on their way to New York.

"There is plenty of room here for all the navies of the world," George observed, looking at the harbor.

"Yes, I believe the bay is forty miles across," replied Clarence. "For all intents and purposes at present, however, San Diego Bay is as good as this."

"Yes, I only wish we had commerce enough for ships to be crowded there."

"If Colonel Scott succeeds in constructing his railroad, there is no doubt that San Diego will be a large city in a few years."

"I believe that, but the question is, will Colonel Scott succeed?"

"I think he will, but he has a hard crowd to fight."

Clarence mused a little, then, changing his position so as to face George, said:

"I have had an idea in my head, a sort of project, I want to talk to you about. Of course, its practicability, I fear, will entirely depend upon the building of the Texas Pacific Railroad; for if San Diego is not to have population, my plan will be impracticable. It is this: The two banks in San Diego, I don't think, have a paid-up capital of more than a hundred thousand dollars. I think we could establish a bank of two or three hundred thousand dollars that would be a paying institution. I heard you say that you thought you would like to come to California, so as to be near your family. That gave me the idea of starting a bank. You could be the president and manager, and I would furnish as much of the capital as suited you."

"Your idea is splendid, nothing could suit me better; but I suppose we will have to see whether we are to have a railroad or not."

"Yes, that is the sole and unavoidable condition."

"I suppose we will know next winter, and if it be decided that the Texas Pacific is to be built, I will immediately accept your proposition, and put in some money with you."

"I can take half, or a third of the stock, and put in some money for Don Gabriel and Victoriano; and Everett can come in, too. You can easily instruct Don Gabriel in the banking business."

"He would make a good cashier; he is a good bookkeeper already. I think I could put in twenty-five or thirty thousand dollars."

"If you put in twenty-five thousand, I will put in that much for each of the others, Don Gabriel, Tano and Retty, and one hundred thousand for myself, or will put in thirty thousand for Don Gabriel and ninety-five thousand for myself."

"You ought to be the president."

"No, I want you and Don Gabriel to have the entire management. You can take in Tano and Retty, if you like, if they prove themselves efficient; but as for myself, I want to be free to attend to those mines (if they are worth working) and take care of my Alameda farm. Don't you think that two hundred thousand will be enough to start? I can put in more, if necessary, by selling some of my United States bonds. I have seven hundred and fifty thousand in United States securities, which I can convert into money at any time."

"Two hundred thousand is more than enough. We can increase the capital, if we wish, afterward. I am glad you are so well fixed in government securities."

"I could have had a round million if I had not sold my stock too soon; but my father kept talking to me so much against dealing in mining stocks, that I ordered Hubert Haverly to sell all I had. Fortunately he held on for a few days to my Crown Point, and sold for nine hundred thousand dollars. I was sorry enough to have lost a million for being so obedient a son, and when in that mood I promised Hubert I would not interfere again, but let him manage my stocks as he thought best. Since then he has done very well, so that now I have seven hundred and fifty thousand in United States bonds, my farm, for which Hubert paid ninety thousand, some town lots in San Francisco, and about one hundred and sixty thousand dollars in bank, besides the interest on my bonds, which I have not drawn for over a year."

"Why, that makes you worth over a million."

"Yes, but if I had kept my Crown Point for a few days longer I could have sold for a million and a half. However, I think the Arizona mines will reward my filial obedience," added he, smiling, "and if we can start that bank I shall be satisfied. I think it is a pity that such men as Don Mariano and his sons do not have some other better-paying business than cattle-raising. It used to pay well, but I fear it never will again, while such absurdities as the '*No-Fence Laws*' are allowed to exist."

"Yes, I heard Don Mariano say to my father: 'I am sure I am to be legislated into a *rancheria*, as there is no poor-house in San Diego to put me into,' he said it smiling, but his smile was very sad. However, when the appeal is dismissed and he is rid of squatters, he will recuperate, provided, of course, there be a Texas Pacific to make San Diego lands valuable. Without it the prospect is gloomy indeed, I may well say dead."

"That's it; it all depends upon that railroad, I am sorry to say, when we are so powerless to counteract hostile influences."

"We must hope and wait."

CHAPTER XV.

Journeying Overland.

The crashing and thundering of Yosemite's falls plunging from dizzy heights, in splendor of furious avalanches, had been left behind.

George and his three companions had given the last lingering look towards the glorious rainbows and myriads of dazzling gems glittering in the sun's rays, which pierced the vertical streams and played through the spray and mist enveloping them.

The memory of the mirror lakes, with their gorgeous borders of green, their rich bouquets of fragrant azaleas and pond lilies, as well as the towering cliffs, the overpowering heights of that wonderful valley, all made a picture to remain forevermore a cherished souvenir.

But alas, for the fatality of human joys, all is evanescent in this world of ours; the moment of parting at last came for the lovers.

The west-bound train would pass the station first, so Clarence must be the one to leave his friends.

"Write to us soon, won't you?" George said.

"Certainly, as soon as I get to San Diego."

"Write before, and let us know what you are doing."

"All right, I will do so," said he, and looked at Mercedes, who with downcast eyes, felt his gaze but dared not look up.

"Don't fail to write the long letter you promised, after you have your talk with papa, and he has explained to mamma your position," Elvira said.

"That is my all-absorbing thought. There is no danger of my failing to see Don Mariano the first minute I can do so. I will write immediately. To whom shall I direct my letter?"

"To me, of course," Elvira replied, "and you will write to Mercita also, after matters have been explained to mamma."

The distant rumbling as if of coming earthquake, and a far off shriek were now heard. In another minute the round-eyed monster was there, and snorting maliciously, rushed off with Clarence, leaving Mercedes leaning on George's arm, scarcely able to stand, and hardly realizing that Clarence had left them.

She was still very pale, and her hands yet trembled, when the thundering of the east-bound train was heard in the distance. Two shrieks pierced the air simultaneously, as the two trains passed each other. Her heart gave accelerated throbs when she heard those shrieks, because she knew that one of them came from the train which bore Clarence away, and it seemed to her as if expressive of his pain at being torn from her. Yes, that magician, the locomotive, understood it all, and shrieked to say he did so, because he knew she, too, wished to shriek like that.

What would you, my reader? She was so young— only seventeen— and in love. The poor child was naturally indulging in all sorts of foolish fancies while looking at the woods through which he had disappeared.

But there was now the east-bound train, and George taking her towards it.

He laughed loudly as they walked to the cars, and Elvira asked why he laughed.

"I declare, Mercedes, you must have fascinated those two fellows more than is good for them— for there they are as large as life."

"Who, George?" Elvira asked.

"Why, who should it be but Selden and Bob Gunther."

"Oh!" ejaculated Mercedes. "Please George get a compartment where we can be by ourselves," implored she.

"I will; you shall have it if money or influence or anything short of murder can get it," said he, helping them up the car steps. "But in the meantime I am going to locate you here, while I go to interview the conductor and porter. This is the last car— you will be here unobserved. Those fellows did not see us get in." So saying, George went off, laughing heartily.

Neither conductor nor porter were to be found in the next car, or the next to that, and George made his way through them as quickly as their jolting and swinging permitted.

At the further end of the fourth car he spied a porter talking with two foreign-looking gentlemen, who were none other than Messrs. Gunther and Selden. Their backs were turned toward him, so he had time to approach them unobserved, near enough to hear Selden say, in his anglicised accents:

"But my good fellah, we were told positively that travelers going from the Yosemite east must get on the train here."

"And so they do," George said, laying his hand on Selden's shoulder.

"By Jove! we've got 'em!" ejaculated Gunther.

"Here they are," Selden said, with radiant face, seizing hold of George's hands, which he shook emphatically.

"Look here! let me have one of his hands, won't you?" said Gunther; "what an all-absorbing fellow you continue to be, I am sure."

While George gave a hand to each, he told the porter he wanted a compartment, if such was to be had.

"There are none disengaged, sir, except some of those little ones at the end of the car, which no one wants; but you can have a section if you like," the porter replied.

"I have that already; but the ladies with me want a good, large compartment."

"We have one which we will be most happy to place at your service," Gunther said.

"And rob you of it. That wouldn't be fair."

"Yes it would, as we don't care for it. And it is very nice and private, and the ladies should have it," Selden said, warmly.

As the section which George's tickets assigned to him was the very next to the apartment in question, it was very clear to Mr. Selden that no arrangement could have been more fortunate, and he said so.

The three then went to bring the ladies to their room.

Mercedes pleaded a headache, and George knew that she wished to be alone, to have a cry all to herself, as most girls would, when their sweethearts have just left them. So he said to Elvira:

"Mercedes had better lie down for a while. If she sleeps she will feel better."

"I think so; I will join you presently," Elvira answered. And hearing this the gentlemen retired.

Mercedes took her hat and gloves and cloak off, and sat at the window *to enjoy* her misery in a thorough womanly fashion. She fixed her eyes on the far-off, flying wall of verdure, seeing nothing, not even the tall trees which, close by, indulged in such grotesque antics, as if forgetting their stately dignity only to amuse her— making dancing dervishes of themselves, and converting that portion of the Pacific slope into a flying gymnasium to perform athletic exercises, rushing on madly, or even turning somersaults for her recreation.

Elvira left her alone with her thoughts, and silently devoted herself to unpacking their satchels, arranging their toilet things, traveling shawls and night-dresses and comfortable slippers all in their proper places. She then took her hat off, and tying a large black veil over her head (Spanish fashion), told her sister to sleep if she could, and not to cry, for, after all, Clarence would soon be in New York.

"Do you really think so?" said Mercedes' sad voice.

"Of course, I do. Clarence is too energetic and too much in love to be kept away."

"But mamma— you know mamma's feelings."

"Which will be entirely changed when she hears that Clarence is no squatter. Leave all that to papa. Come, give me a kiss, and if you can't sleep, put a veil over your head and come out. I am going to join the gentlemen."

"Yes, darling, you go; but at present I'd rather sit here by the window."

And she sat there, but the sad blue orbs saw nothing— for her mental gaze was fixed on that other flying train, that was rushing away, carrying her beloved with such frightful rapidity. She felt, she *knew*, Clarence was sitting by a car window, thinking of her, gazing blankly at his misery.

And so he was.

It is to be feared that his misery would have been greatly intensified had he caught a glimpse of Messrs. Gunther and Selden, as they rushed past him on their eastward journey. This aggravation, however, was spared him. And, as when he arrived at San Francisco, Charles Gunther and his three companions had already left for Oregon, Clarence remained, for the present, in blissful ignorance of the whereabouts of those two persistent young gentlemen, traveling so near Mercedes.

But could magician of old have shown to him in enchanted mirror the image of his beloved, he would have read in those expressive eyes how sadly she felt his absence.

When she had sat there, motionless, for two hours, Elvira came to tell her to get ready for dinner, which she declined doing, saying that she was not a bit hungry. And so the day passed— the night came— and she did not gladden the hearts of their traveling companions, by letting them see her that day. Next day the morning hours also passed. She had her breakfast in her room.

Mr. Selden began to feel piqued and Mr. Gunther nervous. They and Elvira were playing a three-handed game of casino; George was elsewhere, talking to an acquaintance he had met on the train.

Presently, softly and unexpectedly, the sliding-door of the compartment moved, and Mercedes stood beside Mr. Selden, sweet as a rosebud, smiling in her most bewitching way. The blood mounted to Mr. Selden's temples, and those of Mr. Gunther's assumed the same hue. Then she, of course, blushed also— for she could never see any one blush without doing the very same thing herself.

Elvira alone kept her composure, and said: "Why, Baby! I am so glad you feel better. Come, take a hand, for these gentlemen will cut your sister's throat, or she theirs. We are having a fierce battle."

"All right. Will you have me for a partner, Mr. Gunther? I warn you that I am a very poor player," said Mercedes.

"I'll have you for a partner, Miss Mercedes, on any terms, and be most happy to do so," said Mr. Gunther, with more emphasis than the occasion required.

"That being the case, I am ready," said she, sitting by her sister, thereby being diagonally opposite to Mr. Gunther.

From that time the five travelers were constantly together, and the days passed delightfully for all during the entire journey, especially so to Gunther and Selden. They had no occasion to complain of Mercedes for staying away. She most amiably took part in all their games and other amusements, their walks while waiting at stations, their conversations during the sentimental and delightful twilight hours. She had found that both young gentlemen were a most excellent protection against one another, as neither one was ever willing to go leaving her alone with the other. As for ardent loving looks, she knew that the best way of eluding them was by having recourse to her little trick of dropping her gaze, as if she must look down for something missing near by. That little trick came to her from sheer timidity and bashfulness long ago. In fact, she was unconscious of it, until Corina Holman had told her that whenever Clarence Darrell was present she became sly, and did not dare to look at people squarely in the face— that she was the veriest hypocrite. Thus she learned that her bashful timidity had been entirely misunderstood, but she was also made aware that she had accidentally discovered how to avoid looks which were best not to meet— best to avoid by simply dropping her gaze. As her long, curly lashes veiled her eyes with a silken fringe, they could hide under that cover like two little cherubs crouching under their own wings.

CHAPTER XVI.

Spanish Land Grants Viewed Retrospectively.

San Francisco seemed deserted, dusty and desolate to Clarence after his return from the Yosemite and the society of Mercedes. It was the step from the sublime to the ridiculous; so he ran off to his Alameda farm and remained there until the day before the steamer would leave for San Diego. He then came back late to the dusty city and went in search of Hubert to take him to dinner.

"Come for pity's sake to dine with me and talk to me. I can't eat alone, I am too blue," said he, going to Hubert's desk.

"All right, my boy. You are the very man I wanted to see, for I have been slashing into your stocks like all possessed;" and he made cuts and thrusts in the air illustrative of a terrible havoc.

"What have you done?" Clarence asked, laughing.

"Well, in the first place, I have sold all your Yellow Jacket, all your Savage and half of your Ophir, and I bought you some Consolidated Virginia and California. What do you say to that?"

"Not one word, for I suppose you know what you are about."

"I think I do, and, as a proof of it, I made for you twenty thousand dollars clear profit by the operation, besides buying your Consolidated Virginia. So if that last venture is a failure, I shall not feel I have swamped all your cash."

"I should say not. You are the prince of brokers, Berty. You have not made a single mistake in managing my stock."

"Yes I have. I sold your Crown Point too soon."

"But that was my mistake, not yours."

"Yes it was. I ought to have sold half to fool you, and kept the other half ten days longer to make a million with it. I was stupidly honest that time."

"I forgive you."

"But I don't forgive myself, nor you either."

"I know that. You are only piling coals of fire on my head. Now I have to bear twenty thousand more fresh coals, and I forbearingly say: 'Pile on Macduff,' *et cetera*. Where shall we go to dinner— the Poodle Dog or California?"

"Let us go to the California House. John keeps the best."

To the California House they went, and had a most excellent dinner with Chateau Yquem and a bottle of Roderer.

"Don't you know I like some of our California wines quite as well as the imported, if not better? I suppose I ought to be ashamed to admit it, thus showing that my taste is not cultivated. But that is the simple truth. There is that flavor of the real genuine grape which our California wines have that is different from the imported. I think sooner or later our wines will be better liked, better appreciated," Clarence said.

"I think so too, but for the present it is the fashion to cry down our native wines and extol the imported. When foreigners come to California to tell us that we can make good wines, that we have soils in which to grow the best grapes, then we will believe it, not before."

The two friends went after dinner to Clarence's rooms, where they spent the evening together. Twelve o'clock found them still busy talking of a thousand things. Next morning Hubert came to breakfast with Clarence and accompanied him to the steamer.

"Good-by, old fellow; take care of yourself."

"Good-by, my boy; good luck to you," said they, with a lingering grip of the hands.

"I hope Fred has had a safe journey," Clarence added.

"I think so, and I hope soon to get his telegram— about his *'first impression'*— which I shall transmit to you."

Once more Clarence was crossing San Francisco Bay— on to the Golden Gate, on to the broad Pacific.

The surrounding scenery recalled Mercedes' image so vividly to his mind that it made his heart long to see her, and the entire voyage was painful to him with the keen regret of her absence.

But now, again, on the fourth morning— a lovely one in the sunlit July— he was once more making his way between Ballast Point and the sandy peninsula, facing La Playa and then turning to the right towards San Diego City.

San Diego at that time— in July, 1873— be it remembered, was fresh and rosy with bright hopes, like a healthy child just trying to stand up, with no sickness or ill-usage to sap its vitality and weaken its limbs. Only ten months before Col. Scott had come to say that the Texas Pacific Railroad would be built through the shortest, most practicable route, making San Diego the western terminus of *the shortest transcontinental railway*. It was true that on the following winter Congress had done nothing further to help the Texas Pacific. But many reasons were given for this singular lack of interest in so important a matter on the part of Congress. Among the many reasons, *the true one* was not mentioned, hardly suspected; it would have seemed too monstrous to have been believed all at once; incredible if revealed without preparing the mind for its reception. Yes, the mind had to be prepared— slowly educated first. Now it has been. The process began about that time and it has continued up to this day, this very moment in which I write this page. Mr. Huntington's letters have taught us how San Diego was robbed, tricked, and cheated out of its inheritance. We will look at these letters further on.

When the steamer arrived near enough to the wharf for persons to be recognized, Clarence's heart leaped with pleasure, for he saw the well known, tall form of Don Mariano sitting in his buggy leaning back, looking at the approaching steamer. A minute after, he saw Victoriano and Everett standing together near the edge of the wharf ready to receive him.

"Well, Mr. Runaway, welcome back!" Victoriano said, clasping Clarence's hand as soon as he was upon the wharf. He gave the other hand to Everett, who said:

"We will have to *lazo* you to keep you home."

"I think we will have to put a yoke on him," added Victoriano.

"Exactly; only let me select my yokefellow," Clarence said, laughing.

As Don Mariano intended returning home that day, Clarence proposed that Victoriano should drive with Everett, and he go with Don Mariano, an arrangement which was very satisfactory to all parties. He was very anxious to unburden his mind, and Don Mariano's inquiries about his daughters and their voyage to San Francisco soon gave him the desired opportunity. He told Don Mariano what George had said, and how firmly and sincerely Mercedes wished to abide by her mother's wishes. Don Mariano listened very attentively, then said:

"I had intended suggesting to you the same thing. Gabriel has spoken to me about the matter several times, insisting that all the ladies of our family ought to know that *you* paid for your land. Since we cannot divest them of the resentment they have towards squatters, let them know the truth. Let them see that Congress, if it does not always follow moral principles, can certainly subvert them most arbitrarily and disastrously. Do you still wish to keep the matter from your father?"

Clarence thought for a moment, then answered:

"Yes, but only for a short time. I suppose we will have to define our position as soon as the appeal is dismissed. Before that comes, I shall explain all to him."

They rode on in silence for a few moments; then Don Mariano said:

"Very well, I shall tell my wife that, for the present, the matter must not be mentioned outside the family or in the hearing of servants."

"I thank you," Clarence said: "it is very painful to me to find my father adhering so tenaciously to his old conviction that all Mexican grants not finally confirmed to their owners are public land, and being so, they are open for settlement to all American citizens. Thus, he still insists that, being an American citizen, he has the right to locate on your land or any other unconfirmed grant. This idea has been the bane of his life for many years, but for the very reason that in maintaining it he has caused so much trouble to himself and to others, he seems to cling to it most pertinaciously. He believes your land was rejected, and that the rejection will be sustained."

"Yes, my land was reported rejected, but it was by some mistake of the clerks, because at that time the title had not been either finally rejected or confirmed. It had been before the Land Commission, and that (of course) decided adversely, as it generally did. Then I appealed to the United States

District Court. This said that there was not sufficient testimony to confirm my title, but did not affirm the opinion of the Land Commission, nor reverse their decision, nor enter a decree of rejection. It simply left the case in that uncertain condition until 1870, when I discharged my lawyer and engaged another to attend to the suit. Then the case was reopened, and a decree of confirmation was entered. In the meantime, squatters had been coming, and they now have carried their appeal to Washington, to the United States Supreme Court, against me."

"I see it all now," Clarence said, thoughtfully.

"And don't you know," Don Mariano continued, "that I don't find it in my heart to blame those people for taking my land as much as I blame the legislators who turned them loose upon me? And least of all I blame your father, for he has not killed my cattle, as the others have."

"Of course, he couldn't, he wouldn't, he shouldn't do that. That would be worse than the lowest theft."

"That is true, but there is a law to protect him if he did; in fact, to *authorize* him to do so. Thus, you see, here again come *our legislators* to encourage again wrong-doing— to offer a premium to one class of citizens to go and prey upon another class. All this is wrong. I hold that the legislators of a nation are the guardians of public morality, the teachers of what is right and just. They should never enact laws that are not founded upon rectitude, as Herbert Spencer says, no matter if expedience or adventitious circumstances might seem to demand it. But I need not tell you this, for you hold the same opinion."

"Indeed I do, and understanding your rights better than I did, I think you were too generous in making the offer you made to the settlers at the meeting with them last year."

"It was rather generous, but not as much so as you perhaps think. I was looking out for myself, too."

"I heard them talk about an appeal that was pending, and I thought it was your appeal, not theirs."

"The position then was this: In the first place, I was willing to give them a chance of getting good homes for their families, for I shall always consider that the law has deluded and misled them, and helped them to develop their natural inclination to appropriate what belonged to some one else; so they should bear only half the blame for being squatters— Congress must bear the other half. Then, in the second place, about the time I had that meeting, I had just received a letter from George, written at Washington, telling me how the Solicitor General had disobeyed the order of the Attorney General, instructing him to dismiss the appeal against the confirmation of my title. As I did not know that the Solicitor General was acting thus out of pique or personal animosity against the Attorney General, I naturally feared that he was going to make me suffer other worse outrages, judging by his arbitrary, irresponsible conduct. I thought that there might be many more years of delay while waiting for the dismissal of the appeal, and while thus waiting all my cattle would be killed. Reasoning thus, I concluded that it would be less ruinous to me to make the concessions I offered than to wait for tardy justice to restore my land to me— restore it when all my cattle shall have been destroyed."

"I think your reasoning was correct— it did seem as if the Solicitor meant mischief. It was fortunate that he dropped the matter."

"Yes, for which I am devoutly thankful. I hope the mischief he has done may soon be corrected by the Attorney General. Of course, the additional eighteen months of depredations on my cattle which I have had to endure, must go unredressed together with all else I have had to suffer at the hands of those vandals."

"At the hands of our law-givers."

"Exactly. I shall always lay it at the door of our legislators— that they have not only caused me to suffer many outrages, but, with those same laws, they are sapping the very life essence of public morality. They are teaching the people to lose all respect for the rights of others— to lose all respect for their national honor. Because we, *the natives* of California, the Spano-Americans, were, at the close of the war with Mexico, left in the lap of the American nation, or, rather, huddled at her feet like motherless, helpless children, Congress *thought* we might as well be kicked and cuffed as treated kindly. There was no one to be our champion, no one to take our part and object to our being robbed. It ought to have been sufficient that by the treaty of Guadalupe Hidalgo the national faith, the nation's honor was pledged to respect our property. They never thought of that. With very unbecoming haste, Congress hurried to pass laws to legalize their despoliation of the conquered Californians, forgetting the nation's pledge to protect us. Of course, for opening our land to squatters and then establishing a land commission to sanction and corroborate that outrage, *our California delegation* then in Washington, must bear the bulk of the blame. They should have opposed the passage of such laws instead of favoring their enactment."

"Why did they favor such legislation?"

"Because California was expected to be filled with a population of farmers, of industrious settlers who would have votes and would want their one hundred and sixty acres each of the best land to be had. As our legislators thought that we, the Spano-American natives, had the best lands, and but few votes, there was nothing else to be done but to despoil us, to take our lands and give them to the coming population."

"But that was outrageous. Their motive was a political object."

"Certainly. The motive was that our politicians wanted *votes*. The squatters were in increasing majority; the Spanish natives, in diminishing minority. Then the cry was raised that our land grants were too large; that a few lazy, thriftless, ignorant natives, holding such large tracts of land, would be a hindrance to the prosperity of the State, because such lazy people would never cultivate their lands, and were even too sluggish to sell them. The cry was taken up and became popular. It was so easy to upbraid, to deride, to despise the conquered race! Then to despoil them, to make them beggars, seemed to be, if not absolutely righteous, certainly highly justifiable. Any one not acquainted with the real facts might have supposed that there was no more land to be had in California but that which belonged to the natives. Everybody seemed to have forgotten that for each acre that was owned by them, there were thousands vacant, belonging to the Government, and which any one can have at one dollar and twenty-five cents per acre. No, they didn't want Government land. The settlers want the lands of the lazy, the thriftless Spaniards. Such good-for-nothing, helpless wretches are not fit to own such lordly tracts of land. It was wicked to tolerate the waste, the extravagance of the Mexican Government, in giving such large tracts of land to a few individuals. The American Government never could have been, or ever could be, guilty of such thing. No, never! But, behold! Hardly a dozen years had passed, when this same economical, far-seeing Congress, which was so ready to snatch away from the Spanish people their lands (which rightfully belonged to them) on the plea that such large tracts of land ought not to belong to *a few* individuals, this same Congress, mind you, goes to work and gives to railroad companies millions upon millions of acres of land. It is true that such gifts were for the purpose of aiding enterprises for the good of the people. Yes, but that was exactly the same motive which guided the Spanish and the Mexican governments— to give large tracts of land as an inducement to those citizens who would utilize the wilderness of the government domain— utilize it by starting ranchos which afterwards would originate 'pueblos' or villages, and so on. The fact that these land-owners who established large ranchos were very efficient and faithful collaborators in the foundation of missions, was also taken into consideration by the Spanish Government or the viceroys of Mexico. The land-owners were useful in many ways, though to a limited extent they attracted population by employing white labor. They also employed Indians, who thus began to be less wild. Then in times of Indian outbreaks, the land-owners with their servants would turn out as in feudal times in Europe, to assist in the defense of the missions and the sparsely settled country threatened by the savages. Thus, you see, that it was not a foolish extravagance, but a judicious policy which induced the viceroys and Spanish governors to begin the system of giving large land grants."

"I never knew that this was the object of the Spanish and Mexican governments in granting large tracts of land, but it seems to me a very wise plan when there was so much land and so few settlers."

"Precisely. It was a good policy. In fact, the only one in those days of a patriarchal sort of life, when raising cattle was the principal occupation of the Californians."

"I must say that to establish the Land Commission seems to me rather a small subterfuge for the Congress of a great nation to resort to."

"What makes this subterfuge a cold-blooded wrong, of premeditated gravity, is the fact that at the time when we were forced to submit our titles for revision, and pending these legal proceedings, we, the land-owners, began to pay taxes, and the squatters were told that they have the right to take our lands and keep them until we should prove that we had good titles to them. If the law had obliged us to submit our titles to the inspection of the Land Commission, but had not opened our ranchos to settlers *until it had been proved that our titles were not good*, and if, too, taxes were paid by those who derived the benefit from the land, then there would be some color of equity in such laws. But is not this a subversion of all fundamental principles of justice? Here we are, living where we have lived for fifty or eighty years; the squatters are turned loose upon us to take our lands, and we must pay taxes for them, and we must go to work to prove that our lands are ours before the squatter goes. Why doesn't the squatter prove first that the land is his, and why doesn't he pay his own taxes? We, as plaintiffs, have to bear heavy expenses, and as the delays and evasions of the law are endless, the squatter has generally managed to keep the land he took, for we have been impoverished by heavy taxation while trying to prove our rights, and the squatter has been making money out of our lands to fight us with. Generally the Californians have had nothing but land to pay their taxes, besides paying their lawyers to defend their titles. Thus, often the lawyer has taken all that was left out of the cost of litigation and taxes.

"It makes me heartsick to think how unjustly the native Californians have been treated. I assure you, sir, that not one American in a million knows of this outrage. If they did, they would denounce it in the bitterest language; they would not tolerate it."

"They would denounce it perhaps, but they would tolerate it. I used to think as you do, that the American people had a very direct influence upon the legislation of the country. It seems so to hear public speakers in election times, but half of all their fire goes up in smoke, and Congress is left coolly to do as it pleases. And the worst of it is, that this very arbitrary Congress, so impervious to appeals of sufferers, is also led by a few persistent men who with determination do all things, spoil or kill good bills, and doctor up sick ones; and then they half-fool and half-weary the nation into acquiescence, for what can we do? The next batch that is sent to the Capitol will have the same elements in it, and repeat history."

"It seems to me there ought to be some way to punish men for being bad or ineffectual legislators, when sense of honor or dread of criticism fail to make them do their duty."

Don Mariano sighed and shook his head, then in a very sad voice said:

"That should be so, but it is not the case. No, I don't see any remedy in my life-time. I am afraid there is no help for us native Californians. We must sadly fade and pass away. The weak and the helpless are always trampled in the throng. We must sink, go under, never to rise. If the Americans had been friendly to us, and helped us with good, protective laws, our fate would have been different. But to legislate us into poverty is to legislate us into our graves. Their very contact is deadly to us."

"And yet you do not seem to hate us."

"Hate you? No, indeed! Never! The majority of my best friends are Americans. Instead of hate, I feel great attraction toward the American people. Their sentiments, their ways of thinking suit me, with but few exceptions. I am fond of the Americans. I know that, as a matter of fact, only the very mean and narrow-minded have harsh feelings against my race. The trouble, the misfortune has been that the American people felt perfect indifference towards the conquered few. We were not in sufficient numbers to command attention. We were left to the tender mercies of Congress, and the American nation never gave us a thought after the treaty of peace with Mexico was signed. Probably any other nation would have done the same. Why should I then hate them? No, indeed. But I confess my heart collapses when I think what might be the fate of my family if I am not able to avert the ruin which has overtaken the majority of Californians. We have not been millionaires, but we have never known want. We are all ill prepared for poverty; and yet this long-delayed justice, and the squatters crowding me so relentlessly— " he stopped short, then added: "I am not giving you a cheerful welcome with my gloomy conversation."

"But I want you to talk to me frankly and give me your views. You have told me much that I had never heard before, and which I am glad to learn. But as for feeling gloomy about the future of the family, I think a plan that Mr. George Mechlin and myself have been forming will make things rather better for the future, and we trust you will approve it."

"What is the plan?"

CHAPTER XVII.

Doña Josefa at Home.

Don Mariano had only said, "What is the plan?" a very natural and simple inquiry, and yet it threw Clarence into something of a flutter, as it flashed vividly before his mind that the said *plan* was based entirely upon the fate of the Texas Pacific Railroad, and that as a natural sequence it depended upon the wisdom, the moral sense and patriotism of Congress. If Congress acted right and did its duty as the mentor, guardian and trustee of the people, all would be well. But would it? Would it, indeed? The past promised nothing to the future, judging by the light of Don Mariano's experience. But why should the Texas Pacific not be granted aid? The public treasure had been lavished to help the Central Pacific, a northern road— why should the southern people not be entitled to the same privilege? These thoughts flashed through Clarence's mind before he answered, then he said, somewhat timidly:

"The plan is to establish a bank in San Diego, with Mr. George Mechlin for President, and Don Gabriel for Cashier. The only drawback is, of course, the delay there might be in constructing the Texas Pacific Railroad— the delay in the growth of San Diego. As yet, however, we are hopeful, and the prospect seems good."

"The prospect is perfectly good, and I would have entire confidence in it, if the fate of the railroad did not depend upon right and just legislation. The Congressmen from the north do not seem to feel all the interest they should in reviving the south. They are angry yet. The fact that they coerced back into the Union the southern people has not appeased them yet, it seems. I wish Tom Scott would build his road without Congressional aid. The success of your banking project must, of course, depend upon the amount of population in San Diego."

"Undoubtedly. And if there is no railroad, there will be no population. But Mr. Mechlin and myself are ready with our money, and with the least encouraging sign we start our bank. I think we will begin at first with two hundred thousand dollars. Mr. Mechlin says he can subscribe twenty-five or thirty thousand dollars, and I will put the balance in, subscribing thirty thousand for Don Gabriel, twenty-five thousand for Victoriano and twenty-five thousand for Everett, with ninety thousand for myself."

"You must be prudent in incurring risks."

"I am. I have more than two hundred thousand that I can put in this bank without troubling my government bonds or my farm."

Clarence then explained to Don Mariano his financial affairs.

Don Mariano smiled as he said: "I had no idea you were so well off."

"I expect to make a fortune out of my Arizona mines," said he, laughing.

"Take care. Do not put any of your government bonds in them."

"Indeed, I shall not. The interest on those bonds gives me nearly thirty-five thousand dollars per year, and this income is for— " here Clarence blushed and was silent.

"To take care of your wife," Don Mariano said.

"Yes, sir; for that alone. But do you think Doña Josefa will object to me after you explain my position?"

"As her only objection is that she thinks you are squatters, she would be very unreasonable should she hold the same objections after she knows that you are not."

"You make me very happy telling me that. I hope you will let me know soon what answer she gives to you."

"Certainly. You can come to-morrow."

"I have some little packages that Mrs. Mechlin sends. I can bring them this evening— the ladies might wish to see the contents."

"Of course, they will. They wouldn't be women if they didn't. They'll want you to relate all the incidents of the voyage, too, and the trip to the Yosemite. If you can, come this evening. I'll tell them you are coming."

"Thank you, sir."

Everett and Victoriano overtook them now as they entered the valley.

"Say, Clary," Everett called out, "don't you want to get out here and change seats with Tano?"

"I'll take him home," Don Mariano answered; and they all drove toward the Darrell house.

At the door were Mr. Darrell and Alice. Immediately after, Darrell came out to greet his son. He was rather cordial to Don Mariano, and asked him to come in and take lunch. This was so very unexpected to all his hearers, that, with the exception of Don Mariano, all showed their surprise. This kind invitation, however, was politely declined— whereupon Victoriano, pretending to feel slighted because he was not invited, tossed his head at Clarence and Everett, and marched majestically towards his father's carriage.

Everett overtook him, and would not let him get in, insisting upon his remaining to luncheon. Victoriano then indicating that he was entirely pacified, remained, perfectly happy, knowing his seat would be near Alice, and that was the allurement, but he said to Tisha, as she came to set a plate for him:

"Your cooking is so good, Tisha, that I always come sneaking around, begging for an invitation, for I am sure you have something nice to give us."

"La massa! and right welcome ye are, too, by everybody in this 'ere family, and I knows it exactly."

And Tisha winked to herself in the pantry, indicating to the crockery on the shelves that she knew why Massa Tano liked her cooking, "and Miss Alice knows it, God bless her," said Tisha, nodding her head to the rows of preserves and pickle jars, in sheer exultation, for there was nothing so interesting to Tisha on the face of the earth as a love affair.

"*All the world love the lover,*" says Emerson, and Tisha could certify to this aphoristic truth, for who more humble than Tisha? And yet her heart went headlong to the lover, whoever he might be. Therefore, a love affair in the Darrell family was to Tisha perfectly entrancing. She had been in a state of undefined bliss ever since her perceptive organs and other means of information had indicated to her that *Clarence was in love*! She had taken upon herself to watch and see that the affair progressed and ended happily.

In the evening Clarence proceeded to deliver the packages sent by Elvira to her mother and sisters.

With beating heart he timidly ascended the steps of the front veranda of the Alamar house, for he did not feel entirely certain that Doña Josefa's objections would be withdrawn. He was not kept in suspense about the matter, however, as now, preceded by woolly Milord, the handsome matron herself came forward to meet him, extending her hand in welcome most gracious. She never had seemed to him so handsome, so regally beautiful. He thought that he had been right in imagining Juno must have looked like her. And when she smiled, as she extended her hand to him, he thought that such was surely the smile, the manner and the beauty of a goddess.

"I am so glad to welcome you, Mr. Darrell," said she, "and knowing that you wish to speak to me, and as I, too, wish to speak with you alone, I thought I would meet you here by myself."

Milord barked, wagged his tail in token of friendship, and sat up to listen.

"You are very kind," Clarence said, placing the packages on a table near him, not knowing, however, what else to say.

"Sit down," Doña Josefa said, pushing one of the large arm-chairs for Clarence to sit near. "And let me begin our conversation by apologizing for the very wrong, very unjust opinion I have had of you. Believe me, it gives me great pleasure to know I was mistaken."

Her voice, her manner, were more gracious than her words, and Clarence thought that it was not to be wondered that the daughters were so very charming.

"I am the one who should apologize," he hastened to reply; "I ought to have asked Don Mariano to explain my position to you before."

"I wish you had, for that would have saved us many anxious thoughts. But let us not regret the past too much, only enough to cause us to appreciate the present. I understand how you felt, not wishing to seem disrespectful to your father, and yet not agreeing with him."

"It has been the source of very painful feelings to me to see my father so misled, but I have found very great comfort in the fact that my mother agrees with me. She told me she would never come down if I did not pay for the land."

"Yes; Mariano told me this, and I beg of you to convey to her my regrets at having been in error about this matter. Will you do so, please?"

"Certainly, madam; with great pleasure."

"I trust that her good influence will be of great assistance to you in persuading your father to change his views."

"Yes, I hope so; in fact, I feel pretty sure that, more or less warmly, all of my brothers and sisters will agree with me, especially Everett and Alice. Another fact, also, is in my favor, that my father promised to Don Mariano, when he first took up the land, that he would pay for it if the Courts decided against the settlers. That promise, I think, will have a good effect, for he always keeps his word. When the appeal is dismissed I shall remind him of it. In the meantime I shall watch my opportunities to conciliate him, for I feel sure he will resent my having paid for the land without his consent."

"That is a pity. I am very sorry for that."

"It is unpleasant that he should take so decided a view of so clear a subject, but I feel perfectly justified in acting as I did. What I do regret sincerely is that you and— and Miss Mercedes should not have known the truth sooner," said Clarence, reddening to the roots of his hair, for he felt that he was touching on most delicate ground; with anxious, beating heart he waited for her reply.

Her face flushed a little. Was it pride, or was it because the heart of woman must always flutter when in her presence the subject of love is approached, in which ever direction it may be, and no matter if the snows of eighty winters rest placidly on her brow? Love is woman's special province— she has, or has had, or will have, power there. Man might take, and absolutely appropriate, monopolize and exclude her from money-making, from politics and from many other pursuits, made difficult to her by man's tyranny, man's hindrances, man's objections— but in the realms of love he is not the absolute dictator, not the master. He must sue, he must wait, he must be patient. Yes, the lord of creation often has to take snubbing quite meekly, for he can't help it.

Clarence knew all this, but he saw Doña Josefa smile, and grew brave.

"Yes; Mercedes, poor child, was very unhappy, and it went to my heart like a knife to send her away, but I deemed it to be my duty— I hoped it would be for the best."

"And so it was. You did right."

"Yes, but it did not enter into my calculations that you were to jump on board the steamer," said she, laughing.

Clarence's face and ears became crimson.

"I hope you have forgiven me for it," he stammered.

"I suppose I must," said she, still laughing.

"I assure you I had no idea of doing such a thing, but when I saw her going I didn't care what I did."

"And as you received some dispatches, you thought it was best to dispatch other matters as well."

"But, after all, she left everything for *you* to dispatch. My fate is in your hands."

It was now Doña Josefa's turn to blush.

"I thought that George and Mariano had decided that."

"No, indeed. It is all left to you. Please be merciful," he pleaded, feeling very nervous, for he heard steps and voices approaching from through the hall.

"What shall I say?"

"Say *yes*."

"Yes," she said, smiling, with a kind look in her beautiful eyes.

He glanced quickly toward the front door, and seeing no one in sight, dropped on his knees, and seizing her hand, covered it with hurried and vehement kisses, saying:

"Thanks! thanks!"

And all before she knew what he was about.

"Impetuous boy! is that the way you rushed and assaulted my poor little Mercedes?" said she, laughing.

"You have said yes— God bless you for it."

"But, yes to what?"

"Ah! your heart will tell you."

"What is that? What about the heart?" asked Don Mariano, standing in the door. "This looks like love-making. I am interested. Let me hear a little of it," said he, pulling after him a chair, to sit between Clarence and his wife.

"It is love-making, only it is by proxy, and I am to guess at things without being told," said she, still laughing.

Clarence was greatly embarrassed. He knew he had not formally asked for the hand of Mercedes in the serious manner that the subject merited, but he had been carried away by his fears, then by his hopes, and the matter was launched before he could scarcely say how. When for months past he had thought, time and again, of a probable interview with Doña Josefa, he had imagined himself talking to that queenly lady in his most stately Spanish. But now he had taken hold of Cervantes' language— I may say, jumped into it, just as he had jumped on the steamer's deck, thinking of no difficulties in the way, except that they must be overcome in order to reach Mercedes.

He gave a most appealing look to Don Mariano, whose kind heart immediately responded by saying to his wife:

"If it is love-making, and you are to guess at it, there won't be much delay, for no woman was ever slow to guess such matters. I know *you* understood me very quickly."

"Hear him! but please do not learn such frightful lessons in vanity and conceit," said she, laughing again, but blushing also.

"I know she understood what I meant, when I would ride eighty miles on horseback for the pleasure of serenading her. To do that, or jump aboard the steamer after it is under way, means about the same thing, I think."

Don Mariano kept talking in that strain until Clarence recovered his composure.

He then said: "I have been your ambassador before this queen, and her majesty has granted your petition. So you have nothing more to do now than to fall on your knees and kiss her hands."

Whereupon, down went Clarence again on his knees, and seizing her hand, kissed it warmly and repeatedly, in spite of Doña Josefa's protestations, saying:

"That will do. Once is enough— once is enough. Reserve your kisses for younger hands."

"I'll warrant he has plenty more in reserve," Don Mariano said, laughing.

And it was true, for Clarence was so happy that he could have kissed the entire Alamar family— all, all— irrespective of age or sex.

The days now passed pleasantly and peacefully enough at the Alamar rancho.

Don Mariano knew that he would have to go through many disagreeable scenes with the squatters when the appeal should be dismissed, but as the law would be on his side *finally*, he confidently hoped to see the end of his troubles, intending to allow the squatters to keep their homes, provided only that they would fence their crops and pay their own taxes.

Clarence reconciled himself to wait until the fall to take that ring which Mercedes had told him to bring himself. This would be the most judicious plan, as he would thus take the necessary time to have the mines prospected and to decide about their purchase, before going to New York. In the meanwhile he worked in the garden, fenced and prepared ground for planting grapevines and fruit trees. He read and wrote love letters, and passed nearly all of his evenings at the Alamar house, holding Milord, who always came to be held by him as soon as he arrived.

The telegram from Fred Haverly came in due time, a few words only, but how exhilarating they were to Clarence, making his pulse beat high.

It read thus:

"Prospect splendid. Far better than described. Have written to-day. Hurrah!"

Like the telegram, Fred's letter came promptly in the early part of August.

The ledge was so wide, Fred said, that the miners had sunk their prospect shaft in the center of the vein, and consequently all the rock taken out was a high-grade ore. That he was going to run two drifts, and would then have a more correct idea of the character of the mine, its volume, formation, etc. Only a small portion of the hanging wall was visible at the entrance, as the shaft went immediately into the very heart of the broad vein.

"But," Fred added, "If the mine proves to be one-tenth as good as it seems, 'there are millions in it,' literally."

So Clarence must make up his mind to wait developments.

In the meantime the settlers had harvested their crops of hay and grain, and were hauling them to town. Don Mariano, as a matter of course, had paid dearly for these same crops, with the sacrifice of his fine cows, besides very heavy taxes. He had sent half of his cattle away to the sierra, and those left had been as carefully guarded as possible, but still the dumb brutes would be attracted by the green grain, and would obey the law of nature, to go and eat it, in utter disregard of the "no fence law."

Thus, every night the fusilade of the law-abiding settlers would be heard, as they, to protect *their* "*rights under the law*," would be shooting the Don's cattle all over the rancho. In vain did he, or his sons and servants, ride out to find who fired. There was never a man to be seen with a gun or rifle in his hands; it never could be proved that any one of these peaceful farmers had fired a shot. The cattle were killed, but who had done it no one could say. Day after day the *vaqueros* would come in and report the number of cattle found shot, dead or wounded, that morning, and Gabriel would make a note of the number; at the end of the month he would add these figures, and the Don had the sad satisfaction of knowing how many of his cattle were killed *under the law*. For although the law did not enjoin upon any one to kill cattle in this manner, the effect was the same as if it had said so plainly.

"I think Southern California isn't such a very dry country as people try to make it out. The settlers on this rancho, I reckon, will realize nice little sums on their crops this year," Mr. Darrell observed at breakfast one morning.

"And with their little sums they should pay the Don for the cattle they have shot. It is a shame to take his land, have him pay taxes, and then kill his cattle also," replied Mrs. Darrell. "Those heartless people keep me awake sometimes with their cattle-shooting. I think the Don and his family are too kind to bear all these daily (and nightly) outrages so patiently."

"I thought you had given it up as a bad job to be the Don's champion, Mrs. Darrell," said her husband.

"If by being his champion I could save his cattle there would be no danger of giving up my championship. What I regret is that my sympathy should be so useless."

"Never mind, mother, the Don will soon have the power to drive all this *canaille* out of his rancho," Clarence said.

"Do you include me with the *canaille*?" asked Darrell.

"No, father, I do not. I suppose you have not forgotten you promised Don Mariano to pay for the land you located when the title should be approved."

"When there is no more *dispute* about it," Darrell explained.

"I understood you had said that when the government did not dispute it. We all know that the squatters will dispute it as long as they can find lawyers, who for a fee will fight against right and justice," Clarence said.

"I will keep to what I said— but I am not going to have my words construed to suit everybody," Darrell said, doggedly.

"How is the Don to have power to drive off the settlers, Clary? Tell us," Webster inquired.

"Don't you tell him, Clary. He'll go and tell it to the *squatters*," Willie interposed.

"And since when did you learn to call the settlers squatters, Master Willie? Ain't you a squatter yourself?" asked Mr. Darrell.

"No, I'm not. Am I, mamma?" asked Willie.

"I hope not, my dear. If I thought any one in this family were to deserve such a name I would not have come down to this place," Mrs. Darrell replied.

"What is a squatter, anyhow, mamma?" Clementine inquired.

"A squatter is a person who locates a land claim on land that belongs to some other person," Mrs. Darrell explained.

"On land that other persons say belongs to them, but which land, as no one knows to whom it belongs, it is free to be occupied by any American citizen," Mr. Darrell added with emphasis.

"There you are again mixing the wilful squatter with the honest settler, who pre-empts his land legitimately. The dividing line between the squatter and the settler is very clear to any one who honestly wants to see it," Mrs. Darrell said, and three or four of her children started to explain how well they did see that line.

"It is as plain as the nose on your face," Willie's voice said in a high key. "The honest settler only pre-empts government land, but the squatter goes into anybody's land before he knows who has title."

"Bravo!" cried Everett; "you got it straight this time."

"Then a squatter is a land thief?" Clementine inquired.

"That is a severe term," Alice observed.

"But isn't it true?" Clementine argued.

"No, because the squatter might not *intend* to steal. He might mistakenly take land which belongs to some one else. The intention is what makes the action a theft or not," Mrs. Darrell explained.

"But why should they make such mistakes? Ain't somebody there to say to whom the land belongs?" Master Willie inquired.

"Yes, but that somebody might not be believed, Master Willie, and there is where the shoe pinches," Webster explained.

"Ah!" was Willie's exclamation, and he became thoughtful.

"I give it up," said Clementine with a sigh, making them all laugh.

"That is a very wise resolve," Darrell observed.

"I've got it, papa," Willie's voice again was heard saying.

"Well, what have you got?" his father asked.

"The government ought to say first to whom the land belongs, and not let anybody take a single acre until the government says it is public land. Isn't that the way you say, Clarence?"

"Oh, you are quoting Clarence. I thought it was your own original idea you were giving us," Darrell said, and all laughed at Willie.

But he held his ground, saying; "It is Clarence's idea, but I only understood it this minute, so now it is mine."

"That is right, Willie. That is the way correct ideas are disseminated and take root," Everett said.

"And erroneous ones, too," Darrell added.

"Which is the correct, papa?" asked Willie.

"Your mind is even more inquisitive than usual this morning, Willie," said Jane.

"Suppose it is, do you object to it?" Willie queried.

"I think you had better be a lawyer," Lucy suggested.

"I mean to be. Then I will be the Don's lawyer."

"But suppose he don't want you?" asked Webster.

"But he will, for I will be honest."

"Will he want you if you are stupid, only because you are honest?" asked Clementine.

"I hate girls, they talk so silly," said Willie, again bringing the laugh on himself.

CHAPTER XVIII.

At Newport.

Mr. George Mechlin and traveling companions had a most delightful journey across the continent in spite of the hot weather.

Mr. Lawrence Mechlin and wife came to New York to meet George's bride and her sister and take them to Long Branch, where they had been sojourning for the last two months.

Mrs. Lawrence Mechlin was most favorably impressed with her nephew's wife and her sister. The two young beauties captivated her at once. She was enthusiastic.

"My dear," said she after dinner, addressing Elvira, "before I saw you and your sister I had been deliberating in my mind whether we should not go directly to our cottage in Newport and spend the remainder of the summer there. But now I think we had better go to Long Branch first, and then, unless you wish to visit Saratoga, we will go to Newport. How will that do?" She looked at George.

George smiled. He knew his aunt must be much pleased to put herself to the trouble of this traveling in hot weather. He replied:

"I am sure these young ladies will be most happy to follow you, aunt."

"Don't you all get too tired. And this reminds me that people who have been in the cars for ten days should have some rest. The day will be cool to-morrow; we need not go back to Long Branch until the day after," said the senior Mechlin.

"We do not intend going to-morrow. We have something to do in town yet," said Mrs. Mechlin.

"Some shopping, I suppose," Mr. Lawrence observed.

"Exactly," his wife assented.

After Mrs. Mechlin accompanied Elvira and Mercedes to their respective apartments, she returned to the library, where her husband and nephew were engaged in conversation. There was in Mrs. Mechlin's step and manner a degree of pleased elasticity, an amiable buoyancy of contented alacrity, which betokened that her mind was in a state of subdued pleasurable excitement which was to her very enjoyable. She came to George and kissed him twice, saying:

"I must repeat my kiss and congratulations, dear George. Your wife is perfection. Where in the world did such beauties grow? I assure you I am perfectly carried away by those two girls. No wonder you were so impatient to get married. They will be the rage next winter, and I shall give several dinners and receptions in honor of your wife, of course."

"You are always so kind to me, dear aunt."

"No more than I ought to be, but this time pleasure and duty will go together. I know I shall be proud to present my beautiful niece to New York society. Her manners are exquisite. She is lovely. She will be greatly admired, and justly so."

"You will have to arrange for your parties and dinners to be in December and February, because George is going to Washington in January, and the young ladies will take that opportunity to visit the Capital with him," said Mr. Mechlin, senior.

"That is a pity. Couldn't they go in December?"

"No, because George's business is with the Attorney General, and he wrote to me that he would not be ready until January. However, January is six months off yet. For the present, you have enough on your hands with your plans for the summer."

"That is very true. We will order some summer things to be made immediately. But I feel quite sure that we can find imported dresses ready made that will suit. I saw some lovely batists and grenadines at Arnold & Constable's, just from Paris, also beautiful embroidered muslins at Stewart's. We will see to-morrow and be ready to return the day after."

Life at Long Branch in the Mechlin cottage was very delightful to Elvira and Mercedes. When they had been there about two weeks, Mr. Robert Gunther appeared on the scene, and next day Mr. Arthur Selden followed. As they were old friends of the Mechlins, Mrs. Mechlin thought it was a natural thing that these two young gentlemen, on their return from their travels, should come to see her at Long Branch.

"In a day or two we are going to Newport, young gentlemen," she said. "You had better join our party and we'll all go together."

"I shall be most happy. My mother and sister have been with friends in the White Mountains, but will be at Newport next week, so this arrangement will suit me," said Gunther.

"It will suit me, also, as I promised my mother and sisters I should be at Newport in two weeks. Saratoga is too hot for me. I left them there under father's care. He likes Saratoga," Mr. Selden said.

If their sojourn at Long Branch had seemed so delightful to Elvira and Mercedes, their pleasures increased ten-fold at Newport. The Mechlin villa, shaded by tall elms and poplars, and surrounded by shrubbery and flowers, with a beautiful lawn and fountains in front, facing the ocean, and well-kept walks and arbors in different places on the grounds, was certainly a charming abode, fit to please the most fastidious taste. Then the drives, croquet playing, boat sailing and promenades, were also much enjoyed by our two little Californians. In the evenings, music and dancing would add variety to their pleasures, until such life seemed to them too charming to be real.

"And is this life repeated every summer, year after year?" asked Mercedes one evening as in the coming twilight she was sitting with Mr. Bob Gunther in a cozy bower of roses located on a little knoll in the grounds of the Gunther villa. They were looking at the gay equipages which drove by. Gunther sighed as he answered.

"Do you like this life?"

"Very much, but perhaps because it is a novelty to me. However, I am never tired of things that I once like, so I suppose I would like it always."

She did not look at Gunther; her attention was all given to the beautiful carriages driving by. If she had looked at him she would have seen the intensity of his passion in the workings of his features. For a moment the struggle with himself was terrible; but controlling his voice all he could, he said:

"You can have this life if you wish, and continue in the winters in a beautiful residence in New York or in Paris, should you desire it. You know it."

"No, I do not. I have no fairy god-mother to give me palaces. Come, let us go. Where is everybody?" said she, hurrying out of the arbor, looking about the grounds for Elvira and Miss Gunther, who had but a moment before been near her. "Ah! there they are; let us go to them."

"Do I frighten you? or am I tiresome?" said he, pale to the lips, following her.

"Neither; but young ladies who— who are— I mean any young lady, should not have such *tete-á-tetes* with fascinating young gentlemen in rosy bowers."

"Young ladies who are— what?"

"Who are judicious."

"Were you not going to say 'who are engaged?'"

"If I had, I might not have said the truth, *strictly*."

"Oh, in Heaven's name, tell me the truth! Are you engaged?"

"Ask me no questions, and I'll tell thee no lies."

"You are cruel; you are trifling with me!"

She stopped and looked up quickly into his eyes. For a moment she hesitated, then resolutely said:

"Mr. Gunther, I like you very much. Don't talk to me like this. I want to find pleasure in your society, but I shall not if you talk so to me. I am not and have never been cruel, and it never entered my head to trifle with you— never!"

"Forgive me this time. I shall never offend again."

He looked so distressed that Mercedes felt very sorry for him. She would have comforted him if she could. They walked in silence a few steps, but as he still looked pale, she did not wish the other ladies to see him. They were walking towards the house. Pointing to a narrow path leading towards the seashore, she said:

"That path goes to your boat-house, I suppose."

"Yes. I have a new boat; would you like to see it?"

"Is it far? You see it is getting late."

"We can come back in ten minutes."

"Truly? No longer than ten minutes?"

"Not a second longer unless you wish it."

"Come," said she, turning quickly into the little path, and he followed her. She did not care a straw to see the boat, but she wanted to give him time to get back the color to his face. She walked so fast down the hill; she almost ran. She looked back; he was following close. She began to laugh and started to run. He ran after her, and they did not stop until they got to the beach.

"How long is it since we started?" she asked. He looked at his watch.

"Not quite two minutes," he answered.

"I beg your pardon for running, obliging you to run, but I felt like it when I saw the blue water. It reminded me of home, of San Diego."

"No apology is needed. If it gave you pleasure to run, I am glad you did so."

"One look only, and then we must go back. Perhaps we had better return; I hear horses coming," she said, and at the same time Mr. Selden and his youngest sister came down by the boat-house at a gallop. His face flushed and became pale, but he lifted his hat as he passed. Gunther did the same, in answer to Miss Selden's salutation.

"Let us return. More riders might be passing," said Mercedes, and began to walk back.

"What! without seeing the boat?"

"It will be dark inside the house. I'll come some other time, earlier."

"Do you promise me that?"

"Certainly. You see, we can't run as fast up hill; it will take more than two minutes to return."

Again the galloping of horses was heard, and Selden, with his sister, passed on their way back just as Mercedes and Gunther reached the bank at the edge of the lawn and sat down to rest.

Selden's sister had noticed how he flushed and how livid he became a minute after, and faithfully reported the fact to her vigilant mamma as soon as she got home. Arthur would be watched now. His mamma knew that he was a millionaire and considered "a catch."

The Seldens had been abroad many years, the greater time in England, and had acquired some English habits, one of which was to dine late. That evening Arthur did not come down to dinner until half-past eight o'clock. He was afraid he would be questioned regarding the young lady with Robert Gunther. He felt too angry with his friend to hear his name spoken. But it was unavoidable. As soon as he took his seat at the table his mother asked:

"Who was the lady with Robert on the beach?"

"When?"

"This evening as we rode by his boat-house," explained his sister.

"Were they coming out of the boat-house?" asked the elder sister. Arthur's lips became white again.

"Don't be alarmed. They did not go into the boat-house," said he, sneeringly.

"I? I alarmed? It seems to me you are the one alarmed. I might say frightened," she replied, reddening like a peony, trembling with anger, as she well understood her brother meant to allude to her well known fondness for Bob.

"Who is the lady, any way? I ask," reiterated Mrs. Selden.

"She is George Mechlin's sister-in-law," Arthur replied.

"Ah! That is the beauty I hear half a dozen fellows are raving about," said Miss Selden, to pique her brother.

"Is she so very pretty, Arthur?" asked the younger sister.

"I never saw any woman so beautiful in all my life," he answered, with dogged resolution as if about to pull the string of his shower bath.

The mother and daughters exchanged looks. They understood it all now. Poor Arthur, he, too, was raving.

"By-the-by, I met Mechlin in the street to-day, and he asked if any one was sick in our family," observed Mr. Selden, senior.

"I understand. We will call to-morrow," Mrs. Selden said, sententiously. "We will see the beauties."

And they did. When they were in their carriage riding home, Mrs. Selden said:

"I am sorry for Arthur if he is in love with that girl. I fear he will never get over it."

"So much the better if he marries her," said the younger sister.

"Yes, but if he does not, he'll never have any heart left."

"Do you suppose she would refuse him?" said the elder sister, haughtily.

"I don't know; I must have a talk with Arthur."

She had a talk with Arthur, and when he saw evasion would be useless, he told her all about his love and why he believed it hopeless, judging by what he heard George say.

"But if she is not positively engaged to that Darrell, why should you fear him more than you fear Gunther?"

"Because I believe she loves him."

"Perhaps. But we are not sure of it. Moreover, he is far off in California, and you are here."

Arthur shook his head despondingly, but, nevertheless, he was pleased to hear his mother say that they must entertain those two Californians, and Mrs. Mechlin would think it was all intended as a compliment to herself.

The Gunthers being more intimate with the Mechlins, should not be outdone by the Seldens in courtesy to these two ladies (at least such was the opinion expressed by Robert to his mother), and thus a day hardly passed without some entertainment for their amusement.

Arthur closed his eyes to the future and let himself float down this stream of sweet pleasures, knowing that they were but a dream, and yet for that reason more determined to drink the last drop of that nectar so intoxicating, and enjoy being near her, within the sound of her voice, within the magic circle of her personality. The thought that he had seen her with Gunther rambling on the beach had been at first very bitter and disconcerting, but when he had learned that she had intended going to see the boat, but changed her mind, he consoled himself, and more easily yet, when he observed that Gunther and other admirers made no more progress as suitors than he did himself.

Misery loves company, sure. Thus it will be seen that Mr. Arthur Selden did not deceive himself with any very great hopes of success; still, such is the complexity of man's aspirations and man's reasoning, that he determined to speak to Mercedes of his love, for he had never done so— had never offered himself to her. He would know the worst from her own lips. So one morning in the month of September, when George Mechlin and his uncle had gone to New York on business on account of Jay Cook's failure, Selden saw the two Misses Mechlin out driving on the road towards Fort Adams. He concluded that the two Misses Mechlin must be going to call on the officers' wives, stationed at the Fort, and Mercedes must be alone at home. He immediately took a side road thus to avoid meeting the Mechlins and drove directly to the Mechlin villa. He found Mercedes alone in the library, where she had gone for a book to take to her room.

"Mr. Arthur Selden," said the tall servant at the library door, and behind his broad shoulders peeped Arthur's red whiskers.

"I took the liberty of following the servant," said he, "because I hoped we would be less interrupted here."

"Undoubtedly," replied she, laughing and offering him a chair; "very logical deduction."

"Don't laugh at me, please," said he, blushing; "I know you are thinking that others might follow you here as well as I, and it is so, but you see, Miss Mercedes, I am in despair at times. I have been wishing to speak to you alone, but I never have a chance."

"Why, Mr. Selden, you see me very often."

"Yes, but not alone, not where I could tell you all I feel for you, and beg you not to drive me to despair. You know I have loved you from the first instant I saw you. Can I hope ever to win your love? May I hope, or is my love hopeless?"

"Mr. Selden, I like you very much, but please do not ask me to love you. It is not possible."

"Why not? Is it because I am not handsome like Bob Gunther?" said he, with a painful sneer. "Believe me, I shall be a devoted, loving husband; none can love you more passionately and devotedly."

"I do not doubt it. But I cannot. Please don't ask me, and don't hate me."

"Mr. Robert Gunther," said the tall waiter, and Bob's broad brow and good-natured smile shone at the door.

The delightful sojourn at Newport was now over. The Mechlin family were again at their town residence in New York City. Elvira and Mercedes, as it was their habit, were that evening having their cosy chat before going to bed.

"So Clarence will be here next month," Elvira remarked.

"Yes, he says he will spend Christmas with us, and if we'll let him, he will go with us to Washington."

"That will be delightful. I suppose Gunther and your other numerous slaves will disappear when he arrives."

"They ought not, for I have never encouraged any one any more than if I had been married already."

"But you are not, my darling, and that makes a very great difference with young gentlemen."

"Why is it that Mrs. Mechlin does not approve of my being engaged to Clarence?"

"Because she had set her heart upon your marrying Gunther, who is a great favorite of hers."

"I am sorry to disappoint her, for she has been so sweet and good to me, but I can't help it. Here are the letters I got from home. I'll leave them for you to read, and you let me have yours. I hear George coming up stairs, I must go to my room."

"Well, pussy, haven't you had a nice frolic at Newport?" said George, stopping Mercedes at the door and making her come back into the room again.

"Indeed I have," Mercedes answered.

"And haven't you broken hearts as if they were old cracked pottery?"

"They must have been, to be broken so easily. But I guess I didn't hurt any very much."

"Indeed you did. Besides Gunther and Selden who are given up as incurable, there are three or four others very badly winged. Poor fellows, and friends of mine, too. It is like an epidemic, uncle says."

"Clarence will soon be here and stop the epidemic from spreading any further," Elvira said.

"I don't know about that. But I am glad he is coming. When will he be here?"

"About Christmas— perhaps about the twentieth of December," Mercedes answered. "He says he will telegraph to you the day he starts."

"I shall be glad to see him; he is a noble fellow," said he, and embraced Mercedes, saying good night.

CHAPTER XIX.

In New York.

Cards for Mrs. Mechlin's ball, on the 27th of December, had been out for two or three days, when, on the 20th of that same month and year— 1873— Clarence arrived at the American metropolis. He was in a high state of excitement. He could scarcely repress his impatience to see Mercedes, and yet he exerted sufficient self-control to go first to Tiffany and purchase the finest diamond ring in the establishment. He even was patient enough to wait until the diamond which he selected was reset in a ring from which an emerald was removed. When the exchange was made and the jewel paid for, he told the driver to hasten to Mr. Mechlin's house.

George and his uncle had just come from their office when Clarence arrived, so he met them in the hall as he entered. George presented him to his uncle, and the three walked into the library. The cordial manner in which Clarence was received by Mr. Mechlin, demonstrated clearly how favorably this gentleman was impressed.

After conversing with him, while George went to carry the news of his arrival up-stairs, Mr. Mechlin, when George returned, invited him to dine with them, saying:

"I feel as if you were not quite a stranger to us, having heard George speak of you so often, and always most kindly."

Clarence hesitated, but George insisted, and he remained. Then the two friends sat down to chat while the ladies came down. In a few minutes Clarence had given a synopsis of home news.

"And what about mining news?" George asked.

"Splendid," was the reply.

And Clarence quickly told him how rich his mines had turned out, and how he had already sold six hundred thousand dollars' worth of ore, and had an offer of one million dollars for the mines, but the Haverly brothers advised him not to sell. That he thought of putting up crushing mills in the spring.

Mr. Mechlin went into his wife's room without knocking— an omission indicative of great pre-occupation of mind— and his words proved that to be the case.

"But that young fellow is splendid, wife."

"What young fellow?"

"That young Darrell, from California."

"Ah! where did you see him?"

"Down stairs. He is talking with George in the library, and I asked him to take dinner with us."

"He might be splendid— but never superior to Bob Gunther— never!" said Mrs. Mechlin, with firmness.

"Perhaps not superior, mentally or morally, but he is certainly much handsomer."

"Handsomer than Bob? The idea!"

"You wait until you see him," said Mr. Mechlin, going into his room to get ready for dinner.

If Mercedes' hands had not trembled so much she would have been ready to come down stairs much sooner.

"If you had accepted aunt's offer to get you a maid you would not labor under so many difficulties," said Elvira, coming into Mercedes' room as she was going down stairs. "You have never dressed yourself without some one to help you at home, whether it was my squaw, your squaw, or mamma's, or the other girls, or whether it was your own Madame Halier— you always had an attendant."

"That is so," Mercedes said, ready to cry. "I am so utterly useless when— when— sometimes— but how could I accept a maid? It would have been an extravagance after the many dresses and other things bought for me. I couldn't."

"I wish I had thought of sending my maid to help you," said Elvira, coming to Mercedes' assistance.

"I wish so, too, now; but I didn't think I wanted her, as Mrs. Mechlin's maid had dressed my hair. What I dread is that your aunt will be present when I meet him, and— and as she don't like him— "

"Nonsense. She likes Bob Gunther, that's all. But she will not go down before we do if she knows Clarence is here. She will give you time to meet him first."

With Elvira's assistance Mercedes at last was ready, and with trembling knees, which scarcely supported her light weight, she managed to walk down stairs.

"Don't run so fast, dear. I want you by me," said she.

"Take my arm, old lady," said Elvira, laughing.

The rustle of silk approaching put Clarence in a tremor— making him forget what he was saying.

Elvira entered, and he rose to meet her.

"I must salute you Spanish fashion," she said, embracing him.

"Where is pussy?" said George, going towards the door, but as the train of Elvira's dress lay in his way, he looked down and pushed it aside.

Mercedes, who had remained behind the door, saw him do so, and burst out laughing, for it seemed to her as if George was expecting to find pussy entangled in Elvira's train.

"Here she is, laughing at me," said George, taking her arm.

She looked so lovely, that Clarence stood looking at her in silence, not even taking a step to meet her.

"Mr. Darrell, I am very glad to see you," she said, still laughing, all her fear and trembling having left her. She extended her hand to him with perfect composure.

Elvira looked at her surprised. She herself was surprised at her sudden and perfect calmness. Because George made her laugh looking for *pussy* in Elvira's train, she lost all her fear.

"This is a step from the sublime to the ridiculous," she said to herself, as she became of a sudden philosophically calm.

When she explained what had made her laugh, all joined her, remembering that it had indeed seemed as if George was looking for some small object hidden in the ruffles of Elvira's train.

Those rosy lips and pearly teeth looked so sweet, and the little dimples so charming when she laughed, that Clarence would have been satisfied to remain there looking at them for an indefinite length of time without saying anything, only holding her hand in his, and looking into her eyes. But other people were not so entranced, and as now Mr. and Mrs. Mechlin came in, all proceeded to the dining-room, after George had presented him to his aunt.

Mrs. Mechlin was a little cold in her manner at first, thinking that surely Bob must give up all hopes. But being a very courteous hostess, her manner soon became affable, she engaged Clarence in conversation, asking him about fruit-raising in California, and about those wonderfully rich mines, which had given so many millions to the world. Mr. Mechlin also became much interested in what Clarence had to say. Before dinner was over, Mercedes had the pleasure of seeing that Mr. and Mrs. Mechlin were more than favorably impressed with her intended.

After dinner many callers began to arrive. Clarence had not spoken a word yet to Mercedes alone. He followed her with his eyes and watched— without seeming too watchful— for an opportunity of speaking to her without being overheard.

At last the desired moment came, and he was able to whisper a few words.

She blushed as she replied: "Perhaps not this evening— there are so many here."

"I brought you the ring which you told me I was not to send but *bring* in person."

"Bring it to-morrow," she said, with deeper blush.

"At what time?"

"Perhaps between ten and eleven."

Clarence returned to Elvira's side, and had to console himself with studying how Mercedes could have become more beautiful when it had seemed that it would be impossible for any human being to be more perfect.

He was deliciously occupied in pondering upon this problem when ices and cakes, tea and coffee were served by two waiters, in white gloves, and very irreproachable manners, and now Clarence could have the happiness of taking his ice cream beside Mercedes.

Next day, at half-past ten exactly, Clarence ran up the steps of the Mechlin mansion. He gave his card to the servant for Miss Alamar, and asked for no one else, but Elvira came from the library as she heard his voice.

"Aunt and myself are going to attend to some shopping. You will stay to luncheon, won't you? Aunt requests it. I am glad she likes you."

"I am truly grateful to her, and much pleased, indeed. But I shall be making a very long call if I wait. I shall go and return at one— hadn't I better?"

"If you have anything else to do this morning, of course, go and return. We lunch at one."

"I have nothing on earth to do but to see you people and wait on you. I hope you won't get tired of me. I was in hopes you two would go with me to see some very pretty things at Tiffany's."

"We are going there now. I promised aunt to go with her. Mercedes and I, you mean, I suppose, can go with you to-morrow?"

Mrs. Mechlin now came down stairs, and Clarence waited on them to their carriage.

As he closed the carriage door Mrs. Mechlin said: "Elvira has told you we shall expect you to luncheon."

"Yes, madam; thank you," said he, bowing.

The carriage drove off, and Mrs. Mechlin said: "He is certainly very handsome. I am sorry for Bob."

When Clarence returned he met Mercedes in the hall. She was evidently frightened, and so was he, but soon rallied as he followed her into the library.

"Tell me more about home, now that we are alone," said she, pushing a chair for him, and occupying another on the opposite side of the fire-place, with a graceful affability, which reminded him of his interview with Doña Josefa on the veranda at the rancho.

He understood by her manner and the position of the chairs, which had high backs and high arms, that the interview was to be very formal, and so he took his seat accordingly— far off and demurely.

"Where shall I begin?" said he, with mock gravity.

"Anywhere— at the top with papa, or at the bottom with Tisha. It will all be interesting."

"Can't I begin at the middle, for instance, with myself?"

"Yes; but you are here— I see you."

"Do you? At this distance? Don't you want a telescope?"

"You are near enough," she said, laughing.

"I can't talk of anybody but you. What is the use of putting me in this chair like a bad child that must be punished by being roasted alive!"

"Are you too near the fire?"

"And too far from you," said he, rising, and going to sit on a sofa, at the other end of the room. She kept her seat by the fire-place. "Please come here. I have so much to say to you. It will give me a headache to sit so near the fire."

She arose, walked over to where he was, and sat on another arm-chair nearest to the sofa.

"Let us freeze at this end of the room," she said.

"Are you cold? If you are, let us go back to the fire."

She did look a little cold, with her pretty little hands calmly folded on her lap, but she smiled.

He drew a low seat close to hers, and took the soft hands into his, saying in beseeching accents:

"Let me sit by you, please. After so many weary months of absence grant me this happiness. You told me not to send but *bring* our engagement ring. Here it is. Let me put it on the dear little finger myself."

So saying he put the ring on, and covered the hand with kisses. Mercedes' face was suffused with blushes, and she did not dare look at the ring.

"I have been longing for this moment of bliss, Mercedes, my own, my precious. You are pledged to me now. Look at me, my sweet wife!"

"What a foolish boy!" she said, covering her face.

"Now you must set the day of our marriage. Let it be the day after we arrive. Let us be married at San Francisco. Why not?"

"You must ask mamma and papa. Talk to Elvira about it."

"I will. She will not object. Particularly as Mechlin intends going to reside in California, and engaging in business there. So you see, it will be just the thing for our marriage to take place as soon as we arrive. I think it would be so nice for all your family, and my mother and Alice and Everett to come to meet us at San Francisco, and we be married there, and I then take you to your house, which will be ready for you."

"I don't know whether mamma would approve— "

"Oh, my precious! Why not? She will, if you say you wish it so. I will write to-day to Hubert. I shall telegraph him to buy the handsome house he told me was for sale. Shall I telegraph?"

She looked down reflectingly. Suddenly she uttered an exclamation of surprise. She had seen the ring for the first time.

"I had not seen this diamond. Is it not too magnificent for an engagement ring?"

"Nothing is too magnificent for you."

"But, really, will it not attract too much attention?"

"I think not. You are not ashamed of it, are you?"

"No, indeed. Only it might be considered too large for an engagement ring," she said. But observing that he looked pained, she added: "It is very beautiful. It is like a big drop of sunlight."

"I am glad you like it. But perhaps it might not be considered in good taste for an engagement ring. Let us go to Tiffany's now and ask your sister. I'll give you all home news as we drive down. But don't you remove the ring. I am superstitious about that."

Mercedes laughed and arose, saying: "I will not touch it. I'll go now to put on my bonnet. Elvira told me I may drive down with you to Tiffany's, if I wished. I won't be gone but two minutes."

"When am I going to have one sweet kiss?" said he, in pleading tones. "Only one."

"I don't know— I can't tell," she said, running off, eluding him.

The gentle motion of Mrs. Mechlin's luxuriantly cushioned carriage invited conversation, and Elvira soon perceived that her aunt desired to know all about Clarence's family and history and wished to obtain all necessary information in that respect as they drove down Broadway to Tiffany's, Elvira therefore proceeded to enlighten the good lady, remembering, however, that George had cautioned her never to mention that old Darrell had taken land on the rancho in the sincere conviction that by wise enactments of Congress, to rob people of their lands, was and had been made a most honest transaction.

"My aunt will not understand," George had said, "and never realize the effect that our legislation has upon us, as a nation, particularly upon the untraveled, the stay-at-home Americans, and more specially yet, the farmers. She will not believe old Darrell honest in his error, and no matter whether Clarence might be the prince of good fellows, to her he will always be the son of a squatter, of one who *steals land*. No matter under whose sanction— theft is theft to her— and she would snap her fingers at the entire Senate and House of Representatives, if those honorable bodies undertook to prove to her that by getting together and saying that they can authorize American citizens to go and take the property of other citizens (without paying for it) and keep it— and fight for it to keep it— that the proceeding is made honorable and lawful."

Remembering these words of George, Elvira spoke highly of Mrs. Darrell and the other members of the family, but said very little of the head thereof. Still, as there was much to say about Clarence himself, very favorable to that young gentleman, the time was agreeably occupied with his biography, while the two ladies drove through Broadway.

"I noticed last evening that his manners are very good," said Mrs. Lawrence Mechlin, speaking of Clarence. "You know, my dear, that I have a confirmed dread of bad-mannered people. They spread discord and discomfort wherever they are. And *apropos* of manners, I must not omit saying that Mercedes' behavior last evening was all that could be desired in a well-bred young lady. A great many quite nice young ladies on such an occasion would have gone into the library, or the little boudoir, or the other parlors, or would have sat on the stairs, anywhere, to have a whispered *tête-à-tête* with her *fiancé*. Your sister remained in the drawing-room, like a lady, though I know well enough her heart was longing to express how glad she was to see him. And he, too, behaved very well. Did not hang about her, but was courteous to all the ladies. I noticed last summer that Mercedes was not fond of running off to have a *tête-à-tête* with this one, and then with another, as many of our girls do, but I thought she avoided it on account of being engaged. Now, however, I see that her reason is even a better one. That it is inbred self-respect, a lady's sense of decorum."

"I am glad you think so well of my sister, dear aunt; and I think she is naturally refined and lady-like. But as for running off to have *tête-à-têtes* with gentlemen is a thing never seen among our Spanish girls. I know that we, Spanish people, are criticised and much ridiculed for keeping girls too strictly guarded, and in some instances this may be so, but as a general thing, the girls themselves like to be guarded. We have all the freedom that is good for us. Now, for instance, I told Mercedes she may receive Clarence alone, and after they had their talk together, that she might drive down and join us here. I know I can trust her."

"That is right. I am glad you told her to come, for I want to give her a Christmas present, and would like to have some idea of her taste in jewelry."

In due time the two ladies arrived at the jeweler's, and very soon after Mercedes and Clarence joined them. The ring was submitted to Mrs. Mechlin's *dictum*, and she pronounced it superb, not at all inappropriate for an engagement ring. Meantime, however, Clarence had seen another which he liked best, and he bought it at once. It was made of large diamonds, set in a circle, close together, so that the ring looked like a band of light, very beautiful, "and," he said, "just the thing; in fact, symbolical," considering that he wished to surround Mercedes with never-ending brightness and joy.

On Christmas night our Californians attended a *musicale* at Mrs. Gunther's. On the 27th, Mrs. Mechlin's grand ball came off (and a grand affair it was). On New Year's Day George took Clarence on an extensive tour of visiting.

"We will have a regular '*rodeo*,'" said George, laughing, as they were about to start; "and wind up our drive by coming home to make a long visit here, at our *corral*."

"We don't want you, if you call your round of visits a '*rodeo*.' Aren't you ashamed to laugh at us Californians like that?" said Elvira, affecting great resentment, which took several kisses from George to pacify.

Clarence was so pleased with the number and character of the acquaintances he made on New Year's, and he was so warmly invited to call again, that he became convinced that New York was just the nicest city on the continent, and even thought he would like it for a residence, provided Mercedes was of the same opinion.

The Mechlins received in grand style on New Year's, and finished the day with a dance and collation.

Next night Mrs. Gunther's ball took place, which was followed by an equally grand affair at the Seldens, on the 6th.

And now it was time to talk about the trip to Washington. George wanted his uncle and aunt to go with him.

"I have no fears that the Solicitor General will give us any trouble," said

Mr. L. Mechlin; "I think his action in the Alamar case was a *feeler* only for some ulterior purpose, which he has abandoned. But if I could see how I might help Scott with his Texas Pacific Railroad, I should be most happy to go and try— for his sake, for the sake of the southern people, and for the sake of you people at San Diego. But I don't see what I can do now. The failure of Jay Cook has hurt Scott at the very time when Huntington is getting stronger and his influence in Congress evidently increasing."

"Several persons have told me that a certain railroad man is bribing Congressmen right and left to defeat the Texas Pacific Railroad," said George, "and I believe it."

"Bribery is an ugly word," Mr. Mechlin replied; "and if that is the way railroad men are going to work, it will be a difficult matter for an honest man to compete with them and keep his hands clean. However, I might be able to help Scott in some way. I guess we might go for a week or two. Lizzie, what do you think? Would you like to go to Washington for a week or two?"

"I would like it very well. I shall miss these two young ladies very much, and as the best way to cure *ennui* is to avoid it, I think a visit to Washington would be just the thing for me now."

Mercedes clapped her hands in such genuine delight at hearing this, and Elvira and Clarence were evidently so pleased, that Mrs. Mechlin added:

"These dear children seem so pleased that now I would feel great satisfaction in going, even if I did not expect any pleasure in my visit. But I do. I have not been in Washington for years, and I have many warm friends there whom I would like to see."

Thus it was fixed that all the family would go to Washington on the 9th or 10th, and remain for two or three weeks at the gay capital.

Mrs. Mechlin now remembered that the Gunthers and the Seldens had mentioned that perhaps they would accept some invitations to several parties and a wedding, to come off in Washington about the middle of January, and would be going down about the same time.

"I'll tell you what I'll do," Mr. Mechlin said, "I'll get a special car, and you invite the Gunthers and Seldens to go with us, and we will make a pleasant party all together."

"That is a good idea. I'll see Mrs. Gunther to-day, and we will appoint the day to start."

And thus it came to pass that on the 9th of January our Californians were traveling in a palace car on their way to Washington, in company with the most elite of New York.

Messrs. Bob Gunther and Arthur Selden were of the party. They derived no pleasure in being so, but they followed Mercedes because they preferred the bitter sweet of being near her, in her presence, rather than to accept at once the bitter alone of a hopeless separation. They knew they must not hope, but still they hoped, for the reason alone that hope goes with man to the foot of the gallows.

CHAPTER XX.

At the Capitol.

"There is no greater monster in being than a very ill man of great parts, he lives like a man in a palsy, with one side of him dead; while perhaps he enjoys the satisfaction of luxury, of wealth, of ambition, he has lost all the taste of good-will, of friendship, of innocence," says Addison.

If this can be said of a man whose influence is of limited scope, how much more horrible the "palsy," the moral stagnation, of the man whose power for good or evil extends to millions of people, to unlimited time; whose influence shall be felt, and shall be shaping the destinies of unborn generations, after he shall be only a ghastly skeleton, a bundle of crumbling bones!

Would that the power, the wisdom, the omniscience of God had not been repudiated, discarded, abolished, by modern thinkers, so that now but few feel any moral checks or dread of responsibility; for if there is to be no final accounting, morality ceases to be a factor, there being no fear of any hereafter; and as a natural sequence, there is no remedy left for the terrible "*palsy.*" For it is a well demonstrated fact that *sense of justice*, or pure *philanthropy*, alone, is but frail reliance. Fatally has man elevated his vanity to be his deity, with egotism for the high priest, and the sole aim and object of life the accumulation of *money*, with no thought of the never-ending to-morrow, the awakening on the limitless shore! no thought of his fellow-beings here, of himself in the hereafter!

"It is a high, solemn, almost awful thought," says Carlyle, "for every individual man, that his earthly influence, which has had a commencement, will never, through all ages— were he the very meanest of us— have an end! What is done, is done; has already blended itself with the boundless, ever-living, ever-working universe, and will also work for good or for evil, openly or secretly, throughout all time. The life of every man is as a well-spring of a stream, whose small beginnings are indeed plain to all, but whose ulterior course and destination, as it winds through the expanses of infinite years, only the Omniscient can discern. Will it mingle with neighboring rivulets as a tributary, or receive them as their sovereign? Is it to be a nameless brook, and with its tiny waters, among millions of other brooks and rills, increase the current of some world's river? or is it to be itself a Rhine or a Danube, whose goings forth are to the uttermost lands, its floods an everlasting boundary-line on the globe itself, the bulwark and highway of whole kingdoms and continents? We know not, only, in either case, we know its path is to the great ocean; its waters, were they but a handful, are *here*, and cannot be annihilated or permanently held back."

But how many of the influential of the earth think thus? If only the *law-*

givers could be made to reflect more seriously, more conscientiously, upon the effect that their legislation must have on the lives, the destinies, of their fellow-beings *forever*, there would be much less misery and heart-rending wretchedness in this vale of tears. Now, the law-giver is a politician, who generally thinks more of his own political standing with *other politicians* than of the interests entrusted to his care. To speak of constituents sounds well, but who are the constituents? The men who govern them, who control votes, those who guide the majorities to the polls; the politicians, who make and unmake each other, they are the power— the rest of the people dream that *they* are— that's all. And if these law-givers see fit to *sell themselves* for money, what then? Who has the power to undo what is done? Not their constituents, surely. But the constituencies will be the sufferers, and feel all the effect of pernicious legislation.

These were George Mechlin's thoughts as he sat, with his uncle, in the gallery of the House of Representatives, listening to a debate, a few days after their arrival in Washington. The attention of George, however, was divided between the debate and some papers he held in his hands which a member of Congress had given him. These papers contained several arguments, speeches and petitions, praying Congress to aid in the construction of the Texas Pacific Railroad, thus to help the impoverished South to regain her strength wasted in the war. Among these papers there was one which more particularly arrested his attention. It read as follows:

43d Congress, 1st Session.

House of Representatives.

Mis. Doc. No. 68.

CENTRAL PACIFIC RAILROAD COMPANY.

PREAMBLE AND RESOLUTIONS SUBMITTED BY MR. LUTTRELL.

January 12, 1874.— Referred to the Committee on the Pacific Railroad, and ordered to be printed, together with accompanying papers.

"WHEREAS, The Central Pacific Railroad Company was incorporated by the State of California on the 27th day of June, A.D. 1861, to construct a railroad to the eastern boundary of said State; and whereas, by Acts of Congress of the years 1862 and 1863, said company was authorized to extend said railroad eastward through the territory of the United States by an Act entitled 'An Act to aid in the construction of a railroad and telegraph line from the Missouri River to the Pacific Ocean,' and received from the United States, under said Act and the Acts supplemental thereto and amendatory thereof, and from the State of California and counties and corporations within said State, from the State of Nevada, and from the Territory of Utah, the following amounts, estimated in gold coin, to wit:

Land granted by the United States of the value in gold coin of	$50,288,000 00
Granted and donated by various corporations and individuals within the State of California	5,000,000 00
Granted and donated by various corporations and individuals, situate within the State of Nevada	3,000,000 00
Granted and donated by various corporations and individuals within the Territory of Utah	$1,500,000 00
Donated by the State of California	1,500,000 00
Bonds on which the State of California guarantees and pays interest	12,000,000 00
Donated by the County of Placer, in the State of California— Bonds	250,000 00
Donated by the City and County of San Francisco— Interest bonds	400,000 00
Donated by the City and County of Sacramento— Interest bonds	300,000 00
Bonds by the United States Government	27,389,120 00
First mortgage bonds of Central Pacific Railroad Company	27,389,120 00
Second mortgage bonds of said Central Pacific Railroad, legalized by law	15,601,741 83
Second mortgage bonds, issued and sold as above	11,787,378 17

Total	$156,825,360 00

And, whereas, the directors of said Central Pacific Railroad Company made contracts with *certain of their own members* to construct said road, known as the 'Contract and Finance Company,' for consideration in lands, money, and bonds, far in excess of the actual cost of construction; and,

Whereas, said Central Pacific Railroad is, and has been, completed and in running order for, in part and in whole, over six years last past, and the profits accruing from same, amounting to over — — millions of dollars per annum, has been kept and appropriated to their own use, in *violation* of their duties and *in fraud* of the United States Government; and,

Whereas, said directors of the said Central Pacific Railroad Company *issued to themselves, and for their personal profit and benefit*, the second mortgage bonds of said Central Pacific Railroad Company, to the amount of $27,387,120, payable in United States gold coin, with interest at ten per cent. per annum, and have, with said profits accruing to the Central Pacific Railroad Company, from the sales of United States bonds, lands, and other subsidies, as aforesaid mentioned, and the *issue to themselves* of the bonds aforesaid, bought, *in order to defraud* the Government of the United States out of the interest now due from said Central Pacific Railroad Company, other roads in the State of California, and expended in doing the same, all the accruing profits of said Central Pacific Railroad for the benefit of the directors, failing and *fraudulently refusing to pay the Government of the United States*, the interest legally due on said mortgage bonds; therefore, be it

Resolved, That a select committee of seven members of this House be appointed by the Speaker, and such committee be and is hereby instructed to inquire whether or not any person connected with the organization or association commonly known as the 'Contract and Finance Company' of the Central Pacific Railroad Company, now holds any of the bonds, lands, or other subsidies granted said company, for the payment of which, or the interest thereon, the United States is in any way liable; and whether or not such holders, if any, or their assignees of such bonds, lands, or other subsidies, are holders in good faith, and for a valuable consideration, or procured the same illegally, or *by fraud*; * * * and to inquire into the character and purpose of such organization, and fully, of all the transactions of said Central Pacific Railroad Company, and all transactions had and contracted by and between the directors of the Central Pacific Railroad Company and Charles Crocker & Co.; and of all transactions and contracts made by said directors with the 'Contract and Finance Company' for the furnishing of material of every kind and character whatever, and the construction of the Central Pacific Railroad and other branch roads connected therewith; * * *

and to report the facts to this House, together with such bill as may be necessary to protect the interests of the United States Government and the people, on account of any bonds, lands and subsidies of the class hereinbefore referred to, and against the combinations *to defraud the Government* and the people; and said committee is hereby authorized to send for persons and papers, and to report at any time."

Here follows a long recital of *frauds* perpetrated by Messrs. Leland Stanford, Huntington, Crocker and Hopkins, under the name of "Central Pacific Railroad Company" and "Contract and Finance Company," etc. Said frauds, Mr. Luttrell says, were against the Government and against the stockholders of the Central Pacific Company. A Mr. Brannan, in a long complaint, sets forth also how and when these gentlemen *cheated* the Government by presenting *false statements* of the cost of constructing the Central Pacific Railroad, and in other ways, and *cheated* the stockholders of said railroad by issuing *to themselves* the stock, and appropriating other subsidies, which should have been distributed *pro rata* among all the stockholders.

The entire statement is a shameful exposure of disgraceful acts, any one of which, were it to be perpetrated by a poor man, would send him to the penitentiary.

George was shocked to read Mr. Luttrell's "*Preamble and Resolutions*," and Mr. Brannan's "*complaint.*" Mr. Lawrence Mechlin waited to read them in the evening, at his hotel.

"These two gentlemen ever since their arrival had heard strange rumors about Congressmen being '*bribed with money*,' and in other *ways improperly influenced by 'a certain railroad man,' who was organizing a powerful lobby to defeat the Texas Pacific Railroad*." In his endeavors to aid Tom Scott, Mr. Lawrence Mechlin had come across some startling facts regarding the manipulation of railroad bills, especially in the Congressional committees. Still, he was loth to believe that bribery would be so openly used. He was a man of strict probity, slow to think any man dishonorable. George, brought up in the same school, felt, also, a reluctance to believe that the Congress of these United States could be packed, bundled, and labeled, by a few of its treacherous members, who would sell themselves for money, in spite of their honest colleagues.

"Pshaw! the thing is too preposterous," he had said to his uncle, who, with saddened voice, had answered.

"So it seems to me. Let us go to the Capitol again; I want to speak to some of the Representatives; I have only seen Senators; I must talk with the House a little." And they had come, and were now listening to the House.

George's business with the Attorney General had been more satisfactory. The appeal was at last dismissed, and the joyful news had been telegraphed to Don Mariano. There was now no dispute about the validity of his title. The Government itself had said that the land belonged to him; would the squatters vacate now? We will see. Meantime, the remittitur had to be sent to the court below, and it was expected that Congress would soon make an appropriation to defray expenses of surveying lands in California. George wrote to Don Mariano not to engage any surveyor to survey his rancho, as there would be an appropriation made for lands to be surveyed by the Government.

Elvira and Mercedes were made very happy on hearing that the appeal was dismissed. They did not well understand what it all meant; but as they were told that now the Government of the United States had said that the rancho belonged to their father, they naturally concluded that the squatters would go away, and there would no longer be any trouble about the destruction of their cattle, and their father not be so worried and unhappy.

Thus, life seemed very sweet to those two innocents, and they enjoyed their visit to Washington to the fullest extent. The Gunthers and Seldens had stopped at the same hotel with the Mechlins, and the three families were constantly together. Their parlors in their evenings "*at home*" were filled with a crowd of distinguished visitors; other evenings were given to parties and receptions. One cloud only cast a shadow on Mercedes' brilliant surroundings, and this was the obvious misery she saw in Arthur Selden's dejected countenance, and a certain dread she felt at the silent coldness of Robert Gunther. His eyes seemed to her darker than they used to be, but perhaps they seemed so because he was so much paler. But what could she do? she asked herself, and wished very much that these two young gentlemen had remained in New York, for, surely, they couldn't expect that she would give up Clarence! No, indeed. Not for fifty thousand Gunthers, or two million Seldens.

There were times when the coldness of these two young gentlemen was very marked, and, amiable as she was, she felt it. But her Clarence was always near, and his superb eyes were watching, ready to come to her at the slightest indication. It was so sweet to be so quickly understood and so promptly obeyed by him.

There had been a brilliant ball at one of the legations, and on the following morning the Seldens and Gunthers were discussing the event in Mrs. Mechlin's parlor.

"You made two new conquests last night," said the eldest Miss Selden to Mercedes. "Those two *attachés* are now your new slaves. They are awfully in love. I felt pity for them, to see them so completely captivated. You ought to be proud."

"I don't think they are in love, but, admitting it is so, why should I be proud? I should be annoyed, that's all," replied Mercedes.

"Do you expect us to believe that?" Miss Selden asked.

"You may believe it, for it is the truth."

"You are a strange girl, then."

"Why so? Why should I wish men to fall in love with me, when I cannot return their love?" said Mercedes, evidently vexed.

"You are the first girl I ever saw that did not want to have admirers; yes, loads of them."

"Admirers and friends, yes; but you spoke of those young men being *in love*. Now, if I thought so, I would be very sorry, and, as I do not wish to be unhappy, I hope you are mistaken."

The Misses Selden laughed incredulously.

"In my opinion, no kind-hearted girl ought to desire to be loved except by the one she loves. Else, she must be a very heartless creature, who enjoys the miseries of others," added she, earnestly. "Now, I want you to know, I am not cruel; I am not heartless; so I do not wish any man (but one) to be in love with me."

"You are right, my dear," Mrs. Gunther interposed. "But the trouble is, you are too pretty, too sweet, to be let alone; you can't help being loved."

"Then I am unlucky, that's all," she said, with trembling lips, "and the sooner I go home, the better it will be for mutual comfort."

Robert Gunther was talking with Elvira, but he had not lost one word of this conversation. In the evening they went to a Presidential reception. It happened that he was near Mercedes when Elvira proposed to go and see the flowers in the conservatory; he offered her his arm, and they followed Elvira. He had spoken very few words to her since they returned from Newport, but had watched her and feasted his eyes on her loveliness. Now, after walking in silence for some time, he said:

"It is a sad sort of consolation to know that you regret inspiring hopeless love. I heard your conversation with the Misses Selden this morning. I thank you for not enjoying my misery."

"Oh! how could I do that? I wish I could make you happy; please forgive me if I have ever caused you pain?" said she in the sweetest of pleading tones. He looked at her sweet face, turned toward his, and his love for her seemed to rush upon him like an overwhelming wave— like a hot flame rising to his brain.

"Oh! Mercedes, it is frightful how much I love you! What shall I do to conquer this unfortunate infatuation?"

"Forget me; I shall soon be away— far away."

"Oh! darling, I would rather suffer seeing you, than to have your sweet presence withdrawn from my sight. You see my unfortunate situation? I vow it is awful to love so hopelessly! But I shall never talk to you of my love again. I see I pain you," he added, seeing that she trembled and looked pained. "Forgive me, for I am very wretched. My life will now be a blank."

"I wish you could feel for me, as you do toward Elvira. How I envy her your friendship," she said, in very low tones.

"Do you, truly?"

"Indeed I do. I would be so happy."

"I shall try. But how can I, loving you so ardently?"

"As a proof of your love, try to be my friend— only a friend."

"You ask of my love a suicide— to kill itself. Be it so. I shall try," said he with a sad smile. "The request is rather novel, but perhaps it might be done. I doubt it. I suppose you will be my friend then?"

"I am that now— most sincerely," said she, earnestly.

On leaving the conservatory, they saw Clarence coming to meet them. He joined Elvira and walked by her side.

"Thanks, Mr. Darrell. I am glad you have good sense," said Gunther, addressing the back and broad shoulders of Clarence from the distance. Mercedes laughed and felt herself regaining her composure.

They had now been in Washington ten days, and the ladies of the party had only made one very hurried visit to the Capitol. This day Mrs. Mechlin had set apart "to devote to Congress," she said, and it was arranged that they would go in the morning, would lunch at the Capitol, and remain part of the afternoon. A debate on the Texas Pacific Bill was expected that day, and the Mechlins, as well as Clarence and Mercedes, wished to hear it. The President of the Senate put his rooms at the service of Mrs. Mechlin and friends. Thus the ladies had a delightful time, taking a recess in the President's parlor when they liked, or strolling through the corridors, or sitting in the galleries.

After luncheon, the party, walking toward the public reception room, were met by five or six old men with very white beards. Two of them walked slowly as if weakened by sickness, one walked on crutches, and one had lost an arm, his coat-sleeve being pinned to his breast. Mr. Mechlin stopped to shake hands with them, saying to his wife to go on, that he wished to speak with these gentlemen. On rejoining the party, Mr. Mechlin was asked by Miss Gunther where these venerable old gentlemen came from.

"They looked like a little troop of patriarchs," Miss Selden added. "What can they want at the Capitol?"

"They want bread," Mr. Mechlin replied. "Those men should be pensioned by our Government, but it is not done because Congress has not seen fit to do it. The three oldest of those men are veterans of the Mexican War. For twenty-five years they have been asking the Government to grant them a pension, a little pittance to help them along in their old age, but it is not done. Year after year the same prayers and remonstrances are repeated in vain. Congress well knows how valuable were the services of those who went to Mexico to conquer a vast domain; but, now we have the domain, we don't care to be grateful or just. It would perhaps be a matter of perfect indifference to half of our Congress should they hear that all those poor veterans died of starvation."

CHAPTER XXI.

Looking at the Receding Dome.

There was one thing that the gay New Yorkers, under Mrs. Mechlin's *chaperoning*, had to do before they left the capital. They must make an excursion across the Potomac to Arlington, and visit the tomb of Washington. Patriotism, she said, imposed this duty upon them, which must be fulfilled with due reverence.

"Therefore," Mrs. Mechlin added, "they would have a picnic under the glorious trees in the Arlington grounds."

"Let our libations be on that sacred spot," said George; "we will pour wine on the grave of Washington— that is, we will go close to it and drink it."

"You mean that we will drink the wine and rub the bottle devoutly upon the monument, as the Irish woman did when she cured her rheumatism," Bob Gunther added.

"It is awful how unpatriotic and irreverent are the young men nowadays," Miss Gunther said.

"Yes; it makes me weep," added Arthur Selden, blinking.

There would be a day or two before the picnic, and Mercedes told George she wanted to go to the dome of the Capitol, and see Washington City from that elevated place.

"The little puss shall have her wish," George said, and on the following day all the party drove again to the Capitol, and walked through labyrinths of dark corridors leading into committee rooms or may-be into solemn judicial halls, where justice sat holding the scales in terrific silence. Emerging from the cool, musty air of the lower halls, they again visited the upper rooms and galleries, which Elvira and Mercedes liked better than on their former visits. Now all ascended to the highest point they could go, and their exertions were amply rewarded by the pleasure of seeing the beautiful panorama at their feet. Washington City has been viewed and reviewed, and too minutely described to be considered any longer interesting to Eastern people, but to our Californians the view of that city of proud and symmetric proportions, with its radiating avenues lost in diminishing distances, its little triangular parks and haughty edifices, all making a picturesque *ensemble*, was most pleasing and startling.

With Clarence by her side, Mercedes looked carefully at the city that like a magnificent picture lay there beneath them. She wished to carry it photographed in her memory.

The picnic to Arlington was much enjoyed by all. Mercedes would have preferred to walk over the grounds of Mount Vernon with Clarence alone, for her love was of that pure character which longs to associate the cherished object with every thought and feeling having its source in our highest faculties. She thought Mount Vernon ought to be visited reverently, and she knew Clarence would not laugh at her for thinking so. But, alas! those other young gentlemen had no such thoughts. They were in high glee, determined to have fun, and enjoy it; and though Mercedes and Miss Gunther told them they were behaving like vandals, such rebukes only increased their merriment, which continued even after they recrossed the Potomac.

Mr. Mechlin's party had at last to tear itself away from Washington, and hurry to New York, for the "charity ball" was to come off in a few days; then the Liederkranz and the Purim balls would follow— all in the month of February— and Mrs. Mechlin wished that Elvira and Mercedes should see them all. They had been at masked balls in Washington at the house of a Senator and of a foreign minister, but Mrs. Mechlin said that no masked balls in America could or did equal those given in New York at the Academy of Music, consequently it became an absolute necessity that these two young ladies should see those grand affairs. Moreover, she was one of the matrons of the charity ball, and her presence was indispensable to attend to their management.

A special car was again in readiness, and the Mechlin party occupied it one morning at eight o'clock. The party was now increased by the addition of six ladies and eight gentlemen from Washington, who were going to attend the charity ball and Liederkranz. The train was in motion, going out of the city limits, accelerating its speed as it plunged into the woods beyond. George and Clarence sat at one end of the car, separate from the company, looking at the Capitol, as it seemed to retreat, flying with receding celerity. The woods were beginning to intercept its view at times— the dome would disappear and reappear again and again above the surrounding country.

Mr. Mechlin joined the two young men, saying to them, as he turned the seat in front, and sat facing them: "You are watching the receding Capitol. I was doing the same. I wonder whether your thoughts were like mine in looking at that proud edifice?"

"I think my thoughts were about the same subject, uncle. What were your thoughts, Darrell? Tell us," George said.

"I was thinking of your father and of Don Mariano— thinking that under that white shining dome their fate would be decided perhaps, as they both have embarked so hopefully in the boat of the Texas Pacific Railroad."

George and his uncle looked at each other as if saying, "We all were of the same mind, surely."

Mr. Lawrence Mechlin said: "We certainly were thinking nearly alike, Mr. Darrell, with this difference, may-be, that I don't feel as hopeful as I did a few weeks ago, when you and I talked about the fair chances of the Texas Pacific as we looked at that same white dome when we were coming down. Now I am very fearful that the sad condition of the impoverished South is not going to have the weight which it deserves in the minds of this Congress. I talked with many of our law-givers about the matter, and all seemed not to realize the importance, the policy, the humanity of helping the South, and of giving to the Pacific Coast a competing railway, to get California out of the clutches of a grasping monopoly. All agree that it ought to be done, but it looks as if few put their hearts into the matter."

"Their hearts are in their pockets, uncle, and I am afraid that after all our reluctance to believe that our Congressmen can be improperly influenced, we will have to submit— with shame and sorrow— and accept the fact that bribery has been at work, *successfully*. The chief of the lobby is king."

"Not yet— not yet. It is a frightful thought. Let us not accept it yet. Let us think it is an error, but not knavery. I am coming down again, I think, before this session is over. I want to see more before I am convinced. I have my fears and my doubts, but I still hope— *must* hope— that our Congress has many honest men."

"You can hope— but it will be in vain," George said; "the money of the Central Pacific Railroad will be too much for Colonel Scott."

"Don't be so desponding, boy."

"I can't have any hope in this Congress. There never can be any better arguments in favor of the Texas Pacific than are now plain to everybody. So, then, if in the face of all these powerful considerations Congress turns it back and will not hear the wail of the prostrate South, or the impassionate appeals of California, now, *now*, when there is not one solitary reason under heaven why such appeals and entreaties should be disregarded, is there any ground to expect any better in the uncertain future? Certainly not. But still, I do not say that we should abandon all hope. For the sake of my father, who has trusted so much in the Texas Pacific, I am glad you will do all you can to help Colonel Scott."

"I certainly shall," Mr. Mechlin replied. Then, after a few minutes of silence, he said: "If our legislators could only be induced to adopt Herbert Spencer's view of *the duties of law-givers*, there would be far less misery in the United States. If they could but stop to see how clearly it stands to reason that 'legislative deductions must be based upon *fundamental morality*,' that 'the inferences of political economy are true, only because they are discoveries by a roundabout process of *what the moral law commands*.' It is an unfortunate mistake that the words '*moral law*' are generally understood to apply practically only to private conduct; to a man's fidelity to his marriage vows; to his religious belief; this we learn at school. But these words are only loosely applied (if at all) to a man's actions as a legislator. I never heard in election times that any one expects our law-givers to base their legislation upon *fundamental morality*, and regard expediency as a secondary consideration. Congressmen know that they are expected to watch the material interests of their States or counties, but they do not feel any moral responsibility to see that other *constituencies* do not suffer injustice. Thus, if the Congressmen of one State choose to betray the rights of their constituencies, other Congressmen generally look on indifferently, or, perhaps, amused— and do not interfere any more than they would in the domestic affairs of perfect strangers. They do not seem to perceive that on the very instant in which they see that a community, or an individual, is being wronged by the neglect or design of their own representatives, that then any other Congressman should come forward to protect the betrayed community or defenseless citizen. This is clearly their duty. But it seems to be ignored by tacit consent. All Congressmen are ready to offer objections to every conceivable measure. To jump up and shout *against* anything, seems to be thought the proof of a man being a good legislator. Combativeness is the one faculty ever in use to offer *obstructions*, and thus necessary and useful legislation is foolishly retarded, and untold misery is brought upon innocent citizens. All this is a mistake. Because the '*fundamental law of morality*' is not understood. Herbert Spencer says: 'Now, this that we call *moral law* is simply a statement of the *conditions* of beneficial action. Originating in the primary necessities of things, it is the development of these into a series of limitations within which all conduct conducive to the greatest happiness must be confined. To overstep such limitations is to disregard these necessities of things, to fight against the constitution of nature.' Mr. Spencer applies this axiom to the happiness of individuals, as well as of entire communities. If the principles of fundamental morality were better understood and more conscientiously respected, railroad manipulators would find it impossible to organize a lobby to defeat all laws intended to aid the Texas Pacific. But I repeat, in spite of all discouragement, I will use my best efforts to help the Texas Pacific, as I firmly believe every honest man in these United States ought to do, even when not directly interested."

The journey to New York was accomplished safely by our party, and in good time for the charity ball. Mrs. Mechlin and Mrs. Gunther being in the list of its distinguished matrons, busied themselves about that grand affair from the day after their return until its successful *finale*, which was also a success pecuniarily.

To the charity ball follow the Liederkranz and the Purim.

"Are you to go masked, George?" Mrs. Mechlin asked, as they were discussing the coming ball with Miss Gunther.

"No, I think not. I think the best plan is to wear a domino and mask, as we go in with you ladies, so that you may not be recognized. Then after awhile we will leave you and go out into the vestibule and take off our masks and return unmasked."

"But why not keep masked?" Clarence asked.

"Because we will have no fun at all with masks on. The ladies not knowing who we are will have nothing to say to us. But if they see who we are, then they'll come and talk saucily, thinking we will not recognize them. We will, though, and then the fun begins."

"Nobody knows at home what my domino is to look like, but I think Bob will recognize my voice, and know who we all are, as he knows I am going with you," Miss Gunther said.

"But is he not to be of our party?" Mrs. Mechlin asked.

"No; he is going to escort Miss Selden. My brother Charles will be my escort. He will be in our secret, of course. How I wish we could mystify Bob."

"But we can't, if we speak to him, as he will recognize our voices, Mercedes and mine, by our accent immediately," Elvira said.

"You can mimic the German way of talking English, and Mercedes can talk half French and half English, with an Irish brogue," George suggested.

"She talks Irish brogue to perfection," Elvira said.

"But I'll have to practice before I would speak to him," said Mercedes.

"Practice every day— you have six days yet," Mrs. Mechlin said.

"Do, Miss Mercedes. I would like you to fool Bob," Miss Gunther said.

"But you must make your voice sound guttural. Your voice is naturally very musical. You must disguise it," George suggested.

Mercedes followed his suggestion, and by carefully imitating Mrs. Mechlin's French maid (who spoke very broken English and stammered a good deal), she passed herself off for a stammering French girl, who was very talkative, in spite of the difficulty in her speech— maintaining her *rôle* so well that neither Bob nor Arthur recognized her until she took off her mask. Then the faces of the two young men were a study. They both had paid most ardent compliments to her feet and hands, and had earnestly begged for the privilege of calling upon her, which she granted, promising to give the number of her house when she unmasked. She had danced with both several times, and had asked them to present George and Clarence to her. Both of whom also asked her to dance, and while dancing had a good laugh at the expense of the two deluded ones.

When she unmasked, Selden left the ball in the midst of the peals of laughter from those who understood the joke. Bob stood his ground, with the crimson blush up to his ears and eyebrows.

"The fact of the matter is, that you will attract me always, no matter under what disguise," he whispered to Mercedes.

"*Pas si bete*," she answered, stammering fearfully, and looking the prettier for it.

The Liederkranz and Purim balls were highly enjoyed also, but Mercedes, though in domino, assumed no *rôle*. She was very amiable to Bob and Arthur, to heal the wound of their lacerated vanity.

The winter had now passed, and spring came— bringing to our Californians thoughts of returning home.

The sun was shining brightly on Madison Square— there had been a heavy shower that morning, in the early March— which had washed the snow off the pavements into the sewers, leaving the streets clean. Children were out with their nurses in the square, among the trees, which were trying hard to bud out, but as yet succeeded very poorly. Still, there were some little birds of sanguine temperament, chirping like good optimists about the ungainly, denuded branches, calculating philosophically on coming green leaves, though vegetation was slow to awake from its winter sleep.

Clarence, from his window at the hotel, saw that the day was bright, and hastened, in an open carriage, to take Elvira and Mercedes out for a drive in the park. They first went down for George, who had not yet left the bank.

"Did you get letters from home to-day?" Elvira asked.

"Yes; and among them a long one from Don Mariano," Clarence replied.

"What did he say? Any good news for poor papa?"

"He has just made twenty thousand dollars, any way, in spite of squatters. And he will make sixty thousand dollars more if he will do what I asked him in my letter to-day," Clarence said.

"How did he make twenty thousand dollars?" George asked, with a brightened look, which was reflected in the beautiful eyes of the sisters.

"By sending five hundred steers to Fred Haverly."

"Are five hundred steers worth that much?" George asked, surprised.

"Yes— at forty dollars per head— which for large cattle is not too high a price. That is what Fred has been paying for cattle weighing in the neighborhood of four hundred pounds."

"The best thing Don Mariano can do is to sell you all his cattle, even at half of this price," George said.

"That is what I have been writing to him to-day. As I have to buy cattle for the mines, and I am willing to pay him a good price, he ought to sell them all to me, and when he gets his rancho clear of trespassers then buy finer breeds and restock the rancho."

"A most excellent idea," George said.

Robert Gunther passed by, driving his four-in-hand at a furious speed, with a very handsome girl sitting by his side. He bowed as he passed.

Mercedes laughed, saying he looked "sheepish," and though he did not hear what she said, he blushed to the roots of his hair, and ran against a heavy carriage which slowly rolled ahead of him, loaded with four elderly ladies, who screamed terrified. This mishap only increased Bob's confusion, forcing him to check his speed.

"Do you want our assistance?" George asked, laughing.

"No, thanks. If people did not come to drive their funerals through the park, no one would run over them," Bob said.

"And you want to kill them, so as not to have funerals without dead bodies?" Mercedes asked.

"Be merciful! Remember your name is Mercedes," said poor, embarrassed Bob.

Whereupon Mercedes wafted a kiss to him, saying: "That goes as a peace offering."

"Ah, yes; I understand," said he, following her with his eyes. "A kiss to the empty air is all you will ever give me."

CHAPTER XXII.

Perplexities at Alamar.

It has generally been the custom of biographers to treat their subject after he is resting peacefully in his grave, indifferent to the world's opinion. Seldom has a man "*been written*" (in a biography) until he is past knowing what is said of him in print. Epitaphs are non-committal, or laudatory only, and too brief; they are solely a charitable or affectionate tribute to the dead, intended to please the living. Biographies— it is to be supposed— are intended, or should be, admonitory; to teach men by the example of the one held up to view— be this an example to be followed or to be avoided. But if no offense be intended by the biographer, why wait until a man is forevermore beyond hearing what is said of him, before his fellows are told in what and how he surpassed them so much as to be considered worthy of special notice? If he ought to be reproved, let him know it; and if we must worship him as a hero, let him know it also. Only such an irascible man— for instance— as Dr. Johnson was, could have received the homage of admiration and reverence such as Boswell's, so impatiently, almost ungratefully. It is more natural for man to receive incense at least passively, and endeavor to deserve it. Biographies, therefore, ought to be intended, not to mislead readers, but to instruct them. From this point of view, then, it would be difficult to say flattering things of Mr. Darrell, and more difficult yet to say them of the other squatters of Alamar, in a biographical sketch.

Mr. Darrell did not receive the news of the appeal being dismissed as Mrs. Darrell and Clarence had hoped. Mr. Darrell was evidently out of humor with the executive branch of the Government— with the Attorney General— and he discussed the matter with himself in many an animated soliloquy. High as his opinion of Congress was and had always been, he, in his ill humor, even went so far as to say— to himself— that this much respected body of legislators had been entirely too lenient with the conquered natives. Congress ought to have confiscated all their lands and "only allowed them one hundred and sixty acres *each*." The idea that they (the conquered) should be better off than the Americans! They should have been put on an equality with other settlers, and much honor to them, too, would have been thereby, for why should these *inferior* people be more considered than the Americans?

"Inferior? What are you talking about? It is enough to see one of those Alamar ladies to learn that they are inferior to nobody," said Mrs. Darrell, happening to overhear the last words of her lord's soliloquy. "Neither are the Californians considered *better than Americans* because the Government did not take *all* their lands from them. I declare, William, you have gone back to your old unfortunate ideas which brought so many troubles to us in Napa and Sonoma. You forget those troubles, and you are ready to bring them back again."

"No, I ain't; but I always will maintain that the Spanish Californians should not have a right to any more land than Americans."

"And they have not. The Government does not give them any more land; all they ask and expect is that the Government may *not take away what they had*. You see this perfectly well, and you know that every time you have disregarded this truth, we have suffered. This time it might lead to worse suffering, since it is Clarence that might be made very miserable; and if he is, so must I. Then good-by happiness for me."

"Why should Clarence be made miserable?"

"Because he is devotedly attached to Miss Mercedes; and if you are to be the enemy of her family, perhaps she will not marry him."

"Marry him? Does Clarence think she will marry him? She marry a squatter?" He laughed derisively.

"Clarence is no squatter."

"He is the son of a squatter."

"You have been one, but if you keep your word, and this land is paid for, you will not be a squatter."

"I suppose Clarence followed the girl to New York, believing she'll marry him. I thought he would have more sense."

"If he did follow her, he would also be following his father's example."

Mr. Darrell blushed, but he smiled, for he was pleased. The recollection of that tender episode of loving devotion was always very sweet to him. It had been a folly of which he was proud to cherish the memory.

But Mr. Darrell did not pursue the subject any further this time; he felt he would be defeated if he continued it; it was best to beat a masterly retreat before he was routed. He made an orderly march toward the stable, and Mrs. Darrell, remaining master of the field, busied herself with her flower garden, where Alice presently joined her.

"Mamma dear, I overheard your conversation with papa; I hope you won't let him quarrel with the Don."

"I shall do my best to prevent it, but you see, he has all the settlers at his heels all the time worrying him about their claims. Any one might suppose that he induced them to come here, instead of being induced by them. Since they heard that their appeal was dismissed, they have openly said to him that they rely entirely upon his assistance to retain their homes. This pleases him, it flatters him, but it is a piece of hypocrisy on their part, because the Don is too kind-hearted to eject them. Clarence says that the Don will let them keep their homesteads, on the sole condition that they put up fences to keep his cattle off."

"Can anything be more kind and generous?"

"But all his kindness is thrown away."

"At all events, there is this much to be said, that if papa will insist upon wanting to be a squatter, and favor squatters, he will find that not one of his family approves it. No, not even the children."

"I know it; Jane and Lucy feel very badly about it."

"And so does Everett; Webster don't like it either. We all feel very badly to see papa so wrong, and the worst of it is, how it all might affect our darling Clarence, who is so sweet and so good to all of us— yes, to everybody. I do hope he will marry Mercedes. I know she loves him dearly. I am so afraid that papa will quarrel with the Don, and Clarence and Mercedes be separated. It would be awful."

If sweet Alice had said all she held in her dear heart, and which might be affected by the course that her father would pursue between the settlers and the Don, she would have revealed other anxieties besides those she felt on Clarence's account. The thought that Victoriano, too, might be estranged from her, had made that dear heart of hers very heavy with forebodings. Gentle and loving though she was, she could not help feeling exasperated to foresee how miserable she and Clarence, and Mercedes and Victoriano might all be, all on account of this squatter quarrel, which might so easily be avoided if those people were not so perverse, and her father upholding them, which was perversity, also.

Thus ran Alice's thoughts as she helped her mother to trim the fuschias and train them up the posts of the porch, beside the honeysuckle and roses, which already formed an arbor over the front steps. Occasionally she would look up the valley; it was time that Victoriano should be riding out with Gabriel or his father, superintending the gathering of their cattle, to be sent to the Sierra.

Strange as it may appear, now that the Government, by the dismissal of the appeal, acknowledged that Don Mariano's title was good, now, when by this decision, the settlers should have made up their minds to leave the premises or purchase their homesteads from the owner of the land, now their disgraceful destruction of dumb animals was renewed with obvious virulence, and every night the firing of rifles and shot-guns was heard all over the rancho. Don Mariano saw that this devastation was a malicious revenge, which he could not avert, so he began to collect his stock to take them all to the mountains. About that time he received the letter in which Clarence proposed to buy all of his cattle, advising him to restock the rancho afterwards, when cleared of all trespassers. He liked the proposition, and immediately gave orders to drive all the cattle to his sister's rancho as they were got together; there to be put in a valley and kept in a sort of depot, as they were gathered and brought in bands of any number, to wait until Clarence returned. But as afterwards Don Mariano feared that by the time Clarence came back, there would be no cattle left to sell, he now hastened their gathering and decided to send them off as soon as possible. Patiently, and without a word of complaint, Don Mariano and his two sons would ride out every day to superintend personally the collecting of the cattle and sending them off to his sister's rancho to the valley, where the rendezvous or depot had been established. Victoriano named this valley the "*rodeo triste*," insisting that the cattle knew it was a "*rodeo triste*," and walked to it sadly, guessing that they were to be exiled and butchered. "Just like ourselves, the poor natives," he said, "tossed from one cruelty to another still worse, and then crushed out." "*Rodeo triste*" was a very appropriate name, considering the fact of its being different from the gay and boisterous gatherings of other years, when "the boys" of the surrounding ranchos all assembled at Alamar to separate their cattle and have a grand time marking and branding the calves; twisting the tails of stubborn ones by way of a logical demonstration, a convincing argument conveyed in that persuasive form, which was to a calf always unanswerable and irresistible. Then the day's work and fun would wind up with a hilarious barbecue. But this was all in the past, which had been happy, and was now a fading tableau.

Alice, watching from behind the honeysuckle, saw Don Mariano, his two sons and three *vaqueros* ride down the valley. There they separated, each followed by a *vaquero*, going in different directions.

But Alice was not the only one watching the riders going out to gather stray cattle. Though with very different sentiments from those which agitated her loving heart, the entire population of the rancho had been attentive, though unseen, spectators of the Don's proceedings. In the evenings the neighbors would come to relate to Darrell how many head of cattle and horses they had seen pass by their farms, and renew their comments thereon.

Thus six weeks passed. The remittitur from the Supreme Court to the United States District Court at San Francisco came. This caused a ripple of excitement among the settlers. Then a bigger one— a perfect tidal wave— was expected with the surveyors that would come to make the survey of the rancho; and when this should be finished, then the grandest and last effort must be made by the settlers to prevent the approval of it. Thus, at least, they would have more litigation, and while the case was in the courts, they would still be on the rancho raising crops, and paying no taxes and no rent, as they knew perfectly well that the Don would never sue them for "rents and profits."

Everett had gone to town for the mail that day; letters from Clarence were expected. The neighbors knew it, for by dint of asking questions they had learned to time the arrival of his letters, and would drop in quite accidentally, but unerringly, and in an off-hand manner ask if there was "any news from Mr. Clarence?" The Don, with his two sons and three *vaqueros*, had gone out in search of his cattle, as usual, just as if no *remittitur* had come. The settlers thought this was a most excellent subject to ventilate with their neighbor, Darrell; they came in goodly numbers, "to *revolve* the matter, and talk it over in a *neighborly* way," Mr. Hughes had said, with his perennial smile.

"Just so; sit down, sit down," Mr. Darrell replied; and when all having dragged chairs and pulled them forward from between their knees, had dropped upon them, he added, "What may happen to be the matter we are to revolve?"

"Why, the remittitur, of course," Hughes replied, in his oiliest tones.

"Oh, I thought something new," Darrell remarked.

"That is a clincher, you know," Hughes replied.

"Yes, but we knew it was coming."

"Don't you think it queer that the Don be hurrying off his cattle, now that he's won his suit? Don't that look as if he don't put much trust in his victory?"

"He trusts his victory, but he knows that more stock has been shot for the last six weeks than for six months previous. He wants to save *a few* head," said Romeo Hancock, smiling.

"Roper told me," said Hughes, ignoring what Romeo said, "that, if the settlers wish it, this case might be kept in the courts for fifty years."

"After the land is surveyed?" Darrell asked.

"Yes, after the survey."

"We begin our new war by *objecting* to the survey, I suppose; ain't it?" Miller asked.

"That is what Roper says," Hughes replied.

"And, meantime, harass the enemy like the deuce," Gasbang added.

"Exactly; that is Roper's advice," said Mathews.

With a gesture of disgust, Romeo said: "Of course, no cattle having been shot in this rancho before Roper advised it, let the harassing begin now."

"Look here, young man, you had better get more years over your head before you talk so glibly," Billy Mathews snarled at Romeo.

"He is a settler like yourself, Mr. Mathews, and he has as good a right to express his opinion, though he may not have the happiness of being old," interposed Everett.

"It seems to me that all the young bloods on this rancho are either on the fence or have bolted clean over to the other side, Mr. Darrell," said Mathews, addressing his remarks to the elder Darrell, "but they forget that there aren't girls enough to go round. There are only two left, if, as rumor says, Mr. Clarence has taken the blue-eyed one."

"Roper says those girls must have done good service in Washington to get the appeal dismissed so quick." Gasbang said, grinning.

"And Roper is a dirty-minded dog to say that, and I'll make him eat his dirty words, or I'll take his hide off of his filthy carcass," Everett said, jumping up from his seat, livid with anger.

"Sit still, Retty," Mr. Darrell said, "nobody minds what Roper says, except, perhaps, in law matters."

"Some people do mind what the whelp says, as he is quoted here," Everett argued.

"It oughtn't to be so. I don't like women's names mixed up in men's business."

"Roper only said that, because we heard that those girls were in

Washington with a gay crowd, who took them from New York," Gasbang explained.

"Yes, a crowd who went as guests of Mr. Lawrence Mechlin," Everett replied; "a New York banker, and brother of this Mr. Mechlin here. Mr. Mechlin engaged a special car, as George wanted to take his wife and sister-in-law to visit the capital, and then two other families (of the highest and best in New York) were invited, and all made a party to spend three weeks in Washington. Clarence being a friend of George Mechlin's, was invited, also."

"That may all be, but we heard that the crowd was a gay one, running about the corridors and taking lunches at the Capitol with Senators," Gasbang explained. "And as that is the way things are managed when there are any axes to grind, Roper guessed that the girls had been pressed into service to help with their smiles to bamboozle Senators."

"The vile little reptile; I'll put my heel on him yet," said Everett, with white lips.

"It isn't likely that Clarence would have stayed by, seeing Mercedes smiling improperly on anybody, if he cares for her. He wouldn't be a son of mine if he did," said Darrell, frowning.

"No; that is all a very mean talk of Roper's. Attorney General Williams had promised George Mechlin's uncle, six months ago, to dismiss the appeal as soon as the Supreme Court should be session, and, though it cuts us all to pieces, I must say he kept his word like a man; that's all."

"Yes, it was that infernal, dandified puppy George Mechlin, who did the mischief. I'll be even with him yet for it," Old Mathews growled.

"Why shouldn't George Mechlin help his father-in-law? Because it upsets the liver of the amiable Mr. Mathews?" asked Romeo, laughing.

"Keep quiet, Romeo," Old Hancock said, smiling.

"If George Mechlin hadn't helped, the thing would have been done in some other way. It had to come," Darrell said.

"I don't know about that; these Californians are too ignorant to know how to defend their rights, and too lazy to try, unless some American prompts them," Mathews replied.

"They know enough to employ a lawyer to defend their rights," Old Miller observed.

"Yes; but, after all, they have to use influence in Washington," Old Mathews insisted. "And what influence have they, unless it is by the aid of some American?"

"And the pretty daughters," added Gasbang.

"Never mind the pretty daughters," said Miller, seeing that Everett clenched his fists as if ready to pounce upon Gasbang at the next provocation. "The question now is, what is to be done? and who is for us, and who against? The time has come when we have to count noses."

"Yes, what are you going to do, Mr. Darrell?" asked velvety Hughes, with his sickly smile.

"Nothing. What is there for me to do? You heard me promise to the Don that I would pay him for the land I was locating, if it was decided that the title was his."

"You said *when the title is settled*," Gasbang said.

"The title is settled as far as the Government is concerned. As you— the settlers— and the Government were on one side, and the Don on the other, I guess he now naturally supposes I must regard the title as *settled*, since the principal opponent (the Government) has thrown up the sponge," Darrell answered.

"But we haven't," said Mathews; "and as long as we keep up the fight I don't see how the title can be considered settled."

"It is settled with the Government, which was the question when I made my location," Darrell answered.

"But you ain't going to desert our cause?" Hughes asked. "You'll be our friend to the last, won't you?"

"Such is my intention, but what I might think I ought to do, circumstances will point out to me. Probably we will see our way better after the survey is made. Meantime, as the Don don't trouble any one with orders to vacate, the best thing to do is to keep quiet."

"And spare his cattle," Romeo added, looking at Mathews.

"You seem to want to pick a quarrel with me, youngster," growled Mathews.

"What makes you think so? Did *you* ever shoot any of the Don's cattle, that you should appropriate my remarks to yourself? If you never did, I can't mean you."

The boys, the young men, all laughed. Mathews arose, too angry to remain quiet.

"Next time I come to talk business— serious business— with men, with men of my age— I don't want to be twitted by any youngster. Children should be seen, and not heard," said he, putting on his hat energetically.

"Why, Mr. Mathews, you shouldn't call me a youngster. You forget I am a married man," Romeo replied, with great amiability. "I am a papa, I am. Our baby is now six months old; he weighed twelve pounds when he was born. Now, can you show us a baby of *your own*, only as old as that, and weigh half as much?"

The shout of laughter that followed these words was too much for Mathews. The banging of doors as he left was the only answer he deigned to give.

"Mr. Mathews! Five pounds! Two-and-a-half, Mr. Mathews!" shouted Romeo from the window, to the retreating form of Billy, swiftly disappearing in long strides along the garden walk.

"That is the hardest hit Mathews ever got. He is awfully sensitive about having always been jilted and never been married," Miller said.

"He'll never forgive you," added old Hancock.

"He never has forgiven me for locating my claim either, but I manage to survive. One more grievance can't sour him much more," Romeo replied, laughing.

After Mathews had made his exit, the conversation went on more harmoniously. Gasbang was now the only malignant spirit present, but being very cowardly, he felt that as Mathews' support was withdrawn, and the other settlers were inclined to abide by Darrell's advice, he would be politic; he would listen only and report to Peter Roper. Gasbang knew well how unreliable Roper was, but as they were interested in sundry enterprises of a doubtful character, he consulted Peter in all matters when found sober.

Darrell's advice being to "keep quiet," the meeting soon broke up and the settlers went home by their separate ways, all more or less persuaded that, after all, peace was the best thing all around. Old Mr. Hancock gave utterance to this sentiment as he stopped by the gate of the Darrell garden to say good-night to his neighbors.

"I heard the Don say that he does not blame us settlers so much for taking his land as he blames our law-givers for those laws which induce us to do so— laws which are bound to array one class of citizens against another class, and set us all by the ears," Romeo said.

"Yes, I heard him say about the same thing, but I thought he said it because he was a hypocrite, and to keep us from shooting his cattle," Gasbang added.

"No matter what might be his motive, the sentiment is kind anyway," Hancock, senior, said.

"Perhaps," said the others, still unwilling to yield.

CHAPTER XXIII.

Home Again.

On the 25th day of May, of '74, Elvira and Mercedes found themselves again under the paternal roof of their California home, in the Alamar rancho. They could have arrived ten days sooner had they left New York on the first of the month, as was first intended. This they were not allowed to do, because when Mrs. L. Mechlin heard that Mercedes' birthday would be on the 5th of May, she immediately said she could not and would not think of allowing Mercedes to spend her eighteenth birthday in the cars. Consequently, invitations would be issued the following day (which was the 22d of April) for "*A fête in celebration of Miss Alamar's birthday, on the 5th day of May.*"

The invitations were issued thus early to prevent friends of Mrs. Mechlin's from going into the country for the summer, as many of them did every year, in May. All, however, accepted, and waited most graciously.

The season was already too far advanced, and the nights were getting too warm to enjoy dancing, so Mrs. Mechlin thought it would be better to have an excursion to West Point; to charter a river steamer, and thus pass the day on the water; to take breakfast on board on the way to the Point; visit the Post; see the cadets drill and review; and re-embark; take dinner on board, and then the young people dance on deck, as there would be a full band to give them music.

This was the programme— which though decided upon hurriedly, on their return from Baltimore, where they had been visiting— was carried out successfully. All their pleasure excursions had been equally delightful. They had visited Boston first, then they went to Philadelphia, intending to remain only three or four days, but when they were there, Mrs. Mechlin's relatives in Baltimore sent urgent invitations to visit them, so there was nothing else to do but accept. Thus the jaunt to Philadelphia was extended to Baltimore, and might have been prolonged, had not Elvira refused to be separated from George one day more. This young gentleman, on his part, seemed to have thought, too, that Elvira had been away long enough. For as the party were waiting for the train to move out of the depot who should come aboard but this same young gentleman, George Mechlin.

"The darling," said Elvira, perfectly overjoyed at the sight of that beloved apparition, throwing her arms about his neck.

"Precious," said he, clasping her to his heart.

And now Elvira and Mercedes, surrounded by their beloved family, were relating this episode and many other occurrences of their eastern visit, all sitting in their favorite front veranda.

The Holman girls were there, too. They had made several visits to Carlota and Rosario within the last ten months, but this time they came to see Elvira and Mercedes. Mr. Holman himself had accompanied them, that being a good pretext to question George closely regarding Texas Pacific matters. Mr. Holman had invested all his ready money in San Diego, placing implicit faith in the fact that the building of the Texas Pacific was a measure of national importance so manifest that Congress would never have the hardihood to deny it assistance, nor would be so lacking in sense of honor, sense of justice, as to deprive millions of American people of a railway so much needed. These had been the reasons, he alleged, for plunging headlong into real estate speculations, followed closely by his friends, Don Mariano and Mr. James Mechlin.

These three gentlemen now sat at the eastern end of the veranda, listening to what George said that he and his uncle had learned in Washington regarding the prospect of that unlucky railroad; while the ladies were equally entertained, listening to Elvira and Mercedes, on the western end of the same veranda.

"But what has become of the handsome Clarence? Why is he not here?" Corina inquired, seeing Everett and Victoriano riding up with Gabriel towards the house.

Elvira informed her that on their arrival at San Francisco, Clarence found it necessary to visit his farm, and thence to go to Arizona on business, but would return about the first of July.

"We heard that his mine is in bonanza," Amelia said.

"That it has been in bonanza ever since he bought it— hasn't he told you that?" Corina added.

"No; he only said that the ore was very rich," Elvira replied.

Victoriano and Everett now came in and took seats near the ladies. Gabriel joined the gentlemen, and soon was deeply interested in their conversation, it of course being upon that subject— the railroad— which filled the minds and hearts of all the San Diego people, absorbing all their faculties and all their money.

"How are all the ladies of your family? Well?" Amelia asked of Everett.

"Yes, thank you. They are all well, and I think they will be up this evening— at least, some of them will. I heard words to that effect," Everett replied.

"I hope all will come," Elvira said.

"What? Mr. Darrell, senior, also?" Corina asked.

"Certainly. Why not?" Mercedes answered.

"We were speaking of the ladies— but if Mr. Darrell should call, we will be happy to receive him with sincere cordiality," Elvira added.

"All of which would be thrown away upon the stiffest neck in San Diego County," Victoriano observed.

Everett laughed.

"Why, Tano! What makes you talk like that?" Mercedes exclaimed, reddening with evident annoyance.

"Because his '*butt-headedness*' is like that of a vicious old mule, which no one began to break until he was ten years old, and loves to kick from pure cussedness," Victoriano explained, with free use of slang.

"If Mr. Darrell has said or done anything to vex you, the best thing is not to go to his house, but it is not very courteous to speak as you have in the presence of his son," Doña Josefa said.

"I forgive him," Everett said, patting Tano on the back.

"Not go to his house!" Tano exclaimed. "That is exactly what the old pirate wants. It would be *nuts* for the old Turk if I stayed away. Not much— I won't stay away. I'll go when he is at *the colony* with his sweetly-scented pets."

"Where is the colony?" Mercedes asked.

"That is the new name for the large room next to the dining-room, which Clarence said he built for a 'growlery.' Alice called it the '*squattery*,' because father always receives the settlers there; but mother changed the name to '*colony*' to make it less offensive, and because the talk there is always about locating, or surveying, or fencing land— always land— as it would be in a new colony," Everett explained.

"Whether he be at the colony or not, you should not go if he does not wish you to visit his house," Doña Josefa said to Tano.

"But we all wish it— my mother and every one of her children. Father doesn't say anything about Tano's coming or not, but he is cross to all of us, and don't have the politeness to be more amiable in Tano's presence— which, of course, is very disagreeable," Everett replied.

"I think Mrs. Darrell ought to put her foot down, and have it out with the old filibuster," Tano asserted.

"We will see what he will do when Clarence comes," Everett said.

Everett thought as all the family did— that Clarence, being the favorite child of the old man, and having naturally a winning manner and great amiability, combined with persuasiveness, would influence his father, and dispel his bad humor. But if the family had known what was boiling and seething in the cauldron of their father's mind, they would have perceived that, for once, neither Clarence's influence, nor yet the more powerful one wielded by Mrs. Darrell, would at present be as effective as they heretofore had been.

Time alone must be the agent to operate on that hard skull. Time and circumstances which, fortunately, no one as yet was misanthrophic enough to foresee. The fact was, that no one of his family had understood William Darrell. It can hardly be said that he understood himself, for he sincerely believed that he had forever renounced his "*squatting*" propensities, and honestly promised his wife that he would not take up land claimed by any one else. But no sooner was he surrounded by men who, though his inferiors, talked loudly in assertion of their "*rights under the law*;" and no sooner had he thousands of broad acres before his eyes— acres which, by obeying the laws of Congress, he could make his own— than he again felt within him the old squatter of Sonoma and Napa valleys. That mischievous squatter had not lain dead therein; he had been slumbering only, and unconsciously dreaming of the advantages that the law really gave to settlers. Alongside the sleeping squatter had also slumbered Darrell's vanity, and this was, as it is generally in every man, the strongest quality of his mind, the chief commanding trait, before which everything must give way.

Mrs. Darrell had heretofore been the only will that had dared stand before it, but Mrs. Darrell, being a wise little woman, not always made direct assaults upon the strong citadel— oftener she made flank movements and laid sieges. This time, however, all tactics had thus far failed, and Mrs. Darrell withdrew all her forces, and waited, in "masterly inactivity," reinforcements when Clarence returned.

What exasperated Darrell the most, and had ended by putting him in a bad humor, was a lurking self-reproach he could not silence, a consciousness that having promised Don Mariano to pay for his land whenever the title was considered settled, that it was fair to suppose he ought to pay now. But on the other hand, he had also promised the settlers to stand by them, and was determined to do so. Thus he stood in his own mind self-accused, unhappy and unrepentant, but resolutely upholding a lost cause. He avoided the society of his family with absurd persistency. After meals he would fill his pipe, and march himself off to the farther end of his grain fields; resting his elbows on the fence boards, and turning his back upon the house which contained his dissenting family, would puff his smoke in high dudgeon, like an overturned locomotive which had run off its track, and became hopelessly ditched. In that frame of mind, he thought himself ready to do battle against all his family, but he knew he dreaded Clarence's return.

However, that event had at last arrived, and there was Clarence now on the porch— just come from Arizona— kissing all the ladies of the family and hugging all the males, not omitting the old man, who was literally as well as figuratively taken off his feet by the strong arms of the dreaded Clarence.

"Clary is so much in love, father, that he comes courting you, too," Everett said, laughing, as they all went into the parlor.

"I suppose so," Darrell answered, not looking at any one's face, excepting that of the clock on the chimney mantel.

Mrs. Darrel's eyes, however, were not in the least evasive— they met those of Clarence, and he read in them a volume of what was troubling his father's mind. He longed to have a talk with that true-hearted and clear-headed, well-beloved mother, but he must wait— for now came Tisha to announce that luncheon was on the table. She was grinning with delight to see her favorite Massa Clary again, and Clarence jumped up and ran to throw his arms around her, making that faithful heart throb with unalloyed happiness, for she loved him from his babyhood, just if he had been her own child.

"I love them all, missis— all your dear children," she would say to Mrs.

Darrell; "and they are all good children; but Massa Clary I love the best of all. Next comes Miss Alice. But Massa Clary took my heart when he was six months old, and had the measles. He was the best, sweetest baby I ever saw, and so beautiful." Thus Tisha would run on, if you let her follow the bent of her inclination, for Clarence was a theme she never tired of.

All sorts of questions now showered upon Clarence about New York, about Washington, about San Francisco, and about Arizona— all of which he answered most amiably.

"And are the Mechlins very grand? As rich as one might suppose? hearing the Holman and Alamar girls talk of the parties and excursions that Mr. Lawrence Mechlin gave in honor of Elvira?" Jane asked.

"The excursion to West Point was to celebrate Mercedes' birthday," Alice observed.

"Yes, the Mechlins must be rich, to judge by their style of living. Their social position is certainly very high," Clarence replied.

"You had a delightful time, Clary?" Everett said.

"Yes, indeed; most delightful," was the answer.

"We, too, have had lots of fun, with old Mathews on the rampage, like an old hen who got wet and lost her only chicken," said Willie, at the top of his voice.

"Willie!" Mrs. Darrell said, to impose silence, but as Clarence and Everett laughed, and his father did not seem particularly displeased, Willie added:

"And the old man gets so mad, that he perspires, and smoke comes out of his back, as if his clothes were on fire."

"Oh, Willie! how you exaggerate," Lucy exclaimed.

"I don't. He snorts and clucks and growls and snarls. Romeo says he miauls like a disappointed hyena."

"That will do. You must not repeat such unkind criticisms. Romeo is always ridiculing Mr. Mathews," Mrs. Darrell said.

"Old Mathews is in worse humor since the Don began to send his cattle away," Webster said.

"Why so?" Clarence asked.

"Because they made nice targets for his rifle," Everett replied.

"Scandalous!" Clarence exclaimed.

"He threatens to shoot George Mechlin, Tom Hughes says," Webster added.

"Why?" Clarence asked.

"Because he got the appeal dismissed," answered Webster.

"He is foolish to suppose that if George hadn't had it dismissed that no one else would," Clarence said.

"I met the old man this morning. He stopped his wagon to ask me if father knew that Congress had passed the appropriation for money to survey lands in California. I told him I hadn't heard, and he went off whipping his horses, and swearing at Don Mariano and George Mechlin," Everett said.

"I thought there would be a better feeling when the Don's cattle should be sent off, as they were the principal cause of irritation," Clarence observed.

"And it is so. Only those boys— Romeo, Tom and Jack Miller— are always ridiculing or teasing Mathews," Darrell said.

"Why, father!" Everett exclaimed; "the fathers of those boys are as bad as Mathews, and old Gasbang is worse yet!"

"Gasbang was always dishonest, but he is worse now, at Peter Roper's instigation," Darrell said.

"Gasbang says that he and Roper will send the Don to the poor-house," Everett said.

"Not while I live," Clarence replied; adding, "and how is everybody at the Alamar house— all well?"

Up started Willie and Clementine, eager to be the first to tell Clarence the great news.

"They had two arrivals," Mrs. Darrell said.

"Oh, Clary! you never saw prettier babies in all your life! Both have the loveliest blue eyes," Clementine exclaimed, joining her hands, as if in prayer, as Tisha always did when speaking of Clarence's babyhood.

"The boy has gray eyes," Willie interposed, with authority not to be controverted. "He hasn't no blue eyes."

"How do you know? You haven't seen them, but *I* have," Clementine asserted; "and the little girl is exactly the image of Miss Mercedes. She has Miss Mercedes' blue eyes, exactly, with long, curling lashes, the little thing."

"The girl looks like Don Gabriel, as she ought to," Willie stated in a peremptory manner, not to be contradicted, and whilst he discussed with Clementine the looks of the babies, Clarence was informed by his mother and sisters that Elvira was the happy mother of a big, handsome boy, and Lizzie rejoiced in the possession of a beautiful little girl, which weighed nearly as much as her boy cousin. That Doña Josefa and Mrs. Beatrice Mechlin were nearly crazy with happiness, but that the craziest of all was Mr. James Mechlin, who made more "*fuss*" over those two babies than either Gabriel or George, and went from one house to the other all day long, watching each baby, and talking about them by the hour.

CHAPTER XXIV.

The Brewers of Mischief.

Eight delicious weeks passed— the most delightful that Clarence and Mercedes had ever lived. The first of September had dawned, and on the 16th they would be married. With the first rays of the coming morn, Clarence arose and went to the west window of his chamber, which looked towards the Alamar House. As he peeped through the closed shutters, thinking it would seem foolish to open them so early, he saw the shutters of one window— in that well known row where Mercedes' room was located, and which looked to the east— pushed open, and a white hand and part of a white arm came out and fastened it back. His heart told him whose white arm that was, and of course he could not think of going back to bed. He began to dress himself, deliberating whether he should or not go to town that day and telegraph to Hubert to do as he thought best about selling another cargo of ores, or say to wait for him, that he would be at San Francisco on the 20th. When he was dressed, he sat by the west window and tried to read, but that white arm would come across the page and that white hand would cover the letters, so that he threw the book down and began to walk, trying to think about that business of selling the ore to the Austrian house, of which Hubert had been writing to him. Yes, he thought, the best thing would be to go to town that same day and ask Hubert couldn't the matter wait until the 20th. But should Hubert be coming, or should it be necessary to wait for telegrams, he might not be back until the following day in the evening. He would go immediately after breakfast to tell Mercedes that he could not see her that evening.

Mercedes and Doña Josefa were on the front piazza when he arrived, and Gabriel was talking to George in quite an excited manner, for him, as he was always so calm and self-contained. As soon as Clarence came up the piazza steps, George began to tell him that some of the last lot of cattle which had been sent off to the mountains, had got away from the herders and returned to the rancho on the previous day, and that morning a couple of cows of a very choice breed were found shot through the body, in a dying condition. The poor brutes had to be shot dead by Gabriel himself, to save them from further suffering. No one knew who had fired on the poor dumb animals, but circumstantial evidence clearly pointed to Old Mathews.

Clarence was very angry, of course. He reflected in silence for a few moments, then said to Gabriel:

"I think if Don Mariano would make now, to-day, a deed of sale of *all* his cattle and horses to me, they would have a better chance of being spared. Not that Mathews, or Gasbang, or Miller like me any better, but they are not so anxious to annoy me."

"I think Clarence's idea is a good one," George said.

"I think so, too, and have thought so for some time," Gabriel replied. "We are going to drive off the last lot to-day. Father and Tano are down in the valley. I'll tell him what you say as soon as I go down. I think we will return by to-morrow night, and he can draw up the deed then."

"Tell him that I shall consider that the cattle are mine *now*, and will let our friends, the settlers, know it, so that they can have the satisfaction of killing *my cattle*."

"Do you really mean it?" Doña Josefa asked.

"Certainly. Don Mariano can buy all the cattle he wants to restock his rancho after he gets rid of the two-legged animals," Clarence replied.

"That is, if he wants to restock it. He was talking with George and me last night, and he said if the Texas Pacific is built, he will have all his land surveyed to sell it in farming lots, and will not put cattle in it. But if the railroad is not built, then the best use he can make of the rancho will be to make it a cattle rancho again, after the squatters go away," Gabriel said, adding that he must be going to join his father. He then went into the hall to go to the court-yard, where his saddled horse and his *vaquero* waited for him. Clarence and George followed to bid him good-by. Clarence said:

"I wrote to Hubert about procuring for you a place at a bank, to get broken into the banking business, and he replied that he can, and will get you a place. Would you like to try it, now that you will have less to do here, when there will be no cattle at the rancho? I am going to write and telegraph to Hubert to-day— or he might be down in to-morrow's steamer— so that I can tell him about what time you might go up."

"I think you had better go about the time Clarence and Mercedes get married, as they will immediately go to their house in San Francisco," George suggested.

"Yes, I think that will be the best time," Gabriel said.

"Very well; I'll write to Hubert that we will be up by the 20th of this month," Clarence said.

"Gabriel can take his place on the 1st of October. That will do splendidly, as Lizzie and Mercedes will be together," George said.

"But we must live in the hope that we will all come down to make our homes here," Gabriel added.

"Of course. That is understood," Clarence replied.

"Though at times I feel discouraged, still, I can't well see how the Texas Pacific is to be defeated permanently. That would be too outrageous. Let us hope that by next year our banking scheme will be carried out," George said.

"I hope so, and as I have made more money than I had when we first talked about it we can put in more capital. We can, if you advise it, put in a whole million now," Clarence said.

"So much the better," George said, and both shook hands with Gabriel, who quickly jumped on his horse and was off at a gallop, followed by his *vaquero.*

It was the hour when the babies got their morning bath. George had great pleasure in seeing his boy enjoy the sensation of floating in the water; so he let Clarence return to the porch where Mercedes was now alone, and he went to watch the bathing of his boy.

Clarence sat close to Mercedes and said: "Does the sweetest thing that God created realize that this day is the first day of September?"

"If you mean me, though you make me feel very foolish with your exaggerated praise, I must say that I do realize that to-day is the first of September," she replied, smiling.

"And does the loveliest rosebud and the prettiest hummingbird remember that in two weeks more she is to be mine, mine forever?"

"Hush, Clarence, some one might hear you," she said, putting her hand over his lips, blushing and looking around, alarmed. He took that hand and kissed the palm of it, then turned it over and kissed the back of it most ardently, and held it in his own, saying:

"I have a piece of information that is going to make your dear heart glad. What will you give for it?"

"What is it? Do tell me. Is it about papa?"

"No, but it is about Gabriel and Lizzie."

"What?"

"That Gabriel will get a place at a San Francisco bank to learn the banking business, and they will live with us, so you and Lizzie will be together."

"Oh! Clarence, is that so? Oh! you make me so glad! How can I ever thank you?"

"Haven't you said that you love me? Haven't you promised to marry me, and thus make me the happiest man upon the entire face of all this earth? That is enough for thanks. But for telling you the news I want to be paid *extra.*"

Mercedes blushed crimson.

"I am going to town now, to be away a long time; won't you give me one single kiss to say good-by?"

"Must you go? Why don't you write your letters or telegrams and send them from here?"

"Because I may have to answer some dispatches immediately. Or it is possible that Hubert might have run down to see me for a few hours. To-morrow is steamer day."

"Then this will be a good chance to send up your photograph I want to have enlarged and painted."

"Yes; give it to me; I'll send it up."

"I'll bring it," she said, going to the parlor. He followed her. He closed the door, saying:

"Now, one sweet kiss to give me good luck and bring me back all safe. P-l-e-a-s-e don't refuse it."

"Oh, Clarence! Mamma don't approve of such things, and I don't either. You are not my husband yet," she pleaded, but in vain, for he had put his arm around her and was holding her close to his heart.

"I am not your husband yet? Yes I am. In intention I have been ever since January, 1872. More than two years, and, in fact, I shall be in two weeks. So you see how cruel it is to be so distant."

"Do you call this distant, holding me so close?" For sole answer he looked into her eyes, kissed her forehead and blushing cheeks, then he kissed the heavily fringed eyelids, kept partly closed, afraid to meet the radiant gaze of his expressive eyes. Then he put his lips to hers and held them there in a long kiss of the purest, truest love. "My darling! My wife! My own for ever! The sweetest, loveliest angel of my soul!"

No doubt he would have been willing to hold her thus close to his heart for hours, but she disengaged herself from his embrace with gentle firmness. Such warm caresses she intuitively felt must be improper in the highest degree, even on the eve of marriage. No lady could allow them without surrendering her dignity. That was the effect of Doña Josefa's doctrines, which she had carefully inculcated into the minds of her daughters.

"Well, I hope that at last you have kissed me enough," said Mercedes, rather resentfully.

"Never enough, but I hope sufficiently to give me good luck," answered the happy Clarence.

"Oh, Clarence, that reminds me of my horrible dream of last night. I dreamed that papa went to look for you in the midst of a snow storm and never came back. You returned, but he never did."

"You must not believe in dreams, dearest."

"I do not, but this seemed prophetic to me."

"Prophetic of a snow storm in San Diego?"

"The snow was symbolic of bereavement, perhaps."

She rested her head on his shoulder and seemed lost in thought, and he held the little hand, so soft and white and well shaped, and thought of her beauty and lovely qualities and his coming happiness. He was thinking that he would have been content to pass the day thus, when she raised her eyes to his, saying:

"I must not keep you if you must go. Remember how superstitious my dream has made me. I wish you could wait until to-morrow."

"I would, but Hubert might come to-morrow."

"I had forgotten that." One more long kiss and they parted, her heart sinking under a load of undefined terrors.

From the seventh heaven Clarence had to come down again to prosaic earth; and after bidding adieu to Mercedes, he drove back home to speak to his father. The old man was sitting in his easy chair on the porch, smoking his pipe, alone, behind the curtain of honeysuckle, white jasmine and roses, so carefully trained over the porch by Mrs. Darrell and Alice. Seeing his son driving back towards the front steps, he walked down to meet him. Clarence was glad that he seemed in a better humor. He at once said:

"Father, I came back to ask a favor of you."

"A favor? You alarm me. You never did that in all your life," he said, smiling.

"You mean I never did anything else. I know it. But this is a very especial one, and a business favor."

"Let us hear it. Of course I'll do anything I can for you or any other of my children."

"Thanks, father. The favor is this. That in talking with the settlers—especially those who have been most ready to shoot the Don's cattle— that you tell them I have bought all his stock and all will be driven to the Colorado river just as soon as cold weather sets in. I don't think many of the settlers like me any better than they like the Don, but if they think they might displease *you* by killing your son's cattle they might spare the poor animals."

"I'll do it. I expect Mathews and Miller now. They sent me word they are coming to bring me some special news as soon as Gasbang returns from town. But have you really and truly bought the stock? or is it only to— "

"I have made a bona fide purchase; five hundred head are already at the mine, and as soon as the hot weather is over, the others will follow. I must buy cattle somewhere, for we have to feed five hundred men now at work, and as the Don is losing his all the time, I proposed to him to sell all to me."

"But what is he to do with his land? Queer that he should sell his cattle when he gets his land. Doesn't he believe he'll get rid of us— the *squatters*?"

"O yes, but he figures thus: If the Texas Pacific is built, it will pay better to sell his land in farming lots; if not, he can restock it when he gets rid of his troublesome neighbors."

"He has more sense than I gave him credit for. I guess you put him up to that dodge."

"No indeed. He thought it himself, but it seems that Gabriel and George thought the same thing at the same time, and as I was thinking where I could get cattle for my mines, it struck me I might buy his and suit us both."

"All right. I'll speak to the settlers, but of course I cannot promise that they will do what I ask."

"I understand that. Many thanks. Good-by."

"When will you return?"

"To-morrow," and he was off at a tearing speed for his horses were tired of waiting, and longed to be on the road.

There was a little *arroyo* which passed about 500 yards on the west of Don Mariano's house and marked the west line of Darrell's land; as Clarence approached this dried brook, he saw Gasbang and Roper coming down from the opposite hill, evidently unable to check their horses. Roper was so intoxicated that he could with difficulty keep his seat, and as Gasbang seemed much frightened, Clarence took his phæton well off the road and waited so as to lend his assistance, if it should be required. But "the kind Providence which takes care of drunken sailors, children and the United States," was watchful of Roper, and though he swayed and swung beyond possible equilibrium, he stuck to his seat with drunken gravity.

"Going to invest in more real estate?" Gasbang shouted as soon as he felt reassured by passing the great danger of sand and pebbles which his cowardice had magnified to him into a precipice. Roper laughed heartily, but Clarence, not understanding the allusion, made no answer and drove on without looking at them. If a kind fairy could have whispered to him what was the errand of these two men, he most assuredly would have turned back. There being no fairy but the blue-eyed one who had already told her dreams and fears, which he had not believed, he went on to town, and Gasbang took Roper to his house, carefully putting him to bed to take a nap that would sober him before he spoke with Darrell; for it was to speak with Darrell that he came.

While Roper slept, Gasbang went to see Mathews, Miller and Hughes, and together they held a consultation, at the end of which it was decided that, as Roper was too intoxicated yet, and Darrell disliked drunkards, they would go and have a preliminary talk with him themselves, and Roper would be pressed into service, if advisable, in the morning, when he would be sober.

Darrell had got tired of waiting for Mathews; so, after thinking of what Clarence had said, he decided that it would be better to have a talk with Hancock and Pitikin, who were about the most reliable of all the settlers. They perhaps knew what it was that Mathews had to say. He told Webster to saddle a horse and bring it around; he would go on horseback, as the wagon road to Hancock's was very long, around the fields.

But now when Webster had brought the saddled horse to the front steps, Darrell saw Mathews, Gasbang, Miller and Hughes coming in a two-seated wagon, and all seemed to be talking very excitedly.

"Tie the horse there. I'll wait for those men," said Darrell, sitting down again. Webster did as he was told, and then walked straight up-stairs to his mother's room. Everett and Alice were with her.

"Mother, if I were you, I would go and sit in the parlor and do my sewing there by the windows on the piazza, while those bad men are talking to father," Webster said.

"Why, Webster, go and listen unseen!" Mrs. Darrell exclaimed.

"Certainly, and do it quickly, for those old imps mean mischief to Clarence."

"To Clarence!" exclaimed Alice and her mother at the same time.

"Yes, mother, Web. might be right. You might just be in time to unmask some lie against Clary," Everett suggested.

"One thing is sure, that those men already have too much influence over father, and we have done nothing to oppose it," Alice said. Mrs. Darrell was silent, then, looking at her children, said:

"You might be right, my children, but that would not justify my listening at the keyhole." Everett shrugged his shoulders, saying:

"All right, mother. Come on, Web." And both boys left the room. When they were out, Everett said: "Web, get a horse saddled and tie him at the back porch for me. I am going to listen from Jane's room; one of her windows is right over those men. If what I hear makes it necessary for me to see Clarence, I shall go to town. Get a horse saddled immediately and come to me."

CHAPTER XXV.

THE SQUATTER AND THE DON.

Everett found Lucy in Jane's room. Both were sewing by the window he wanted. He squeezed himself into a seat between his sisters, saying:
"Girls, I want to hear. Hush! Listen!"

Voices were heard below. All listened. As Webster was coming down stairs he saw John Gasbang going out at the other end of the parlor, pushing a large arm-chair out upon the porch. He heard them laughing at some of Gasbang's coarse, vulgar jokes, and then all sat down. After some desultory talk, Mathews, evidently anxious to begin at what they had to state, said:

"I am afraid, neighbor Darrell, that somebody has been fooling you and laughing at you, or if not, then the thing will look as if *you yourself* had been fooling us and laughing at us. This we can hardly believe."

"We don't believe at all," Hughes explained, seeing Darrell's brow darken.

Jane's window was possessed of most favorable acoustic qualities. Every word could be distinctly heard.

"I don't understand you," says Darrell, gruffly. "I am not given to joking or laughing much, and I never knew that anybody dared to laugh at me."

"Precisely!" Hughes exclaimed, bowing deferentially.

"Did you ever give us to understand that this land you occupy you had bought and paid for?" Mathews asked.

"No. I said to the Don I would pay when the title is settled; that's all. You all heard that."

"But you never paid him any money?"

"Not a red cent. But see here, what do you mean by coming here to catechise *me*? You don't know William Darrell, if you think you can set a trap for him in this way. I tell you he would kick your trap to the old 'Nick' in two minutes," Darrell said, getting white with anger.

"I know it," Gasbang said, shaking with laughter.

"Stop your nonsense," Darrell said to him; then to Mathews, "Speak out like a man— what is it all about?"

"That we are told that it is recorded that you paid six thousand four hundred dollars to the Don for six hundred and forty acres of land," Miller explained.

"When did I do that?" Darrell asked, with increasing pallor, the sight of which his interlocutor did not relish.

"On the 13th day of February, 1872," Gasbang replied.

"Who saw the record?"

"I did. I saw the entry made by the notary."

"Well, the notary lies, that's all."

"He couldn't. He could be prosecuted for it," Miller said.

"Very well, he shall be; for it is a lie that I bought any such land or paid any such price for it."

"Perhaps the Don had the entry made," Hughes suggested.

"Then the Don lied, and I'll tell him so," Darrell retorted.

"Are you sure that Mr. Clarence did not buy the land unbeknown to you?" Mathews asked.

"What do you mean, sir? Do you mean to say that my own son would put me in such a ridiculous position? No, I think it is more likely that, as Hughes says, the Don had the false entry made on the strength of my having promised to pay him for the land I would take. But I'll teach him that I am not to be dragged into a bargain like that."

"What would the Don gain by that? Nothing. No, if you will not be offended, I'll tell you what I heard is the most likely theory of it all," Gasbang began.

"And who in the devil has been building theories on my affairs? I'd like to see the fellow who does that," thundered Darrell.

"It was my lawyer, who casually discovered that entry in the notary's books, and told me of it. He meant no harm," Gasbang explained, with conciliatory amiability.

"Of course, he meant no harm. Lawyers of the Peter Roper stamp never do. When they go sticking their noses into people's business, they do so *casually*. And your lawyer— Mr. Roper, I suppose— being a very innocent and straightforward and honorable, high-toned man, who never gets drunk, he did not mean any harm, and *accidentally*, purely so, made this discovery, and no danger of his having been too drunk to read straight, either. Look here, John, don't you talk to me as if you thought me idiotic, for I am not. But what is this innocent theory of this unsophisticated, honorable Peter Roper? Let us see."

"Well, he thinks that Mr. Clarence being in love with the Don's daughter, probably bought the land to propitiate the family, and dated back the deed of sale," Gasbang said.

Darrell was silent, but shook his head.

"You see, the Don could have had no object in putting on record that he had received six thousand four hundred dollars, unless he did so," said Miller.

"So you think he received the money?" Darrell asked.

"No doubt of it," all the others answered.

"There he goes now," said Hughes, and all could see the Don riding towards home, accompanied by his two sons. Behind them the *vaqueros* were driving a lot of cattle towards the "*corral*" at the back of the house.

Seeing the cattle, Darrell said: "By the way, these cattle now belong to Clarence. He bought every head on this rancho belonging to the Don, and will drive them to the Colorado River as soon as the weather cools off. So I hope that if any stray cows or calves come up to your places you will corral them and send *me* word. I ask this of all of you, as a favor to me, not to Clarence."

"Certainly! certainly!" said Hughes, Miller and Gasbang.

"Will it be too much trouble to do that?" Darrell asked Mathews, who had remained silent.

He was compelled to reply: "Of course not— not for you."

"Well, you see, I ask only what the law gives."

"I know that."

"And Clarence knows that if his cattle go to your fields you must corral them and give him notice. And now I want to go and speak with the Don."

All arose.

Hughes said: "As we all wish to know more about that land sale, we will come back this evening to hear what the Don says."

"Very well. I am going to ask all he knows about it."

"He knows everything, the greaser!" Mathews growled.

"But you think Clarence paid the money?" asked Darrell.

"Of course he did, to get the girl," laughed Gasbang; then added: "It was all a put-up job, and they kept the secret well, so we never smelled the rat, while they laughed at us. But I don't care so long as you, Mr. Darrell, wasn't in it."

"So says I," added Miller.

"And I," said Hughes, and they drove off, laughing.

Darrell remained standing on the front steps. He ground his teeth and clenched his fists as he heard the laughter from the wagon, which sounded louder as the wagon went further away. He walked to the stable and took a heavy whip, one of those which teamsters call "black snakes," which are used to drive mules with. The old man trembled with suppressed anger, so much that he could not fasten on his spurs, and this only increased the more his senseless rage.

Everett was scarcely less angry or less pale. He was waiting for his father to start, to follow him. Webster came up-stairs and said to him:

"Retty, father means mischief. He has a 'black snake,' and trembles with rage as if he had the ague."

"Poor father, how unfortunate it is that he got into such a wrong train of reasoning," Jane said.

"He is bound to keep wrong as long as he permits such men to influence him. I am ashamed of father," Lucy added.

"No, don't say that," Jane begged.

"But I am," Lucy maintained; "very much ashamed."

"And I also— bitterly ashamed," Everett said.

The old gentleman at last succeeded in fastening his spurs and getting on his horse. He trotted off to meet the Don. Everett and Webster went down stairs. Webster had saddled two horses; he was not going to let Everett go alone, when he might need help. So the two boys followed their father at a short distance.

Lucy and Jane went to Clarence's room, from which they had a better view of that part of the valley through which passed the main road, in front of the Alamar house. They saw their father take the main road. The Don was coming slowly with his two sons, watching the *vaqueros* driving the cattle up the hill.

"Mamma, see father going to meet the Don. What does he mean?" exclaimed Alice, alarmed.

Mrs. Darrell went to the window, and both sat there to watch proceedings.

Two or three head of cattle got separated, and Gabriel turned back at a few paces to head them off. Don Mariano and Victoriano kept on, and soon after met Darrell.

"Good afternoon, Mr. Darrell," said Don Mariano, pleasantly. "You see we are Clarence's *vaqueros* now."

Darrell muttered something gruffly, and stopped his horse in the middle of the road. The others did the same. Don Mariano saw that Darrell was very angry, and waited for him to speak first.

The enraged man gasped twice, but no sound came. On the third effort his harsh tones said:

"I want you to tell me what is all this trickery and lies about my having paid you six thousand four hundred dollars for land. You know that to be a lie."

"Of course I do. You never paid me a cent, nor the other settlers either. No settler wants to pay, and I never said you had, or expected they would, for I know they believe themselves authorized by law to appropriate my property."

"Didn't Clarence pay you for the land I took?"

"Look here, Mr. Darrell, business matters between Clarence and myself are not to be mentioned, and unless he authorizes me to speak I cannot repeat anything which he wishes to keep quiet."

"Then you have some private business together."

Don Mariano bowed, but did not speak. Darrell came closer to the Don, and shaking at him the fist in which he held the whip, said:

"Then I tell you, you ought to be ashamed of yourself to be bargaining with my son in a clandestine manner, fooling me, and making me appear ridiculous. But I tell you to your face— for I am not a sneaking coward— I tell you, that you have acted most dishonorably, inveigling Clarence into bargains unbeknown to me, inducing him, with seductive bribes, to act most dishonorably towards me."

"What were those bribes?" Don Mariano asked.

"What were they? Your daughter's pretty looks, by G— !"

"Oh, father!" exclaimed Everett, turning very pale.

"Pshaw! That is too low," the Don said, turning his horse towards his house.

Darrell spurred his and stood in the way.

"Too low, you say? And isn't it low to act as you have? And now you want to sneak off like a coward, and not give me any satisfaction."

"I am ready to give you any satisfaction you want, but demand it like a gentleman. I am no Peter Roper, or Gasbang, or Billy Mathews, to have a tumble-down fist-fight in the dirt with you. If you forget your dignity, I do not," the Don replied, again trying to go towards his house.

Darrell again placed his horse in front to intercept his road, and said, livid with rage:

"And why didn't you think of your dignity when you paraded your daughter (like a pretty filly for sale) before my son, to get his money! Damn you! can't I make you fight? Won't you be insulted, you coward? I'll publish your cowardice all over California."

So saying, he lifted his whip and struck a severe blow at the Don. Quickly, at the same instant, Victoriano and Everett had dashed their horses between, and the blow fell right upon the backs of the two young men.

This act of devotion was scarcely necessary, for as Darrell lifted his whip, and before it fell down, Don Mariano touched his horse with one spur only, giving a quick touch to the reins to one side. The horse jumped aside, sat on his haunches for an instant, half-crouching, half-rearing, and in a second he was up again. Don Mariano smiled at Darrell's clumsy horsemanship, conscious of being able to ride him down and all around him before the belligerent squatter could tell what was happening. Still smiling, the Don rode slowly away. Darrell followed close, and again lifted his whip to strike, but instantaneously he felt as if he had been struck by lightning, or as if an aerolite had fallen upon him. His arm fell powerless by his side, and an iron hoop seemed to encircle him. He looked down to his breast surprised, and there the coil of a *reata* held him in an iron grip, and he could not move. He looked about him amazed, and saw that the other end of the *reata* was neatly wound around the pommel of Gabriel's saddle, and that young gentleman sat quietly on his horse, as if waiting Mr. Darrell's orders to move, his handsome face a little pale, but quite composed.

"Go home and bring me my pistols, Webster. I'll fix this brood of greasers," said Darrell, half choked with rage and the tight embrace of the *reata*.

Webster hesitated, and looked towards his brother for advice. Everett winked, and Webster understood at once that Everett meant that he should go, but bring no pistols. He galloped off towards home.

The horse that Darrell was riding was the mate of the one that Webster rode, so that when he saw his partner go off towards home, he thought he must do the same, and followed. As the reins hung loosely upon his neck, he naturally supposed that he was to follow at the pace his companion went, so he started at a gallop to catch up with Webster.

Thus now began a most ridiculous steeple-chase going home. Darrell could not check his horse or do anything but hold to the pommel of his saddle, his arms being pinioned to his body. Gabriel, fearing to let go the *reata*, which, if loosened, might entangle the horse, and thus pull the old man off his saddle, followed, maintaining the *reata* at an even, gentle tension, carefully keeping at the same distance. Victoriano and Everett saw nothing to do but follow, trying to get near Darrell to catch him in case he should lose his balance going over the rough ground of the plowed field.

The two Indian *vaqueros* after putting their cattle in the *corral*, came down to inquire for further orders, and seeing the race going on, they thought they could join in, too. So, putting spurs to their horses, they began to run and shout in high glee. Noticing that the patron, Don Gabriel, held a *reata* in his hands, the *lazo* end of which was attached to Darrell, they thought that for sport Don Gabriel had thrown the *lazo* on the old squatter. Having come to this conclusion, they began to shout and hurrah with renewed vigor.

"Apa! viejo escuata ó cabestreas ó te órcas," cried one.

"No le afloje patroncito Gabriel," said the other.

Now the ground being very rough, Darrell began to sway, as if losing his balance.

"Apriétate viejo! apriétate míralo! ya se ladea!" cried again one *vaquero*.

"Creo que el viejo escuata va chispo," said the other.

"Que es eso? A que vienen acá? Quien los convida? Cállense la boca, no sean malcreados, Vallense!" said Victoriano, turning to them in great indignation.

This rebuke and imperative order silenced them immediately, and not understanding why these gentlemen were having all that fun, and did not laugh, nor wished any one else to laugh, quietly turned and went home.

Darrell's horse now came to a hollow made by the old bed of a brook where the road passed diagonally. To gallop down hill was too much equestrianism for the pinioned rider; he began again to topple to one side. Quick as a flash Victoriano darted forward, and grasping the bridle with one hand, caught with the other the body of Darrell, which having entirely lost balance, was toppling over like a log.

Gabriel immediately gathering the *reata* quickly in successive loops, all of which he hung on the pommel of his saddle, came to Darrell's side.

"I'll take that *lazo* off, Mr. Darrell, if you permit me," said Gabriel, very quietly, when Victoriano had straightened him on the saddle, and he had again a perpendicular position.

"Yes, damn you, and you'll pay for it, too!" was Darrell's courteous reply.

"Very well, but don't be abusive. Use better language; and if you want to fight I'll accommodate you whenever you wish, with any weapons, except the tongue," Gabriel answered.

"I suppose you think a *lazo* is a very genteel weapon. It is good enough for cowardly, treacherous greasers," said the irate Darrell, eager to be as insulting as possible.

"And to subdue wild cattle," Gabriel added. "I threw my *lazo* on you to keep you from striking my father. He was unarmed, and you made a brutal attack upon him with a heavy mule whip. I would *lazo* you again fifty times, or any other man, under the same circumstances. If you think it was cowardly to do so, I will prove to you at any time that I was not prompted by cowardice. Victoriano, loosen the *reata* off Mr. Darrell's arms."

Victoriano dismounted, and endeavored to loosen the tight noose, but it was so firmly drawn that he could not move it. Everett came to his assistance, but he, too, failed.

"I cannot loosen the noose without hurting Mr. Darrell," said Victoriano, giving up the task.

Gabriel dismounted, and examined the noose carefully. He shook his head, saying:

"No, sir; we cannot loosen that *reata* while you are sitting down. We will have to put you on your feet, Mr. Darrell, and you will be slimmer then. Thus by collapsing a little the loop will lose the tension that keeps it tight."

"Come on, Mr. Darrell, Retty and I will let you down nicely," said Victoriano.

"Lean on me, father," said Everett, but as he held up his arms towards his father, he became convulsed with laughter. Victoriano was laughing, too, so heartily, that Darrell was afraid to trust his weight into their hands.

"For shame, Victoriano, to be so discourteous," said Gabriel, reprovingly— his handsome features perfectly serious.

But Victoriano had suppressed his desire to laugh too long, and now his risibility was beyond control. Everett was overcome in the same manner, so that he hung on Victoriano's shoulder, shaking with ill-suppressed laughter.

"Mr. Darrell, be not afraid to trust to my strength, I am slender, but I am stronger than I look. Lean your weight on me slowly, and I'll take you off your horse while those boys laugh," Gabriel said, putting up his hands for Darrell to lean on them.

"I think we had better go home first," he said.

"No, sir. It will be painful for Mrs. Darrell to see you as you are, and then you ought to have that *reata* off now, quickly. It will sicken you."

"Yes, I feel a very strange sort of cold feeling."

Gabriel was afraid that impeded circulation might make the old man faint, so he said:

"Come, Mr. Darrell, quick."

He slipped off one stirrup, then quickly went around slipped off the other, and pulled Darrell to him gently. Down like a felled tree came the old fighter, almost bearing Gabriel down to the ground. Everett and Victoriano, checking their laughter somewhat, lent their assistance to hold him up, and as he had begun to look bluish, they saw the necessity of establishing the old man's circulation. While Everett and Victoriano held him up, Gabriel loosened the coil, rubbing briskly and hard the benumbed arms to start circulation by friction, moving them up and down.

"Can you get on your horse now?" Gabriel asked, after Darrell had moved his arms several times.

"Yes, I think I can," he said, looking towards his house. A new shadow passed over his face.

Webster was coming back, leading his horse. Would he bring pistols? No. His mother was walking with him. Mrs. Darrell saluted the Alamares, and they lifted their hats respectfully in response. Webster had told her all that had happened, and she understood everything, excepting the steeple-chase performance. She had seen all running behind her husband, but she did not know that the chase was most involuntary on his part. Seeing them stop for so long a time in the hollow she thought he had fallen.

"What is the matter, William? Did you fall?"

"No. And if I had, you couldn't pick me up. What did you come out here for?" was the characteristic answer.

"Because, not seeing you when down in this hollow I feared you were hurt, but since it is only foolish anger that ails you, I need not waste my sympathy," she said in her sweet, low voice— which Clarence insisted always was like Mercedes' voice, having that same musical vibration, so pleasing to the ear and sure to go straight to the heart.

"Mrs. Darrell, allow me to assure you that all this trouble came most unexpectedly to us. We don't know what caused it, but no matter what the cause may be, I certainly could do nothing else than prevent anybody from striking my father," Gabriel said.

"Certainly, Don Gabriel, you did your duty. I do not blame you— no one of you— at all. Express my regrets to your father, please. I am grieved to the heart about this," she said, and there was a sad note in her tones, which plainly told that her expressions of regret were but too true.

"I will tell my father what you say, and let us hope that the cause of all this misunderstanding may be explained," Gabriel replied.

"I hope so," she said, offering her hand to him, which he took and pressed warmly.

When Darrell saw that friendly demonstration, he turned his back upon all, and muttering that he was "to be made the scape-goat of all," walked home.

Mrs. Darrell then asked Gabriel to explain everything to her, which he did, while she listened to him very attentively.

"If you only had heard what those squatters said, and prevented father from riding out," Everett exclaimed.

Mrs. Darrell sighed, shook hands with the Alamares, and, followed by her sons, walked home.

CHAPTER XXVI.

Mrs. Darrell's View of Our Land Laws.

Of all the horrible tortures that the human mind is capable of conjuring up with which to torment itself, none was greater to William Darrell than the consciousness of being ridiculous— the conviction that people were laughing at him. He had seen Victoriano and his own Everett so convulsed with laughter, laughing at him, laughing in his presence, laughing so heartily that they could scarcely stand up. This laughter of the two boys was the most vivid picture in the panorama of living scenes which he himself had evoked. Surely if his own son laughed so heartily, everybody else would do the same. And when on his return home, Clementine had said to him most unceremoniously:

"Why, papa, what made you sit on your horse so stiff? Why did you want to keep that rope? You looked so funny." And Clementine laughed heartily.

"Get out of my way," said he, and went to the "colony" straight and banged the door; which meant that he wanted no one else within the precincts of that asylum. "So I looked funny and stiff; they were all laughing at me," he said, and with a groan of mental and physical pain, flung himself on the lounge.

Presently, Tisha came to say that supper was on the table. "I don't want any supper," said he in the gruff tones he used when he was angry, or pretended to be. Tisha retired, but in about ten minutes she returned, carrying a tray, which she deposited on a table, saying:

"Missus says that mayhap when you rested awhile you might feel a little hungry."

"Give me a cup of tea; I want nothing else," he said, and Tisha fixed his tea just as she knew he liked it with plenty of rich cream and four lumps of sugar, for Darrell's teacup held a pint; she placed the tea on a little table by the lounge and retired.

The tea seemed to refresh him in spite of himself, and he accepted the improvement with an inward protest as if setting down an exception (as lawyers call it) by which he renounced all obligation to be grateful.

Early the settlers began to arrive at the "colony" through the side door of the back hall. Everett joined the meeting, as Romeo came to request his company. Darrell gave his son a withering look, but did not speak to him. He kept his reclining position on the lounge and his satellites sat in a semi-circle around him. He soon told them he had nothing satisfactory to say, as the Don had refused to make any explanation, alleging that he had promised Clarence to say nothing. When Clarence returned he would clear the mystery. The settlers again recommenced their conjectures, and discussed the motives which must have actuated the Don to make a false entry, to record having received money which he never got. Land was the discussion, but there seemed no dissenting voice as to the Don's culpability, and the sinister motives which actuated him in acting in that underhand manner. When the altercation was at the highest, and could be heard all over the house, Mrs. Darrell walked in and, bowing to the astonished squatters, came slowly forward and stood about the middle of the semi-circle, though outside of it. Darrell sat up and all the others stood on their feet and stared as if they had seen some Banquo spectre or other terrible ghostly apparition.

"Be seated, gentlemen, I beg of you. I have but a few words to say. Please sit down," she reiterated, seeing that every one remained standing.

Slowly all one by one dropped into their seats and all the faces were turned towards her. No one thought of offering her a chair, and she did not want one either. When all had resumed their seats, she said:

"All those amongst you, gentlemen, who think that Don Mariano Alamar induced my son Clarence to purchase land from him are much mistaken; and all those who think Don Mariano made a false entry of a land sale, do him an injustice."

"Who made the entry then?" Darrell asked, sharply.

"That is what I came to say. The land was bought and paid for at *my* request. If there is any blame, or crime, or guilt in the matter, *I* am the criminal— *I* am the guilty one. I told my son, Clarence Darrell, that if he did not pay for the land which his father had located, I would never, *never* come to live upon it. Moreover, I told my son not to mention the fact of having paid for the land, because his father would think we were interfering in his business, and I did not wish him to know that the land was paid for until the question of the Don's title was settled. Then we would have avoided painful discussions, and the eloquence of facts (I trusted) would clearly show to my husband that his wife and son had acted right, when we had paid the legitimate owner for his property."

"And now, gentlemen, let me add this, only this, that I do not mean to criticise anybody's actions or opinions, but, from my point of view, I say, those laws which authorize you to locate homesteads upon lands claimed as Mexican grants, those laws are wrong, and good, just, moral citizens should not be guided by them. Settlers should wait until the titles are finally approved or rejected. See! look back and see all the miseries that so many innocent families have suffered by locating in good faith, their humble homes upon lands that they were forced to abandon. Our law-givers doubtless mean well, but they have— through lack of matured reflection, I think, or lack of unbiased thought— legislated curses upon this land of God's blessings. I love my country, as every true-hearted American woman should, but, with shame and sorrow, I acknowledge that we have treated the conquered Spaniards most cruelly, and our law-givers have been most unjust to them. Those poor, defenseless ones whom our Government pledged its faith to protect, have been sadly despoiled and reduced to poverty.

"I have only expressed my opinion, gentlemen; I mean no slur upon yours.

I hope you see now that I alone, *I am* the one to blame for the purchase of the land which has given so much offence. Good night, gentlemen."

So profound was the silence following Mrs. Darrell's exit, that a pin could have been heard drop. Romeo Hancock was the first to find utterance to his amazement.

"By George," he said, "but ain't she superb! I see now where Clarence gets his good sense and correct ideas."

At any other time, Darrell would have been proud of this tribute paid to the wife he adored, with passionate, secret, unrevealed tenderness, but now he was too angry. He even felt angry at the longing to take to his heart that darling so resolute and yet so gentle. This longing, when his pride clamored that she was wrong and should be reproved, was an additional torture to him. He remained silent.

"Well, I suppose that— in the language of the poets— 'this settles our hash,'" Gasbang said, and laughed at his witticism, as it was his habit to do.

Hughes and Miller laughed with him, but no one else. All were deeply impressed with Mrs. Darrell's words.

"I wish she had told me this before," Darrell said, and resumed his recumbent position.

"Yes, why didn't she?" Gasbang asked.

"Because women are bound to do mischief," Mathews replied.

"She stated her reasons very clearly," Romeo said.

"What were they?" Mathews asked.

"Can your memory be failing you already, Mr. Mathews, that you forget what you just heard, or are you getting hard of hearing?" Romeo answered.

Mathews snorted and turned his back on Romeo. Everett answered him, saying:

"My mother said that she wished the purchase to be kept quiet until the Don should have his title. Then the fact of the land being his, would prove the correctness of having paid for what we took, and thus all discussions would have been avoided. Unfortunately some busybody went to see the entry, and came to herald his glorious discovery."

"How did she know that the Don's title would not be rejected?" Mathews inquired.

"Her good sense told her," Romeo answered.

"I wasn't talking to you," Mathews retorted, making all laugh— and even Darrell smiled— but he looked very pale, and Everett began to feel anxious, to see his pallor.

The conversation had now drifted to the subject of the coming survey of the rancho.

"I heard that the surveyor will be on the ground by the first of October," Miller said.

"All right; that will give us plenty of time," Gasbang observed.

Everett said something to Romeo, who then went and whispered to his father, whereupon Old Hancock nodded an assent and in a few moments said:

"Well, my friends, let us go home. For the present I don't see that anything can be done. Mr. Darrell looks fatigued, and I don't wonder at it, for we have bored him nearly to death. Let him go to bed and rest."

Evidently Mathews, Gasbang and others had no idea of going home so early, but as Darrell said nothing, they reluctantly arose and took their departure.

If Darrell had obeyed the impulse of his heart when he went up-stairs to his bed-chamber, he would have taken his wife in his arms and, with a kiss, made his peace with her; for he knew her to be true, and always acting from the best motives. But there was that streak of perversity within, which impelled him to do or say the wrong thing, when at the same time an inner voice was admonishing him to do the opposite.

"I am sorry, William, that I kept that matter of the land purchase from you. Believe me, my husband, I did so out of a desire to avoid discussions always painful to me. You seemed so happy here, that I hated to bring up for argument any disagreeable subject. It was a mistake; I regret it."

"Yes, wise women generally put their foot in it," said he, turning his back on her.

"Can you forgive me? I am very sorry. And now I want you to take a nice warm bath; after so much excitement it will soothe you, and you will sleep sweetly. After all, it is better that you know the whole thing now."

"No thanks to you, though."

"That is true, but you know my maxim."

"Which one? Wise women have so many."

"To accept blessings thankfully, even when they come in disguise," she replied, taking no notice of his sarcasm.

"I have yet to see the blessing in this."

"You will to-morrow if you will only take care now of your physical comfort— your health. Come, take a bath; it will prevent your having a fever."

"I don't want a bath; I feel badly."

"That is why you should have it. I know your constitution well— nothing would be better for you than warm bathing. Be reasonable, please. I feel tired, too; I would like to go to bed."

"Why don't you, then?"

"Because I wanted first to see you resting for the night."

"I don't know that I'll go to bed. I think I'll sleep in this chair."

"Very well, then, I shall go into Clarence's room and sleep there! It would keep me awake to know that you were sitting up."

"Do as you please."

"Can it be possible, William, that you refuse to go to bed because you are too angry with me to have me lie by your side?"

He said nothing, but looked very pale. She waited; he never said a word.

"Very well, William, I am dismissed I suppose. If you are sick or require anything, knock at Clarence's door. I shall be there. Good night."

"Good night."

She went quietly into Clarence's room and lit a lamp. She went to a hall closet and took a soft merino wrapper, came back, locked her door, undressed herself, put the wrapper on, and sat by the window to think.

"What fools men are? Such small vanity guides them. To think that William should fling away happiness at the instigation of a reptile like Gasbang! And you, my sweet boy, my darling Clarence, how will this affect your happiness?" This thought gave her the keenest pain.

While Mrs. Darrell was thus sadly meditating, her angry lord was nearly choking with smothered rage— intensified a hundred fold by his disappointment at being left alone without his adored, worshipped Mary. Mrs. Darrell knew that her husband loved her, but she had never guessed that torrent of passion and devotion which rushed through that rugged nature like a river plunging from Yosemite hights into unknown abysmal depths.

Why would he not yield to her sweet entreaties to bathe and take his comfort? Was it all perverse obstinacy? Partly, yes. He had refused a warm bath and her sweet society, for the very reason that those two were the things he most desired on earth— he felt as if even his bones clamored for them. But there was yet another equally strong motive in that very complex nature— a motive stronger than obstinacy— compelling him in spite of himself, and this was *his bashfulness*. He feared that his wife might see the bruises on his arms and the heavy welt that he knew there must be around his body, made by the coil of the *reata*. He felt very sore, and his bruises became more painful, but he would rather die than let any one see his pitiful plight. And thus he sat up all night and would not undress, or go to bed, or be comforted.

Towards morning he walked to the window and looked into the valley, then his gaze wandered towards the Alamar house. All the windows had the shutters closed and no light was seen from them excepting one. He did not know what room that was or who occupied it, but unconsciously he watched it— watched the light he could see through the lace curtains. The light became intercepted at regular intervals; so he concluded that some one must be going and coming before that light. He smiled, hoping that the Don might be as miserable as he was— unable to sleep.

But the Don was sleeping. She who was awake, walking in her solitary vigil, was Mercedes. Those beautiful blue eyes had never closed in sleep all night.

She had been embroidering a *mouchoir* case for Clarence that unfortunate afternoon of Darrell's performance, when she heard loud talking in the piazza. At first she paid no attention to it and went on with her work, hoping that Clarence would return early, because her dream troubled her. The talking becoming louder, and more voices being heard, she felt alarmed, imagining that Clarence's horses had run away and he had been hurt. She went out to inquire.

The entire Alamar family, as well as Mrs. Mechlin, George and Lizzie, were in the veranda. All had seen Darrell's attempt and subsequent steeple-chase. Now Gabriel and Victoriano had returned and related what had passed in the hollow. Victoriano was again overcome with laughter, which, being so hearty and uncontrollable, became contagious. Even Gabriel and Mr. Mechlin, who were less disposed to indulge in hilarity, laughed a little. Mercedes was the only one who not even smiled. She did not understand a word of what was said. Gradually she began to comprehend, and she stood motionless, listening, her pale lips firmly compressed, her eyes only showing her agitation and how grieved she was; their dark-blue was almost black, and they glowed like stars.

"Cheer up, little pussy. When Clarence comes he will undeceive the old man, and all will be right," said Don Mariano, putting his arms around her yielding form and drawing her to his heart.

"*Palabra suelta, no tiene vuelta*," Doña Josefa said. "Darrell can never recall his insulting words."

"But he can apologize for them," Don Mariano said.

"And would that satisfy you?" Carlota asked.

"It would have to," was the Don's answer.

"Oh! papa!" Rosario exclaimed.

"What then? Shall I go and shoot the old fool?"

"I believe he would enjoy that, he is so full of fight," Victoriano said, recommencing his laughing.

"I fear his anger will not abate as long as the bruises of the *reata* remain painful," Gabriel said, thoughtfully.

"Did you draw the *lazo* very tight?" Don Mariano asked.

"Not intentionally, but he himself did so by stooping forward as his horse galloped. Every time he did so the noose became more closely drawn until he could scarcely breathe."

"This is a bad business, George," the Don said to his son-in-law, who had remained a silent listener to all.

"Yes, sir; but let us hope that between Clarence and Mrs. Darrell they will pacify the old man. The thing now is to give him time to cool off his anger," George replied.

"If those squatters could be kept away, Darrell would come to his senses much sooner," Mr. Mechlin said.

"That's it exactly," Gabriel added; "they make the mischief."

"But why does he allow it?" Doña Josefa said.

"Because he loves the smell of gunpowder, and they are full of it," Tano explained.

"I think Mrs. Darrell ought to prevent those horrible creatures from invading her house," Carlota said.

"They only go to the 'colony.' The old buster wants them there. He would smash the furniture if his pets were not allowed to come to lick his boots," Victoriano asserted, positively.

"You don't speak very respectfully of your future father-in-law," George said to Victoriano, laughing.

"Not at present. Not when I have just seen him running away like a chicken thief, just caught with a turkey under each arm," Tano replied, lapsing into another fit of laughter.

"Oh, Tano! if you care for Alice, how can you so ridicule her father?" Mercedes exclaimed, speaking for the first time. And without waiting for a reply, she turned away and went to her room.

There she remained inconsolable, her lovely face often bathed in tears. She did not go to bed; she hoped that Clarence might possibly have finished his business in town and hurried back. She watched for the faintest sound all night.

In the morning Madame Halier came to see her, and immediately went to report to Doña Josefa the state of Mercedes' eyes. Don Mariano came in at once and took his pet in his arms.

"Papa, you said you were going to-day. Please don't go," she begged.

"Why not, my pet? I shall go only a little ways with those stupid Indians who keep letting the cattle turn back. I shall return before dark," he said, smoothing her golden hair.

"Papa, please don't go. I want you to be here when Clarence returns. Let the cattle be. I want you here. You may never see Clarence again in this world if you go." And she put her pale cheek against her father's and sobbed convulsively.

"What an idea! Why shouldn't I see Clarence again if I ride one or two miles? My baby darling, you are too nervous. You have cried all night, and now your mind is in a whirl of sad visions. Do not exaggerate the mischief that Darrell might do. He will probably say very insulting things to Clarence, but Clarence is as true as steel, and has a very clear head."

"I know that. I am sure of him. He is so true. But, papa, can I marry him after what his father said to you, and when he tried to strike you? Can I marry him after that, papa?"

"Why not, pray? What he said is an infamous lie, and because Darrell chooses to indulge in mean thoughts and atrocious language, is that a reason why you and Clarence should be made wretched for life? If Darrell did not permit men like Gasbang, and others influenced by Peter Roper, to come near him, his ears would not hear such low, vulgar suggestions. As long as we know that Clarence is a gentleman, and he behaves as such, I shall not permit that you two be separated by anything that Darrell may do or say."

"But, papa, you will keep out of Mr. Darrell's way."

"Certainly, my poor little darling. Don't be afraid; Darrell will not attack me again."

The Don talked in this consoling and reassuring way to his favorite child until he saw that he had quieted her. She promised to eat breakfast and then try to sleep.

"It won't do to look at Clarence through such swollen orbs. You had better let Tano give you one of his graphic accounts of the battle of Alamar, as he calls Darrell's performance, and make you laugh."

"No, I couldn't laugh. I wouldn't if I could."

"Very well. To sleep is the best for you."

He kissed her and soon after he and Gabriel went on their way. They quickly overtook the herders, who were driving the lot of cattle which had started at daylight. The Don was confident of returning at sundown, and glad to leave Mercedes more contented and hopeful, he rode away cheerfully.

CHAPTER XXVII.

Darrell Astonishes Himself.

Mercedes felt so comforted by what her father had said, that in less than ten minutes after he left she was sleeping like the good child that she was. Madam Halier watched her slumbers, coming to the door every few minutes. And when she had slept and felt refreshed, she had a bath and a luncheon of tea, cold chicken, fresh peaches with cream, and fresh grapes just cut from the vines; then she was ready to dress herself and take up her embroidery. She was afraid her eyes would yet be too swollen for her to go into the parlor or veranda, and perhaps meet George or Mr. Mechlin. So she stayed in her room.

But she was missed, and George came to knock at her door, and being asked to come in, he did so, making a profound bow. Then counting on his fingers as he spoke, began:

"Doña Josefa, Doña Beatrice, Doña Carlota, Doña Rosario, Doña Elvira, Doña Carolina, Doña Elizabeth, all request the pleasure of your company at a canning performance to take place this afternoon in the kitchen of Doña Beatrice."

Mercedes laughed, asking: "Are they really going to do the canning? Who knows about it?"

"They all know, theoretically, but as to practice, that '*quién sabe.*' However, they are going to peal peaches by the bushel this evening, so they will all dine there."

"Doesn't mamma expect papa to dinner?" asked she, alarmed; "I hope so."

"I'll go and inquire," George said, going; but she followed him, trembling— she did not know why. She took George's arm, and both went to the piazza, where Carlota, Rosario and Doña Josefa were waiting for George to go with them.

"Mamma, don't you expect papa to dinner?" asked she.

"Yes, but he might be late; so we will dine at Mrs. Mechlin's, and he and Gabriel will take supper here on their return."

"I will wait for them here."

"Will you not go to Mrs. Mechlin's?"

"No, please. I'll stay home."

"Take my advice, and don't see Clarence yet," Carlota said.

"Why not, pray?"

"Because, after what his father did and said, the least you have to do with the Darrells the more it will be to your honor," Rosario said, sententiously.

"And must I give up Clarence because— because his father gets mad, and— and— "

"And insults your father, and insults you," Carlota said.

"But that would be awful," said she, looking at George, who full of sympathy for his favorite sister-in-law, said:

"Do not worry about that now— you have suffered enough. No doubt, Clarence will make it all right, if we only give him time. All will be explained."

"I doubt that," Carlota said.

"I don't think Mercedes knows all that Darrell said. I think Clarence himself will see the impossibility of his marrying Mercedes as things are now," Doña Josefa said.

"What are we to do?" Mercedes exclaimed, in low, tremulous tones, that revealed all the desolation she felt.

"Try to be courageous, little sister," Carlota said.

"What to do? Clarence himself ought to know— to separate for the present. Will you marry the son of a man who said of you and your father such horrible things?" Doña Josefa asked.

"But Clarence is innocent, and so am I," pleaded Mercedes, with white lips.

"My daughter, do you not see that I *must* withdraw my permission to your marriage now?"

"Will you tell that to Clarence?" asked Mercedes, frightened.

"Certainly, as soon as I see him."

"And break our engagement?" she asked, with a voice scarcely audible.

"Certainly. What else, my daughter?"

"I want to go to my room," she said, slowly turning to go back, walking as if in a dream.

George put his arm around her shoulder, and walked with her.

"Don't be discouraged, my dear *humanita*. Doña Josefa is justly indignant now, but her anger will pass off, and she will see how absurd it will be to punish you and Clarence for the sins of his ill-tempered, foolish father. The only thing now is to drop the matter. 'Least said, sooner mended,' applies to this case exactly."

"I wish papa were here. He don't think as mamma does. If mamma sees Clarence first, she will send him away. Oh! that will be awful to me."

"We will keep your mamma at our house until Don Mariano returns. Tano will see Clarence first."

When George left, Mercedes hurried to her bedside to pray. In all the sad tribulations of her mind, her heart turned to her Redeemer and the Blessed Virgin Mary. To them she told all her grief, all her trials, and after begging to be strengthened, she always arose from her bended knees comforted.

This time, however, her convulsive sobs only became more uncontrollable, as she poured out her great sorrow and terrible fears before the pitying Mother of suffering humanity.

When her sobs were almost a paroxysm, Madame Halier, who had come to the door to listen, went, and much excited, told Doña Josefa that Mercita would certainly be ill if some one didn't show a little humanity to her.

Doña Josefa hurried to Mercedes' room, and found her still at her bedside sobbing and praying. Gently the mother lifted her child and pressed her to her heart.

"Mercedes, darling, have courage. Your father and Clarence will talk this matter over, and determine what is best to do. Perhaps it might all be arranged."

"You will not tell Clarence to— that— to go away?"

"Certainly not. But there must be some other arrangement about the wedding. It will be postponed, perhaps. Darrell could not be expected to be present, or he might wish the engagement broken off."

Carlota and Rosario came in to see how Mercedes felt, as Madam Halier seemed to be so anxious and indignant with everybody for their cruelty to Mercedes.

"If old Darrell wants the engagement broken off, then my dear sister you must break it— else he will have a good reason to say that papa wants to sell you, or to entrap Clarence, for his money, into marrying you," Rosario said.

"Did Mr. Darrell say that?" Mercedes asked, blushing, so that her pale face became suffused to the roots of her hair.

"He said worse— but you had better hear no more."

"That is awful!" the poor child exclaimed, clasping her hands in eloquent protestation; then adding: "Mamma, I will try to have courage. I don't know what I am to do. But if my father has been so grossly insulted, I must feel for him. I must not be selfish. I don't know what I'll do," and the unhappy girl pressed her hands to her forehead, as if to keep together her distracted thoughts.

"I think the best thing for you to do is to go to bed. To-morrow your father will see Clarence. That is George's advice, and I think it is good," said her mother, as she kissed and embraced her, adding: "the sweet, blued-eyed baby is too young to get married, any way, and can well wait four years, and then be only twenty-two years old." But seeing the blank despair in those expressive eyes, Doña Josefa hastened to add: "I don't say that you will wait that long, but that you are young enough to do so."

When Mercedes was again alone, she tried to think it was her duty to her father to break her engagement. Her mind utterly refused to see the matter in that light, but as her older sisters had said her engagement ought to be broken off, and her mother spoke of the wedding being postponed, it was clear that she could not be married on the 16th. Would Clarence be willing to wait? and these thoughts revolved around her mind in a circle of coils, worse than the one which so enraged and hurt Darrell.

Madam Halier and Victoriano ate their dinner alone— with Milord for sole company. Poor Tano, though he had laughed heartily at Darrell's plight, was scarcely less distressed than Mercedes, and anxiously looked for Clarence's return.

In the meantime this young gentleman was traveling at the rate of twelve miles per hour, and would have come faster had the road been better. He had been obliged to delay, because Hubert had telegraphed that if he waited two hours he would give him a definite answer about Gabriel's business. The answer came, and it was all that could be desired. Gabriel could go at any time, or wait until the first of October to take his place at the bank. Clarence was delighted to have this good news to carry to Mercedes, with the addition that Fred said that the mines developed richer ores every day. He had an offer of two million dollars for his mines— but both Hubert and Fred advised him not to sell.

With these cheerful thoughts, he was getting into his phæton, when the notary, who had made the entry of Don Mariano's conveyance, came close to him, and said in a low voice, and looking mysteriously around:

"Look here, it may be nothing, but those two fellows are so tricky and slippery that I always imagine they are up to something, and both have been twice to look in my books at the entry of the land conveyance which Señor Alamar made to you. They might mean mischief, though I don't see how."

"Of whom are you speaking?" Clarence asked.

"Of Roper and Gasbang. Why should they wish to know about that conveyance?"

"I don't know; but I am sure it is for no good. When did they look at the entry?"

"About two days ago, the last time. When they first looked at it I was not at home. My wife was at my office when Roper came and asked permission to see the date of a conveyance which he himself had made. This was only a ruse. Two days after he came and told me that one of his clients wanted to buy land from Darrell, and wished to see what sort of a title he had. I, of course, let him see it. Gasbang came after, and that made me suspicious."

Clarence thanked the notary, and drove home as fast as the uneven road permitted. He felt that he must at last disclose to his father all about that land transaction, and feared that he would be angry. His fears, he saw, were only too well founded as soon as he arrived home.

The family were at supper when he drove up to the door. On hearing the sound of wheels, Everett left the table and hastened to meet him. All his brothers and sisters would gladly have done the same, but a look from their mother kept them in their chairs.

In a few words Everett condensed the unfortunate occurrences of the previous day and evening, ending his hurried statement by saying that the entire family hoped that Clarence's influence might appease their father's irritation when nothing else would.

"No; I am sure that if mother has failed, I shall have no effect at all," Clarence said. "But are you sure that there is nothing else to anger him? The fact alone of my having paid for the land, and at my mother's request, would not so infuriate him while in his normal state of mind. There must be some *other* irritating circumstance."

"None that we know of."

"I am glad he did not strike the Don."

"So am I, though I have a big bump to testify that he struck *me*, and I suppose Tano has another to speak for him."

Clarence told the servant who came to take the horses to the stable to leave them where they were, only throwing a blanket on, as he had driven them very fast. He and Everett then walked into the hall, carrying some small parcels which he (as usual) had brought home— one of those parcels being a beautiful pipe, for which he had paid forty dollars, and a lot of fine tobacco, for his father.

Placing them on the hall table, he said to Everett: "I suppose father would rather throw this tobacco into my eyes than put it in his pipe and smoke it."

Everett laughed at this, thinking it rather a witticism under the circumstances, and was still laughing when both went into the dining-room.

Clarence said good evening to all, kissing his mother as he took his seat beside her. Darrell never lifted his eyes, paying no attention to his son.

"What made you laugh just now, Retty?" Willie asked.

"Something that Clary said," answered Everett.

"Was it anything funny?"

"It must have been; but you needn't hear it."

"But I want to hear it," he insisted.

"It must have been about your father, he is the funny man now— the laughing stock," said Darrell to Willie; then to Clarence: "We have had circus performances. Your father distinguished himself by performing *in* the tight rope, with Don Gabriel— a very tight rope," he said, making a semi-circular sign around his body with both hands, and nodding his head at Clarence by way of emphasis, or as if he challenged him to contradict his statement.

"Oh, father! I am very sorry," was all that Clarence could answer.

The entire family were almost choking with suppressed laughter, but none dare give vent to it.

"Why don't you laugh— all of you?" asked he, looking around fiercely.

"Because you frighten their laughter away," Mrs. Darrell replied. "They fear to offend you."

"Offend me? *Me?* And since when such consideration? Since when, I say?"

"Since they were old enough to know you as their father," calmly replied Mrs. Darrell.

"Ah! I am glad to hear it. Well, sir," he said, addressing Clarence again, to the terror of all the family, "I have at last learned that you have been making clandestine bargains with your future father-in-law, placing me in a most ridiculous position, for which I don't thank you."

"I am sorry, father. My intention was most kind," Clarence answered, respectfully, but very calmly.

"You only thought that as I was a fool, you would be my sense-bearer, and act for me— you, the man of brains."

"No, sir. All I thought was, that as you seem to love my mother, you would prefer to give her the kind of home that she desires. I thought that when you came to know all, you would approve of my having obeyed my mother's wishes."

"If you were so sure of my approval, why didn't you tell me the whole thing before?"

"Because I was pledged to my mother not to do so. I was bound to be silent."

"By George!" said Darrell, striking the table with his fist, making all the glasses and cups dance; "and for all that nonsense I have been made a laughing stock, a ridiculous, trusting fool— an ass!"

"No one will think that but yourself," Mrs. Darrell said; "and you will change your mind, I hope."

"And how do you know that?"

"I was supposing that people reason in the way that in all my life I have believed to be correct."

"Yes, what *you* believe to be correct no one else has any right to think differently."

"Whether they have or not, I shall not interfere."

"No, you only wanted to interfere with me."

"Certainly. As my life is united to yours, I am obliged to try and prevent such of your actions as will make me unhappy."

"An excellent doctrine for wives— for mothers to teach their children— and we see the result now."

Mrs. Darrell was pleased that his attacks seemed directed to herself instead of Clarence, but she felt prematurely relieved, for now he came down upon Clarence. He said:

"Well, sir, since yourself and your mother have bought this land, and since I am an unreclaimed *squatter*, I suppose I had better leave this place, and go back to Alameda again. I suppose I can have that place again?"

"You will not have to lease it, father; you can have it rent free, as long as you live, if you prefer to reside there," Clarence replied.

"How is that?"

"I bought the place, and if you wish you can live in it."

"You? *You* bought the place! Then, by George! *you* have managed to coop me up," said Mr. Darrell, drawing down the corners of his mouth and elevating his shoulders deprecatingly, as if he thought Clarence was a voracious land-grabber, who wanted to appropriate to himself all the vacant land in the United States.

"Don't say that, please. The place was for sale, Hubert telegraphed me, and I telegraphed back to buy it."

"I didn't know you were so rich," he answered, sneeringly.

Clarence made no reply.

"Well, I must admit you have cornered me completely; but as I don't want to live on the bounty of my rich son, I must get out of this place."

"You can refund me the price of one hundred and sixty acres, father, if you are too proud to accept that from me, which is little enough, considering your generosity to me all my life. The other two claims, you know, you said would be one for Retty and the other for myself. This house and the orchards are all on your claim."

"I have taken a dislike to the whole thing," said he, waiving his hand, as if to shift the position of the land in question. "You can have it all, together with the Alameda farm. There are other lands in California."

Mrs. Darrell and Clarence looked at each other. The case seemed hopeless. All were silent.

Mr. Darrell continued: "All I want before I leave here is to give your greaser father-in-law a sound thrashing and another to that puppy, Gabriel, who is so airy and proud, and such an exquisite, that it will be delightful to spoil his beauty."

"But why should you wish to do that? What has Don Mariano done to you? and if Don Gabriel threw his *lazo* on you, it was to protect his father."

"What has the old greaser done? He inveigled you into that land business, and you together have made me ridiculous. That is what the matter is."

"Then you don't believe me?" Mrs. Darrell said.

"Don't you take so much credit to yourself, and throw yourself into the breach like a heroine. If the Don hadn't had that pretty daughter, Clarence would not have been so obedient to his mother, perhaps."

Clarence rose to his feet, very pale, but he sat down again, and controlling himself, said as calmly as possible:

"I had never seen one, not one of Don Mariano's daughters when I went to offer to pay for this land."

"Do you mean that you wouldn't have done so if your mother hadn't wished it?"

"No sir, not that. I think I would, for I felt great sympathy with the Don for the contemptible manner in which the squatters received the propositions he made them. I was convinced then that the land belonged to him, and nobody had a right to take it without paying for it."

"Aha! I knew we would come to that," said Darrell, sternly, glaring at his son. "I was a thieving squatter, of course, and that is what you said to your greaser father-in-law, who to reward your high sense of honor, took you to the bosom of his family. The cowardly dog, who will take insults and not resent them, but has puppies at his heels to throw *lasooing* at people."

"Pshaw! I never thought you capable of— "

"Of what? Insulting those greasers?"

"They are gentlemen, no matter how much you may wish to besmear them with low epithets."

"Gentlemen that won't fight."

"They told you they would fight *like gentlemen*."

"Who told you that?"

"I did, father. I heard Don Mariano and Don Gabriel both tell you that," Everett said.

"If they are so ready to fight, why didn't they do it when I told the old dog that the bait to catch you was his daughter?"

"What! Did you say that?" asked Clarence, reddening to the roots of his hair, his face quickly blanching again.

"I did— in clear language."

"In dirty, low, nasty language, and it is you who are the coward, to insult *me* under the shelter of your paternal privileges," said Clarence, rising. "You have been taunting me until I can bear it no longer. I suppose you wish to drive me from your house. Be it so. I leave now— never to enter it again."

"That suits me. You are too *greasy* for both of us to live under the same roof," said Darrell, contemptuously, with a gesture of disgust.

"Good-by, mother; good-by, my sisters; good-by, boys— take care of mother and the girls. God bless you."

With a piercing cry, that rang through the house, Alice ran to Clarence, and throwing her arms around his neck, said:

"Kiss me, my darling, for if you leave us I shall be wretched until you return. Oh! I can't let you go."

Tenderly Clarence pressed his sister to his heart. He felt her arms relaxing, her head fell back, and she closed her eyes. Lovingly he then lifted her, and placing her upon a lounge, said:

"Alice has fainted, mother. My sweet sister, how dearly I love her, God only knows."

He covered her face with kisses, while his own was bathed in tears. Without lifting his eyes or saying another word, he walked out into the darkness.

The delicious, fragrant air, loaded with the perfume of roses and honeysuckle and heliotrope, seemed to breathe a farewell caress over his heated brow, and the recollection of the loving care he had bestowed upon these flowers when he planted them to welcome his mother, flashed through his memory with a pang. He sighed and passed into the gloom, overpowered with a dread that made him feel chilled to the heart. It seemed to him as if an unseen voice was warning him of a dire misfortune he could not perceive nor avert. What could it be? Was Mercedes to be taken from him? Would her family object to him on account of his father's ruffianly behavior? Could he claim to be a gentleman, being the son of that rough? These thoughts flashed through his mind, filling him with sickening dismay and inexpressible disgust. Would he dare stand in the presence of Mercedes now? Or, would he return to town at this late hour? Where could he go for a shelter that night?

Mechanically he walked to the phæton, got into it and took the reins to drive off.

CHAPTER XXVIII.

Shall it be Forever?

Everett followed Clarence and got into the phæton with him.

"My dear brother," said Clarence, in a hoarse voice that sounded unnatural, as if coming from a great depth, "I would like to have your company, but as I am not coming back, I can't take you with me."

"No matter; drive off. I'll go with you a little ways, and will walk back," said Everett. Clarence turned his horses and drove away through the middle drive in the front lawn, and was out of the gate before he fully realized that he himself was driven away from the paternal roof.

"Retty, you did not tell me that my father had insulted my darling so grossly. I wish you had, for I would not have gone inside the house," Clarence said, with a sigh.

"It was so horrible, I couldn't. Forgive me, dear Clary."

"Certainly; I can't blame you."

"Are you going to Don Mariano's?"

"Yes. I will ask Tano to give me a place to sleep; that is, if Doña Josefa is not too disgusted to tolerate a Darrell under her roof."

"I am sure they feel nothing but kindness for you."

"I hope so; but should she wish to break the engagement, I will not stay. I'll drive to town to-night and take the boat for San Francisco, which is not to leave until to-morrow at daylight. I'll have time, I think."

"Don't do that. Wait for the Don, if he is not in now."

"I may, but I don't know. I dread to see Mercedes. I feel so humiliated, so ashamed. What can I say to her?"

At the foot of the hill Clarence stopped his horses to send to his mother and sisters— especially to Alice— loving messages. He also said if he should miss seeing Don Mariano, Everett would say that he would write from San Francisco, and would return at any moment, if Mercedes called him.

"But you will see her yourself," Everett said.

"I hope so," said the disheartened Clarence, driving up toward the house in which he felt his fate would be decided. Victoriano had heard the phæton's wheels and came out to meet it.

"I am so glad to see you, old fellow," said he to Clarence; "it seems an age since sundown."

"I was detained in town about that business of Don Gabriel, but it is all arranged. He can take his place at the bank now, whenever he wishes, or wait until the 1st of October; it will be kept for him. Then I had my own business about the mine. That is all right, too. I only wish that things had gone on as well at home."

"So do I, but it has been awful. Retty told you."

"Yes, I know it all now."

"Unfortunately I did not tell him father's insulting remarks about Miss Mercedes," sadly observed Everett.

"Yes, had I known that, I would not have gone into the house. But I went, and father had the satisfaction of saying it to me himself; and on my telling him what I thought about it, he expressed himself willing that I should take myself off. So here I am, driven from home, and I came to ask you for a bed to-night, as I am very tired."

"And hungry, too. Father spoiled his supper with his courteous remarks," added Everett.

"Come, my dear boy; no one is more welcome to this whole house," Victoriano said, with true Spanish hospitality, much intensified by present circumstances. "Come; father will soon be here. At present, Mercedes, Madame Halier Milord and myself only are at home. Mother and the rest are at the Mechlins. Come in; come, Retty."

"No. I'll say good-by to Clary now and walk home."

"But this is awful," Victoriano said, as if beginning to realize the situation. "For Heaven's sake, where are you going? And why must you go?"

"I will not if Mercedes does not send me away. If she does, I shall go first to San Francisco, and thence God only knows where," was Clarence's reply.

"She won't send you away; she shan't. If you only knew how the poor little thing cried, so that this morning literally she could not see out of her eyes, you would then know how she feels. She told me that if she lost all hope of being your wife she would lie down and die. She felt better this morning when father left, as he told her he would arrange everything with you so that the wedding should not be postponed. Then she was comforted and went to sleep. But— " And Victoriano stopped.

"But what? Better tell me all, dear Tano," said Clarence.

"Well, I was going to say that she is again unhappy because Lotte and Rosy told her what your father said. She had not heard that part of the trouble before."

Clarence stood silent with one foot upon the first step. He was calculating the chances against him. He turned to Victoriano, and, with a sickly smile that was truly painful to see, said:

"My heart misgives me, dear Tano; I cannot blame her if she considers my father's words unpardonable."

"But they were not *your* words," Everett interposed. "You are not to blame if your father forgets *himself* and makes a brute of *himself*. I almost hate him. Courage, dear Clary."

"Yes, remember, 'Faint heart never won fair lady,'" Victoriano added, and the quotation brought such sweet recollections to poor Clarence's troubled mind, that he staggered as he went up the steps. But, with a renewed effort over himself, he managed to stand firmly, and to say to Everett:

"I suppose we must part now, dear brother."

Everett threw his arms around him, and for a few moments both brothers held each other in close, silent embrace.

"Cheer up, boys. Don't think you are to part," said Victoriano, with assumed cheerfulness. "You must come to breakfast with us to-morrow Retty. When father comes he and Clary will concoct some plan so as not to postpone the wedding. Come, I'll take you home. I'll let Mercedes know first that Clarence is here." So saying he walked into the house. Returning in a few moments, he said:

"Walk in, Clary. Mercedes will be in the parlor in a minute. Now, Retty, I'll take you home."

While both drove to the Darrells, Clarence went in the parlor to wait with beating heart Mercedes' coming. He walked about the room looking at every object in it without seeing anything. When he heard the rustle of her dress, he stood by the piano with his arms crossed over his breast as if trying to compress the wild throbbing of his heart. He was pale to the lips and his eyes had an expression of longing, of beseeching tenderness, that was far more sad and eloquent than tears would have been. Mercedes came in, followed by her faithful Milord, who, seeing that Clarence paid no attention to him, turned up his nose in mild resentment and went to lie down upon the rug in front of the fire-place. She offered to Clarence her hand in silence. In silence he took it, kissed it and led her to a sofa, sitting down by her side. She was the first to speak. Looking into his eyes, she said:

"Clarence, must we part? I have such, faith in your truth that I believe you will candidly tell me your opinion, even if it kills both of us. Am I right?"

"My darling, what is it? Do not put me to a test that may be too hard, for I tell you frankly I can give up my life, but not my love. Not you! my own! Oh, no; anything but that. Not that." So saying, he took both her hands— the beauty of which he so loved— and kissed them warmly, all the time fearing that if she said to him that she must break off their engagement, he must submit, as he could not blame her if she considered him beneath her love. "What is it you wish to ask me? Oh, my angel! be merciful!"

"I wish to ask you what must I do when your father has said such frightful things to my papa? Am I obliged and in duty bound to decline a tie which will create any relationship with him?"

Clarence was silent, still holding the dear little hands. His face flushed with shame, but became pale again as he replied:

"It would have been more difficult to solve that problem if my father himself had not done so by driving me off. I am exiled now— driven away from home. I doubt whether he would consider you related to him by being my wife now."

"I am glad of that," said she, quickly, but then checking herself, and a little abashed by what she thought the hasty expression of a selfish feeling, she said: "Forgive me; I don't mean I am glad he should drive you away, but that since he has cut you off— and yet— he cannot do that. How can he?"

"He has done so. That proves he can, doesn't it?"

"No, Clarence. No matter what he does he is still your father."

Clarence leaned his head back on the sofa and looked at the chandelier in silence for some moments, then said:

"Yes, he is my father, but not the father he used to be. There are different kinds of fathers. Some are kind and good, others are most unnatural and cruel. Are they entitled to the same love and respect?"

"But was he ever cruel to you before?"

"Never. He has been always most kind and indulgent to all his children, but especially so to Alice and myself."

"Then, Clarence, for this one fault, all his life of kindness and devotion must not be forgotten."

"Oh, my darling! are you going to plead for him and forget my misery? My heart is bleeding yet with the pain of leaving home, and if your indulgence to him means that I must bear the burden of his fault, *I then—I must suffer alone*!"

"I do not wish you to suffer at all. If there is to be any suffering, I shall share it with you. No. All I say is that if Mr. Darrell is so angry at my papa and myself, we had better postpone our wedding until— "

Clarence sprang to his feet, and with hands pressed to his forehead, began pacing the room, greatly agitated, but without speaking a word.

"Clarence, hear me. It will only be for a little while."

He shook his head, and continued his walk— his mind a prey to the wildest despair.

"Would it not be very unbecoming for us to marry now, and your family not be present at the wedding?"

"Why shouldn't they be present? All would be but father, and in the furious state of his feelings he had better be away— a great deal better— far, far away."

"Since he is so furious, I don't think he would like his wife and children to be at our wedding."

"Mercedes, tell me frankly," said he, resuming his place at her side: "tell me, has my father's outrageous conduct made me lose caste in your estimation? If so, I shall not blame you, because when a man acts so ungentlemanly, so ruffianly, it is fair to suppose that his sons might do the same."

"Never! Such an idea never entered my mind. How could it?" said Mercedes, with great earnestness.

"If it did not, it is because you are good and generous. Still, perhaps, it is selfish in me to keep you to your engagement with the son of such a rough. I release you, Mercedes. You are free," he said, and he closed his eyes and leaned his head again on the back of the sofa. A sensation of icy coldness came over him, and he thought that death must come like that. But for all that mental agony, he still thought Mercedes would be right in rejecting him.

The whole scene as described to him by Everett, when his father was uttering those low insults to Don Mariano, came vividly before him, and he thought it would be impossible for Mercedes not to feel a sense of humiliation in uniting herself to him— he, the son of that brutish fellow— that rough. He arose, and his pallor was so great that Mercedes thought he must be ill.

"Mercedes, we part now. Heaven bless you."

"Clarence, you are ill. What do you mean? Will you not wait for papa?"

"No. I had better go now."

"You misunderstood me, I think, else how could you think of going?"

"Did you not say that our wedding had better be postponed? And does that not mean that it may never, *never* be?"

"Why should it mean that?"

"Because, how can we measure the duration of an anger so senseless? It might last years. No, Mercedes, I feel that you have the right to reject me. I shall be so very wretched without you, that I would beg and entreat, but— "

"Clarence, I do not reject you, and I have no right, no wish, to do so. Please do not say that."

"Will you be mine— my wife— after all the ruffianly words my father has said?"

"Certainly. Why should I blame you?"

"My own, my sweet wife. Oh! how dearly I love you! The strength of my love makes my heart ache. Will you call me when you think you can consent to our wedding?"

"What do you mean by asking if I will *call* you?"

"I mean that if our marriage is to be postponed, I shall leave you, but shall be ready to obey your call, and I pray I may not wait for it a long time. And I say this, also, that if upon reflection you decide to cast me off, I shall not complain, because— because my father has lowered me. I am not the same Clarence I was two days ago. You cannot feel proud of me now."

"But I do. Please do not say those dreadful things. Why should you go away?"

"Because it is best, as long as our marriage is to be postponed. My presence here will be a cause of irritation to my father, and goodness knows what he might not do in his angry mood. If you would not feel humiliated by marrying me, the best thing would be to have a quiet wedding immediately, with only the members of your family present, and not invite guests at all, and then we would take the steamer to San Francisco, and go to our home there."

"I don't think mamma would consent to that."

"Then, my darling, I must leave you now. I will return to town, and take the steamer which leaves at daylight, I shall abide implicitly by what you decide. Make known your wishes, and I shall obey."

"You are offended, Clarence, and I do not know how I have incurred your displeasure," she said in those tones of her voice which were the most thrilling to him— most sure of going straight to his heart.

Silently he approached her, and kneeling at her feet, he put his arms around the slender and graceful form he idolized so fervently. He rested his head on her shoulder for a few moments, then with a sigh, that seemed to come from his very soul, he said:

"I am not offended, my sweet rosebud, but I am very miserable. Pity me. You see, on my knees I beg you to marry me now— immediately— in two days. If not, I must go now— to-night. Say, will you marry me, as I *beg* of you?"

"Oh, Clarence, why do you ask me? How can I tell? You will have to ask papa and mamma."

"Will they consent?"

"Papa, perhaps; but I fear mamma will not approve of such a hasty marriage."

"That is so. Perhaps I am unreasonable. Good-by, my beloved. Will you call me back soon?"

"Clarence, you are not going? How can you?"

"I must. Do not ask me to remain, under the circumstances, unless it is to make you my wife. I cannot."

He pressed her to his heart in a long, tender embrace. He arose, and gazed at her sweet face so sadly, that she felt a pang of keen distress and apprehension.

"Clarence, do not look at me so sadly. Please remain until papa comes. Do not go. You might never see him."

"I must, or I will lose the steamer. Farewell, my own sweet love."

He clasped her to his heart, and wildly covered her face with kisses. Then, without daring to look back, hurried out of the room into the hall, across the piazza and down the garden-path to the gate, where his phæton had been left by Victoriano, after having taken Everett home.

"She must naturally hesitate to marry the son of a man who can act and has acted as my father did. I cannot blame her. I ought to respect her for it. Oh, pitying God! how wretched I am! Farewell, happiness for me."

Muttering this short soliloquy, Clarence drove quickly down the incline leading to the main road.

When the last sound of his footsteps died away, a feeling of utter desolation rushed upon Mercedes. The silence of the house was appalling. In that silence it seemed to her as if a life of lonely misery was suddenly revealed. To lose Clarence, was to lose happiness forevermore. Shocked and terrified at her loneliness, with no hope of seeing him again, she rushed out and ran to the gate, calling him. She saw that he was driving fast, and would soon be crossing the dry bed of the brook to take the main road. Once there he would be too far to hear her voice. She ran out of the gate and turned to the right into a narrow path that also led to the main road, going across the hill through the low bushes and a few elder trees near the house, thus cutting off more than half the distance. Loudly she called his name, again and again, running in the narrow path as fast as her strength allowed. She heard the sound of the phæton's wheels as they grated harshly on the pebbles of the brook, and then all was silent again.

"Oh, my darling is gone," said she, and the ground swelled and moved under her feet, and the trees went round in mad circles, and she knew no more. She had fallen down fainting, with no one near her but her faithful Milord, who had followed her, and now nestled by her side.

Clarence had heard her voice call to him, and tried to turn his horses immediately, but they were going down the hill too fast to turn without danger of upsetting; he saw he must first get to the foot of the hill, and turn when he reached the brook. He did so, and with heart-throbs of renewed hope, he re-ascended the hill and hurried to the house. At the door he met Madam Halier, who was blinking at the hall lamp as if just awakened from a sound sleep. Clarence asked for Miss Mercedes.

"I think madamoiselle has just gone down to Madame Mechlin's. I heard her calling Tano, and that woke me up. I had just dropped off into a short nap of five minutes— *just* five minutes."

"I thought I heard her voice in this direction," said Clarence, pointing to the opposite side.

"Oh, no. I think she was afraid to go to Mrs. Mechlin's alone, and she called her brother. But she has been anxious to see you all day. I will send a servant to say you have come. Walk in. Had you a pleasant drive from town?"

"Madam, I have seen Miss Mercedes since my return from town. I had said farewell, and was driving away, when I thought I heard her voice calling me. Perhaps I was mistaken, but I think not. Where has she gone, I wonder?"

"To Madam Mechlin's, monsieur."

"Be it so. Good-by, madam," said he, extending his hand.

"But will you not wait for madamoiselle?"

"No, madam; if she did not call me, I need not wait."

This time Clarence drove slowly down the hill, looking at both sides of the road, peering under the trees and bushes, still impressed with the idea that he might see her form or hear her voice. The moon was just rising, casting long shadows as it arose, but the shadow of that beloved, graceful form was nowhere to be seen. This added disappointment was added bitterness to his cup of misery, and he began to feel sick in body and mind, and he saw in himself a most wretched outcast.

Tano and Doña Josefa now came and saw the phæton ascending the hill on the other side of the brook.

CHAPTER XXIX.

Hasty Decisions Repented Leisurely.

When Victoriano had left Everett at his front door, exacting the promise that he would come to breakfast with Clarence next morning, he merely delayed long enough to learn that Alice was quiet, and Mrs. Darrell thought that with a night's rest she would be well next day. He then drove back home, and thinking that Clarence was going to stay, left the phæton at the front gate to run down through the side gate to Mrs. Mechlin's, to call his mother and say to her that Clarence had been sent off by his father, and had come to their house to pass the night. But as he hurried through the front garden, Victoriano remembered that the horses had to be put in the stable and taken care of, so he went in the kitchen to tell a servant he must attend to the horses immediately.

"Yes, *patroncito*, I'll do it right away," said the lazy Indian, who first had to stretch himself and yawn several times, then hunt up tobacco and cigarette paper, and smoke his cigarette. This done, he, having had a heavy supper, shuffled lazily to the front of the house, as Clarence was driving down the hill for the second time, and Doña Josefa and Victoriano returning from Mrs. Mechlin, came in through the garden side gate.

"Who is going in that carriage?" was the first question put by Victoriano to Madame Halier.

"It is Monsieur Clarence."

"And where is Mercedes?"

"She called you to go to Madame Mechlin's."

"No such thing," said Victoriano, going to look in the parlor; returning immediately to renew his questions.

But the madame could do no more than repeat all she knew, which was little enough, and that little thoroughly mixed in her mind.

All that Victoriano and Doña Josefa could ascertain, with some clearness, was that Clarence was going, and had come back, thinking that Mercedes had called him, but that on being told that Mercedes had called Tano to accompany her to Mrs. Mechlin's, he had gone away.

"I must overtake Clarence. There is some misunderstanding here, that is plain," said Victoriano, going to the back piazza to call a servant.

This time Chapo came a little quicker, not knowing whether he would be to blame, because the *Americano* went off with his horses before he had time to put them in the stable.

"Bring me my bay horse, saddled, in two minutes, do you hear? Two minutes— not two hours— go quick."

"We cannot find Mercita. She is not in the house," said Doña Josefa to her son, much alarmed.

"She must be, mother. Call the other girls. Look again for her. I must run after Clarence, and learn why he is going, instead of passing the night here."

Fifteen minutes after Clarence had left, Victoriano was galloping behind him, wondering why he could not see him anywhere on the road.

Madame Halier and Doña Josefa continued looking for Mercedes most anxiously, but in vain. George now came up, and joined in the search for the missing girl.

As Victoriano crossed the brook and ascended the hill beyond it, Don Mariano and Gabriel came up into the court-yard. They immediately hurried into the house, Don Mariano knowing that Mercedes would be anxious for him to talk with Clarence.

Doña Josefa and the madame met them at the door, and related as well as they knew all that had occurred. They all agreed that the matter had better be kept from the servants, if possible, and they all went out by the front gate again, since it was useless to search in the direction of Mrs. Mechlin's house. Don Mariano and Gabriel saw George follow the path to the right and disappear. They followed him. George had heard the barking of a dog in the distance, and at first paid no attention to it, but when the barking would be followed by most piteous howls, he listened, and thought he recognized the plaintive whining of Milord. He followed the path, and as he did so, came nearer to the barking, and soon after Milord himself met him, with demonstrations of great satisfaction.

George had no doubt now of finding Mercedes. He let Milord be the guide, and run ahead, he following. In a few minutes he saw something white on the ground, and immediately after recognized Mercedes' form lying motionless across the path, as she had fallen. In a moment George had lifted her insensible form in his arms, calling out he had found her.

Don Mariano ran to him, but Gabriel, being more active, passed him, and was quickly at George's side, gazing anxiously at his sister's face.

"Give her to me, George," said Don Mariano, in a hoarse whisper, for he was so agitated he could scarcely speak. "Give my baby to me."

"Wait a little while. I'll carry her a little longer," said George, holding the unconscious girl.

"Father is too agitated to be steady enough just now," said Gabriel. "I'll carry her."

"Let me see her face, for God's sake! Has she no life?" Don Mariano exclaimed.

"Oh, yes. She has fainted only. We will soon restore her to consciousness. Don't be alarmed. I think the parting with Clarence has nearly killed her— but she is alive," George said.

"But why did they part? Why did he go?" Don Mariano asked.

"That is as much a mystery to me as to you," George replied.

The fainting girl was tenderly placed in her bed, and all the care that loving hearts could bestow was lavished on her. But nearly two hours elapsed before she returned to consciousness. Then, after looking vaguely about the room for some minutes, an expression of pain came over her face, and looking at her father, she asked for Clarence.

"Victoriano has gone to call him," Don Mariano replied, hoping that this little fiction would come true, and believing it would if Victoriano could overtake the fugitive.

"I am so glad," she said, and with a sigh closed her eyes, lying so calmly that it was difficult to see whether she had relapsed into a swoon, or lay so quiet from sheer exhaustion.

In the meantime, he for whose love all this misery was suffered— and who shared it fully— was flying onward as rapidly as a couple of fast thoroughbreds could take him. Victoriano followed at full gallop, confident of overtaking him, or if not, of being in town before the steamer left. But the fates decided it should not be as the heart of the anxious rider wished, and when he rode up to the wharf the steamer was leaving it. He could see its lights moving swiftly away, and hear the shaking and revolving of the wheels on the smooth bay, as the black, floating mass glided off, like a cruel monster swimming away with the happiness of so many loving hearts.

Victoriano stood looking at the steamer with a disappointment so keen that it seemed unbearable. He could have rebelled against any power. Then a sense of realization of the inevitable came like a revelation to him, and he felt overpowered, surrounded by dangers that he might not avoid, because they would come upon him unawares.

In this perturbed state of mind he was still looking at the steamer passing over the moonlit bay, when the freight agent for the steamer came to say that Mr. Darrell had left a note for him, and he would bring it if he waited. Victoriano not only would wait, but followed to the door of the freight office.

The agent said, as he handed the note, that Mr. Darrell had left orders at the stable to keep the two horses and phæton until Don Victoriano sent for them. Eagerly Victoriano read the note. It ran thus:

> DEAR TANO:
> Forgive me for not waiting to bid you good-by. I feared to miss the boat; and since Doña Josefa desired to postpone the wedding, I thought it was best for me to be away, under present circumstances. It would be too unendurable in my painful humiliation to be constantly dreading some other unexpected outbreak from my father. My presence would be a source of irritation to him, which might lead to worse results.
> Say to Don Mariano and Don Gabriel I will write to them as soon as I reach San Francisco, perhaps before. My love to all of you, my good and beloved friends. Heaven bless you all.
> I don't ask you to think kindly of me, for I know you will. I feel sick in mind and body; and how I wish I could have slept

under your hospitable roof.

Tell Retty to write or telegraph how Alice is. I was so disappointed not to find Miss Mercedes when I drove back. I had felt so sure I heard her voice calling me, that I was faint with disappointment and thoroughly heartsick.

Good-by, dear Tano, again. God bless you all.

Ever your true friend,
Clarence.

P. S.— I leave you my horses and phæton

There was nothing for Victoriano to do now but return home. He went to the stable, ordered fresh horses put to the phæton, and leaving his own horse with the other two, said he would send for them when they were thoroughly rested. He went to see Clarence's horses himself to be sure that they were well groomed. Two men were rubbing them down, and he saw that neither of the two fine animals had been hurt by their furious drive. He patted them, and they turned their pretty heads and intelligent eyes, expanding their nostrils as they recognized him.

Victoriano was so depressed that he felt a presentiment of never more seeing Clarence. He looked at the two horses as if they were a last token of his friendship, and he hurried out of the stable and out of town quickly, to be alone with the silent moon and his own thoughts; his thoughts of Alice, of Clarence and Mercedes going with him, as he drove home. But Victoriano's thoughts of those three interesting persons were shared by many others.

Don Mariano and Doña Josefa sat by Mercedes' bedside. Her heavy slumber began to alarm them. She lay motionless, with closed eyelids, but she was not sleeping, for she would open her eyes when they spoke to her.

About midnight Doña Josefa asked her if she had been sleeping. She shook her head and whispered:

"I am waiting for Clarence. He is coming, sitting on a water lily. I see him. I am waiting."

The look of dismay that Doña Josefa exchanged with her husband, revealed to each other their terrible anxiety and dread.

"We must wait for Victoriano, and if Clarence does not come, then we must send for a doctor," Don Mariano whispered.

But Mercedes heard him, and said, scarcely audibly: "He will come. I am waiting. He loves me. He don't want to kill me."

When Victoriano arrived it was near daylight, but Don Mariano was up and came out to meet him. Seeing the phæton with only one occupant, he knew the sad truth. Victoriano gave him Clarence's letter, which he read with the keenest regret, feeling that if he had stayed at home, as Mercedes had begged, Clarence would not have felt compelled to go, but would have been made happy under that roof, as he deserved to be. Vain regrets now. He was gone, and there was nothing to be done but wait until he arrived at San Francisco. It would only be a matter of three days, Don Mariano tried to argue to himself, but the experiences of the last two days had taught him how much mischief might be effected in a very short space of time.

When he returned to Mercedes' room he found that she was sleeping, but her sleep was restless, and now a high fever had set in. Her cheeks were like red roses, and her pulse beat with telegraphic velocity. She moaned and moved her head, as if it pained her, but did not awake. It was evident that a doctor must be sent for immediately.

Victoriano never drove or rode past Darrell's house without looking at a certain window next to that of Clarence's room. As he came from town now, before driving into the court of his own house, he looked towards the well-known window. His heart beat with alarm, seeing a light through the shutters. Alice must be ill, he thought, and that light has been burning all night. The lover's heart had guessed the truth. Alice was ill with a raging fever, and when daylight came, instead of the fever passing off, as Mrs. Darrell had hoped, she became delirious.

Victoriano did not go to bed. He preferred to walk out to the front piazza and have another look at that window of Alice's room. Yes the light was still burning. He felt sure that she was ill. Was she to be sick, and he not able to see her? or inquire for her? How angry he felt at old Darrell. Poor Tano, he was a prey to contending emotions. He now wished to see Mercedes, and had told his father that he would lie in one of the hammocks in the veranda, instead of going to bed, so that he would be called to Mercedes' room as soon as she awoke.

Presently Don Mariano came and said to him: "Victoriano, Mercedes is awake, but so entirely out of her head that she does not know any one of us. We must send for a physician."

"I will go at once," Victoriano said, jumping to his feet.

"No, you have been up all night. We don't want too many sick to take care of. Gabriel will go."

Victoriano looked towards the fascinating window, and hesitating a little, said:

"I am afraid Alice is sick too. Evidently a light has been burning in her room all night. She fainted when Clarence was leaving them, and for the last two days she has been so nervous, Everett says, that she was almost in convulsions."

"There is some one going out in Clarence's buggy. Perhaps they are sending for a doctor," Don Mariano said.

"I believe it," Victoriano said, watching the buggy. "It is Everett. Alice is ill, I am sure. Retty is coming this way."

Everett was driving fast, and in a very few minutes was at the gate, and coming to the piazza.

"I ventured to come up," he said, "because I saw you here. It is a most unchristian hour to go into a neighbor's house."

"Is Alice sick, Retty?" Victoriano asked, without heeding Everett's apology for coming.

"Yes, she has a high fever, and is very delirious. I am going for a doctor, but as she has been calling for Clarence most piteously, mother thought he would come to see her."

Don Mariano and Victoriano turned several shades paler than they were before, but they related to Everett what had happened, as far as they knew. Still the reason *why* Clarence left must yet remain a mystery to them until Mercedes could explain it.

Everett was greatly disconcerted and pained. He had hoped to find Clarence, and as his father seemed moved and grieved at Alice's illness, all the family inferred that he would be only too glad to see Clarence restored to them.

"I must hurry for a doctor," said Everett, with trembling lips, "and when Clarence arrives in San Francisco he will find a telegram awaiting him there."

"He will find two," said Don Mariano.

"He can never stay away if he knows that Miss Mercedes and Alice are sick— sick with grief at his going from us," Everett said; adding: "are you not going to send for a physician for Miss Mercedes?"

"Yes; Gabriel will go very soon," Don Mariano replied.

"Who is your doctor? Can't I call him for you?"

On being told the doctor's name, Everett said that he was the one he proposed to bring for Alice. Don Mariano then wrote a line asking the doctor to come, and Everett hurried off on his sad errand.

Clarence had passed the night on deck, walking about in the moonlight, or sitting down to muse by the hour, with no one near— no company but his thoughts. He felt ill and weary, but wakeful, and could not bear to lie down to rest. He must be moving about and thinking. He felt convinced that his father had some *other* cause of irritation than the mere fact of the land having been paid for, but what that cause could be he had not the remotest idea. Then his thoughts would go back to their center of attraction, and pass in review, over and over again, the last scene at the Alamar house, and every word that Mercedes had said. The more he reflected upon them, the clearer it seemed to him that Mercedes could not help thinking it would be humiliating to marry him, for how could a lady marry the son of a man who used such low language? And if she did, out of the purest devotion and tenderest love, could she avoid a feeling of loathing for such a man? Certainly not; and such a man was his father; and Clarence's thoughts traveled around this painful circle all night.

On arriving at Wilmington, he heard the puffing of the little tug boat, coming to ferry the passengers to Los Angeles. He had nothing to do at Los Angeles, but he would go with the passengers, rather than wait all day in the steamer at anchor, rolling like a little canoe, and whose fate was too much like his own— as he, too, was tossing over a broad expanse, a boundless ocean, like a block of wood, helpless, compelled to obey, as though he was an infant. He took a cup of coffee, and joined the passengers on the little tug boat, which was soon meandering over the shallow, muddy creek, or rather swamp, with its little crooked channels, which is to be made into an harbor, with time, patience and money.

At Los Angeles a surprise awaited Clarence, an incident which, coming after those of the previous night, was delightful, indeed. He was sauntering past a hotel, when he heard the well known voice of Fred Haverly, calling him.

"You are the very man I came to see. I am now expecting at any moment, a dispatch from Hubert in answer to my inquiry for your whereabouts," Fred said, conducting Clarence to his room, where they could talk business without being interrupted.

The business which brought Fred up from the mines was soon explained, and in conclusion Fred said:

"I wish you could go with me, see the ores yourself, and talk with the men who wish to buy the mines. But the weather is frightfully hot, and you are not looking well. What is the matter? May I inquire?"

Clarence soon told Fred all that had happened at home, and how he was exiled, and did not care where he went. Fred was truly distressed, for he had never seen Clarence take anything so much to heart and be so cast down.

"I'll tell you what we had better do to-day. Let us take a carriage, and go for a drive among the orange groves. Then we will come back to dinner. After dinner we will kill time somehow for a couple of hours, then you go to bed. To-morrow you will decide what to do."

"But to-morrow there will be no steamer to take me to San Francisco."

"Then wait for the next. The matters you have under consideration are too important to decide hastily."

"That is true. I wish some one had reminded me of that fact last evening. I'll let the steamer go, and if I do not decide to go with you, I'll take the next boat. But now, as to our drive, I think I would rather have it after I had some breakfast, because I begin to feel faint, having eaten nothing for twenty-four hours."

Clarence sat down to a very nice breakfast, but did not succeed in eating it. He had no appetite. All food was distasteful to him. They had their drive and dinner, and he managed to get some sleep. This, however, did not refresh him, and he felt no better. Still, he decided to go to see his "*bonanza*," and talk with the men who wished to buy the mines. If he did not sell them, Fred thought stamp mills ought to be put up, as the ore heaps were getting to be too high and too numerous and very rich.

Clarence devoted that day to writing letters. He wrote to his mother, Alice and Everett, to George, Gabriel and Victoriano; but his longest letters were to Mercedes and Don Mariano.

On the following day he and Fred took the stage for Yuma. When they reached that point, the river boat was about to start, thus Clarence and Fred lost no time in going up the river to their mines. But as the navigation up the Colorado River, above Fort Yuma, was rather slow, having to steam against the current following the tortuous channel of that crooked, narrow stream, and the mines were more than three hundred miles from Yuma (about thirty from Fort Mojave), they did not arrive as soon as they would have wished, and Clarence had been stricken down with typhoid fever before they reached their camp.

CHAPTER XXX.

Effect of Bad Precept and Worse Example.

The whir of threshing machines was heard in the valleys of the Alamar rancho, and wagons loaded with baled hay went from the fields like moving hills. The season had been good, and the settlers, forgetting their past conduct, were beginning to calculate on the well-known good nature and kind heart of the Don, to get their lands by purchasing them from him at a low price and easy terms when he got his patent.

Gasbang and Mathews were the only ones who still slandered the entire Alamar family, in the vilest language, having for their instigator and legal adviser the little lawyer, Peter Roper, *protegé* of Judge Lawlack and partner of Colonel Hornblower.

Everybody in San Diego knew that Roper had made for himself a most discreditable record, unblushingly vaunting of his degradation, but because he managed first to become a partner to the pompous Colonel Hornblower, and then— "for some secret service unexpressed"— to be a special favorite of Judge Gryllus Lawlack, Roper was not only tolerated but well treated. Even among the respectable people of San Diego Roper had clients who, when he was intoxicated, or when he was obliged to keep his bed because, as it often happened, he had been too severely whipped in some drunken brawl, would patiently wait for him to get sober and on his feet again. Why did those respectable people employ such a low, disreputable character? strangers in town asked. The answer was: "*Because Roper says he has so much influence with the Judge?*" And verily Roper, intoxicated or sober, won his cases, for when in ignorance of the law, he made any mistakes, which he generally did, being only an amateur lawyer, the Judge, with his rulings, would remedy the harm done, thus unwittingly, or not, assisting Roper, giving him a seemingly good cause to boast that he had *retained the Judge*, and by so boasting get clients. Of course, many of Judge Lawlack's decisions were constantly reversed, but the serene majesty of the law in his Honor's breast was not in the least disturbed by this; on the contrary, he spoke jestingly about being constantly reversed, and said jokingly to lawyers that if they desired to win their suits they should not wish him to decide in their favor, as the Supreme Court was sure to reverse him.

Nevertheless, on the strength of his vaunted influence with the Judge, Roper had gone to the Alamar rancho to solicit the patronage of the settlers. He was willing to take contingent fees, he said, as he was sure to win.

"But what if your friend, the Judge, is reversed, as he always is?" Roper would be asked.

"Well, then we will make a motion for a new trial, or we will call the same suit by some other name, and file a new complaint, or do something else, so as to keep in possession of the property. Possession, as long as it lasts, is ownership."

"But in the end you don't win?"

"Who says we don't? Isn't it to win if you keep in possession as long as you live? Or, any way, as long as *my Judge* is in office? And in office he shall be, for I shall keep him there, if I have to swill whisky by the barrel in election times, see if I don't."

And with this low bragging and bar-room swagger Roper managed to impose upon people, saying that his influence kept the Judge in office, because he had advocated his cause and worked to have him elected. So, with his delusive sophistry, Peter got clients among the Alamar settlers. While making inquiries about the Alamar lands he came across the entry made by Don Mariano of the land sold to Clarence. This discovery he communicated to Gasbang, and we have seen what resulted.

Now these two worthies were rejoicing at the effect they had caused, and would have been happier had they known the full extent of the misery they had inflicted. They guessed enough, however, to furnish them with matter for their coarse jests, and Roper got intoxicated to celebrate his triumph. He, of course, came out of the tavern with a black eye, but being the chosen friend and political *factotum* of the Judge, this public degradation was kindly condoned, and San Diego threw its cloak over the prostrate Roper, as usual, when overcome by whisky.

It would have seemed unbearable to Darrell if he had known how amused and pleased Roper and Gasbang were to know that they had brought trouble to the Alamares, and made him ridiculous. This additional misery, however, was fortunately spared to the already much-afflicted, proud spirit. But, indeed, he suffered enough to have satisfied the most relentless *Nemesis*. No one guessed the extent of his misery. In fact, Clarence was the only one who suspected the existence of some secret source of irritation goading him, and had that kind son been permitted to remain at home, he would have coaxed and persuaded his father to say what was torturing him. For torture it was—mental and physical. A band of purple and black encircled his body, and his arms were of that same hue from the elbow to the shoulder. The bruises made by the tight coil of the *reata* had left a narrow ring, which became blacker as it grew daily wider and wider. He had done nothing to relieve the soreness, and he went about aching so much that he could scarcely walk, and with a fever to intensify his pains, he was indeed a wretched man. But all this physical suffering was nothing compared to the mental distress of being bereft of his wife's cherished society. He knew that Mrs. Darrell was grieved to think that he was the cause of all the unhappiness brought upon two innocent families, and this thought almost made him crazy.

He was willing to accept his bodily aches as a retributive penance for his cruelty to Clarence, but to endure the loneliness of his room when his infirm body could hardly bear the weight of his bitter remorse, that indeed seemed beyond human strength. He would go to his solitary bedroom, close the door, and extend his aching, bruised arms in silent appeal, in mute supplication to the adored wife who was now in another room, at the bedside of Alice, forgetful of the entire world except the suffering child before her, and the exiled one, for the sight of whom her heart yearned with aching pulsations.

And where was he, the best beloved, now? He lay on a sick bed, delirious, with a raging fever that seemed to be drying the very fountain of his young life. They had not made a very quick trip to Yuma, for the hot sands of the desert seemed to burn through the very hoofs of the horses, and they were obliged to stop at ten o'clock A.M., and not resume their journey until past three in the afternoon. The exposure to this excessive heat was more than Clarence had strength to endure, for he was already ill when he arrived at Los Angeles. He was only partially conscious when they arrived at the mine, and Fred now gave all his time and attention to the care of his friend. By a great effort of his mind, Clarence had succeeded in impressing upon Fred that he was, on no consideration whatever, to tell to his family or write to anybody in San Diego that he was ill. "They must not be made anxious," he whispered. "If I get well, I'll tell them myself; if I die, they'll know it soon enough." He closed his eyes, and in a short time delirium had come to make him forget how miserable he was.

Immediately Fred telegraphed to Hubert to send the best physician he could induce to come to that terribly hot climate. No money or trouble was spared, for the two brothers valued Clarence too highly to neglect anything that might be for his benefit. The doctor went at once. The sum of five thousand dollars was paid down to him, and five thousand more he would get on his return after leaving Clarence out of danger, if he lived.

In the meantime, his letters, sent from Los Angeles, had arrived at Alamar, and were answered immediately. In his letters to Gabriel and George, Clarence had explained that his absence must not make any difference in the business arrangement they had made, and the projected bank would be established by George whenever he thought fit to do so— whenever the prospect of the Texas Pacific Railroad justified it. For this purpose, and to pay for the cattle sent to the mines, he had instructed his banker to pay to Don Mariano three hundred thousand dollars.

Gabriel replied, thanking him, and saying that he would adhere to the original plan of going to San Francisco by the first of October, when he hoped Mercita would be out of danger. If Clarence could only have read these letters!

George answered him that he did not intend returning to New York until Mercita got better (Elvira not wishing to leave home while her sister was yet in danger), but that he would be ready to return to California and establish their projected bank at any time that the business outlook justified it; that the chances seemed much in favor of the Texas Pacific, and all were hopeful. If Clarence could only have read this!

Don Mariano wrote a cheerful letter, telling him to return at once. The fact of the matter was that he confidently expected to see Clarence's bright face very soon; to see those eyes of his, with their brilliant glow of kindness, emanating from a generous, manly heart. How could it be otherwise when all that was necessary would be to recall him, and recalled he had been?

But days and days passed, and Clarence did not come, nor any letters from him either, and the month of September, which was to have brought so much happiness, had been passed in sadness, and was now ending in gloom.

Mercedes and Alice were no longer delirious, but their condition was still precarious, and the anxious parents could not lay aside their fears.

Thus the month of October passed, and November came, bringing the United States Surveyors to measure the Alamar rancho in accordance with the decree of the United States District Court. This advent, though fully expected, did not fail to agitate the settlers of Alamar. It brought before their minds the fact that the law, though much disregarded and sadly dilatory, did sometimes, as if unawares, uphold the right.

Gasbang and Mathews, inspired by Roper, were very active in trying to urge the settlers to some open demonstration. Roper wanted lawsuits, and he saw a chance now to originate several; but the settlers were rather disposed to be quiet, and disposed to wait until the survey was finished and approved, for, after all, what had they to do? The Don took no steps to eject them. What pretext had they to complain?

"I expect we will have to kick *him* out of his own house," said Peter Roper, and laughed, thinking it would be such a good joke to do that; "and by — —, if you only show me the ghost of a chance, we'll do it!"

"Why are you the Don's enemy, Roper? Did he ever do you any injury?" Romeo asked.

"Oh, my! No; why should he? I am nobody's enemy; but if I can make any money by kicking him out of his house, don't you suppose I'd do it? You don't know me if you think I wouldn't," was Roper's characteristic reply.

But his sharp yellow eyes clearly saw that Gasbang and Mathews were the only ones really anxious to be aggressive, yet aggressive only according to the natural bent of their dispositions. Mathews was unscrupulous, vicious and murderous; Gasbang, unscrupulous, vicious and cowardly— he would use no weapons but the legal trickery of Roper, aided by the indulgence of Judge Lawlack's friendship. In fact, Judge Lawlack was a host in himself, and when that host was led on to battle by the loquacious Roper against clients who had only justice and equity on their side, everybody knew that Roper's brow would be crowned with honorable laurels of fraud and falsehood and robbery, while innocent people were cruelly despoiled and left homeless. This, however, was (according to Roper) the *secret bargain* between Judge Gryllus Lawlack and his favorite. This shameful debauchery of judicial power was the wages of the *political factotum*; and Roper unblushingly acknowledged it, and *boasted* of it— boasted openly, in his moments of exultation, when he had imbibed more whisky than was consistent with discretion; when he would become loquacious, and following the law of his being, which impelled him to swagger and vaunting, he longed to make known to people his "*influence with the Court.*" Wishing at the same time that he was facetious, to be considered a wit, he would relate several stories illustrative of *his power over the Judge*. One of these stories was that of two litigants, who had had a lawsuit for a long time; at last, one litigant came to the other and said:

"See here; you had better compromise this suit. Don't you see, on my side I have the law, the equity, the money and the talent?"

"Very true," answered the other. "You have the law, the equity, the money and the talent, but *I have the Judge.*"

And Roper would laugh, thinking himself very funny, and with a wink would say: "Didn't I tell you I run this whole town? Of course I do, because *I have the Court in my pocket.* Give us another drink." And he staggered for more whisky.

Could the Judge ignore that his name and office were thus publicly dragged in the mire? Certainly not, but he would merely remark that "Mr. Roper was joking," seeing no disgraceful reflection upon himself.

In the full reliance of secured power, Gasbang and Roper decided that they would do nothing while the survey of the rancho was going on, but would watch and wait for developments, and then, relying upon the Judge's friendship to serve their purpose, start some plot to rob the Alamares or the Mechlins.

"Yes, we will watch and pray, brother John," Roper said, with a nasal twang. Gasbang was a church deacon.

But Mathews had no Judge Lawlack to bedraggle justice for his sake. So while Gasbang and Roper were jubilant, he became gloomy and morose. He could not give vent to his ill humor by shooting stray cattle now; not that he liked Clarence any better than he liked the Don, but he had promised Darrell not to shoot his son's cattle, and he could not afford to break his promise and make an enemy of so useful a man as Darrell. So Mathews went back to his old love of whisky, and as his whisky was of the cheapest, burning poison circulated in his veins. Miss Mathews, his maiden sister, was seriously alarmed, observing her brother's ways of late, and would kindly remonstrate against his drinking such poor liquor.

"For you see, William, all liquor is bad, but bad liquor is worse," the poor old maid would say, in unconscious aphorism, pleading with her hardened brother to the best of her ability.

One morning, when Mathews had been on a debauch of several days' duration, Miss Mathews walked over to Mrs. Darrell, and apologizing for not having been to see Alice, because she had had so much trouble at home, said she wished to speak to Mr. Darrell. On being told by Jane— who received her— that her father had gone to the fields where grain was being threshed, she left word that she would thank Mr. Darrell to call on her that evening. Agreeable to this request, Mr. Darrell started for Mathews' house after supper.

Slowly Darrell went over the field and across the little hollow where Gabriel had taken him off his horse. Then he followed the path he had galloped with the *reata* around his body, and came to the road where he had met the Don and tried to strike him. This was the first time Darrell had been over this ground since that memorable day which was now recalled to his mind so painfully. He wondered how he could have been so blind, such a fool, not to take the right view of Clarence's actions. Ah! and where was Clarence now, that beloved first-born boy, of whom he was so proud? In this sad meditation, with head bowed down most dejectedly, Darrell followed the path until he came to a fence. He looked up and saw this was the south side of Mr. Mechlin's garden. He turned around the southeast corner and followed along the fence, remembering that going by that path he would shorten the distance to Mathews' house. For a few rods Darrell walked in the path, but not wishing to be seen by the Mechlins, he left the path and walked close to the fence, hidden by a row of olive trees. Presently he heard a man's voice, talking and walking up and down the piazza. On the next turn he saw it was George Mechlin carrying his baby boy in his arms, kissing him at every few words.

Darrell was pleased to see the young man kissing his child so lovingly. It reminded him of his young days when he held his own first boy like that. Then he felt a pang shoot through his heart as he thought that if it had not been for his wicked folly, Clarence in another year might have held his own child, too, in his arms, as George was now holding his, and that baby would have been his own grandchild! Darrell trembled with the strength of his keen remorse— a remorse which now constantly visited him, invading his spirit with relentless fury, like a pitiless foe that gave no quarter. He leaned against the fence for support and stood still, wishing to watch George caressing his baby. Meantime, George continued his walking, his talking and caressing, which Darrell could hear was occasionally reciprocated by a sweet little cooing from the baby. Elvira came out on the piazza now, and he heard her say:

"Indeed, George, that baby ought to be in bed now. See, it is after seven, and he is still awake. You keep him awake."

Mr. Mechlin also came out and took the baby, saying he, too, must have a kiss. Then Mrs. Mechlin followed, and Caroline, and all caressed the baby, showing how dearly they loved the little thing, who took all the petting in good part, perfectly satisfied.

At last Elvira carried him off to bed, and Darrell saw George and Mr. Mechlin go into the library and sit by the center-table to read. He then, with down-cast eyes, continued his walk towards Mathews' house.

He found Miss Mathews alone, with eyes that plainly showed sad traces of tears, she was sitting by the lamp darning her brother's stockings, which, like those of Darrell himself, had always holes at the heels, for the tread of both was alike, of that positive character which revealed an indomitable spirit, and it soon wore out the heels of their socks.

After the customary inquiries for the health of the family, and the usual remarks about the crops being good, Miss Mathews went on to say that she could no longer bear the state of her mind, and thought it was her duty to tell Mr. Darrell her fears, and prevent mischief that might occur, if her brother was not spoken to by somebody.

"What mischief do you fear?" Darrell asked.

"Well, you see— I can scarcely explain— for, after all, it might be all talk of William, when he has drank that horrible whisky."

"What does he say?"

"Well, you see, he is awful sore about the appeal being dismissed, and he blames it all on Mr. George Mechlin, and says he ought to be *shot dead*, and all other horrible talk. And now, since the surveyors came, he is worse, saying that the Don will drive us off as soon as the survey is finished!"

"He will do nothing of the sort. He is too kind-hearted," Darrell said, and he felt the hot blush come to his face— the blush of remorseful shame.

"That's what I think, but William don't, and I wish you would talk encouragingly to him, for he is desperate, and blames Congress for fooling settlers. He says Congress ought to be killed for fooling poor people into taking lands that they can't keep, and Mr. Darrell I hope you will talk to him. What is that?"

She started to her feet, and so did Darrell, for the report of a rifle rang loud and distinct in the evening air.

"That is William's rifle. I hope he did not fire it," she said.

Darrell went to the door to listen for another shot, but none was heard, so he came back and resumed his seat.

"Three times I have taken that very rifle from William. He was going to shoot cattle, he said, and I had to remind him that the cattle now belong to your son."

Steps were heard now, and Mathew's face peered through the window. Miss Mathews gave a half-suppressed shriek, and dropped her sewing. Her brother's face looked so ghastly pale that it frightened her. He pushed the door and came in.

"What makes the old maid shriek like a fool?" said he.

"Your death-like face," Darrell replied.

"Nonsense!" he said, going to a side-table to pour out whisky from a demijohn he took from under it.

"Oh, William! for pity's sake! don't drink more," she begged. "It will make you crazy, I am sure."

"Anybody might suppose I have drank a river, to hear the old hag talk like that," he snarled.

"You have not said good evening to Mr. Darrell."

"You don't give me a chance, with your infernal chatter. Mr. Darrell knows he is welcome," he said, without looking at him.

"Where is your rifle, William?" she asked.

With an oath he turned and glared at her, with distorted features.

"It is none of your business where it is. Have I to give you an account of everything?"

"I thought you might have loaned it to somebody, for we heard it fired a little while ago."

"Is there no rifle but mine in this valley?"

"I am sorry to say there are plenty, but I know the report of yours. I never mistake it for any other."

Mathews became so enraged, hearing this, and so violent and abusive in his language, that Darrell had to interfere to silence him.

"If you talk like that to your sister, I would advise her not to stay alone in this house with you," Darrell said; "her life might be in danger."

"I wish the devil would take the old hag," he retorted. "She torments my life. I hate her."

"What is the matter with you, Billy?" Darrell asked. "Why are you so excited?"

"It makes me mad to hear her nonsense," he said, in a calmer voice, but still much agitated, and he again went to pour himself another drink.

Miss Mathews whispered hurriedly to Darrell: "Take away his rifle."

"Neighbor Mathews," said Darrell, "I want to send my rifle to have it fixed, will you lend me yours for a few days?"

"Take it," said he gruffly, then folding his arms on the table and leaning his head upon them, immediately sunk into a heavy sleep.

"Take the rifle with you now, Mr. Darrell, he might change his mind when he awakes. I'll bring it directly," said Miss Mathews, hurrying out of the room. Presently she returned, and in her dejected countenance keen disappointment was depicted. Dropping into her seat she whispered: "The rifle is not in the house. Somebody has taken it and fired it. I am sure that was the shot we heard. I know the ring of it."

"I'll go and see. Perhaps I'll find out who fired it," Darrell said, walking towards the front door, followed by Miss Mathews, who preferred to make a few parting suggestions outside, not sure of Billy's soundness of sleep.

As both stepped outside the first object that met their eyes was Billy's rifle, peacefully reclining against the window.

Darrell took it up and looked at Miss Mathews perplexed. She was looking at him aghast.

The undefined fears that neither one expressed were only too well founded. The rifle had been fired, and fired by Mathews with murderous intent. For several weeks, instigated by Roper and bad whisky, Mathews had been watching an opportunity to shoot George, because he had the appeal dismissed. This evening he at last saw his chance when George was walking the porch caressing his baby. He could not take good aim while he was walking, but when Elvira at last took the baby away and George walked into the library, then, as he went to put the window down, Mathews aimed at his heart and fired. Fortunately the ball struck the window sash, deflected and glanced down, striking the hip-bone instead of the heart.

Darrell and Miss Mathews were still looking at the rifle, as if expecting that by a close examination they might guess who fired it, when they were startled by Mathews uttering frightful curses and smashing the furniture. The noise brought two hired men, who were smoking their pipes by the kitchen fire, and they helped Darrell to grapple with the maniac and pinion his arms, tying him to a chair.

Miss Mathews was greatly shocked to see her brother crazy, but she had been expecting it. She quietly consented to have him taken to an insane asylum.

CHAPTER XXXI.

A Snow Storm.

George Mechlin's wound was not mortal, but it made it necessary to convey him to town to have medical attendance near at hand, and no doubt it would be of a long and painful convalescence, with the danger, almost a certainty, of leaving him lame for life. This danger was to him far more terrible than death, but he concealed in the deepest recesses of his heart the horror he felt at being a cripple, for he knew the keen anguish that Elvira suffered at the thought of such a probability. Her lovely black eyes would fill with tears, and her lips would tremble and turn white, when he or any one else spoke of the possibility of his being lame. So he had to be consoler, and soothe her grief, and be the one to speak of hope and courage.

There was no possibility of his being able to return to his duties at their bank in New York at present, and he, to cheer Elvira's desponding heart, would say that he could attend to a bank in San Diego.

"Don't be despondent, my pet," he said one day, when she looked very sad; "things will not be so bad, after all, for in the spring I will be well enough to attend to bank business here, even if I cannot stand the trip to New York. With the money that Clarence sent, and with what I will put in myself, we can start quite a solid bank. Gabriel will have learned a good deal by that time, and though I will not walk much, I can be a very majestic President, and give my directions from my arm-chair. All we want is the success of the Texas Pacific— and my uncle writes that Tom Scott is very confident, and working hard."

"But will he succeed?" Elvira asked.

"He has powerful enemies, but his cause is good. The construction of the Texas Pacific ought to be advocated by every honest man in the United States, for it is the thing that will help the exhausted South to get back its strength and vitality."

"Will it really help the South so much?"

"Certainly. Don't we see here in our little town of San Diego how everything is depending on the success of this road? Look at all the business of the town, all the farming of this county, all the industries of Southern California— everything is at a stand-still, waiting for Congress to aid the Texas Pacific. Well, the poor South is in pretty much the same fix that we are. I am sure that there are many homes in the Southern States whose peace and happiness depend upon the construction of the Texas Pacific. Look at our two families. All the future prosperity of the Alamares and Mechlins is entirely based upon the success of this road. If it is built, we will be well off, we will have comfortable homes and a sure income to live upon. But if the Texas Pacific fails, then we will be financially wrecked. That is, my father will, and

Don Mariano will be sadly crippled, for he has invested heavily in town property. For my part, I'll lose a great deal, but I have my bank stock in New York to fall back upon. So my poor father and yours will be the worst sufferers. Many other poor fellows will suffer like them— for almost the entire San Diego is in the same boat with us. It all depends on Congress."

"But why should Congress refuse to aid the Texas Pacific, knowing how necessary the road is to the South? It would be wicked, George, downright injustice, to refuse aid."

"And so it would, but if rumors are true, the bribes of the Central Pacific monopolists have more power with some Congressmen than the sense of justice or the rights of communities. The preamble and resolution which Luttrell introduced last session were a 'flash in the pan,' that was soon forgotten, as it seems. In that document it was clearly shown that the managers of the Central Pacific Railroad Company were guilty of undeniable and open frauds. Enough was said by Luttrell to prove those proud railroad magnates most culpable, and yet with their record still extant, their power in Congress seems greater every year. Still, uncle writes that Tom Scott is to make a big fight this winter, and that his chances are good. I am bound to hope that he'll win."

"But why has he to *fight*? What right have those men of the Central Pacific to oppose his getting Congressional aid? Does the money of the American people belong to those men, that they should have so much to say about how it should be used? Is it not very audacious, outrageous, to come forward and oppose aid being given, only *because they don't want to have competition*? Isn't that their reason?"

"That's all. They have not an earthly *right* to oppose the Texas Pacific, and all their motive is that they *don't want competition* to their Central Pacific Railroad. They have already made millions out of this road, but they want no one else to make a single dollar. They want to grab every cent that might be made out of the traffic between the Atlantic and Pacific Oceans, and they don't care how many people are ruined or how many homes are made desolate in the South or in California."

"Oh, George, but this is awful! If those men are so very rapacious and cruel, what hope have we? They will certainly sacrifice San Diego if their influence in Congress is so great! Poor San Diego! my poor, little, native town, to be sacrificed to the heartless greed of four or five men."

"And what claim have these men upon the American people? Think of that! Have they or their fathers ever rendered any services to the nation? None whatever. All they rely upon is their boldness in openly asking that others be sacrificed, and backing their modest request with money earned out of the road they built with Government funds and Government credit. But they have tasted the sweets of ill-gotten gain, and now their rapacity keeps increasing, and in a few years— if they kill the Texas Pacific— they will want to absorb every possible dollar that might be made on this coast. The only thing that will put a check upon their voracity is the Texas Pacific. If this is killed, then heaven knows what a Herculean work the people of this coast will have to destroy this hydra-headed monster, or in some way put a bit in each of its many voracious mouths."

"I am awfully discouraged, George. I am so sorry that papa put all his money into town property."

"Let us yet hope Tom Scott might succeed."

And thus this young couple went on discussing San Diego's chances of life or death, and their own hopes in the future. They were not the only couple who in those days pondered over the problem of the "*to be or not to be*" of the Texas Pacific. It is not an exaggeration to say that for nearly ten long years the people of San Diego lived in the hope of that much-needed and well-deserved Congressional aid to the Texas Pacific, which *never came!* That aid which was to bring peace and comfort to so many homes, which at last were made forever desolate!

Yes, aid was refused. The monopoly triumphed, bringing poverty and distress where peace might have been!

Yet in those days— the winter of '74-'75— everybody's hopes were bright. No clouds in San Diego's horizon meant misfortune. Not yet!

And of all of San Diego's sanguine inhabitants, none surpassed in hopefulness the three friends who had invested so heavily in real estate, viz.: Mr. Mechlin, Señor Alamar and Mr. Holman. They exhorted all to keep up courage, and trust in Tom Scott.

Many of the cattle sent to Clarence's mines had returned to the rancho from the mountains, and now it was necessary to collect them again and send them back.

Don Mariano himself, accompanied by Victoriano and two of his brothers, would start for the Colorado River, intending to see that the cattle got to the mines safely.

The evening before leaving Victoriano enjoyed the great happiness of seeing Alice by herself and talking to her of his love. For three long months her illness had kept her a close prisoner in her bedroom, and she had not seen Tano.

Now they enjoyed a two hours' *téte-à-téte*, which was very sweet to them, and which pleasure they had not had since Clarence left.

Mercedes' convalescence was very slow. Her despondency at Clarence's absence retarded her recovery. The wounding of George had also impressed her painfully, for she was devotedly attached to him; and now she was worrying about her father having to go away.

Don Mariano told her that as soon as the cattle were on the other side of the mountains he would not feel any apprehension of their running away; that once in the desert they would go straight to the river, but that while in the mountains there was danger of their "*stampeding*" and being lost. She heard all this, but still she dreaded her papa's going out of her sight. She could not forget that had he been at home when Clarence came that last evening all might have been right. She had no faith in human calculations any more. She was sick, and wanted her papa near her.

"I think the best thing you can do is to send Mercita to town, to remain with us while you are away," George had said to Don Mariano, hearing how badly she felt at his going.

"Yes, you are right. The surroundings at the rancho bring to her painful thoughts which will be gloomier when Tano and myself are away. She will have the two babies, of whom she is so fond, to amuse her here," said Don Mariano.

"Besides all of us, the Holman girls will be good company for her," added George.

Mercedes, therefore, was told by her papa that she was to remain with Elvira and Lizzie in town during his absence.

"Papa, darling, I shall not cease to be anxious about you and Tano until I see your dear faces again. I am a thoroughly superstitious girl now. But still, I do agree with you and poor, dear George, that the babies will be a sweet source of consolation to me. Yes, take me to them. I'll play chess or cards with George, and we'll amuse each other. He will read to me; he is a splendid reader; I love to hear him."

Mercedes, therefore, was conveyed to town by her loving father, who went away with a much lighter heart, thinking that she would be less desponding.

The *mayordomo*, with about twenty *vaqueros*, were nearly at the foot of the mountains with twenty-five hundred head of cattle, when Don Mariano and Victoriano overtook them, and as the cattle had been resting there for two days, their journey to the Colorado River would be resumed at daybreak.

The weather had been intensely cold for the last two days, so that the benumbed animals could scarcely walk in the early morning, but now the air felt warmer.

"I fear it is going to rain. We must try to reach the desert and leave the storm behind us," said Don Mariano to his *mayordomo*.

A good day's journey was made that day, and night overtook them as they descended into a small valley, which seemed to invite them to rest within its pretty circumference of well-wooded mountain slopes, from which merry little brooks ran singing and went to hide their music among the tall grasses that grew in rank solitude.

The bellowing of cattle and shouts of the *vaqueros* soon awoke the mountain echoes, and the silent little valley was noisy and crowded with busy life. Camp-fires were quickly lighted, from which arose blue columns of smoke, making the lonely spot seem well populated.

"With a good supper and good night's rest, we will make a long march to-morrow," said the *mayordomo* to Don Mariano. "There is plenty of feed here for our cattle."

"But the weather looks so threatening. I wish we were out of this," said Don Mariano.

"And I, too. We are going to get a wetting," added Tano.

About midnight Don Mariano awoke, startled; he had heard nothing, and yet he awoke with a sense of having been summoned to arise. He sat up and looked around, but saw nothing. The darkness of the sky had changed from inky black to a leaden hue, and the clouds hung down among the tall trees like curtains of ashy gray, draping them entirely out of view. The fires were out, and yet he did not feel cold. He thought it strange that all the fires should have burned out, when they had put on such heavy logs before going to sleep. He struck a light to look at his watch, for he had no idea what the hour might be. By the light he saw that his blankets seemed covered with flour. He brushed off the white dust, and found that snowflakes had invaded even their retreat under the shelter of oak trees.

"There must have been some wind to blow this snow under the thick foliage of these oaks," said he, hurriedly putting his coat and shoes on, these being the only articles of his dress he had removed, "and I did not hear it. How stealthily this enemy came upon us. I fear it will be a winding-sheet for my poor cattle." He now proceeded to awake everybody, and a hard task it was, for the treacherous drowsiness spread over them with that snow-white coverlet was hard to shake off. But he persisted, and when he made believe he was losing his patience, then all arose, slowly, reluctantly, but they were on their feet.

"Come on, boys, let us build fires, fires! Fires under every tree, if we have to put up barricades to keep off snow-drifts. Come on; we must drink coffee all night to keep us awake."

In a short time several fires were started under oak trees which had widely-spreading branches or under pines which clustered together.

Don Mariano had a consultation with his *mayordomo*, and both agreed that it would be best to drive the cattle back for a few miles and wait until the snow had melted sufficiently for them to see the trails, else all might plunge unawares into hidden pitfalls and gulches covered over by snow-drifts.

"Yes, this is our only course," said Don Mariano, "and now we must start them up. Sleep under snow cannot be any better for cattle than it is for men. Let us have some coffee, and then we must whip up and rouse the cattle; they seem dead already; they are too quiet."

He was going back to the tree where he had slept, when he was met by his brother Augustin, who came to say that Victoriano wished to see him.

"What? Still in bed?" said he, seeing Victoriano lying down. "This won't do. Up with you, boy."

"Come here to me, father," said Victoriano's voice, very sadly. His father was quickly by his side.

"What is the matter, my boy?" asked he.

"Father, I cannot stand up. From my knees down I have lost all feeling, and have no control of my limbs at all."

"Have you rubbed them to start circulation? They are benumbed with the cold, I suppose."

"I have been rubbing them, but without any effect, it seems. I don't feel pain though, nor cold either."

This was the saddest perplexity yet. There was nothing to be done but to wait for daylight to take Victoriano home. In the meantime, a fire was made near his bed. His limbs were wrapped in warm blankets; he drank a large cup of warm coffee and lay down to wait for the dawn of day to appear.

As soon as all the herders had drank plenty of warm coffee, all mounted their horses, and the work of rousing the cattle began.

The shouts of the *vaqueros*, bellowing of cattle and barking of dogs resounded throughout the valley, the echo repeating them from hill to hill and mountain side. In a short time everything living was in motion, and the peaceful little valley seemed the battle-ground where a fiercely contested, hand-to-hand fight was raging. The great number of fires burning under the shelter of trees, seen through the falling snow as if behind a thick, mysterious veil, gave to the scene a weird appearance of unreality which the shouts of men, bellowing of cattle and barking of dogs did not dispel. It all seemed like a phantom battle of ghostly warriors or enchanted knights evoked in a magic valley, all of which must disappear with the first rays of day.

Don Mariano and his two brothers also mounted their horses, but remained near Victoriano's bed to keep him from being trampled by cattle that might rush in that direction.

About four o'clock the *vaqueros* had a recess. They had put the cattle in motion, and could conscientiously think of cooking breakfast. By the time that breakfast was over, daylight began to peep here and there through the thick curtains of falling snow. Giving to the *mayordomo* the last instructions regarding the management of the cattle, Don Mariano got Victoriano ready to start on their forlorn ride homeward. It was no easy task to put him in the saddle, but once there, he said he was all right.

"I am a miserable chicken from my knees down, but a perfect gentleman from my knees up. Don't be sad, father; I'll be all right again soon," said he, cheerfully.

The snow had not ceased falling for one moment, and if the *mayordomo* had not been so good a guide they might not have found their way out, for every trail was completely obliterated, and no landmarks could be seen. After a while, Don Mariano himself, aided by a pocket compass, got the bearings correctly. The entire band of cattle were driven back, so that all began their retreating march together, preceded by Victoriano, with his limbs wrapped up in pieces of blanket, an expedient which he found very ridiculous and laughable, suggesting many witticisms to him.

About ten o'clock they came to a grove of oak trees which covered a broad space of ground and afforded good shelter for man and animals. Don Mariano told his *mayordomo* that he thought this would be a good place for him to stay with the stock until the storm had passed, for although the snow might fall on the uncovered ground, there would be shelter for all under the trees.

After resting for an hour and eating a good luncheon, Don Mariano, aided by his brothers, again put Victoriano on horseback and started homeward, all the country being still enveloped in snow. About nightfall the snow was succeeded by rain, and this was much worse, for it came accompanied by a violent wind which seemed as if it would blow them away with their horses. Having left the *mayordomo* and all but one *vaquero* with the cattle, Don Mariano had with him only this one *mozo* to wait on them, and his two brothers to assist him in the care of Tano. The night was passed again under the friendly shelter of trees, but in the morning it was found necessary to ride out into the storm, for now Victoriano's limbs ached frightfully at times, and it was imperative to reach home. This was not done until the following day, when Victoriano's malady had assumed a very painful character, and when Don Mariano himself had taken a severe cold in his lungs. A doctor was immediately sent for, and now Doña Josefa had two invalids more to nurse.

For six weeks Don Mariano was confined to his bed with a severe attack of pneumonia, followed by a lung fever, which clung to him for many days. In the latter part of January, however, he was convalescing. Not so Victoriano; his strange malady kept him yet a close prisoner. When his father was out already, driving and riding about the rancho, poor Tano had to be content with sitting by the window in an arm-chair, and looking at that other window which he knew was in Alice's room. Everett came daily to sit with him, to read to him, or play chess or cards, and he helped the invalid to take a few steps, and little by little, Tano began to walk.

CHAPTER XXXII.

A False Friend Sent to Deceive the Southerners.

"Great men are the Fire Pillars in this dark pilgrimage of mankind; they stand as heavenly signs, ever living witnesses of what has been, prophetic tokens of what may still be— the revealed embodied Possibilities of human nature," says Carlyle.

If conspicuousness or notoriety could mean greatness, we have our *great men* in California. But are they the Fire Pillars in our dark pilgrimage? Verily, no. They are upas trees, blighting life, spreading desolation, ruin, death upon all they overshadow. Only the cruelist irony could designate them as *heavenly signs*, for surely they march before us in the opposite direction from that in which heavenly Fire Pillars would be expected to stand.

And who are the most conspicuous in our State? The *monied men, of course*— the monopolists. They are our *Fire Pillars*! Unfortunate California! if thou art to follow such guides, thy fate shall be to *grovel for money* to the end of time, with not one thought beyond, or above, money-making, and not one aspiration higher than to accumulate millions greedily for rapacity's sake— without once remembering the misery that such rapacity has brought upon so many innocent people— the blight it has spread over so many lives. Thy ambition shall be to control the judiciary and utterly debauch the legislative branch of our Government; to contaminate the public press and private individual until thy children shall have lost all belief in honor, and justice, and good faith, and morality. Until honesty shall be made ridiculous and successful corruption shall be held up for admiration and praise.

And are not *our* "Fire Pillars" dragging us already in that direction? blinding us instead of guiding and enlightening? Yes, alluring, tempting, making rapacity and ill-gotten wealth appear justifiable, seen through the seductive glamour of Success!

The letter Mr. James Mechlin received one morning about the latter part of November, 1875, would seem so to indicate. He and Mr. Holman met often at the postoffice each winter since 1872, always hoping to get railroad news from Washington. These two gentlemen religiously went to the postoffice every day again this winter— particularly since the Mechlins had taken their temporary residence in town— and religiously they expected that *good news* would come at any time while Congress was in session— news that a bill to aid in the construction of the Texas Pacific Railroad had been passed. But days and days went by and no news came. This morning, however, Mr. Mechlin received two letters from his brother, the first he had got since he brought the wounded George to town.

One of these letters said that early in that month (November) Mr. C. C.

had taken east from California in his special car ex-Senator Guller, for the purpose of being sent South *to persuade* the Southern people into believing that the Texas Pacific Railroad would be injurious to the South; that it was being built for the benefit of Northern interests, but that *the Southern Pacific*, of Mr. Huntington and associates, was truly the road for the South. Mr. Huntington instructed Senator Guller in all the fictions he was to spread in the South, and with that burden on his soul (if the old man has one), the hoary headed ex-Senator started from Washington about the 12th of November, 1875, on this errand to deceive, to betray. To betray cruelly, hiding under the cloak of friendship and good will, the worst, blackest, most perfidious intent. "He is going about the South making public speeches," Mr. Mechlin said, "and using his influence to mislead Southern newspapers and Southern influential men; trying to convince all that the Texas Pacific will do the South great harm. The Southern people and Southern Press have fallen into the trap. They never doubted, never could doubt, the veracity of ex-Senator Guller, who had espoused their cause during the war of the rebellion, and had always held Southern sentiments. Who could believe that now, *for money*, he would go to deceive trusting friends? That, *for money*, he would cruelly mislead Southerners to their ruin? Who would believe that this old man, calling himself a friend, was the veriest, worst, most malignant Mephistopheles, holding in the heart so wicked a purpose, such an infamous design?"

In the second letter Mr. Lawrence Mechlin spoke of ex-Senator Guller being still at work in the South, and that his patron, Mr. Huntington, seemed to think that the old man was not telling as many fictions as he (Huntington) wished. But that what more false statements he desired, it did not appear, for in reality Dr. Guller had prevaricated and misrepresented all that he could within the limits of possible credibility.

"And now," Mr. Mechlin's letter added, "old man Guller will soon return from his Southern trip. Let us hope that the old man will be well paid for his unsavory work. I cannot believe that in making his public speeches he does not occasionally feel a pang of regret, of remorse, when seeing the faces of those unfortunate, betrayed Southerners upturned to him, listening in the sincerity of their hearts to the atrocious concoctions which he is pouring upon their unsuspecting heads."

Mr. James Mechlin read to Mr. Holman this portion of his brother's letter, and both looked at each other in dismay.

"Come with me," said Mr. Mechlin. "Let us go and talk with George about this." When they had walked in silence a few minutes, Mr. Mechlin turned suddenly around and said:

"I have an idea. Let us (you, Don Mariano, and myself) go to see Governor Stanford and find out from him directly whether they really mean to kill the Texas Pacific, or whether those tricks of Huntington are intended only as a ruse to bring Tom Scott to terms."

"But would Stanford tell us?"

"Whether he does or not, by talking with him we will find out the truth."

"I don't think the sending of Guller to the South can be a ruse only; it must have cost them money."

"True. You are right," said Mr. Mechlin, sadly, resuming his walk. "And it proves conclusively that these men of the Central Pacific Railroad will stop at nothing to obtain their end; and yet, I have always thought so well of Governor Stanford that I am unwilling to believe he is a party to any trickery of Huntington's."

On arriving home, Mr. Mechlin, followed by Mr. Holman, went directly into George's room to lay before him his idea of interviewing Governor Stanford. After listening attentively, George said:

"I have not the slightest doubt that the railroad men of the Central Pacific wish to establish an iron-bound monopoly on the Pacific slope, to grasp all the carrying business of the entire coast, and to effect that, they will do anything to kill the Texas Pacific, or any other road that might compete with them. Still, as you are going to San Francisco to escort Lizzie, you can then, for your own satisfaction, have a talk with Governor Stanford, and Mr. Holman and Don Mariano can join you."

"Yes, after I see him, I shall know the truth whether he tells it to me or I see it myself," said Mr. Mechlin.

"Well, I shall join you at any time. Let us go to see Don Mariano to-morrow and find out when he thinks he will be well enough to travel," said Mr. Holman.

"Very well; I shall call for you about nine A.M.," said Mr. Mechlin. Mr. Holman then arose, and, saying he wished to speak with the ladies and try to forget railroads, went into the parlor. Mr. Mechlin followed him, saying to George as he was leaving the room:

"Here is a lot of letters and papers that came this morning which I was almost forgetting to give to you."

Among the various letters of less interest to George, there was one from his uncle, one from Bob Gunther and (would he believe his eyes!) one from Clarence! The sight of that writing made George start, and he immediately thought of the effect it would have on Mercedes. He hastily tore open the envelope and found four letters besides the one for himself. One was for Don Mariano, one for Gabriel, one for Tano, and one for Mercedes. "The noble fellow forgets no one," said George, beginning to read his letter, and thinking it was best not to give to Mercedes hers until all the visitors had left, was soon absorbed in what Clarence said. Knowing that all would repeat the contents of his letters to one another, Clarence related to each different incidents of his travels, leaving for Mercedes alone the recital of his heart's longings, and sufferings, and fears, and hopes. To George he related his travels in the interior of Mexico, speaking with great enthusiasm of the transcendent beauty, the sublimity of the scenery in that marvelous country. He had passed several weeks in the Sierra Madre, had ascended to the summits of Popocatepetl and Orizaba, viewing from the snow-clad apex of this last named mountain, at an elevation of more than three miles above the sea level, a vast panorama of the entire Mexico, bordered on each side by the Pacific and Atlantic Oceans. Clarence also spoke in highest terms of praise of the delta of the Sumasinta River, and beautiful scenery of the Rio Verde and Rio Lerma, and Chapala Lake, so large and picturesque that it looks like an ocean set apart by the jealous gods so that men may not defile its beauty and break its silence with the hurry scurry of commercial traffic. Clarence dwelt, also, upon his visit to Yucatan, where he went more especially to see the ruins of Urmal. Those ruins which are the irrefragable witnesses of a past civilization, lost so entirely that archæology cannot say one word about its birth or death. Clarence found those ruins intensely interesting, and would have spent much longer time than the month he passed there, examining, studying and admiring them, had his traveling companions been willing to remain longer, but they were anxious to visit the City of Mexico, and so he was obliged to leave those majestic ruins whose silence spoke to him so eloquently. They seemed to him symbolical of his ruined hopes, his great love, in fact, himself. Was he not like those crumbling edifices— a sad ruin of lofty aspirations? Poor Clarence, his sad heart was only made sadder when, upon his arrival at the City of Mexico, he found no letters there. He inquired at the American Legation whether any letters had come for him, and was told by the Secretary that *no letters*, but one package, only one, had been received, which had been kept for six months, at the end of which time Mr. Hubert Haverly had written saying that if Mr. Darrell did not call for the package soon, to return it to him (Haverly) at San Francisco. This had been done about two weeks previously. On hearing this, Clarence sat down, wrote letters to all his friends, and then started for South America, intending to cross that continent and embark at Brazil for Europe. His letter to Mercedes he ended with these words.

"I do not blame you for renouncing me, for it must be repugnant to you to unite yourself with one who has such rough blood in his veins. But, Oh! Mercedes, can you not pity me enough to say one kind word? What have I done to deserve being the miserable outcast that I am?"

Mercedes was in despair. Where could all their letters be? Why did he not get them? He wrote to his mother, to Everett and Alice, and to them he made the same complaint, and yet, all had written to him repeatedly.

Mr. Mechlin, accompanied by Mr. Holman, arrived at the rancho about luncheon hour. Their drive had given them a good appetite and they enjoyed their repast. After it, they all adjourned to the parlor to discuss, by the fire, their intended visit to San Francisco. Don Mariano would have preferred to sit out doors on one of the verandas, but Doña Josefa reminded him that a whole year had passed since he was overtaken by that disastrous snow-storm, and he had not yet regained his usual health; neither had Victoriano. The injury to his health seemed even greater and more difficult to remedy, for every two or three months he had attacks more or less serious of the same lameness which deprived him of the use of his limbs.

As for the cattle, the poor, dumb brutes who had never seen snow, they became so frightened at the sight of that white pall, enveloping everything, that they were absolutely unmanageable after Don Mariano had gone in advance with Victoriano, and the *mayordomo* thought they would wait until the storm had passed. Next day the *mayordomo* went about in hopes of finding such stray animals as might have ran less wildly, but none were to be seen, excepting those which lay stiff in death under the snow.

The loss of his cattle made it more imperative that Don Mariano should look closely into land matters, into the prospects of a railroad for San Diego. He therefore listened attentively to what his friends said about Mr. Lawrence Mechlin having written, and their proposed visit of inquiry to ex-Governor Stanford as to what might be the fate of San Diego's railroad.

"It seems to me incredible that Doctor Guller should have lent himself for such service, no matter how well paid," said Don Mariano. "If he had been sent to deceive the North, to fool the Yankees, the errand would have been– if not more honorable– at least less odious for a Southerner, not so treacherous; but to go and deceive the trusting South, now when the entire country is so impoverished, so distressed, that act, I say, is inhuman, is ignominious. No words of reprobation can be too severe to stigmatize a man capable of being so heartless."

"Truly, but the instigators are as much to blame as the tool they used. They should be stigmatized also as corrupters, as most malignant, debasing, unscrupulous men," said Mr. Holman. "Men who are harmful to society, because they reward dishonorable acts; because they reward, with money, the blackest treason!"

"Can it be possible that Governor Stanford had any knowledge that his associate was sending Doctor Guller on that disgraceful errand?" Don Mariano queried.

"It looks like it, but let us hope he did not," Mr. Holman replied.

"Yes, let us hope also that Mr. Lawrence Mechlin was misinformed, and Doctor Guller has not been guilty of anything so atrocious," the Don said.

It was finally decided that the three friends would go to San Francisco at the same time that Lizzie would be going. She had made a flying visit to her family at San Diego, and Gabriel was calling loudly for her to return, saying that after banking hours he felt lonely and missed her dreadfully.

Lizzie, therefore, had three gentlemen for her escort, and in a few days they all steamed away for the city of the sand dunes.

The first day in the city Don Mariano devoted to raising a sum of money by a mortgage on his rancho, as he needed the money to pay taxes on the land occupied by the squatters; but the day after, the three friends presented themselves at the railroad office and inquired for Governor Stanford. They were told that he had just left the office, but that he would be there on the following day. As they were leaving the office, they met a Mr. Perin, a friend whom they had not seen for some time. When they had exchanged greetings, Mr. Perin asked them if they had come to see Governor Stanford. On being told that such was the case, he said:

"It is well that you did not see him, for he is not in a very good humor today, and as for Mr. C., he is like a bear with a sore head— furious at Tom Scott."

"What is the matter? What has Tom Scott done to anger his persecutors?" asked Mr. Holman.

"It seems they need money and can't raise as much as they want, while Huntington keeps clamoring for more to kill Tom Scott together with the Texas Pacific," was the answer.

"The earnings of the Central Pacific this last year were seventeen millions of dollars. How are they in such need of money? Is not that enough to kill Colonel Scott?" Mr. Mechlin asked. "Why do they want more?"

"Because, if their earnings had been seventy millions, these men would still be in need of money," Mr. Perin said.

"Why so?"

"Because, as they wish to absorb all the carrying business of this coast— in fact, all sorts of business— they want money, money, money. They want to buy steamboats, ferry-boats, ocean steamers; street railroads and street cars; coal mines and farms; in fact, they want everything, and want it more when some poor devil loses his business thereby and goes, frozen out, into the cold world. So you see, to go into such a variety of business besides railroading and killing Tom Scott, it costs money. It takes millions and millions to kill and freeze out so many people."

"I hope they'll be disappointed in killing Colonel Scott," said Don Mariano. "That would mean death to many others."

"I hope so, too, but I hear that Mr. Huntington devoutly prays that a kind Providence may enable him '*to see grass growing over Tom Scott,*'" Mr. Perin replied.

"Yes, my brother wrote me that Huntington does say that he hopes to worry Scott to death, and '*see grass growing over his grave.*' I fear he will see grass growing over many graves if he succeeds in killing the Texas Pacific," said Mr. Mechlin.

"He is trying hard to do that, and his associates are backing him up with millions," Mr. Perin said.

"Then Heaven help us poor people who have invested our all, believing that San Diego would have a railroad," said Mr. Mechlin, bitterly.

Next morning the three friends went again to the railroad office and sent their cards to Governor Stanford. In a few minutes the servant returned to say that the Governor was very busy, but if the gentlemen could wait he would see them as soon as possible. The gentlemen waited; they read the morning papers and looked over railroad guides to while away time.

Yes, they waited, but they would have spared themselves that trouble, and they would have never made that pilgrimage from San Diego to consult the oracle at San Francisco, could they have read what Mr. Huntington was about that time writing to his *associates* concerning his *modus operandi* in Washington to "*convince*" Congressmen to do as he wished, to defeat the Texas Pacific; writing all about sending an ex-Senator to "*switch off the South*," and there to pretend to be an anti-subsidy Democrat, and to state falsely that the Texas Pacific would injure the South. All this, however, was only known lately, when Mr. Huntington's letters were made public. At that time the three friends, thinking it impossible that the rights of Southern California would be so utterly disregarded, did not see any absurdity in interviewing the Governor.

While they waited they had an opportunity of hearing several instructive matters freely mentioned. One of these was the way of avoiding the payment of taxes, and how to fight the cases in the courts. The gentlemen who discussed the subject evidently understood it and were waiting to have an audience. Their talk suggested a very sad train of thoughts to Don Mariano, as he heard that the railroad people did not mean to pay taxes, and would resist the law. He thought how those millionaires would pay no taxes, and defy the law openly and fight to the bitter end, whilst he was not only obliged to pay taxes upon a too highly appraised property, but must also pay taxes for the land occupied by the squatter and on the improvements thereon! As a necessary sequence to such unjust, unreasonable, inhuman taxation, Don Mariano had been obliged to mortgage his rancho to raise funds to pay the taxes of the squatters. With the yearly sales of his cattle he had always been able to pay his own taxes as well as those of his unwelcome neighbors, but as his cattle were now lost, his only resource was his land. Not yet having the patent, he could not sell to advantage at all. He must therefore mortgage.

"If I were a railroad prince, I suppose I would not be forced to pay taxes for the squatters on my land," said Don Mariano to his friends, smiling sadly to hear how the taxes on railroad property were to be fought.

"If you were a railroad prince, you would not pay your own taxes, much less those of the squatters," said Mr. Holman.

"I think you ought not to hesitate to use the money that Clarence paid for your cattle. If they ran away, it was not your fault," Mr. Mechlin said.

"No, not my fault, but my misfortune; a misfortune which I have no right to put on Clarence's shoulders. I did not deliver the cattle; I don't take the pay. I am going to mortgage my land, but I can't avoid it," Don Mariano replied.

"It is certainly a very hard case to have to mortgage your property to pay taxes for the squatters," observed Mr. Holman.

"If these railroad men will only let us have the Texas Pacific all will be right, but if not, then the work of ruining me begun by the squatters will be finished by the millionaires— if they kill our railroad," said Don Mariano sadly, adding: "Our legislators then will complete their work. Our legislators began my ruin; our legislators will end it."

CHAPTER XXXIII.

San Diego's Sentence is Irrevocable.

After waiting in the reception room for nearly two hours, Don Mariano and his two friends were at last ushered into the presence of ex-Governor Stanford. He was so well hid behind his high desk, that looking around the empty room, Mr. Holman observed:

"Well, I hope this is not to be a second stage of waiting."

Mr. Stanford arose, bowing from behind his desk, said:

"Be seated, gentlemen. Excuse my having kept you waiting." Then seeing that there were but two chairs near by, and only one more at the furthest corner of the room, he added, going to bring the chair: "I thought that there were chairs for you."

Don Mariano, too, had started for the same chair, now that its existence was discovered, but the Governor got there first, and brought it half way, then the Don took it and occupied it.

When all were seated, Governor Stanford said in his low, agreeable voice, which any one might suppose would indicate a benevolent, kind heart:

"What can I do for you, gentlemen?"

Don Mariano laughed outright. The situation struck him as being eminently ridiculous. Here was this man, who held pitilessly their destiny in his hands— held it with a grip of iron— and not one thought of the distress he caused; he, through his associate, Huntington, was lavishing money in Washington to kill the Texas Pacific, and thus snatch away from them (the three friends) the means of support, absolutely deprive them of the necessaries of life, and he asked them what he could do? and asked it with that deep-toned, rich melody of voice which vibrated softly, as if full of sympathy, that overflowed from a heart filled with philanthrophy, generosity and good will. This was a sad and cruel irony, which to Don Mariano made their position absurd, to the point of being laughable.

"This is like laughing at a funeral," said Don Mariano, apologetically. "Please pardon me. What made me laugh was that I felt like answering you by saying, 'Governor, you can do for us all we ask.' But— but— "

"Say it out. But what?" said the Governor, smiling.

"But will do nothing for us," finished Mr. Holman.

"That is to say, for San Diego," added Mr. Mechlin, afraid that it might seem as if they came to ask a personal favor.

"Ah! it is of San Diego that you wish to speak to me? Then, truly, I fear I can do nothing for you," the Governor said.

"But you can hear what we wish to say to you," Mr. Holman interposed, with a sickly effort at smiling.

"Certainly. But really, gentlemen, you must excuse me for saying that I am very busy to-day, and can only give you a half hour."

They all bowed.

Mr. Mechlin and Don Mariano looked at Mr. Holman, as it was understood that he would be spokesman. But Mr. Holman's heart was leaping with the indignation of a lion, and then shrinking with the discouragement of a mouse into such small contractions— all of which he in no way must reveal— that for a minute he could not speak.

"I suppose the San Diego people wish me to build them a railroad, isn't that it?" said the man of power, slowly arranging some papers on his desk.

"Or to let some one else build it," said Mr. Holman.

The Governor colored slightly, in evident vexation.

"Tom Scott, for instance," said he, sneeringly. "Take my advice, gentlemen, and don't you pin your faith on Tom Scott. He'll build no Texas Pacific, I assure you."

"Then why don't you build it?" asked Mr. Mechlin.

"Because it won't pay," was the dry reply.

"Why won't it pay? We have plenty of natural resources, which, if developed, would make plenty of business for two railroads," Mr. Holman said.

"Only the San Diego people say so. No one else thinks of San Diego County, but as a most arid luckless region, where it never rains."

"That is the talk of San Francisco people, Governor, because they want all the railroads to come to their city, and nowhere else," said Don Mariano.

"We have less rainfall in Southern California, on an average, but on average, too, we get better crops than in the northern counties in dry years. How it is I can't tell you, unless it be that a given quantity of rain is all that crops require, and above that it is superfluous, or else that for certain soils a certain amount of rainfall is all that is required. It is undoubtedly true that in dry years more crops have been lost in some of the northern counties than in ours," said Mr. Holman.

"Perhaps, but when we have such magnificent wheat country in our northern valleys, it isn't to be supposed that we can give any attention to San Diego."

"If our county does not take the lead as wheat-growing, it certainly can take it as fruit-growing. We have no capital to make large plantations of vineyards or trees, but what has been done proves, conclusively, that for grapes, olives, figs, and in fact all semi-tropical fruits, there is no better country in the world."

"That may be so, but you see we are not engaged in the fruit-growing business. We build railroads to transport freight and passengers. We do not care what or who makes the freights we carry."

"Exactly. But surely there cannot be any reason why, if San Diego should have freights and passengers to be carried, that we should not have a railroad."

"Certainly not. If you can get it, do so, of course."

"Then, Governor, that is why we came to talk with you. *Is San Diego's death sentence irrevocable?* Is it absolutely determined by you that San Diego is not to have a railroad?" asked Mr. Holman.

"Well, that is a hard question to answer. No, perhaps for the present San Diego will *not* have a railroad," said he, with cool nonchalance.

"What do you call *for the present*? How long?"

"That is a harder question yet. You see, if we effect a compromise with Mr. Scott, we will keep on building the Southern Pacific until we meet his road, and then, as all the Eastern freight can come by the Southern Pacific, there will not be any necessity of another railroad."

"In other words, San Diego must be strangled. There will not be any Texas Pacific?" said Mr. Holman.

"No, not in California," the Governor calmly asserted, passing over the subject as of no consequence, if a hundred San Diegos perished by strangulation.

"By the terms of the Southern Pacific charter were you not to build to San Diego?" asked Mr. Mechlin.

"Yes; that is to say, through San Diego to the Colorado River, but that wouldn't suit us at all. Still, I think that after a while, perhaps, when we have more time, we might build to San Diego from some point of the Southern Pacific that we see is convenient," said he, as if it didn't matter what the terms of the Southern Pacific charter were, knowing that Congress would not enforce them.

"A little branch road," observed Mr. Holman.

"Yes; that is all we think is necessary for our purpose."

"Then to sum up, what we must understand is, that San Diego cannot hope to be a western terminus of a transcontinental railway; that all we may hope to get is a little branch road from some point convenient to the Southern Pacific Railroad." Mr. Stanford bowed. "And yet," Mr. Holman continued, "by right, San Diego is the terminal point of a transcontinental railway, and San Diego ought to be the shipping point for all that immense country comprising Arizona, Southern California and Northern Mexico. We are more than five hundred miles nearer to those countries than San Francisco, thus you will be making people travel six hundred miles more than is necessary to get to a shipping point on the Pacific."

"So much more business for our road," Mr. Stanford said, laughing, in a dignified way, and slightly elevating his eyebrows and shoulders, as if to indicate that really the matter hardly merited his consideration.

"But without asking or expecting you to take any sentimental or philosophic or moralizing view of our case *as a benefactor*, will you not take into consideration, as a business man, the immense benefit that there will be to yourselves to have control of the trade which will be the result of uniting

Southern California with Arizona, with the Southern States and Northern Mexico, and developing those vast countries now lying useless, scarcely inhabited."

"Oh, yes; we have thought of that, I suppose, but we are too busy up here. We have too much business on hand nearer us to think of attending to those wild countries."

"Then, Governor, let some one else attend to them. We have only one life to live, and, really, much as we would like to await your pleasure, we cannot arrest the march of time. Time goes on, and as it slips by, ruin approaches us. We invested all our means in San Diego, hoping that Colonel Scott would build his railroad. Now we see plainly that unless you withdraw your opposition to Scott we are ruined men, and many more innocent people are in the same situation. So we come to you and say, if you will not let any one else build us a railroad, then do build it yourself. It will save us from ruin and give you untold wealth. We will be glad to see you make millions if we only secure for ourselves our bread and butter," said Mr. Holman.

"Our bread; never mind the butter," said Don Mariano, smiling.

"Why, you at least have plenty of cows to make butter," said Mr. Stanford, addressing Señor Alamar, evidently wishing to avoid the subject, by turning it off.

"No, sir, I haven't. The squatters at my rancho shot and killed my cattle, so that I was obliged to send off those that I had left, and in doing this a snow-storm overtook us, and nearly all my animals perished then. The Indians will finish those which survived the snow."

"Those Indians are great thieves, I suppose?"

"Yes, sir; but not so bad to me as the squatters. The Indians kill my cattle to eat them, whereas the squatters did so to ruin me. Thus, having now lost all my cattle, I have only my land to rely upon for a living— nothing else. Hence my great anxiety to have the Texas Pacific. My land will be very valuable if we have a railroad and our county becomes more settled; but if not, my land, like everybody else's land in our county, will be unsaleable, worthless. A railroad soon is our only salvation."

"That is bad," Mr. Stanford said, looking at his watch. "But I don't see how I can help you San Diego people. If Mr. Huntington effects some compromise with Mr. Scott, we will then build a branch road, as I said."

"And what if there is no compromise?"

"Then, of course, there will be no road for you— that is to say, no Texas Pacific in California."

"Why not, Governor? 'Live and let live,'" Don Mariano said.

"You don't seem to think of business principles. You forget that in business every one is for himself. If it is to our interest to prevent the construction of the Texas Pacific, do you suppose we will stop to consider that we might inconvenience the San Diego people?"

"It is not a matter of inconvenience— it is ruin, it is poverty, suffering, distress; perhaps despair and death," said Mr. Mechlin. "Our merchants, our farmers, all, the entire county will suffer great distress or ruin, for they have embarked their all in the hope of immediate prosperity, in the hope that emigration would come to us, should our town be the western terminus."

"You should have been more cautious; not so rash."

"How could we have foreseen that you would prevent the construction of the Texas Pacific?"

"Easily. By studying business principles; by perceiving it would be to our interest to prevent it."

"We never thought, and do not think now, that it is to your interest to prevent it. But even if we had thought so, we would not have supposed that you would attempt it," Mr. Mechlin replied.

"Why not?"

"Because it would have seemed to us impossible that you could have succeeded."

"Why impossible?"

"Because we would have thought that the American people would interfere; that Congress would respect the rights of the Southern people."

Mr. Stanford laughed, saying: "The American people mind their business, and know better than to interfere with ours. All I can tell you, gentlemen, is that if Mr. Scott does not agree to come no further than the Colorado River, he shall not be able to get the interest of his bonds guaranteed by our Government, which means that he will not have money to build his road—no Congressional aid at all."

"You seem very sure of Congress?"

"I am sure of what I say."

"But, Governor, the Government helped you to build your roads, why don't you let it help ours?"

"Who told you that?" said he, with an angry expression, like a dark shadow passing over his face. "Who told you that the Government helped us to build the Southern Pacific?"

"The Government gave you a grant of many millions of acres to help build it, as the Central Pacific was constructed with Government subsidies, and the earning of the Central Pacific were used to construct the Southern Pacific, it follows that you were helped by the Government to build both," said Mr. Holman.

"You are talking of something you know nothing about. The help the Government gave us was to guarantee the interest of our bonds. We accepted that help, because we knew that, as private individuals, we might not command the credit necessary to place our bonds in the market, that's all. As for the land subsidy, we will pay every cent of its price with our services. We do not ask of the Government to give us anything gratis. We will give value received for everything."

"That is certainly a very ingenious view to take of the whole matter, and so viewing it, of course the killing of the Texas Pacific seems justifiable to you," said Mr. Mechlin.

"Carlyle, in your place, would not view your position like that, Governor," said Don Mariano, rising.

"Nor Herbert Spencer, either. His ideas of what you call business principles are different," added Mr. Holman.

"Pray, what would those great thinkers say?"

"Carlyle would think you are much to blame for flinging away a magnificent chance to be great and heroic. Carlyle worships heroes, but his idea of heroism is not only applicable to warriors and conquerors, but to any one capable of rising to a high plane of thought or heroic endeavor, doing acts which require great self-denial for our fellow-beings, for humanity's sake, with no view or expectation of reward in money," Mr. Mechlin said.

The Governor smiled, and with the least perceptible sneer he asked:

"And how does Mr. Herbert Spencer differ with my ideas of business principles?"

"He differs in this, that he thinks that commercial honor, business morality, should be based on strict rectitude, on the purest equity. That so soon as any one in the pursuit of riches knowingly and wilfully will injure any one else, that he then violates the principle upon which commerce should rest," Mr. Holman replied.

"But that is absurd. Would he stop competition?"

"Not at all. Competition generally has the effect of securing the preference to whomsoever deserves it. No, what Mr. Spencer maintains is that monopolies should not exist when they have become so powerful that they defy the law, and use their power to the injury of others. The fundamental principle of morality is then subverted," said Mr. Holman.

"Fundamental morality forbids us to injure any one because we would be benefited by that injury," said Don Mariano.

"The same old axiom of the French revolution, that 'the rights of one man end where those of another begin.' Danton and Marat sang that to the music of the guillotine," said the Governor, a little bit contemptuously.

"That is so; but you see, Governor, the devil might sing psalms, and it won't hurt the psalms," Don Mariano replied.

"We have made you waste your time talking to us, Governor," said Mr. Holman; "can we not hope that you will reconsider this matter, and examine more carefully the advantages of making San Diego the direct outlet for all that country that needs a railroad so much? Believe me, sir, such road will bring you more millions than the Central and Southern Pacific Railroads. If you do not build it, and prevent Col. Scott from building it, sooner or later some one else will, for it stands to reason that such a magnificent enterprise will not be left neglected after other less advantageous routes are tried. Then you will have the regret of having spurned this golden chance."

"And besides the chance of making millions for yourselves. Think of the blessings you will bring to so many hearts who are now sadly discouraged, and will be desolate if our hopes are frustrated," Mr. Mechlin said.

"Corporations have no souls, gentlemen, and I am no Carlylean hero-philanthropist. I am only a most humble *'public carrier.'* I do not aspire to anything more than taking care of my business," Mr. Stanford answered.

"But, Governor, you cannot be indifferent to the distress your action will cause?" insisted Mr. Mechlin, with sad earnestness.

"As for that," replied Mr. Stanford, smiling; "if I don't cause distress some one else will. Distress there must be, bound to be in this world, in spite of all that your philanthropists might do or say to prevent it."

"But do you not think that if all and every one of those who have it in their power to be beneficent were not so indifferent to human suffering, but were to be benevolent, that then the combined result would be great alleviation and diminution of human distress?"

"No; because those who have power to do good are very few, and the improvident, the vicious, the lazy are in myriads; and they and their folly and vices and improvidence will, forever, more than counterbalance the good that the beneficent might effect," Mr. Stanford asserted.

Mr. Mechlin arose and turned towards the door. Mr. Holman followed his example. Señor Alamar looked sadly at the floor, saying:

"Well, Governor, I am sorry we have failed in bringing you to our way of thinking. Time will show who is mistaken."

"Oh, yes! Time will show. We can't cast any astrological horoscope at the birth of a railroad. All we can do is to take care that it thrives."

"To clear away competition."

"Exactly. The country is not settled enough yet to divide profits. Besides, we think that Eastern people ought not to build any roads to the Pacific Coast, when we of California are ready to do it. Let Tom Scott keep away. We don't build roads in Pennsylvania."

"But are you sure you will always be able to prevent a competing road? Would it not be cheaper for yourself to build than to fight Tom Scott?"

"No indeed. For the present, it is cheaper to fight. It don't cost so much money to make friends," said he, smiling.

"You seem very confident of success."

"Money commands success, you know."

"Yes, money is everything! And it weighs not a feather, all the ruin and squalor and death you will bring to a people who never harmed you! Not a feather's weight, as against the accumulation of money for yourselves," said Mr. Mechlin, forgetting his usual consideration for others' feelings.

"If I did not cause this misery you apprehend, some one would. Be sure of it, for there will always be misery in the world, no matter who causes it," the Governor replied, with an air of being satisfied with his philosophy, inasmuch as he was to be exempt from human suffering, no matter who went under.

Mr. Mechlin, still lingering sadly, and veiling his great disapprobation of

Mr. Stanford's practical philosophy, said:

"Mr. Herbert Spencer also, in elucidating his principles, reminds us of the fact that 'Misery is the highway to *death*, while happiness is added life, and the giver of life.' Think of this, Governor. Surely, you do not wish to make us so miserable that you cause *death*! Yes, death from poverty and despair. Poverty, overwork and discouragement are the causes of sickness and death oftener than it is supposed, and this Mr. Spencer also maintains unswervingly."

"You have a very vivid imagination; you color up things too dark," said the Governor, also rising.

"I hope you will not be sorry to have thought so. I hope you will not regret that you closed your heart and your mind against us, against justice, humanity and reason." So saying, Mr. Mechlin slowly walked off; then at the door he turned, and lifting his finger, said to Don Mariano: "I feel a prophetic warning that neither you nor I will ever see light in this world. These men— this deadly, soulless corporation, which, like a black cloud, has shut out the light from San Diego's horizon— will evermore cast the shadow that will be our funeral pall. But let them look to it, they might yet carry their heartless rapacity beyond limit. The mighty monopoly, that has no soul to feel responsibility, no heart for human pity, no face for manly blush— that soulless, heartless, shameless monster— might yet fall of its own weight." So saying, Mr. Mechlin walked away, as if he intended this prophecy to be a parting salutation to the men who had blighted his life and made him utterly hopeless.

CHAPTER XXXIV.

THE SINS OF OUR LEGISLATORS!

"'*Assey de Bonaparte!*' cried France, in 1814. Men found that his absorbing egotism was deadly to all other men," says Mr. Emerson. "It was not Bonaparte's fault. He did all that in him lay to live and thrive without moral principle. It was the nature of things, the eternal law of the man and the world, which balked and ruined him; and the result in a million experiments would be the same. Every experiment by multitudes or by individuals, that has a sensual or selfish aim, will fail. The Pacific Fourier will be as inefficient as the pernicious Napoleon. As long as our civilization is essentially one of property, of exclusiveness, it will be mocked by delusions. Our riches will leave us sick; there will be bitterness in our laughter, and our wine will burn our mouth. Only that good profits which serves all men."

Yes, only that good profits which does not represent the misery of others; only that wine should be sweet which is not drunk when the tears of those we have rendered desolate are silently running over pale cheeks from eyes that have kept the vigil of want, mourning for the beloved to whom poverty brought death!

In heavenly-inspired words Emerson and Carlyle and Herbert Spencer have repeated those burning aphorisms, but our California "*Fire Pillars*" differ with them— differ widely and differ proudly.

Mr. Stanford says that if *he* did not cause misery some one else would, for "*misery there must always be in this world*!" Sound philosophy, truly! Why should he recoil from adding to the sum total of human misery when so many others do the same!

Mr. Huntington was about the same time writing from Washington that he *would* "*see the grass grow over Tom Scott*" before he stopped his work of *convincing* Congressmen. And he kept his word.

He carried *conviction* to Washington, distress to the South and ruin to San Diego.

Mr. Crocker was answering, "*Anything to beat Tom Scott!*" The thing was to prevent the construction of San Diego's railroad, no matter to whom ruin came thereby. "No matter how many were sacrificed."

Nothing was more hopeless, therefore, than to suppose that any of those men would swerve one iota from their course of greedy acquisition, out of respect for equity or humanity.

Not a word was spoken until the three saddened friends reached Don Mariano's parlors at the hotel. They had walked silently out of the railroad building, silently taken the street car and silently walked out of it, as it happened to stop in front of their hotel.

"Well, we have failed sadly, but I am glad to have had the chance of studying that piece of humanity, or rather I should say inhumanity," Mr. Mechlin exclaimed.

"How confident he is of their power over Congress! And he certainly means to wield it as if he came by it legitimately. He is proud of it," added Mr. Holman.

"Yes, but he is wrong to be proud of a power he means to use only for selfish ends. Sooner or later the people will get tired of sending men to Congress who can be bought so easily. I am disappointed in Governor Stanford. I thought him much more just and fair; a much higher order of man," said the Don. "How coolly he laughed at us for quoting Carlyle and Spencer! As if he would have said, 'You quote the philosophers, gentlemen, and I'll make the millions. You might die in poverty, *I* shall revel in wealth.'"

"I ought to have quoted Emerson, when he says: 'I count him a great man who inhabits a higher sphere of thought into which other men rise with labor and difficulty.' This might have pointed out to him how groveling it is never to rise above the mere grubbing for money. No, he is not half as large-minded as I had believed," said Mr. Mechlin.

"How can he be if he is cognizant of the means employed by Huntington to defeat all legislation in favor of the Texas Pacific?" observed Mr. Holman.

"Yes, I fear now the Governor gives his sanction to Huntington's work. I never believed it before. I am disappointed in the Governor as much as in our fruitless errand," the Don said.

"How irksome and distasteful it is for him to hear about '*the rights of others.*' He almost takes it as an insult that any one but himself and associates should have *rights*; and he seems to lose all patience at the mention of the distress they have brought upon the people of San Diego and the financial ruin that their rapacity and heartless conduct will cause the Southern people," said Mr. Holman. "Did you notice how he frowned at the allusion to the fact that the Central Pacific was built with Government money? The mere mention irritates his nerves."

"Does he suppose we don't know that they had no money, and that it was with capital *given* as absolute gifts, or loaned to them on the guarantee of the Government, that they built and are building their roads?" said Mr. Mechlin. "I never saw such complete subversion of the laws of reasoning as these men exhibit. Good luck has made them think that to genius they owe success. Thus their moral blindness makes them take as an insulting want of proper deference any allusion to those *rights of others* which, in their feverish greed, they trample. For this reason they hate San Diego, because San Diego is a living proof of their wrong-doing; a monument reminding California of their deadly egotism, of the injury done by unscrupulous men to their fellow-men. Hence, my friends, I say that San Diego must have no hopes while those men live."

"I am afraid you are right, and as I have invested in San Diego all I have in the world, I see no hope; nothing but hard-featured poverty staring me in the face," said Mr. Holman, sadly.

"If it were owing to natural laws of the necessities of things that San Diego is thus crippled, our fate would seem to me less hard to bear," said Don Mariano; "but to know that the necessities of commerce, the inevitable increase of the world's population, the development of our State, all, all demand that Southern California be not sacrificed, *and yet it is*, and our appeals to Congress are of no avail! All this adds bitterness to our disappointment. Yes, it is bitter to be reduced to want, only because a few men, without any merit, without any claims upon the nation's gratitude, desire more millions."

Thus the disheartened friends discoursed, fully realizing their terrible proximity to that financial disaster which was sure to overtake them. In the generosity and kindness of their hearts, they felt added regret, thinking of so many others who, in San Diego, were in the same position of impending ruin; so many good, worthy people, who certainly did not deserve to be thus pitilessly sacrificed; so many who yet clung to the hopes of '72, when all rushed to buy city lots; so many out of whose hopes three years of disappointment had not quenched all life. The failure of Jay Cook in the fall of '73 had made the financial heart of America shrink with discouragement and alarm, but San Diego did not realize how much her own fate was involved in that sad catastrophe, and continued her gay building of proud castles in the air and humble little cottages on the earth— very close to the earth, but covered with fragrant flowers, with roses, honeysuckles and fuchsias. These little one-story wooden cottages were intended for temporary dwellings only. By and by the roomy stone or brick mansions would be erected, when the Texas Pacific Railroad— the highway of traffic across the continent— should bring through San Diego the commerce between Asia and the Atlantic seaboard, between China and Europe. San Diego lived her short hour of hope and prosperity, and smiled and went to sleep on the brink of her own grave, the grave that Mr. C. P. Huntington had already begun to excavate, to dig as he stealthily went about the halls of our National Capitol "offering bribes." But such "foul work" was then only surmised and scarcely believed. It was reserved for Mr. Huntington himself to furnish proof that this was the fact. His letters were not published until years after, but the world has them now, and the monopoly, with all its power, cannot gainsay them.

The three friends were yet discussing this painful topic of their pilgrimage, when Mr. Mechlin observed that Don Mariano was looking very pale, and asked if he felt ill.

"Yes," Don Mariano replied; "I feel very cold. I feel as if I was frozen through and through. When we were at the Governor's office I felt very warm, and when we came out my clothing was saturated with perspiration. Now I feel as if I had been steeped in ice."

"This won't do. You must change your clothes at once," said Mr. Mechlin. Mr. Holman also became alarmed at seeing the bluish pallor of his face.

"Why, this is a congestive chill," said he, hurrying off to call the doctor, who resided at the hotel, and who fortunately was at home.

Prompt and efficient medical attendance saved Don Mariano's life, but he was too ill to leave his bed for several days. His two friends remained with him, writing home that business matters detained them.

Doña Josefa did not feel anxious; she thought that her husband was busy negotiating a loan on his land, and this detained him.

Gabriel and Lizzie also were in constant attendance, and thus the sick man was kept in a cheerful frame of mind, a thing much to be desired in sickness always, but more especially in his case, accustomed as he was to be surrounded by a loving family.

Still he was anxious to return home. Reluctantly the doctor allowed him to do so, hoping that the salubrious climate of Southern California would be beneficial. But he said to him:

"I let you go on condition that you pledge me your word to be very careful not to get into a profuse perspiration and then rush out into the cold air. If your lungs had not been originally so healthy and strong you could not have rallied so soon, if ever; but they are yet filled with phlegm, and the least cold might give you pneumonia." To Gabriel the doctor repeated the same words of warning, adding: "Not only is the condition of your father's lungs very precarious, but also that of his heart. He must not task either too much."

Gabriel was thoroughly alarmed at hearing the doctor's opinion, and immediately wrote to his mother how careful his father ought to be, and how she should watch him.

Don Mariano tried to be careful, but having been very healthy all his life, he did not know how to be an invalid, nor guard against fresh colds.

About two weeks had elapsed since his return from San Francisco, when a notice that many of his city lots would be sold for taxes brought Don Mariano to town. He still held to the belief that a railroad to San Diego would surely be built at some future day, but had ceased hoping to see that day. However, he would willingly have waited for a rise in real estate before selling any of his city property, but he saw it was ruinous for him to pay taxes— taxes for town property and taxes for squatters— it was too much; so he reluctantly concluded that it would be best to lose a great many lots (yes, whole blocks), permitting them to be sold for taxes, hoping to redeem them on the following year if Tom Scott was more successful with the Texas Pacific. Mr. Mechlin and Mr. Holman did the same, and many other unlucky ones followed their discouraging examples. Thus city lots by the hundreds were sold every year.

Don Mariano saw his city property thus sacrificed before his eyes at public sale, just as he had seen his cattle buried under the snow. He submitted in both cases to the inevitable without a murmur; but this time the blow seemed heavier. He was pecuniarily less able to bear it, and being in bad health and discouraged, his misfortunes were more depressing. He rode home saddened indeed.

Victoriano, who was now able to be about (but said he *mistrusted* his legs), was with him.

"Father, why don't you use some of that money Clarence sent you? I am sure he would approve your doing so, and feel glad, *very* glad, indeed, that you did it," said Victoriano, when they had driven for a long time without uttering a word.

Don Mariano turned sharply and said: "Why should I use Clarence's money? If I had delivered the cattle to Fred Haverly, as it was agreed I should, then I would have a right to take from Clarence's money the price of the cattle delivered. But having delivered no cattle, I take no money."

"Everett was saying that Clarence distinctly stated to his father that the cattle in the Alamar rancho with your brand were all his, and would be driven as soon as the weather permitted. Mr. Darrell thinks that the cattle lost belonged to Clarence, and not to you."

"Mr. Darrell is wrong, then. I cannot expect to be paid for cattle I did not deliver."

"But he says you had sold them already. If they were lost on the way it was neither your fault nor your loss."

"No, but was my misfortune, not Clarence's."

"The cattle were going to Clarence's mines, which goes to prove that they had been bought by him."

"I cannot view the matter like that," Don Mariano said, and Victoriano saw his mind was settled upon the subject, and it was best not to annoy him by insisting in opposition.

When they arrived home they found that Doña Josefa had received a telegram from Gabriel, sent the night before, saying that he, Lizzie and the baby would spend Christmas and New Year's Day at the rancho. This was glad news, indeed, and most unexpected, for inasmuch as Lizzie had just been down on a visit and hurried back, so that Gabriel would not be all alone on Christmas, they did not think that Lizzie would want to take the trip so soon again. But Lizzie would travel many more miles to be with her family. And the reason that Gabriel had for coming was, moreover, a most powerful one.

He had one day casually met the doctor who attended his father, and after inquiring whether Don Mariano was better, added:

"I tell you frankly, Don Gabriel, your father may yet live many years, but he is in danger, too, of dying very suddenly."

"How? Why so?" Gabriel asked, pale with alarm.

"Because his heart may give out if his lungs don't work well, and as he is not very careful of himself, you see he might task his heart with heavier work than it can perform. If he is kept from excitement and gets rid of all that phlegm which has accumulated in his lungs, he will be well enough. So write to him to be careful in avoiding colds," said the doctor.

"I will go and tell him so myself," Gabriel said.

"That is right. The case is serious, I assure you."

This short dialogue brought Gabriel home.

From the time he had entered the bank he had never been absent from it one minute during office hours, so a three weeks' vacation was readily granted to him.

All the Mechlins would come to Alamar to pass the holidays. George told his father that they might as well go back to their home again since his lameness did not require daily medical attendance.

Mr. Mechlin replied that they would decide upon that after New Years, but he was evidently pleased at the prospect of returning to Alamar.

The Alamar house looked once more as it had in the days of old, before squatters invaded the place; it was full of people, and music and laughter resounded under the hospitable roof. Mercedes, however, sat silent, and though she smiled her own sweet smile, it was too sad; it failed to deepen the cunning little dimples as it did in other days. The Don and Mr. Mechlin, too, were not as cheerful as they used to be. In that visit to San Francisco "*a change came over the spirit of their dream*," and it seemed to have come to quench the light of their lives.

But the young people wanted to decorate the house with green boughs and have a huge Christmas-tree, and the Don himself went to help them to get pine branches and red "*fusique*" berries. The tree would be in honor of his two grandchildren; they were now eighteen months old, and the proud mammas said they were so intelligent that they would surely appreciate the tree.

Everett, Alice, Rosario and Victoriano were the committee on decorations; Carlota, Caroline, Lucy and Webster were the committee on refreshments. While the laughter of the young people came ringing out through the parlor windows, Don Mariano and Mr. Mechlin slowly walked up and down the back veranda in earnest conversation.

"Yes," Mr. Mechlin said, as if to reiterate some previous assertion, "yes, I have lived my allotted term; my life is now an incumbrance— nay, it is a burden on those who love me. If I were not living, George could take his wife, his mother and sister, to reside in New York, but because I cannot live in that climate, all those dear ones remain in this exile."

"But why should you call it exile? They don't think it is; and even if it were, my friend, you have no right to cut your life off at your will," said Don Mariano.

"Why not? Life is a free gift, and often a very onerous one. Why keep it, when to reject it would be preferable? when it would release others from painful obligations?"

"But are you sure that the grief and horror of knowing that you took your own life would not be a million times worse than the supposed exile you imagine to be so objectionable?"

"Perhaps so; but I assure you, since I have lost all my money, and when I am too old to make another fortune, my health has begun to fail again. I hate life without health, and these constant annoyances of financial difficulties will end by prostrating me on a sick-bed again. Now, when I have lost nearly all the money I invested in San Diego, now they come down on me to pay a note of ten thousand dollars which I endorsed, with five others. Why don't the others pay their share? I am willing to pay two thousand dollars, but not the entire sum."

"I don't see why you should, either. What does your lawyer say?"

"He shrugs his shoulders, caresses his side-whiskers, and says he *thinks* that some of the other indorsers are insolvent, because their property has depreciated so much that it would bring nothing if sold; while those that have some means, no doubt, put everything out of their hands, so I am left alone to pay the entire sum."

The sad dialogue of the grandpapas was now interrupted, as they were called to witness the glee of the babies at the sight of the illuminated Christmas-tree. When the surprise of first sight was over, little Mariano Mechlin stretched out both hands for the colored candles. His uncle Tano gave him a tin trumpet, teaching him how to blow it; whereupon baby Mechlin gave the company a blast, and looked so surprised at his own performance, and gazed around so triumphantly and yet so perplexed, that he made everybody laugh. Josefita looked at her cousin distrustfully and gave her arms to her papa, as if she thought Marianito was entirely too martial for the vicinity of peaceful babies like herself. Gabriel took her near the tree to select any toy she liked. She fancied a string of bright balls, which her father gave her. The babies were allowed to be in the parlor for nearly an hour, and they were so bright, trying to repeat what was taught them, that it was really amusing to watch them. Marianito sang for the company; all were surprised to hear so young a baby sing so well. None enjoyed more heartily their cunning ways than the two grandfathers, especially Don Mariano, and both babies clung to him when the nurses came to take them to bed.

When the babies had made their exit, the children of larger growth had their music and dancing until ten, supper being then announced. On returning to the parlor, after supper, the clock upon the mantel struck twelve; at the same time a curtain ran up, and an altar was disclosed to view, tastefully decorated in the Roman Catholic style, having statues of the Virgin Mary, the divine infant, enveloped in fleecy drapery, and St. Joseph standing by his side. Behind the cradle were three magi, and further off, the hills of Judea were seen. As all the company were Roman Catholics, all entered into the spirit of the commemoration, and joined with true feeling in the carol led by Mrs. Darrell and Alice. Other sacred songs were sung, and then all retired for the night; the Darrells promising to come on the following evening to have another dance, because— said Victoriano— it must be celebrated that they had heard from Clarence, and that he had found his legs, meaning that he

(Tano) had again the use of his limbs.

Christmas Day was passed very happily, and in the evening the young people assembled in the parlor for a dance. Don Mariano excused himself to Mr. Mechlin, saying he felt badly, and thought that he ought to be in bed.

At about eleven o'clock he sat up in bed and looked around as if wishing to speak. Gabriel and Mercedes were sitting by his bed, and promptly asked if he wished for anything.

"The sins of our legislators have brought us to this," he exclaimed, leaning back. Presently he said: "Call your mother, my son."

Gabriel called his mother, who being in the next room, talking with Mrs. Mechlin, was quickly by his side.

"Call Elvira and Tano. Call Carlota and Rosario and George. Call all, all, quickly! I fear, my beloved son, I fear I am dying! Bring all my girls; I must bless them all!"

Mercedes had her arms around him. He looked at her lovingly.

"My baby, kiss me. Tell Clarence I bless him with my last breath." His voice began to fail him, but his eyes seemed glowing with an intensity that was startling. He sat up again, looking at each one of the anxious faces around his bed. "God bless you all, my beloved ones," said he, hoarsely.

"Papa, darling, can't we do something to relieve you?" asked Mercedes. He shook his head and whispered:

"Too late. The sins of our legislators!"

"Do you feel pain, father?" Gabriel asked.

"Not now," he whispered, extending his hand to George as if to say good-by. He looked again to see whether every one of his family was there; he forgot no one; he seemed anxious to see them all for the last time. He extended his arms to his wife; she came to him. "Pray for me," he whispered, moving his lips as if in prayer, and leaning on Gabriel, who held him, closed his eyes and sighed. A few aspirations followed that last sigh, and all was over— his noble soul had passed away.

For some moments no one believed that his lofty and noble spirit had left the earth, but when the truth was at last realized, the scene of grief, of heart-rending agony, that followed would be impossible for me to describe.

Closely in the sad train of this mournful event, and as a fitting sequel and a complement of such dire misfortune, another disaster, more unexpected, more dreadful and tragic, followed, which must now be related. It shall be told as briefly as possible.

A few days had passed after the funeral, and the Alamar family were still in town. Doña Josefa and Mercedes were at the Mechlins. Victoriano, Carlota and Rosario were at the Holmans; that is, they slept there, but as Mercedes was again prostrated with fever, they, as well as the Holmans, divided their time between the two houses.

One morning Mr. Mechlin arose from the breakfast table and said he was going hunting.

"Don't go far, James; you are too weak," said Mrs. Mechlin.

"I think, papa, you ought not to carry that heavy gun. You eat nothing, and walk too far, carrying it," Caroline said.

"Will you carry it for me?" he said, smiling.

"I will," Gabriel said; "I'll take George's, too, and go with you, if you'll permit me."

"It isn't necessary," he replied, going towards his room.

"I think papa has taken to heart the death of Don Mariano more than any one sees," said Caroline.

"I know he has; he has hardly slept or eaten enough to sustain life since that awful night," Mrs. Mechlin said, "and constantly talks about soon joining his best friend."

"I have observed how very sad he is. I wrote uncle to come; I think to see his brother will be great consolation to him," said George.

The report of a gun was heard in Mr. Mechlin's room, and all jumped to their feet. Gabriel was the first to run and got to the room in advance of the others. He found Mr. Mechlin shot through the heart.

"Oh, God! Was it accidental?" Mrs. Mechlin exclaimed, clasping her husband to heart. The dying man smiled, whispering:

"Do not mourn for me; it is best so; I shall be happier." He looked lovingly at the anxious faces surrounding him, and closed his eyes forever.

CHAPTER XXXV.

The Fashion of Justice in San Diego.

If those kind eyes of the Goddess of Justice were not bandaged, but she could see how her pure white robes have been begrimed and soiled in San Diego, and how her lofty dignity is thus lowered to the dust, she would no doubt feel affronted and aggrieved. And if she is so irreverently maltreated, can she afford any protection to those who must rely on her alone, having no riches to maintain protracted litigation or carry their plaints to higher tribunals? To the moneyless laity Justice thus defiled seems as helpless as themselves. She is powerless to accomplish her mission upon earth whenever a Judge, through weakness or design, may choose to disregard her dictates. At present the dignity of a Judge's personality is more sacred than the abstract impersonality of justice. Because the accepted theory being that Judges are always just and incorruptible (and generally the supposition is correct), there is a broad shelter for a Judge who may be neither just nor impartial. What mockery of justice it is in our fair land of freedom to say that a bad Judge can be impeached when impeachment is so hedged with difficulties as to be impossible— utterly ineffectual to protect the poor, victimized laity! Who is the poor litigant that would dare arraign an unjust Judge, well sheltered in his judicial ermine, and the entire profession ready to champion him? "*Libel*" would be the cry against any one who would dare hold the mirror for such Judge to see himself! Ah, yes, when the real libel is to distort the law and degrade the mission of justice on earth!

Peter Roper, knowing well with what impunity he could violate justice and decency, conceived the brilliant idea of taking the Mechlin house at Alamar, now that the family were sojourning in town. Peter did not like to divide the spoils, but as accomplices were absolutely necessary, there was no alternative but to take his friend and client Gasbang into the plot.

On a Sunday evening Peter proceeded to unfold his plan before John, who had come from his farm to attend church and was attired in a white vest and black coat, having just come from evening service. For, as I have said before, John Gasbang was a pillar of the church now, and never failed in his attendance every Sunday. People knew that in old times, when John was very poor, he used to play "*monte*" with the Indians and cheat them out of their money. Many times he had been known to spend almost the entire night sitting cross-legged on a blanket with a tallow candle set in a bottle to light his high-toned game, surrounded by the select company of naked Indians, who were too fascinated to see how plainly John was robbing them. Pitilessly would John strip his unsophisticated tattooed comrades of everything they owned on this earth. Their reed baskets, bows and arrows, strings of beads, tufts of feather-tips, or any other rustic and barbaric ornaments. All, all, John would gather up with his skillfully shuffled cards. The spoils he thus collected he would sell to other Indians from whom he would presently gather in (like the good Sexton he was), gather in, with high-toned and highly skillful shuffling. But John now was a rich man. Kindly San Diego had forgiven John's petty thieving. The money won from the poor Indians had helped him to thrive, and consequently convinced him that, after all, cheating was no worse than other sins, the gravity of which entirely depended upon the trick of hiding them. He would now try to hide his humble, predatory gambling, he said to himself, and seem respectable.

Yes, he would wear a white vest and try to look honest, but on hearing Roper's project, his dull, fishy eyes revolved quickly in their little sockets, and his square jaws expanded like those of a snake before it shakes its rattle and coils up to spring. His mouth watered in anticipation of the sweets of ill-gotten gain as he listened attentively to all that Roper had to say.

"I'll see Hogsden the first thing in the morning," said he, joyously.

"But wait. Can you trust him?"

"Trust him? I should say I could, and if he weakens, there is his wife to brace him up with her good advice. He owes a big sum of money to old Mechlin; so old Hoggy will be only too glad to get even by jumping the house. I suppose our friend, the Judge, is with us."

"Don't be silly. Do you suppose I would do a thing of this kind if I wasn't sure of him? He won't fail me. He'll do as I say. Be sure of that, and don't talk. Come to my house now and I'll draw up the conveyance. Hog. must sign his quit-claim deed, and then I'll see that his location of one hundred and sixty acres is properly filed. But, mind, if Hogsden betrays us, he'll spoil our game," observed Roper.

"Leave that to me," said John, rubbing his hands and giving his vest a downward pull.

The result of this dialogue was that Hogsden quit-claimed all his, "right, title and interest in a certain parcel of land, etc., etc., with a dwelling house and other improvements, etc., etc.," and the description of the property might have applied to a hundred others in the county. This transaction accomplished and recorded, they took the furniture that had been left in the house by the Mechlins and put it temporarily in the barn; Mrs. Hogsden taking only such articles as she wished to keep. She stole them brazenly, saying she had bought them.

It was further agreed that they would work the farm in partnership, dividing profits equally, and a contract in writing to this effect was signed by them.

Roper now being a property holder, besides being so influential with *the* Judge, thought he could soar to higher altitudes. By the assistance of Gasbang and a few others, whom he said belonged to his *gang*, he managed to get himself nominated for Representative to Congress. Bursting with pride, puny Peter started on his way to glory, to *stump* his district. He would begin at San Bernardino and carry the county by storm, with the force of his eloquence and personal magnetism, he said, with characteristic modesty.

He made speeches at San Pascual, and Poway, and San Bernardo, and Bear Valley, and Julian, but his greatest effort, the achievement that would crown his brow with laurels, that effort he reserved for Los Angeles. Quite a big crowd was marshaled to hear him. He had paid a good deal of money in advertisements so as to collect an audience. He succeeded; a crowd was there ready to make up in quantity what it lacked in quality.

Roper came forward. His face was red as usual, but he seemed sober— he stood straight. He was as loquacious as ever, of course, and talked incessantly for quite a while, making the crowd laugh. After he had all his audience in a laughing mood with his coarse anecdotes and broad jokes, he thought he would capture their votes beyond a doubt if he then and there proved himself— by his own admissions— to be *low*, the lowest of the lowly— so very low, so very disreputable, that no one could be lower.

"You cannot doubt," said Peter, "that my sympathies as well as my interests, are with you, the working people, the poor who must work or starve. I have nothing in common with bloated bondholders or pampered monopolists who have enriched themselves with the earnings of the poor. I don't know how I came to be a lawyer. I suppose it happened because I don't like to work. I would rather talk and let others work. [Laughter.] I am a child of the people, and *for* the people— the poor people I mean. My mother was a cook, a poor cook— poor in pocket I mean. Her cookery may have been rich [laughter], but upon that point I couldn't enlighten you, for I have forgotten the flavor of her dishes. But she was a cook by profession, just as I am a lawyer by profession, and one is as good as the other. [Laughter.] As for my father, of him I know nothing to speak of— literally— [laughter], so the less said on that head, the sooner mended; for if the fact of my being here goes to prove *to you* that I had a father, that is all the proof *I* ever had myself."

Here Peter laughed, but he laughed alone. He thought that a burst of laughter and applause would follow this last shameless, revolting admission, but not a sound was heard. He had overstepped the bounds of decency so far, that even such a crowd as made his audience was silent as if unanimous disgust was beyond utterance. Roper was evidently disconcerted.

"We don't want to be represented in Washington by a fellow who exults in degradation and has no respect for the memory of his mother," said a loud voice, and the crowd began to disperse.

Soon Peter's native impudence came to his aid and he tried to recommence his discourse. "Look here," he cried, "where are you going? You ain't going to send my mother to Congress! Did you think I came to ask you to vote for her?" He went on in this coarse, bantering style which had taken so well at first, but in vain. Nobody wanted to hear him now. It seemed as if the ghost of the poor reviled cook had come, like that of Banquo, to frighten off the audience. In a few minutes only about half a dozen of his supporters had been left, and they remained to scold.

"Well," said one, looking back at the receding crowd, "that cake is all dough, Peter. I hope your mother would have made a better job of it."

"A delightful dough," said another; "and his goose is well cooked. I say, Peter, you cooked your goose brown, browner than your mother ever cooked hers, and I bet on it."

Peter answered with an oath.

"The worst of it is, that in cooking your goose, you burnt ours to a cinder. We haven't the ghost of a chance now, and the Republican candidate will have a walk-over to Congress," said a third supporter.

Alas for human delusions! This fiasco was the crowning glory of Roper's political campaign. Like the celebrated ambitious toad which cracked its sides by the force of its own inflation, Peter came to grief, ignominious grief; that is to say, it would have been ignominious to any one not thoroughly inoculated with disgrace as he, *according to his own version*, must have been from the day of his birth.

"Let me ask you a question, Roper," said a fourth friend. "Why did you bring out such a thing against your mother? It was your misfortune as long as you kept quiet about it, but now it is your shame. What was the good of telling against your own mother? Don't you know that people, even the humblest, must censure and despise you for it? Few, very few decent men, like to have anything to do with a man who reviles his dead mother, no matter if she was a poor cook. What pleasure can you find in proclaiming your shame?"

Roper laughed loud and derisively, saying:

"What will you bet that I'll have just as good and just as many friends in San Diego as I ever had before?"

"Do you mean to say that the people of San Diego *approve* of language such as you used to-night? Approve your conduct?"

"Never mind about that, only will you take my bet?"

The henchman shrugged his shoulders and walked off, but if he had taken that bet, he would have lost.

When Colonel Hornblower received the news of Roper's fiasco, it occurred to him that he would take a trip to Europe. He had now made money enough out of the troubles and distress he and Roper brought upon others, to indulge in that luxury, the pleasure of saying he had been to Europe.

"My dear," said the Colonel to his wife, "I think now is the best time to take that trip to Europe we have had in our hearts for so long. Get ready; let us go."

"What has happened?" Mrs. Colonel Hornblower asked.

"Nothing, except that that partner of mine made a fiasco of his political campaign," and the Colonel related to his swarthy lady Roper's speech, and how it was received.

"How absurd! so unnecessary!" she exclaimed.

"Perfectly, but you see, for a man of *my* dignity the thing is awkward. What will the town say of *me*, ME?"

"The town will say nothing. As long as Roper has the friendship of Judge Lawlack he can have clients; and as long as he has clients the San Diego people will be indulgent to him, no matter how debased he says he is. However, drop him, and let's go to Europe. I wish we could get letters to distinguished people abroad."

"What for? Our American ministers can present us to the best society, and besides, I am sure I am well known abroad. My name— the name of Colonel Hornblower— must be as familiar to Europeans as the names of other distinguished Americans. I am the most prominent man in San Diego. All the world knows San Diego, all the world must know Colonel Hornblower."

"Still, I would like to get letters."

"Not at all necessary, I assure you. I'll tell our minister in England that Mrs. Colonel Hornblower wishes to be presented to Queen Victoria, and he'll present you. The Queen, no doubt, will wish to make our acquaintance."

"I would like to see other royal people. I would like to see the Pope, also."

"You shall see as many princes and princesses as you like. We Americans are princes, all of us. We are the equals of princes. As for the Pope, I would not take one step to make his acquaintance, unless he met me half way; but if you like to see him, we'll get an introduction easily. Perhaps he might invite us to dinner. If he does, I hope it won't be on Friday, as fish don't agree with me."

"Does he ever invite people to dinner?"

"Distinguished people, of course."

The Hornblowers sailed for Europe before Roper returned from his stumping tour. He was detained at Los Angeles, where he had been beaten so badly in a bar-room brawl that he was obliged to keep in bed for several days. The Colonel then wisely slipped off for Europe, to hob-nob with royal people and take dinner with the Pope, perhaps.

Mrs. Hornblower conjectured rightly. Roper's disgrace was condoned by San Diego, because he was under the patronage of Judge Lawlack, and in San Diego everybody has a law suit.

But has the Judge no moral responsibility in this? *Has he the right to impose upon the community* a man so self-debased and noxious? If the Judge were to withdraw his support Peter would collapse like a pricked gas-bag, to be swept off into the gutter. But the Judge is the genii, "*the Slave of the Ring*" and his power keeps the little gas-bag afloat, soaring as high as it is in the nature of little gas-bags to soar. The Judge keeping in his hand the check-string, kindly preventing him from going to destruction.

With characteristic coarseness, amounting to inhumanity, Peter Roper and Gasbang decided to throw down their masks, and reveal their fraud in "*jumping*" Mr. Mechlin's house. They came to this decision about ten days after Mr. Mechlin's death.

Gabriel had returned that same day from San Francisco, where he had accompanied the remains of his father-in-law, and deposited them in a vault to await until Mrs. Mechlin should be able to travel, when she, with all the family, would go East.

Mr. Lawrence Mechlin had also arrived. He started from New York on the day of his brother's death, two hours after receiving George's telegram conveying the terrible news. He reached San Francisco on the night before the steamer for San Diego sailed. Thus he and George came together.

The Deputy Sheriff presented himself to announce to Mrs. Mechlin that her furniture left at her country house had been taken out by order of Peter Roper, and put on the road about two miles from the house. As Mrs. Mechlin was too ill to see any one, excepting the members of her family, the Sheriff made his statement to George, in the presence of his uncle and Gabriel, just arrived.

The proceedings seemed so atrocious that at first no one could understand the Sheriff.

"Do you mean to say that Peter Roper claims to own our house, and because he is the owner, has taken out the furniture and left it lying on the road?" asked George.

"Yes; that's what I was told to say," the Sheriff replied.

"But why? How is he the owner of our house?"

"Because he and Gasbang bought it from Hogsden, who located a claim there after you abandoned the place."

The trick was infamous. George and Gabriel saw through it. There was nothing to do but to bring a suit in ejectment to get rid of them, but in the meantime they would hold possession (perhaps for years), and that was what they wanted, to get the property into litigation.

Gabriel went to state the matter to the lawyer who had attended to Mr. Mechlin's law business, and he corroborated their opinion, that there was no other course to pursue but to file a complaint in ejectment to dispossess the thieves.

"Is there no quicker way to obtain redress?" George asked.

"No, sir," the lawyer answered; "as the deed is done by Peter Roper and John Gasbang, the Judge will decide in their favor, and you will have to appeal."

"But this is atrocious," Mr. Lawrence Mechlin said; "Do you mean to say that people's houses can be taken like that in this country?"

"Not generally; but Peter Roper might, if there is the ghost of a pretext, and if there is a dishonest servant, like Hogsden, left in charge, who will steal and help to steal; then, you see, the thing is easy enough, as long as the Judge befriends trespassers. But the Supreme Court will put things to right again. That is to say, if the Judge's findings are not a string of falsehoods which will utterly mislead the Supreme Court."

This property, Mr. Mechlin had repeatedly said, he intended should be a homestead for his wife, so the suit in ejectment was brought in her name. She at the same time filing a petition for a homestead before the Probate Court, and asking that Gabriel Alamar be appointed administrator of her husband's estate.

All this would, of course, involve the property in tedious legal proceedings, there being the probate matters, beside the suit in ejectment to litigate in the District Court. The attorney employed in the case advised George to have a deed executed by Doña Josefa, conveying the property to Mrs. Mechlin, as it had been agreed before the death of their husbands that it should be done. Doña Josefa cheerfully assented, remembering that Don Mariano had said to her:

"If I should die before I get my land patented, the first thing you must do is to make a conveyance of his place to Mr. Mechlin."

The shock caused by his father's death when that of Don Mariano was yet so recent, acted most injuriously upon George's health. It made him feverish, inflaming his wound again very painfully, as the ball had never been extracted; now it chafed the wound, and gave him as much pain as before.

Mrs. Mechlin, Doña Josefa and Mercedes were also in their beds, suffering with nervous prostration and night fevers. It seemed impossible that people could be more bereaved and disheartened than these ladies, and yet exist. Mr. Lawrence Mechlin saw that George must have skillful medical attendance without delay, and wanted his own doctor to take him under his care. So he and Gabriel arranged all business and other matters in order that George should go East. It was heart-rending to Elvira— the mere thought of leaving her mother and sister sick, and all the family in such distress— but she must go with her husband. Gabriel would attend to the lawsuits. He had powers of attorney from George and Mrs. Mechlin, and was the administrator.

The answer to Mrs. Mechlin's complaint was a masterpiece of unblushing effrontery that plainly showed it had originated in a brain where brazen falsehoods and other indecencies thrived like water-reptiles growing huge and luxuriating in slimy swamps. The characteristic document ran in the following manner:

> *In the District Court of the —— of the County of San Diego, State of California.*
>
> BEATRICE MECHLIN, *Plaintiff,*
>
> v.
>
> PETER ROPER, JOHN GASBANG, and CHARLES HOGSDEN, *Defendants.*

And now come the defendants, Peter Roper, John Gasbang and Charles Hogsden, and for answer to plaintiff's complaint, on file herein, they and each of them say:

That they deny that in the year of 1873, or at any other time before or after that date, James Mechlin was owner of the premises described in this complaint; deny that the said James Mechlin ever purchased from William Mathews the aforesaid property or any part thereof, or paid any money or any other valuable consideration; deny that the said Mechlin ever built a house, or planted trees, or resided on the said property himself, with his family, or by agent or servant occupied said premises; deny that respondent, Charles Hogsden, was ever put in charge of the aforesaid premises or any part thereof, as the agent, or servant, or tenant of the said James Mechlin; deny that the said James Mechlin ever was in the possession of the said premises, but on the contrary, these defendants allege that if James Mechlin had any kind of possession, it was as a naked trespasser, and his title to said property was at all times disputed and contested by other parties.

These defendants allege that defendant Charles Hogsden was the rightful owner of the said premises; that defendants Peter Roper and John Gasbang are the innocent purchasers of the legal and equitable title, and are now in actual and lawful possession of the said premises, having paid a just and fair price to the rightful owner, Charles Hogsden.

These defendants further allege, that the plaintiff Beatrice Mechlin wrongfully, unlawfully, fraudulently and maliciously, and for the purpose of cheating and defrauding the aforesaid innocent purchasers, Peter Roper and John Gasbang, out of their rights in said property, entered into a fraudulent conspiracy with one Josefa Alamar and one Gabriel Alamar, wherein it was agreed by and between them that said Josefa Alamar, as executrix of the estate of Mariano Alamar, and purporting to carry out the wishes and instructions of her deceased husband, the said Mariano Alamar, would execute a deed of sale or a confirmatory deed of said property.

And these defendants aver, that in pursuance of the fraudulent conspiracy aforesaid, the said Josefa did execute a fraudulent deed of sale to the said Beatrice Mechlin, for the purpose of cheating and defrauding these innocent purchasers, etc.

This string of prevarications ran on for about twenty pages more, repeating, *ad nauseam*, the same falsehoods with all legal alliteration and more than legal license.

Gabriel was left to attend this suit and other matters, and with grief, which was too profound for description and too heart-rending almost for human endurance, the two loving families separated.

Elvira must leave her beloved mother in her sad bereavement; Lizzie must see hers go to perform the painful duty of accompanying the remains of a beloved husband.

In sorrow and silent tears the Alamar family returned to their country house the day after the Mechlins left.

Mrs. Mechlin's suit in ejectment against the "*innocent* purchasers," Peter and John, was, as a matter of course, decided in favor of these *innocents* of Judge Gryllus Lawlack. The Judge knew, as well as any one else, that the allegations of these men were brazen falsehoods strung together for the purpose of robbery. Nevertheless, his Honor Lawlack made his rulings, and set down his findings, all to suit the robbers. Among the findings that his Honor had the hardihood to write down, were these: That "James Mechlin had never possessed the premises in question; had never lived there in person or by proxy, and had never made any improvements, etc." And these premeditated falsehoods went to the Supreme Court. The case was, of course, reversed and remanded for new trial, but with additional misstatements it was *again* decided by Judge Lawlack in favor of his friends. Thus, in fact, the Supreme Court was *reversed by Judge Gryllus Lawlack*. The case was the second time remanded by the Supreme Court, but in a new trial it was *again* decided in favor of Peter and John. This being the same as "reversing the Supreme Court," but Lawlack laughs at this, saying that the Supreme Court decides according to their opinions, and he (Lawlack) does the same.

As for Peter Roper, he made no concealment of there being a *private bargain* between himself and Judge Gryllus Lawlack. Peter to render political or other services, Gryllus to reward them with judicial ones.

At a political meeting a friend of Roper (a lawyer in the pay of the monopoly), urged him to make a speech in favor of the railroad. Peter declined, saying that as Gryllus Lawlack wanted to run again for the Judgeship, and knew how anti-monopolist San Diego County was, it would hurt the Judge politically to have him (Peter Roper) speak for the monopoly, as everybody knew that he (Peter) was the principal support of the Judge, and exponent of his principles.

"And," concluded Peter, "if I speak for the monopoly the Judge will grant a rehearing in a suit I am opposing, and will not decide my case as I want. That is understood between us."

This is the fashion of dispensing justice in San Diego, just as Peter bargains for.

But this order of things (or rather disorder) could not have been possible if the Texas Pacific Railroad had not been strangled, as San Diego would not then be the poor, crippled and dwarfed little city that she now is. In this unfortunate condition it is that she submits to the scandalous debaucheries of judicial favorites; debaucheries and violations of common justice, social decorum, of individual rights; debaucheries tolerated because the local power sanctions with his encouragement such proceedings.

If San Diego had been permitted to grow, to have a population, her administration of the laws would have been in other hands, and outrages like breaking into the Mechlin house could not have occurred. The voters of the county would not then have elected a Judge that could reward such vandalism, by allowing the thieves to keep the stolen premises. Now, however, without a railroad, San Diego is at the bottom of a bag, the mouth of which Mr. Huntington has closed and drawn the strings tight.

CHAPTER XXXVI.

Clarence and George with the Hod-carrier.

The lawsuits forced upon the Mechlins, to resist the fraudulent claims trumped up by Roper and Gasbang, obliged Gabriel to delay returning to his place at the San Francisco bank. It was very painful to leave his mother and Mercedes still so sick and depressed, but they themselves urged him to go, fearing that his place would be given to another, and now, when their pecuniary circumstances were so embarrassed, he could ill afford to lose his position. But he did, for as the bank could not wait for him longer, they took some one else instead. He wished to spare his family the regret of knowing this, and tried to get anything to do to earn a living. Thus he began that agony endured by so many young men of good families and education, trying to find employment to support themselves decently. Gabriel found the task most difficult. He was dignified and diffident, and could not be too pressing. He was persevering and patient and willing to work, but he dreaded to seem importunate, and never urged his services upon any one. But he tried everything, every means he could think of or Lizzie suggest to him. At times he would find some writing to do, either copying or translating English or Spanish, but this did not give him permanent employment, and between one job and another Lizzie's jewelry had to be sold for their daily expenses. They gave up the nice little cottage they had had before, and took two small rooms at the house of a widow lady who kept a few boarders. Their living was simple, indeed; but their landlady was kind and courteous and obliging, and her house clean and very respectable. Thus many months went by.

George and Elvira and Caroline wrote to them, constantly telling them how and where they were. Now they were in Germany, as Mr. Mechlin's physician advised George to try some German baths in which he had great faith. His faith was justified in George's case, for he began to improve rapidly before he had been taking the baths a month, and he was confident of regaining his health perfectly. This was cheerful news, and Lizzie felt great reluctance in writing to George how unsuccessful Gabriel had been, thus perhaps checking his recovery by making him again despondent; for it was a noted fact, well recognized by the two families, that misfortunes made them all more or less physically ill.

The winter of 1876 now set in, and Gabriel thought he must make up his mind to find some manual labor, and by that means perhaps get permanent occupation; but here other obstacles, no less insuperable, confronted him. He had had no training to fit him to be a mechanic, and what could he do? He did not know, and yet his family must be supported. He had not been able to send to his mother any money, as his scant earnings were inadequate to support his wife and babies. There was now another little girl to provide for—

a little darling, eight months old. Poor people are bound to have children.

About this time he got a letter from Victoriano, telling him how his miserable legs had failed him again, giving out in the midst of his plowing. Everett had come to help him plow up a fifty-acre piece of land he had intended to put in wheat, but lo! before he had plowed two acres, his legs seemed to disappear from under him as if the very Old Nick had unscrewed his knees and carried them off. Tano added: "And here I am, a perfect gentleman from my knees up, but a mean chicken, a ridiculous turkey, a kangaroo, from my knees down; and this, too, when we can so ill afford to have me lying in a sick-bed, perfectly useless. If land was not so valueless now, we might perhaps be able to sell some, although the price would have to be very low, on account of the delay in getting our patent and its being mortgaged; but as all hopes in the Texas Pacific are dead, land sales are dead, too, and we might as well all be dead, for as we have nothing but land to get a living from, and that is dead, you can draw the inference. However, don't worry about us; for the present, we are getting along very well. Several of the cattle lost in the mountains have come and keep coming, and Everett puts our *'venta'* brand on, and pays mamma, on Clarence's account, cash down for them. To-day he paid mamma three hundred dollars, and he says he heard that more cattle are on the way here."

Gabriel was very glad that his mother and sisters would have this little pittance at least, but he was much alarmed and anxious about Victoriano, and hastened to tell Lizzie he thought they ought to go home.

"I am truly sorry for poor Tano. Really, my sweet husband, you must let me write to George, telling him our circumstances. He can and will help us, and we might go back to the rancho."

"No, don't write to him about that yet. I'll try to get money enough to take us home. If Tano is sick, I certainly should be there. If he was trying to plow, I think I can do that, too. Yes, I ought to have stayed at home and worked in our orchard, and we would not have suffered the distress of mind at my repeated failures. As soon as I make money enough to pay the board bill I owe and have enough left to pay our fare to San Diego, we'll go home. Don't write to George to help me, I don't like that. I can work and help myself."

"Forgive me, my darling," said Lizzie, blushing crimson; "I have already written to George. I told him I was going to persuade you to go home. I wrote him a month ago. I expect his answer very soon." Seeing that Gabriel also blushed, Lizzie added: "I am sorry if I offended you."

"You have not offended me. I blushed because I, too, have been keeping a secret from you, thinking you might not approve of it, or feel humiliated."

"What is it, pray?"

"I have been trying to learn a trade."

"A trade! What trade, for gracious sake?"

"A very respectable one. That of a mason."

"But can you learn that? Where?"

"Anywhere. I have been taking some lessons and earning my two dollars per day besides."

"Oh, Gabriel, why did you do that?" said Lizzie, her face suffused with blushes.

"There! See how you blush because I want to learn an honest trade, and yet see how your people, the Americans, deride us, the Spanish, for being indolent, unwilling to work. For my part, I am willing to prove that I will work at anything that is not absolutely repulsive, to earn a living."

"But how did you come to select that trade?"

"Because to go down town I had to pass by the houses of the railroad millionaires which have been in process of construction. There are two Californians from Santa Barbara, whom I know, working there, and to see them earning their two dollars per day, while I have been losing months in search of more gentlemanly work to do, suggested to me the idea of also earning my two dollars a day while the gentlemanly occupation is being found. Then I thought, too, that I might learn to be an architect, perhaps."

"That is why you have been reading those books on architecture?"

"Yes, and I think I understand a good deal about it already, but I'll combine practice with theory. The thing now is, as Tano is sick, I must go home."

"Yes, let us go. I don't like the idea of your being a mason. Give it up. I think I'd rather see you plowing."

"Yes; in my own land, you mean. Don't be proud. Let me work a little while longer at *my trade*, and we'll go home."

But Lizzie was not willing he should, though she said nothing more about it to him. She wrote to Doña Josefa, saying that if she could spare fifty dollars, to, please, send that sum to her to enable them to come home.

There would be ten days, however, before she could get Doña Josefa's reply. This was not so agreeable, but Lizzie thought she would get ready to start as soon as the money came.

The cause of Victoriano's second severe attack of lameness, of which he spoke in his letter, was again exposure— exposure to cold and dampness. About the same time that Gabriel was trying to be a mason, and working as a common day laborer at two dollars per day, Victoriano had been pruning trees, fixing fences, repairing irrigating ditches and plowing. He had only two men to help him, so he worked very hard, in fact, entirely too hard for one so unused to labor. Work broke him down.

"Plowing is too hard work for poor Tano," Doña Josefa said, looking at Victoriano working in a field near the house, while the sad tears ran down her pale cheeks.

"Yes, mamma, it is; and I begged him not to try to plow again, but he insisted on doing so," Mercedes replied.

"What is the matter? Did he fall down?" Doña Josefa exclaimed, alarmed, drawing her chair close to the window.

Mercedes arose from hers, and came to look down the orchard. Yes, there was Victoriano sitting on the ground, and Everett standing by him. Presently Everett sat down beside him, and an Indian boy, who had also been plowing with another team, came up, leading his horses towards the house.

Doña Josefa thought that they wanted to put the boy at some other work, and that Tano was resting, so she sat quietly waiting to see whether he would walk.

Mercedes now sat by her mother, also to watch Victoriano. She said:

"Mamma, tell Tano not to try plowing, the ground is very damp. He will have that lameness again."

"I have told him, but he says he must work now, since we are so poor, and have only land with a title that no one believes in, and no one will buy. So what is he to do but work? And he has been working very hard all the fall and winter, but I fear he is getting that lameness again. He walks lame already."

They now saw that the Indian boy had run to the house to hitch his horses to Clarence's phæton and drive to where Tano was sitting. Assisted by the Indian, Everett put Victoriano in the phæton, and brought him to the house.

It was as his mother and sister had feared— Victoriano was again unable to walk. With great difficulty, assisted by Everett and the servant boy, he reached his bed.

"Don't write to George or Gabriel that I am sick. Wait until I get better, or worse," said he.

Seeing, however, that there was no change in his condition, he wrote to Gabriel himself, telling him of his second attack. Willingly would Gabriel have taken his little family and started for home, but he did not have money enough to pay their fare, and he owed for their last month's board. So there was nothing to do but to wait and work as a day laborer yet for a while. He knew what he earned in a whole month would scarcely be enough to pay their board, and that to go home he must write his mother to send him money for their fare. But his pride revolted. He hated to do this. He could not bring his mind to it. He hesitated.

About the time that Victoriano was taken sick and Gabriel was trying to be a mason, George and family arrived in Paris on their return from Germany. They would only spend a week or ten days in that city, and then sail for New York.

The day before they were to start, a card was sent to Elvira from the office of the hotel. Elvira took it very indifferently and read the name, but the words she read seemed to be cabalistic, for she started, turned red and then pale.

She handed the card to George, who read aloud, "Clarence Darrell."

"Ask the gentleman to please come up," said George to the servant, and followed him, going to meet Clarence.

The two friends met and clasped each other in a tight embrace; to shake hands seemed to both too cold a way of greeting, when they felt so much pain and joy that to express their sentiments, words were inadequate.

When Clarence came in, he stretched both hands to Elvira, and she, on the impulse of the moment, threw her arms around his neck and sobbed. Mrs. Mechlin and Caroline were also affected to tears. Clarence brought back to them vividly the happy days at Alamar, when Mr. Mechlin and Don Mariano lived so contentedly in each other's society.

All were so anxious to learn how Clarence came to be in Paris, and where he had been in all these years, and Elvira showered so many questions upon him, that George told him he must remain with them and tell them everything.

The family of Mr. Lawrence Mechlin were also in the same hotel, on their way to New York.

George said to Clarence: "Prepare yourself to be cross-questioned by aunt, for she has been very anxious about you."

Clarence replied he was willing to be questioned, and began his narrative by saying how he came to miss all the letters written to him. He said:

"When I was delirious and at the point of death in a cabin at the mines, all the letters that came addressed to me the doctor put in a paper bag, and when he left he considered me still too weak to read letters that might cause me excitement, so he took the paper bag and placed it behind a camp looking-glass which hung over a little table beside my bed. I was so impressed with the conviction that I might not be considered fit to marry Miss Mercedes, that when, upon asking if any letters had come for me, and Fred Haverly, thinking that I meant other letters besides those handed to the doctor, answered in the negative. I did not explain that I had not received any at all. I accepted patiently what I considered a natural result of my father's conduct, and said nothing. I went to Mexico, and there a fatality followed my letters again. I missed them twice— once through the mistake of a clerk at my bankers, the second time by a mistake of the Secretary of the Legation, who misunderstood Hubert's request about returning the letters to him. From Mexico I went to South America, crossed to Brazil, and went to England. From England I went to the Mediterranean, and since then I have been on the go, like the restless spirit that I was, believing myself a miserable outcast. It was almost accidentally that I came to Paris. I got a letter from Hubert, and in a postscript he said that he hoped I got my letters at last, for he had sent them with a remittance to my bankers, requesting that my letters should be kept until I called for them. I was far up the Nile when I received his letter, but next morning I started for Paris with a beating heart, I can assure you. Twenty-six letters I found, and I am more grieved than I can express to you to think that I did not get them before."

Clarence arose and paced the floor in great agitation, and his friends were much moved also, for they knew he was thinking that never again, in this world, would he see his noble friend, Don Mariano.

On the following morning the Mechlins, accompanied by Clarence left Paris. Before leaving, Clarence telegraphed to Mercedes:

"I have just received your letters written in '73. I leave for New York to-morrow with the Mechlins, thence for California.

— — CLARENCE DARRELL."

Everett, who had been to town, religiously, to see whether there might be a letter from Clarence, or news about him, brought Mercedes the cablegram.

Poor Mercedes, she read the few words many times over before she could realize that they were from Clarence. When she did so, she was seized with a violent trembling, and then completely overcome by emotion. Ah! yes she would see him again, but where was now her darling papa, who was so fond of Clarence?

Mercedes sent the dispatch for Mrs. Darrell to see, and when Everett brought it back, Carlota made a copy of it to send to Lizzie in a letter next day. The Darrells were truly overjoyed, thrown into a perfect storm of pleasure. The old man said not a word. He went to his lonely room, locked the door, and there, as usual since he lived the life of a half-divorced man, battled with his spirit. This time, however, he allowed tears to flow as he blessed his absent boy, and thanked God that he was coming.

"If I had a decent pair of legs to speak of," said Tano to Everett, "I would dance for sheer joy, but having no legs, I can only use my tongue and repeat how glad I am."

When Gabriel came home in the evening of the day in which Lizzie received the copy of Clarence's telegram, she said to him:

"Darling, don't go to that horrid work again. Clarence is coming, and now he and George will establish the bank."

"Yes, but in the meantime I must earn enough to pay our board; remember, we owe one month's board already. Be patient for a few days longer." And she was patient, but anxious. A few days more passed, and she received Doña Josefa's letter, inclosing seventy dollars, and saying she hoped they would come immediately, for she wanted Gabriel at home.

"Now we have money enough to pay our board bill, and as George will surely come to our assistance, why should you go to work as a mason? Darling, leave that work," Lizzie begged.

"Let us see; Clarence's cablegram was dated twenty days ago. They must have arrived in New York a week ago, and if he don't delay at all, he'll be here in two or three days," Gabriel said.

"Then why should you work like that?"

"I'll stop to-morrow, but I must give notice of a day or two, at least, for the foreman to get somebody else in my place."

When Gabriel arrived at his place of employment near Nob Hill, he found that his occupation that day would be different from what it had been before, and in the afternoon he was put to work at another place in the building. He would have to carry bricks and mortar up a ladder to quite a high wall. He told the foreman that he would rather not do that, as he had never done such work and was very awkward about it. The foreman said he had no one else to spare for that job, and Gabriel at last said he would try. He had carried many loads, and was beginning to tremble with fatigue, when upon going up, carrying a hod full of bricks, the ladder slipped to one side a little. In his effort to steady it, Gabriel moved it too much, and it fell to one side, taking him to the ground. As he fell, the bricks fell upon him. He was insensible for some time. When he regained consciousness he was being carried to a wagon which would take him to the city hospital. Lizzie, to whom the foreman had sent a message notifying her of the accident, now met the wagon.

"Where are you taking my husband?" she asked the driver.

"To the city hospital, ma'am."

"But why not take him home?"

"Because he will get attendance there quickly, Madam," said the foreman, who evidently felt he was to blame for a very painful accident.

"If that is the case, let us go to the hospital," Lizzie said, getting into the wagon. She sat beside Gabriel, and placed his head in her lap. Gabriel smiled, and his beautiful eyes were full of love, but he could scarcely speak a word.

The jolting of the wagon gave him much pain, and Lizzie asked the driver to go very slow. "He ought to be carried on a stretcher, ma'am; he is too much hurt to go in a wagon," said the driver.

They now came to a street-crossing, and several wagons were standing still, waiting for a line of carriages to pass first.

"Oh, why do we wait? He is suffering so much!" Lizzie exclaimed. "He is bleeding; he might bleed to death!"

"We are waiting for them carriages to pass, ma'am. They are carrying people to a reception on Nob Hill, ma'am," said the driver.

On the other side of the street, in a carriage which also had been stopped that the guests for the Nob Hill festivities might pass, sat George and Clarence, just arrived, and on their way to see Lizzie and Gabriel. They saw that a man lay in a wagon which stood in front of them, and noticing that a woman sat by his side holding his head in her lap, bending over him anxiously, Clarence said to the driver that there seemed to be some one sick in that wagon, and that it should be allowed to pass.

"Yes, sir; but he is a hod-carrier who fell down and hurt himself. I suppose he'll die before he gets to the hospital," said the driver, indifferently, as if a hod-carrier more or less was of no consequence. "The carriages must pass first, the police says."

As Lizzie raised her head to ask the driver to take some other street, they saw her. Both uttered an exclamation of surprise, and left their carriages immediately, walking hurriedly to the wagon where she was.

"Lizzie, my sister, why are you here?" George asked.

"Oh, George! Gabriel fell down!" she replied, sobbing, her courage failing now that she had some dear ones to protect her. "Oh, Clarence, see how you find my darling! We are taking him to the city hospital, but because those carriages must pass first my darling may die here— bleeding to death!"

"Let me go for a physician immediately," said Clarence.

"Wait," George said, "Which is the nearest from here, Lizzie, your house or the hospital? We must take him to the nearest place."

"The hospital is nearer, sir," the driver answered.

"Then let us go the hospital," George said, getting into the wagon beside his sister, shocked to find Gabriel in a situation which plainly revealed a poverty he had never imagined.

"I shall go for a surgeon, there might not be one at the hospital," said Clarence. "I shall be there when you arrive."

The wagon went so slowly that Clarence, with a doctor, overtook them before they reached the hospital. Meantime, Gabriel had whispered to Lizzie and George, in a few words, how he had fallen down.

On arriving at the hospital he was carried to the best room, with best attendance, two rooms adjoining were for his nurses, one to be occupied by Lizzie and the other by George and Clarence, for neither of them would leave Gabriel now.

The doctor would give no opinion as to his recovery. If he had internal injuries of a serious character, they might prove fatal, but of this it was impossible to judge at present. About eight o'clock Gabriel seemed to be resting a little more comfortably, and Lizzie took that opportunity to go to see her babies. She found them already asleep. The kind landlady had given them their supper and put them to bed. She told Lizzie of a good nurse who could be hired to take care of the baby, and that she would engage her to come the next morning. Lizzie thanked her, and then returned to her husband's bedside, and there, accompanied by George and Clarence, she passed the night.

About daylight, with great reluctance, she was prevailed upon to lie down on a lounge at the foot of Gabriel's bed, and as the patient seemed to be resting quietly, George and Clarence went into the next room to partake of a light collation.

George poured a glass of wine for Clarence and another for himself, and both drank in silence. Evidently they could not eat.

"Was it possible to imagine that Gabriel could have become so poor that he had to be a hod-carrier?" George said at last, scarcely above a whisper.

Clarence being as much moved, took some time to reply.

"The thing is to me so shockingly preposterous and so very heart-rending that it does not seem possible. And to think that if I had not gone away, I might, yes, could, have prevented so much suffering! Oh! the fool, the idiot that I was to go," said Clarence, rising and pacing the room in great agitation. "I will never forgive myself nor my bankers either, and shall take my money to some other bank. They should never have given Don Gabriel's place to anybody else, for it was at my request, and to oblige me that they employed him, and they have had the use of my money all this time. Oh! how I wish you could have established a bank here with the three hundred thousand dollars I placed to Don Mariano's credit, since he would not accept any payment for the cattle— *my* cattle, mind you— lost in the snow. But perhaps three hundred thousand dollars would have been rather small capital."

"It would have been plenty to begin with, but as the understanding was that the bank was to be in San Diego, none of us felt authorized to change the plan. I doubt if Don Mariano would have drawn any of the three hundred thousand dollars. You know he mortgaged his rancho rather than take any of your money."

"His money, you ought to say, for I had already bought his cattle. I wish he had not taken so different a view of the matter. Really, the money was his from the moment I agreed to make the purchase. But tell me, why is it that Mrs. Mechlin lost her homestead. It might have been sold to help the family."

George related how Peter Roper "*jumped*" the Mechlin house in true vandalic style, breaking open the doors with axes and dragging out the furniture when the family were in great grief, and how this outrage as well as others were indulgently passed over by San Diego's august tribunal of justice. George, however, did not know all. He did not know that Judge Lawlack upon one occasion, when he had made a decision in favor of Peter Roper and against the Mechlins, discovering upon reflection that he had made a gross mistake, because the authority upon which he based his decision, obviously favored the Mechlins, had changed his decision. He actually called the attorneys of both sides into court and then amended his own decree and had an entirely different judgment entered— a judgment based upon another authority, which, with his construction of the law, favored Peter. Then again when the Mechlins tried to file another complaint, Peter got up, and in his coarse loquacity, vociferously exhorted his Honor to send all the plaintiffs and their attorney to jail for *contempt of court* in daring to renew their complaint when his Honor had decided that they had no case; that the *innocent purchasers*, Roper and Gasbang, were the legitimate owners of the Mechlin place. Whereupon, his Honor Lawlack hurriedly slid off the judicial bench, under the judicial canopy, in high tantrums, and shuffled off the judicial platform, gruffly mumbling: "I have passed upon that before," and slouchingly made his exit.

The plaintiffs, their attorneys and their witnesses, were left to make the best of *such legal proceedings*! They could not even take an appeal to the Supreme Court, for they had no record; they could make no pleadings; Judge Lawlack had carefully and effectively done all he could to ruin their case. Peter winked and showed his yellow teeth and purple gums in high glee, proud to have exhibited his influence with the Court, and, as usual, went to celebrate his triumph by getting intoxicated and being whipped, so that he had a black eye and skinned nose for several days.

It was obvious to George and Clarence that the position of Gabriel and Lizzie in San Francisco must have been painful in the extreme, and yet they did not know all. Lizzie had never told anybody all the disagreeable, humiliating, repugnant experiences she had had to pass through. She had tried to help her husband to find some occupation more befitting a gentleman than that of a day laborer. But she gave up her sad endeavors, seeing that she was only humiliating herself to no purpose. She met at times gentlemen and kind-hearted men, who were courteous to her, but oftener she found occasion to despise mankind for their unnecessary rudeness and most unprovoked boorishness. More painful yet was the evident change she noticed in the manners of her lady acquaintances.

Years before, when she was Lizzie Mechlin, she had moved in what was called San Francisco's *best* society. Her family, being of the very highest in New York, were courted and caressed in exaggerated degree on their arrival in California. Afterwards, for the benefit of Mr. Mechlin's health, they went to reside in San Diego. When Gabriel came to his position in the bank, she was again warmly received by all her society friends. But this cordiality soon vanished. Her family went back to New York, and she and Gabriel returned from San Diego to San Francisco to find that he had lost his place at the bank. Then he endeavored to get something else to do. This was bad enough, but when *she* tried to help him, then her fashionable friends disappeared. Nay, they avoided her as if she had been guilty of some disgraceful act. The fact that Gabriel was a *native Spaniard*, she saw plainly, militated against them. If he had been rich, his nationality could have been forgiven, but no one will willingly tolerate a *poor native Californian*. To see all this was at first painful to Lizzie, but afterwards it began to be amusing and laughable to see people show their mean little souls and their want of brains in their eager chase after the rich, and their discourtesy to an old acquaintance who certainly had done nothing to forfeit respect. About that time the fever for stock gambling was at its height. The *Big Bonanza* was, in the twinkling of an eye, making and unmaking money princes, and a new set of rich people had rushed into "San Francisco's best society." The leaders of the *ton* then, who held title by priority of possession, not forgetting that many of them had had to serve a rigorous novitiate of years of probation before they had been admitted to the high circles, were disposed to be exclusive and keep off social "*jumpers.*" But the weight of gold carried the day. Down came the jealously guarded gates; the very portals succumbed and crumbled under that heavy pressure. Farewell, exclusiveness! Henceforth, money shall be the sole requisite upon which to base social claims. High culture, talents, good antecedents, accomplishments, all were now the veriest trash. Money, and nothing but money, became the order of the day. Many of the newly created money-nobility lived but a day in their new, their sporadic, evanescent glory, and then, with a tumble of the stocks, went down head-foremost, to rise no more.

But some of the luckiest survived, and are yet shining stars. Lizzie saw all this from her humble seclusion. Occasionally, at the houses of those few friends who had remained unchanged in her day of adversity, she met some of the newly arrived in society as well as a few of the fading lights, taking a secondary place. All the new and the old lights she saw, with equal impartiality, shifting their places continually, and she began to think that, after all, this transposing of positions perhaps was right, being the unavoidable outcome in a new country, where naturally the raw material is so abundant, and the chase after social position must be a sort of "*go-as-you-please*" race among the golden-legged.

Therefore, like the true lady that she was, Lizzie had quietly accepted her fate, and forgiven fickle society, without a murmur of complaint or a pang of regret. But what certainly was a perennial anguish, a crucifixion of spirit to her, was to see in Gabriel's pale face,— in those superb eyes of his,— all his mental suffering; then courage failed her, and on her bended knees she would implore a merciful heaven to pity and help her beloved, her beautiful archangel.

What Gabriel suffered in spirit probably no one will ever know, for though he inherited the natural nobility of his father, he was not like him communicative, ready to offer or receive sympathy. He was sensitive, kind, courteous and unselfish, but very reticent.

But if Gabriel had never complained, the eloquence of facts had said all that was to be said. In that hod full of bricks not only his own sad experience was represented, but *the entire history* of the native Californians of *Spanish descent* was epitomized. Yes, Gabriel carrying his hod full of bricks up a steep ladder, was a symbolical representation of his race. The natives, of Spanish origin, having lost all their property, must henceforth be hod-carriers.

Unjust laws despoiled them, but what of this? Poor they are, but who is to care, or investigate the cause of their poverty? The thriving American says that the native Spaniards are lazy and stupid and thriftless, and as the prosperous know it all, and are almost infallible, the fiat has gone forth, and the Spaniards of California are not only despoiled of all their earthly possessions, but must also be bereft of sympathy, because the world says they do not deserve it.

George and Clarence entertained a different opinion, however, and in suppressed, earnest tones they now reviewed the history of the Alamares, and feelingly deplored the cruel legislation that had ruined them.

Lizzie, unable to sleep, had again taken her place by the bedside, and sadly watched the beautiful face which seemed like that of slumbering Apollo. Would he recover, or was it possible that her darling would die, now when relief had come? Oh, the cruel fate that made him descend to that humble occupation.

Lizzie shuddered to think of all the suffering he would yet have to undergo. Oh, it was so inexpressibly sad to think that his precious life was risked for the pitiful wages of a poor hod-carrier!

CHAPTER XXXVII.

Reunited at Last.

The life of Gabriel hung by a very frail thread for several days, and Clarence did not have the heart to leave him. He did not telegraph to Mercedes their arrival, for he would then have been obliged to give a reason for delaying. He wrote her saying that Gabriel had accidentally fallen from a ladder, and not knowing how seriously he might have been hurt, George and himself had decided to remain with Lizzie, who was very much frightened and distressed.

Mercedes answered, thanking him in the warmest terms of gratitude for remaining with her darling brother, adding that much as she wished to see the long-lost Clarence, she preferred to endure the pains of waiting rather than to have him leave Gabriel now.

The proudest man in America was Clarence. He knew that in the gratitude of her heart she would allow him to press her to his, and he longed to have that bliss. But faithfully he kept his watch at the hospital, and Gabriel lived yet. No doctor dared say whether he would die or survive his terrible fall, or his health remain impaired. No one dare venture a prophecy for so dark a future.

In the meantime Clarence got his house ready for occupation, and as soon as Gabriel could be removed without danger, they took up their residence there. In the silent recesses of her heart Lizzie thanked God that her surroundings were again those of a lady. She shuddered to remember the poverty she endured for so long a time, and she would have felt really happy could she have been sure that her beloved Gabriel would live.

"George," said she to her brother, as they walked towards the library, when Clarence had relieved their watch, and was sitting by Gabriel's bedside, "I have an idea in my head which I think we might put into practice, if you will help me."

"What is it, dear sister?" asked George, tenderly, observing how thin and haggard she looked.

"It is this, that if you and I write to Mercedes that she ought to marry right away, so that Clarence can bring her to be with me, to help me take care of Gabriel, that she will do so."

"By, Jove! It is a splendid idea, little sister, and I'll write to Mercita and to Doña Josefa at once."

"It is little enough, George, for you and I to do, when Clarence has been so devoted to my darling," said she, her eyes filling with tears of heart-felt gratitude.

"Of course it is, but it comes so natural to Clarence to act always like the noble fellow he is, that it would surprise me if he had acted otherwise than nobly."

"But we ought to consult him about our project."

"Certainly. I'll go and stay with Gabriel and send him to you that you may disclose your plan."

"No, let me go to Gabriel, while you tell him the plan," said she, hurrying off to the invalid, whom she found sleeping.

She whispered to Clarence that George wished to speak to him, and took his place by the bedside.

Clarence could find no words to express to George his joy and gratitude. He flushed and paled by turns, and finally, stroking his mustache with trembling fingers, and trying to bite it, in his agitation, sat down in silence, while George went into the details of the matter.

"But will she consent?" Clarence exclaimed at last.

"I think she will, for you know how all of them love Gabriel, Mercedes more than all,— and the thought that he is suffering, and Lizzie's distress, and your kindness to him,— all that will furnish a most excellent excuse to do what her heart has been begging for," said George. "I am going to write now about it."

"Oh, I shall be so grateful!" Clarence exclaimed.

"Send Lizzie to me, we both must write," George said.

Clarence went back to the sick room, and said to Lizzie that George wanted her.

Kissing her hand most fervently, he exclaimed in a tremulous whisper: "You are my angel!"

George and Lizzie's letters were very pleading. Clarence wrote also, imploring Mercedes to forgive the stupidity that took him away, and beseeched her to yield to his prayer, and be his wife, after so many years of suffering.

Mercedes kissed the letter, and cried over it, of course, as women must, but referred the subject to her mother. Doña Josefa must also cry a good deal before she said anything, for the memory of her husband made such subjects most painful to her.

But Victoriano stormed from his bed. He would have no delay. He sent for Everett, so that he would in person carry a dispatch to town, saying to Clarence, by telegraph, to come in the very first steamer. Victoriano would have no contradiction.

"If Mercedes don't marry Clarence, as George advises, I want to be taken by the legs— my mean, cripple legs, my ridiculous kangaroo legs— and dragged out of this bed, and out of this house. I don't want to live under the same roof with people that will refuse so just and reasonable a request."

"But who has refused it, Tano? Wait, won't you?" said Rosario, seeing that Tano had hidden his head under the covers.

Victoriano's head came out again, and said: "Nobody says yes."

But the *yes* was said.

Everett took a dispatch from Doña Josefa to George, saying that whenever

Clarence came, Mercedes would go with him, as George suggested.

There would be five days only before another steamer would arrive, but by telegraphing to Clarence on that day, he would have time to take the steamer next morning, or go on the cars to Los Angeles, and take the steamer at Wilmington. And this was what Clarence telegraphed he would do, suggesting that if Mercita would be ready, they could take the same boat, and by again taking the cars at Los Angeles, be with Gabriel in two days.

Was it a dream? To see Clarence within five days, and be his wife, when she thought she might never see him on this earth again! Thus ran Mercedes' reflections, when she had gone to her room to open a wardrobe which had been locked for three years. That wardrobe held the *trousseau* sent by Mrs. Lawrence Mechlin in '74, and the jewelry which Clarence had given her in New York.

Mercedes thought of those days, and the image of her father arose before her vividly. She sat by the window to think of him with loving tenderness and ever living regret.

"But, *mon Dieu*, mademoiselle," said Madame Halier, coming in, "why don't you come? Miss Carlota is waiting to begin getting your things ready."

"I beg pardon; I had forgotten," said Mercedes, rousing herself from her reverie. Carlota, Rosario and Alice now came in, and soon the contents of the wardrobe were distributed all over the room. Madame Halier was to pack in trunks all Mercedes' things, leaving out only her bridal attire and traveling dress. The madame did her work with pleasure, as she was going with Mercedes, and had been wishing to visit the city of San Francisco for a long time.

Everything was ready. A dispatch came from George saying that Clarence had started; that Gabriel was a little better, and anxious to see Mercedes. This made Doña Josefa feel that it was her imperative duty to send Mercedes to her brother at once.

Mrs. Darrell went to see the priest about going to the rancho to perform the marriage ceremony there. The good man would have preferred that it were solemnized in the church, but, considering that Victoriano could not leave his bed and Doña Josefa was still in very deep mourning, he consented.

There would be no invited guests except the Holmans and Darrells. There would be no bridesmaids either, though there were plenty of young girls that could act as such.

Everett went to town the night before the arrival of the steamer to bring Clarence as soon as he landed, and they came from town so quickly and noiselessly that no one knew when they arrived at the rancho.

The ladies were all in Mercedes' room discussing the wedding outfit and other matters, when it occurred to her to go out and from the veranda look towards the road, as she might perhaps see the carriage in the distance. What was her surprise when, on passing by the parlor door, she saw Everett coming through the gate, and there, right there, where Clarence had stood on that terrible night when he left her, there he stood again, looking at her with those same speaking, glowing, loving eyes. He seemed to her like an apparition, and she uttered an exclamation of surprise, turning very pale and tottering as if about to fall. In an instant he was by her side pressing her to his heart and covering her face with kisses.

Surely this was no ghost. His warm kisses and beating heart spoke of the lover full of life and hope, trembling with the realization of years of longing to hold her thus close, very close in his loving, chaste embrace.

"Mercedes, my own, my sweet wife," he said, and his voice had so much the same tone and vibration as in that last memorable night, that the rush of sad memories and painful emotions made her for a moment feel confused, bewildered, almost losing consciousness. As her yielding form relaxed in his arms he carried her to the sofa and sat there holding her, scarcely realizing it was not all a dream.

Everett had gone to Victoriano's room, and now that impatient invalid was screaming for Clarence to come. His loud calling brought Doña Josefa to him, and then all the family learned that Clarence had arrived.

"Come here, you truant," said Victoriano to Clarence, "come here, you ugly man." And as Clarence stooped to embrace him, he clasped him to his heart, making him lie down by his side. "There," said he, "I have given you a good hugging; now go and kiss the girls."

Which Clarence did gladly, but his mother and Doña Josefa he kissed first. He then went to the parlor, where he was kindly greeted by no less than fourteen girls, counting thus: three Alamares, three Holmans, four Darrells, and four other Alamares, cousins of Mercedes.

Clarence was a brave fellow, so he never flinched and kissed them all, very deliberately. "Not to give offence," he said.

There was one duty which Clarence shrank from performing, but which he submitted to quietly, and that was meeting his father.

Darrell came to the Alamar house for the first time in his life, and as he said he would like to be alone when he met Clarence, Rosario conducted him to *the office*, a room used by her father when he saw people on business and where he wrote his letters, but where others of the family scarcely ever entered.

Clarence was shocked to see how aged his father was. When he left, the auburn hair of the old man showed no white lines at all. Now he was so gray that his hair was almost white. The sight of that white hair swept from Clarence's heart all trace of resentment, and his love for his father seemed to rush back to him with pain, but with great force.

"Oh, father!" exclaimed Clarence, seeing the open arms before him.

"My boy, my best beloved," said the old man, with a sob and a checking of breath, holding his son close to his breast.

"Father, why are you so gray?" Clarence asked.

"Because I did you a great wrong. Because I murdered the Don, and he was the best man I ever saw." When Darrell said this he completely lost his self-control and wept like a child. Clarence wept with him, for he felt deeply Don Mariano's death, but thought he must speak kindly to his father.

"You did not murder him; don't think that," he said.

"Yes, I did. My wickedness helped the wickedness of others to kill him. And our wickedness combined brought infinite misery upon this innocent family. But a merciful God brought you back, and I know you will devote your life to repair as much as it is possible the wrong your father did. I know you will be a good husband, but for *my sake*, also, I beg you to be a devoted son to the widowed lady whom I have injured so frightfully. A wrong legislation authorized *us squatters*, sent us, to the land of these innocent, helpless people to rob them. A wrong legislation killed the Texas Pacific, and such legislation is the main cause of the Don's death. But I, too, helped the wrong-doers."

"Don't blame yourself so much," Clarence remonstrated gently, trying to soothe his father. "George and Lizzie told me that all the family believe that the disappointment at the failure of the Texas Pacific was what killed Don Mariano. It preyed upon his mind; it saddened, worried and sickened him until it utterly undermined his health and broke down his nervous system. It did the same with Mr. Mechlin. So, you see, those who defeated the Texas Pacific are to blame for the death of these two most excellent men, but not yourself."

"Yes, I am. No man can injure his fellow-man, and then shift the blame on some one else's shoulders, because others had a share in the wrong done. Each man must stand and bear his proportion of blame. I could and should have prevented the settlers from destroying the Don's cattle. If I had done so, he would not have been obliged to take them all at once. He could have sent them in small bands, but he was afraid of the murderous rifles of *my friends*. So the poor, dumb animals perished in the snow. But this was not the worst; the saddest was yet to come. Victoriano lost his health, and the Don lost his life. The good, the best of men, was right when, in his dying moments, he said: '*The sins of our legislators brought me to this.*' That was a truth uttered by a just and noble soul as it passed away. Still, I must feel I am individually to blame for the sorrow brought upon this family. I know that if the railroad had been built the Don could have recuperated his fortune, but yet my share of wrong-doing stands there all the same; I must bear it myself. If I had not driven you away, you could have prevented their misfortunes. I was a monster. So now I beg and entreat, for my own sake, and as a slight reparation for my cruelty, that you be kind to that lady, as kind as if you were her own child."

"I will, father; I vow I will."

"That is enough. I know you'll keep your word. Now, my boy, heaven bless you, and your father's blessing will go with you always. Now, go, and when the ceremony is to be performed, send Willie to call me."

As everything was ready, the marriage ceremony took place as soon as the priest arrived. Victoriano was brought to the parlor in an arm-chair, and managed to stand up, held by Everett and Webster. Doña Josefa wept all the time and so did her daughters, but everybody understood that memories of the sad past, but no fears for the future, caused those tears to flow.

The parting with her mother and sisters was most painful to Mercedes. Clarence feared she would make herself ill with weeping. He put his arms around her waist and said:

"Don't be disheartened. I have been thinking that Doña Josefa and all the family had better come to San Francisco to live. If she does, I think we can persuade George to bring his family also to reside there."

Doña Josefa shook her head doubtingly, but Mercedes asked:

"Do you think George might come?"

"I do, and he can then carry out there our plan of establishing a bank. San Diego is dead now, and will remain so for many years, but San Francisco is a good business field. So we can all locate ourselves there, and Gabriel and Tano go into business easily."

"Business without capital? See where my poor Gabriel is now," Doña Josefa answered, sadly.

"That is true, but if you will sell your rancho, they will have plenty of capital. Even at two dollars per acre, your rancho, being forty-seven thousand acres— if sold at that low figure— would bring you ninety-four thousand dollars."

"But who, who will buy mortgaged land, full of squatters, and without a patent, in this dead place?"

"I will. I will pay you more than ninety-four thousand dollars— more than double that amount— besides paying you for the lost cattle, which will be no more than what is right."

"Oh, no, I couldn't agree to that, but as for selling the land, if my children are willing, I shall be, for this place is too full of sad memories, and will be sadder yet if I cannot have my children with me. When Gabriel and Victoriano get well, talk to them about buying the rancho, though I don't think you ought to pay any such high price. You are too generous to us."

"Indeed, I am not. Don't forget I am a money-making Yankee. I think four— or even three— dollars per acre is a high price for land in this county *now*, but I can wait years, and then I shall double the price paid now. So, you see, I am not a bit generous. I am trying to make money out of you."

"Talk to the boys. See what George and Gabriel say," Doña Josefa said, smiling sadly at Clarence's wily argument and earnest manner.

The last adieux were said, but the parting was less painful to Mercedes, with the new hope held out by Clarence of a probability of being reunited soon in San Francisco.

When Clarence and Mercedes arrived at their home they found that

George and Lizzie had propped up Gabriel with pillows, and he was sitting up to receive his sister. From that day he began to improve slowly but perceptibly.

The letters from home spoke of Victoriano's marked improvement, but still his malady was not cured; so Clarence proposed that Doña Josefa, the two girls and Tano should come up immediately. She could then make up her mind whether she would like to make San Francisco her home, and the change of climate would perhaps do Victoriano good. The idea was highly approved by all, and that same evening Mercedes wrote to her mother, begging her to come and see whether she liked San Francisco for a home; that she and Clarence were going to Europe on a visit in the fall, and she wanted to leave her mamma and sisters and brothers all together; that George and Gabriel liked the plan of selling the rancho to Clarence very much, and wanted to talk to her and Tano about it. Thus Doña Josefa was enticed and persuaded to leave the home of her joys and sorrows, where she had lived for thirty years. Carlota and Rosario were willing to go, and Tano was most anxious to find a way of making a living, for he was every day more in love with Alice, but could not think of marrying her until he knew how he was going to support a family.

Doña Josefa, Carlota and Rosario, therefore, escorted by Victoriano, found themselves, on a bright morning, in the Southern Pacific Railroad cars, on their way from Los Angeles to San Francisco. There were only about a dozen persons besides themselves on the entire train.

"I wonder why they put on so many cars. One would carry all the passengers," said Rosario.

"Half a car would be more than enough," Carlota added.

"They must lose money running empty cars," Tano observed. "I am glad of it. They were so anxious to leave San Diego out in the cold, I hope they will lose money with this road."

"Don't wish that, it is unkind, unchristian, ungenerous," said Doña Josefa, with a sigh.

"And why not? Didn't they kill our road, the Texas Pacific, to build this road? What consideration had they for us? I am glad that many years will pass before they will run crowded cars over this desert. They are old men, they won't live to see this, their pet road, with well-filled cars, running over it, and I bet on that," said Tano, exultingly.

"Perhaps they will," said Carlota.

"I know they'll not," Tano retorted, emphatically.

In the afternoon, Clarence and Mercedes met them in Oakland, and together they crossed the bay.

And now on that same night as Doña Josefa looked from her bedroom window upon the lighted city, she noticed that a large mansion near by, was very brightly illuminated, and Mercedes told her that one of the railroad kings, who had killed the Texas Pacific, lived there, and was giving a "*silver wedding*" party to the *elite* of San Francisco. Doña Josefa sighed, and sat at the window to think.

Truly, San Francisco had been in a flutter for ten days past, and the "best society" had stretched its neck until it ached to see who got invitations for "*The Great Nob Hill Silver Wedding Ball*" of one of San Francisco's millionaires. Mrs. Grundy ascertained who were to be the best-dressed ladies, what their pedigree was, and how their money had been made, and then Mrs. Grundy went to the ball, too.

When all the elegance of San Francisco had arrived, nobly sprinkled with a Baron or two, and ornamented with a Lord and Lady and a Marquise or Count, the great millionaire proceeded to astonish his guests in the manner he had conceived to be most novel and startling.

The band struck up a wedding march, and Mr. Millionaire, with his wife leaning on his arm, proceeded to the last of an elegant *suite* of rooms, where, under a canopy of fragrant flowers, a mock marriage ceremony was to be performed. After conducting the blushing bride to the mock altar, and the ceremony being over, the millionaire thought he would treat his guests to what he imagined to be a real hymenean oration. He prefaced his homily with what he believed to be witticisms and quotations of his own. He then thought it was time to wax eloquent and didactic, above prejudices, truly large-minded.

"But let me read to you a short, telling lesson now," he said, swelling with just pride; "I speak most particularly to the young men, to those who have yet their fortunes to make. Be not discouraged if you meet with hardships and trials. Go ahead and persevere. Look at all these luxurious appurtenances surrounding us! I might well say, look at this wealth! Look at this splendor! Well, ladies and gentlemen, sixteen years ago we were in Sacramento, so poor, that we had to put tin pans over our bed to catch the water that leaked through our roof, and keep our bed-clothes dry. I had not money enough to get a better roof over our heads," and the millionaire looked around for applause, but none came, because the guests possessed the good taste, or, perhaps, bad, which their host lacked, and were pained and mortified; they did not see the good of waking up memories of unsavory poverty. The foreign nobility was not so proud, perhaps, as they had been at the hour of receiving an invitation to all this so very newly created splendor. But the rich man, still inflated with pride, hurriedly wound up his peroration as best he could, feeling vague misgivings that he had marred the *eclat* of his magnificent illumination shining over his costly furniture, by trying to rise above himself to make a high-minded, witty speech. "Be plucky, and persevering, and go ahead, as I did," said he to close his oration, bowing to his foreign guests.

The company scattered in couples or in groups over the luxuriously furnished and richly decorated rooms, and Mrs. Grundy hurried about everywhere to catch the comments made by the grateful guests upon "the brilliant speech of their amiable host." At the very first group she heard a young man say:

"Yes, I would be *plucky and persevering* if I had an associate in Washington with plenty of money to bribe people so that no other railroad could be built to start competition in California."

"I could be plucky, too, if the Government had given me millions of money and more millions of acres to build two railroads, and which millions I never intended to pay back," said another.

"And for which millions you never paid taxes," added another.

"Taxes? Bah! Let the poor people pay taxes. Why should railroad magnates pay taxes when they have money to fight the law? Absurd!" said a fourth. "Let us go and take ices; the brilliancy of our host's oration makes me thirsty."

And while all this went on in the brilliantly lighted mansion, Doña Josefa sat at her window in the dark, thinking of what "*might have been*" if those railroad men had not blighted San Diego's prosperity. Her husband would have been alive, and Mr. Mechlin, also, and her sons would not have been driven to poverty and distress, and perhaps lost their health forever.

"God of Justice, is this right, that so many should be sacrificed because a few men want more millions? Our family is one of the many who have suffered so much. Oh! so much! And all to what end? For what? Ah! the same answer again, because a few heartless men want more millions," said she, with her face bathed in tears.

Doña Josefa evidently did not believe that because "*misery there must always be in the world, no matter who causes it,*" that she was called upon to stoically submit to unmerited infliction. In a mild and dignified way, her mind rebelled. She regarded the acts of the men who caused her husband's ruin and death with genuine abhorrence. To her, rectitude and equity had a clear meaning impossible to pervert. No subtle sophistry could blur in her mind the clear line dividing right from wrong. She knew that among men the word business means inhumanity to one another; it means justification of rapacity; it means the freedom of man to crowd and crush his fellow-man; it means the sanction of the Shylockian principle of exacting the pound of flesh. She knew all this, but the illustration, the ocular demonstration, had never been before her until now in that gay house, in that brightly illuminated mansion, and she sadly contrasted her sorrow with their gayety, and continued her soliloquy: "No doubt those people think they have a right to rejoice and feast with the money extorted in crushing so many people— the killing of my darling. Doubtless they say that they earned the money in BUSINESS, and that allegation is all-sufficient; that one word justifies in the pursuit of riches everything mean, dishonest, rapacious, unfair, treacherous, unjust, and fraudulent. After a man makes his money no one cares how he made it, and so those people dance while I mourn for my beloved."

For hours Doña Josefa sat at that window, weeping sadly, while the others danced gayly.

Afterwards, when she had been for some time in San Francisco, she had yet stronger demonstrations, and her sense of justice and her ideas of moral adjustment of men's actions with principle, received additional shocks, quite as painful as seeing the millionaire's palace illuminated, while the humble houses he had desolated must remain dark.

Doña Josefa frankly spoke to the ladies who had called on her, of the cause of her husband's death. She did so in answer to their inquiries. She, on two or three occasions, mentioned how painful it had been to sit by the window looking at that house of rejoicing, while thinking that if those rich men had had more sense of justice and less greed of money, that her husband could have been spared to her.

"Don't say that, my dear lady, for you will give great offense," said an old friend, who having heard that Clarence was worth twelve million dollars, had called on her, suddenly remembering that she used to know the Alamares years ago.

"Why should I give offense? It is the truth," Doña Josefa replied.

"That may be, but you cannot speak against such rich people; San Francisco society will turn against you," was the rejoinder.

"Then it is a crime *to speak* of the wrongs we have suffered, but it is not a crime *to commit* those wrongs."

"I don't know. I am not a moralist. But this I do know, that if you accuse those rich men of having done wrong, the society people will give you the cold shoulder."

"Oh, very well, let it be so. Let the guilty rejoice and go unpunished, and the innocent suffer ruin and desolation. I slander no one, but shall speak the truth."

CONCLUSION.

Out with the Invader.

"Let infamy be that man's portion who uses his power to corrupt, to ruin, to debase," says Channing, in righteous indignation, speaking of the atrocities perpetrated by Napoleon the First to gratify his vanity and ambition. Further on, with increasing earnestness, Channing adds: "In anguish of spirit we exclaim: 'How long will an abject world kiss the foot that tramples it? How long shall crime find shelter in its very aggravations and excess?'"

If Channing lived now, his 'anguish of spirit' would be far greater to find in his own country, firmly enthroned, *a power that corrupts, ruins and debases* as utterly as that which he so eloquently deplored, and his own fellow-citizens— the free-born Americans— ready and willing to *kiss the foot that tramples them*!

Not infamy, but honor and wealth, is the portion of the men who corrupt and ruin and debase in this country. Honor and wealth for the Napoleons of this land, whose power the sons of California can neither check, nor thwart, nor escape, nor withstand. And in California, as in France, "crime finds shelter in its very aggravations and excess," for after ten years of fighting in Congress against legislation that would have given to the people of the Southern States and the Pacific Coast a competing railway; and after fighting against creating a sinking fund to re-imburse moneys due to the Government, and fighting against laws to regulate freights and fares on a fair basis, they (the Napoleons) refuse to pay taxes on their gigantic property, thus making it necessary for the Governor of California to call an extra session of the Legislature to devise some new laws which will compel those defiant millionaires to pay taxes, and not leave upon the shoulders of poor people the onerous duty of defraying public expenses.

Is not this "aggravation of excess?" Excess of defiance? Excess of lawlessness? How insidiously these monopolists began their work of accumulation, which has culminated in a power that not only eludes the law of the land, but defies, derides it! They were poor men. They came before the Government at Washington, and before the people of California, as suppliant petitioners, humbly begging for aid to construct a railroad. The aid was granted most liberally, and as soon as they accumulated sufficient capital to feel rich they began their work of eluding and defying the law. They became insolent, flinging defiance, as if daring the law to touch them, and truly, the law thus far has been powerless with them. At Washington they won their first victories against the American people; and now California has the shame of seeing that she has not the power to enforce her laws upon the men she made rich. The Legislature convened and adjourned, and there is no way yet of compelling the insolent millionaires to pay their taxes or regulate their rates on freights and fares!

It seems now that unless *the people of California take the law in their own hands*, and seize the property of those men, and confiscate it, to re-imburse the money due *the people*, the arrogant corporation will never pay. They are so accustomed to appropriate to themselves what rightfully belongs to others, and have so long stood before the world in defiant attitude, that they have become utterly insensible to those sentiments of fairness animating law-abiding men of probity and sense of justice.

These monopolists are essentially dangerous citizens in the fullest acceptance of the word. They are dangerous citizens, not only in being guilty of violation of the law, in subverting the fundamental principles of public morality, but they are dangerous citizens, because they *lead others* into the commission of the same crimes. Their example is deadly to honorable sentiments; it is poison to Californians, because it allures men with the glamour of success; it incites the unwary to imitate the conduct of men who have become immensely rich by such culpable means.

Mr. Huntington in his letters (made public in the Colton suit), shows the truth of all this; shows how bribing and corrupting seemed to him perfectly correct. He speaks of "the men that can be *convinced*" (meaning the men that will take bribes), as naturally as if no one need blush for it. And with the same frankness he discloses his maneuvering to defeat the Texas Pacific Railroad, and elude the payment of moneys due the Government. It is surprising, as well as unpleasant, to read in Mr. Huntington's letters the names of men in high positions whom he reckons in his list as "men who can *be convinced*" and he speaks of them in a cool way and off-hand manner, which shows how little respect he has for those whom he can *convince*. Perhaps there are some in his list who never did take a bribe from him, but then those gentlemen are in the position of "Old Dog Tray," who suffered for being in bad company.

"I have set matters to work in the South that I think will switch most of the South from Tom Scott's Texas and Pacific bill," etc., etc., Mr. Huntington wrote in April, '75, and in November of the same year he concluded to send Dr. Gwin to work on the credulity of the Southerners, to switch them off.

"I think the doctor can do us some good if he can work under cover. * * * He must not come to the surface as *our man*. * * * Not as our agent, but as an anti-subsidy Democrat and a Southern man," etc. When the deceiver returned, Mr. Huntington wrote: "I notice what you say about the interest that Dr. Gwin should have. I have no doubt that we shall agree about what his interest should be," says Mr. Huntington, speaking of the price to be paid the ex-Senator for his work of helping to "*switch off the South!*"

In another letter Mr. Huntington says: "I had a talk with Bristow, Secretary of the Treasury. He will be likely to help us fix up our matters with the Government on a fair basis."

Another letter says: "I am doing all I can to have the Government take six million acres of land, and give the railroad company credit for fifteen million dollars, etc. I wish you would have the newspapers take the ground that this land ought to be taken by the Government and held for the people, etc. Something that the demagogues can vote and work for," etc.

Mr. Huntington also says: "I think there should be a bridge company organized (that we are not in) to build over the Colorado River, etc. In this way we could tax the through business on this line should we so desire," etc.

In another letter, dated March 7th, 1877, he says: "I stayed in Washington two days to fix up a Railroad Committee in the Senate. * * * The Committee is just as we want it, which is a very important thing for us." * * *

He again says: "The Committees are made up for the Forty-fifth Congress. I think the Railroad Committee is right, but the Committees on Territories I do not like. A different one was promised me. Sherrel has just telegraphed me to come to Washington," etc.

Mr. Huntington mentions in other letters the fact of bills being submitted to him before being put to vote; and also about being consulted concerning the formation of Committees and other Congressional matters, much as if Congress really wished to keep on the good side of Mr. Huntington. But it looked also as if he did not have everything his own way always, for at times he loses patience and calls Congress a "set of the worst strikers," and "the hungriest set" he ever saw.

In his letter to his friend Colton, of June 20th, '78, he exclaims: "I think in the world's history never before was such a wild set of demagogues honored by the name of Congress. We have been hurt some, but some of the worst bills have been defeated, but we cannot stand many such Congresses," etc.

The thing that annoyed Mr. Huntington the most was that he could not persuade Governor Stanford to tell the bare-faced falsehood, that the Southern Pacific did not belong to the owners of the Central Pacific.

Again and again Mr. Huntington urged the necessity of this falsehood being told, childishly forgetting the fact that such prevarications would have been useless, as all Californians knew the truth.

In the Congressional Committees, however, he himself attempted to pass off that misstatement. It is not likely that he was believed, but he succeeded in killing the Texas Pacific, and in "seeing the grass grow over Tom Scott." The subterfuge no doubt was useful.

Mr. Huntington having buried the Texas Pacific, and also Colonel Scott, as well as other worthy people (of whom no mention has been made in this book), now proceeded to demand that the Government surrender to him and associates, the land subsidy granted by Congress to the Texas Pacific.

This, surely, is an "*aggravation of excess!*"

The House Committee on Public Lands in their report on the "*forfeiture of the Texas Pacific land grant*" reviewed Mr. Huntington's acts with merited severity. Amongst many other truths the report says: "The Southern Pacific claims to 'stand in *the shoes*' of the Texas Pacific. Your committee agree that 'standing in the shoes' would do if the Southern Pacific *filled the shoes.*" But it does not. It never had authority or recognition by Congress east of Yuma. For its own purpose, by *methods which honest men have denounced*, greedy to embrace all land within its net-work of rails, to secure monopoly of transportation, surmounting opposition and beating down all obstacles in its way, and in doing so, crushing the agent Congress had selected as instrument to build a road there, *doing nothing, absolutely nothing, by governmental authority or assent even, and having succeeded in defeating a necessary work and rendering absolutely abortive the attempt to have one competing transportation route to the Pacific built, it coolly asks to bestow upon it fifteen millions of acres of lands; to give it the ownership of an area sufficient for perhaps one hundred thousand homes, as a reward for that result.*

And the committee (with one dissenting voice only) reported their opinion that the Southern Pacific Railroad Company had *neither legal nor equitable* claim to the lands of the Texas Pacific which Mr. Huntington wished to appropriate.

But is it not a painful admission that these few men should have thwarted and defeated the purpose and intent of the Government of the United States of having a competing railway in the Texas Pacific? Not only Colonel Scott, and Hon. John C. Brown, and Mr. Frank T. Bond, the President and Vice President of this road, but also Senator Lamar, Mr. J. W. Throckmorton, Mr. House, Mr. Chandler, of Mississippi, and many, many other able speakers, honorable, upright men, all endeavored faithfully to aid the construction of the Texas Pacific. All failed. The falsehoods disseminated by ex-Senator Gwin, which Senator Gordon and others believed, and thus in good faith reproduced, had more effect when backed by the monopoly's money.

But Tom Scott is laid low, and so is the Texas Pacific; now the fight for greedy accumulation is transferred to California. The monopoly is confident of getting the land subsidy of the Texas Pacific— after killing it; of getting every scrap that might be clutched under pretext of having belonged to the decapitated road. Thus the lands that the City of San Diego donated to Tom Scott *on condition* that the Texas Pacific should be built, even these, the monopoly has by some means seized upon. No Texas Pacific was built, but nevertheless, though clearly specified stipulations be violated, San Diego's lands must go into the voracious jaws of the monster. Poor San Diego! After being ruined by the greed of the heartless monopolists, she is made to contribute her widow's mite to swell the volume of their riches! This is cruel irony indeed.

And now those pampered millionaires have carried their defiance of the law to the point of forcing the Governor of California to call an extra session of the Legislature to compel them to obey the law. Speaking of these matters a very able orator said in one of his speeches in the extra session:

"It is stated in the proclamation of the Governor to convene this Legislature, that for three or four years past the principal railroads in this State have set at defiance the laws of the people; that they have refused to pay their taxes; that they had set up within our borders an *imperium in imperio*; that they had avowed and declared themselves free from the laws of the State under which they hold their organization; that there were no laws in this State to which they were bound to submit and pay such taxes as would have fallen to them had they been subject to the laws of the State, etc., etc. It has not occurred before in the United States that a great Commonwealth has been defied successfully by its own creatures."

Other speakers followed, and we of California have now, at least, the satisfaction of knowing that faithful hearts and bright intellects have been aroused and are watching the strides of the monster power.

The Spanish population of the State are proud of their countryman, Reginaldo del Valle, who was one of the first to take a bold stand against the monopoly. This young orator with great ability and indomitable energy, has never flagged in his eloquent denunciations of the power which has so trampled the laws of California and the rights of her children.

Mr. Breckinridge, another brilliant orator, speaking of the pertinacious defiance of the law exhibited by the monopolists, said: "Nothing but a shock, a violent shock, a rude lesson— such as the old French noblesse got when they saw their chateaux fired and their sons guillotined— will awaken them from their dream of security."

The champions of right fought well, fought nobly, in the legislature, but alas! the gold of the monopoly was too powerful, and the *extra session*, called to devise means of compelling the railroad corporation to obey the law, adjourned— adjourned, having *failed* in accomplishing the object for which it was called.

The legislators themselves acknowledged that corruption was too strong to be withstood. Mr. Nicol said:

"There was once a belief that the legislature of California was a high, honorable body, into which it should be the pride and glory of fathers to see their sons gain admission. I have been here two sessions, and instead of being a place to which an honorable ambition should prompt a young man to aspire, I believe it to be the worst place on the continent. *We are surrounded by a lobby which degrades every man here by constant temptation and offers of corruption; the monopoly has made it no place where a careful father will send his son.*"

If these powerful monopolists were to speak candidly, would they say that the result of their struggle for money in the last fourteen years of their lives has compensated them for that shoulder-to shoulder fight with opponents who were in the right, and must be vanquished by foul means? "I shall see the grass grow over Tom Scott," prophetically wrote Mr. Huntington several times. He had his wish. The grass grows over Tom Scott. Mr. Huntington can claim the glory of having laid low his powerful opponent, for it is well known that the ten years' struggle for the Texas Pacific undermined Colonel Scott's health beyond recovery. Broken down in health, he left Mr. Huntington master of the field. But is the victory worth the cost? The fight was certainly not glorious for the victor. Is it to be profitable? Many lives have been wrecked, many people impoverished, much injustice done, and all for the sake of having the Southern Pacific Railroad without a rival, without competition. This road runs mostly through a desert; how is it to be made profitable? In their eager pursuit of riches, the projectors of it miscalculated the inevitable, and did not foresee that other capital could, in a few years, build competing lines through more favorable routes; did not foresee that it would have been a better policy to adhere honestly to the terms of their first charter; did not foresee that it would have been better not to sacrifice San Diego. No, they deemed it a wiser plan to kill Tom Scott, to kill San Diego, and then take the money earned in this manner to go and build railroads in Guatemala and in British America. To men who do not think that in *business* the rights of others should be considered, this policy of crushing or desolating everything in the path of triumphant accumulators no doubt is justifiable. But why should the rich enjoy rights that are "deadly to other men?" It is alleged in defense of the California railroad monopolists that as they do not think it would be lucrative to run a railroad to San Diego, they do not build any. If this were a true allegation, why did they fear the Texas Pacific as a competing road? Why did they spend so much money and ten years of their lives to kill that railroad? Surely, if they knew so well that a road to San Diego would not pay, why were they so anxious to prevent its construction? Was it out of a purely disinterested and philanthropic solicitude for their rivals? Did Mr. Huntington wish "to see grass grow over Tom Scott" because he kindly desired to prevent his financial ruin?

Obviously, to maintain that the monopoly did not build a road to San Diego because it would not pay, and that they would not allow Tom Scott to build it either, for the same reason, is not logical. If to construct and run such road would have been ruinous, that was the very best of reasons for allowing it to be built. This would have been as effective a way of getting rid of Colonel Scott as by seeing grass grow over his grave.

But no, it is not true that the San Diego road would not have been profitable; the truth is, that because it would have been profitable, it was dreaded as a rival of the Southern Pacific. But the monopoly had no money to build two roads at once, so they (characteristically) thought best to kill it. As they could not have it, no one else should. And for this reason, and because one of the railroad kings conceived a great animosity against the people of San Diego and became their bitter, revengeful enemy, they were not allowed to have a railroad. This last fact seems incredibly absurd, but if we remember how a Persian tyrant razed a city to the ground because he ate there something that gave him an indigestion, we ought not be surprised if a modern king— one of California's tyrants— should punish a little city because it did not turn out *en masse* to do him humble obeisance. Doubtless, to indulge in such petty malice was not lofty; it was a sort of mental indigestion not to be proud of; it was a weakness, but it was also a wickedness, and worse yet, it was a *blunder*.

Time alone, however, will prove this. In the meanwhile, the money earned in California (as Californians only know how) is taken to build roads in Guatemala. Towns are crushed and sacrificed in California to carry prosperity to other countries. And California groans under her heavy load, but submits, seeing her merchants and farmers ground down with "special contracts" and discriminating charges, and the refractory punished with pitiless severity. Thus, merchants and farmers are hushed and made docile under the lash, for what is the use of complaining? When the Governor of this State sought in vain to curb the power of the monster and compel it to pay taxes by calling an extra session of the Legislature, and nothing was done, what more can be said?

Ask the settlers of the Mussel Slough what is their experience of the pitiless rigor of the monopoly towards those who confidently trusted in the good faith of the great power. These poor farmers were told by the railroad monopoly to locate homesteads and plant orchards and vineyards and construct irrigating canals; that they would not have to pay for their land any higher price than before it was improved. With this understanding the farmers went to work, and with great sacrifices and arduous labor made their irrigating canals and other improvements. Then when this sandy swamp had been converted into a garden, and valueless lands made very valuable, the monopoly came down on the confiding people and demanded the price of the land after it had been improved. The farmers remonstrated and asked that the original agreement should be respected; but all in vain. The arm of the law was called to eject them. They resisted, and bloodshed was the consequence. Some of them were killed, but all had to submit, there was no redress.

And what price did the monopoly pay for these lands? Not one penny, dear reader. These lands are a little bit of a small portion out of many millions of acres given as a subsidy, a *gift*, to build the Southern Pacific Railroad, which road, the charter said, was to pass through San Diego and terminate at Fort Yuma.

The line of this road was changed without authority. [Mr. Huntington talks in his letters about *convincing* people to make this change.] Thus the Mussel Slough farmers got *taken in*, into Mr. Huntington's lines— as was stated by the public press.

But these, as well as the blight, spread over Southern California, and over the entire Southern States, are historical facts. All of which, strung together, would make a brilliant and most appropriate chaplet to encircle the lofty brow of the great and powerful monopoly. Our representatives in Congress, and in the State Legislature, knowing full well the will of the people, ought to legislate accordingly. If they do not, then we shall— as Channing said "kiss the foot that tramples us!" and "in anguish of spirit" must wait and pray for a Redeemer who will emancipate the white slaves of California.

THE END

Detailed Historical Context
The Squatter and the Don

LITERATURE IN THE 19TH CENTURY

The 19th century was a fascinating and essential developmental time in Western literature since it served as the primary context for the future expansion and emergence of current writings and styles as we know them now. The Romantic, Symbolist, and Realist movements, as well as numerous social and economic conditions that prevailed in the 20th century, for example, all had their origins and predecessors in the 19th century.

LITERARY MOVEMENTS

ROMANTICISM IN LITERATURE

Romanticism, a new style with a contrastive focus on emotion and the irrational, emerged in the 19th century. In contrast, the 18th century was thought of as the age of reason, logic, and intellect. Romanticism was characterized by a focus on the unique, the subjective, the mystical, emotional, and inner life. It had its origins in the German *Sturm und Drang* ("Stress and Storm") style of the late 18th century, which was noteworthy because it included Goethe and Friedrich Schiller. It had a big influence on music, art, literature, and even architecture.

- *Jean-Jacques Rousseau*

Rousseau, a Swiss philosopher who lived in the 18th century, had an influence on the Pre-romantic and Romantic movements, as well as the *Age of Enlightenment* and some elements of the French Revolution, with his attention on the individual and the necessity of inspiration.

- *Early Romantic poetry*

The *Lyrical Ballads* collection of poetry by the Romantic English poets William Wordsworth and Samuel Taylor Coleridge, published in 1798, is regarded as the precursor to this style in the late 18th and early 19th centuries. The Romantic poetry movement spread throughout Europe and beyond, as seen by the works of Ugo Foscolo and Giacomo Leopardi in Italy, Pushkin in Russia, and José de Espronceda in Spain.

- *Romanticism in America*

A few examples of the Romantic movement's influence and growth in America include the historical adventure novels of James Fenimore Cooper, the occult and mystical works of Edgar Allan Poe, Walt Whitman's poetry, and the Transcendentalist writings of Emerson and Henry David Thoreau.

- *The second generation of Romantic poets*

The Romantics looked to people's emotions, which were rooted in and illustrated by contact with nature and the primal self, in order to discover the "truth" of things rather than via logical investigation. The writings of the second generation Romantic poets John Keats, Lord Byron, and Percy Bysshe Shelley provide as excellent examples of these viewpoints.

POST ROMANTICISM

- *Parnassianism*

Examples of Parnassianism may be found in the poetry of the French authors Théophile Gautier and Charles Baudelaire. With its emphasis on aesthetics and the idea of art for art's sake, Parnassianism can be seen as an extension of the early Romantic perspectives. Schopenhauer's philosophical viewpoints also had an effect. The Romantic movement's excess emotion and sentimentality was rejected in favor of a more controlled, formal approach to handling the exotic and ancient topics that fascinated its followers.

- *Impressionism and Symbolism in art*

The development of impressionism, which was first evident in painting and then in music, in France at the end of the 19th century was aided by Claude Monet and other Paris-based artists. Impressionism was a painting movement that sought to authentically depict the world as it was perceived through human perception and experience by utilizing the changing qualities of light and color.

Symbolism may be defined as a transition away from naturalism and realism and toward a harsher, more realistic depiction of the world, with an emphasis on the ordinary rather than the spectacular. Symbolist poets, such as Gustave Kahn and Ezra Pound, utilized lighter, freer verse form strategies and meant to "evoke" rather than portray or explain through imagery.

GOTHIC FICTION

This was a popular subgenre of European Romantic fiction that began in the late 18th century with novels like Horace Walpole's *Castle of Otranto* (1765) and Ann Radcliffe's *Mysteries of Udolpho*. The term "gothic" refers to Gothic architecture, which commonly featured as the background and setting for writings in this genre. It set itself apart from previous supernatural or ghost narratives by employing the idea of its heroes' present-day lives being tormented by their pasts.

Famous and renowned 19th-century gothic novels include *Frankenstein* by Mary Shelley, *Wuthering Heights* by Emily Brontë, *Bride of Lammermoor* by Walter Scott, *Dracula* by Bram Stoker, *The Devil's Elixirs* by E.T.A. Hoffmann, and *The Strange Case of Dr. Jekyll and Mr. Hyde* by Robert Louis Stevenson. Other well-known Victorian works, such as Charles Dickens' *Bleak House* and *Great Expectations*, exhibit the influence of the Gothic style.

WESTERN PHILOSOPHY

- *German Idealism*

This school of thought included Johann Gottlieb Fichte, who established Kantian metaphysics and asserted for a self that is a "self-producing and changing process," Georg Wilhelm Friedrich Hegel, whose writings highlighted the importance of the historical thought pattern in which the spirit conceives of itself, and Arthur Schopenhauer, who, in contrast to Hegel, argued for a return to Kantian transcendentalism.

- *Marxism*

A school of thought created and propagated by Karl Marx and Friedrich Engels. Their *Communist Manifesto* (1848), which asserted that capitalism will inevitably self-destruct and be supplanted by socialism and finally communism, laid the groundwork for the modern communist movement.

- *Positivism*

August Comte's empiricist philosophical theory held that authentic knowledge may be perceived to be true by definition or positive— that is, an *a posteriori* truth determined by utilizing reason and logic, from sensory experience, as opposed to instinct or theology.

- *Social Darwinism*

Natural selection and survival of the strongest theories, such as those developed and detailed in Charles Darwin's *On the Origin of Species*, were intended to be applied to social Darwinism views. Francis Galton was among those who claimed that mental qualities, like physical ability, were inherited and that over-breeding by "less fit" members of society must be discouraged. Herbert Spencer, whose book *The Social Creature* (1860), sees society as a living organism that evolves and progresses in the same way. Francis Spencer was also a supporter.

SOCIAL, ECONOMIC AND POLITICAL EVENTS

- *The Industrial Revolution*

The Industrial Revolution, which occurred between the late 18th century and the years 1820-1840, was a period of great social, political, and economic upheaval and change that involved the dynamic shift from primarily manual methods of production to mechanical manufacturing techniques, especially in the industries of textiles, steam power, iron making, and the invention of machine tools. Agriculture had previously formed the cornerstone of the European economy, and it was also a time when fundamental political, scientific, and religious ideals were dismantled.

As a byproduct of this mechanisation, a considerable number of people were transported from rural villages to metropolitan regions, resulting in a major rise in population and the establishment of new, bigger cities. The advancement of new technology led to the creation of factories, a dehumanizing and horrifying manner of labor, particularly child labor, and a capitalist way of life. Because cities were unable to handle the rapidly rising population, there were overcrowded slums and terribly deplorable living conditions, as described in publications such as Friedrich Engels' *The Condition of the Working Class in England*, published in 1844.

The Cry of the Children by Elizabeth Barrett Browning, *Tess of the D'Urbervilles* by Thomas Hardy, and works by author and philosopher Thomas Carlyle, in his novels *Hard Times* and *Oliver Twist*, cautions of the danger to society presented by these inhumane conditions and the profit-focused, materialistic ideals of what Carlyle referred to as the "mechanical age."

- *Science and Non-Fiction*

Throughout the nineteenth century, Victorians' ambition to comprehend and categorize the natural world played a significant role in the creation of scientific theory and understanding. Charles Darwin's works, such as the well-known *On the Origin of Species* (1859), would have a profound and far-reaching effect due to the innovative concept of evolution, which contradicted many of the time's established assumptions and religious beliefs.

The French Revolution: A History, published in 1837, and *On Heroes, Hero-Worship, and the Heroic in History*, published in 1841, are two additional important non-fiction works from the time that influenced political ideas in the mid-nineteenth century.

KEY HISTORICAL EVENTS

- *The Acts of Union and Treaty of Amiens*

Following the French Revolution and the Irish Rebellion in the late 18th century, both ushered in times of unpredictability and instability, the Acts of Union were approved in 1800, uniting Britain and Ireland to form the United Kingdom.

The Treaty of Amiens ended the War of the Second Coalition, as well as the issues between France and the United Kingdom. However, the effect was very ephemeral, as the Napoleonic Wars began in just three years.

- *Westward expansion of the United States*

With their freshly obtained independence, the United States decided to double its size and expand their jurisdiction over the Mississippi River by acquiring the Louisiana Purchase in 1803. Native Americans inhabit a sizable chunk of the territory, which was purchased from the French First Republic for $15 million.

- *The Napoleonic Wars*

In 1805, Napoleon destroyed the Russian and Austrian armies, but his plans to invade England were thwarted when Admiral Nelson soundly defeated the French and Spanish armies at the Battle of Trafalgar, solidifying the nation's dominion over the oceans.

The French army sustained significant losses during the invasion of Russia— up to 380,000 troops died— and Napoleon's prior reputation as an unstoppable leader was destroyed. As a result of his defeat in the War of the Sixth Coalition in 1814, the French monarch abdicated and was banished to Elba.

- *Expansion of the British and Russian empires*

Following France's defeat, the British and Russian empires became known as the world's two leading powers, with Russia continuing to expand its sphere of influence to include Central Asia as well as the Caucasus and Britain expanding its overseas territories to include Canada, Australia, South Africa, and Africa. The British East India Company was dissolved as a consequence of the Indian Rebellion of 1857, a broad revolt against its rule. Later, the British Crown established direct administration and created the British Raj.

- *China and the Opium Wars*

By the middle of the nineteenth century, China had major opium issues due to the opening of commerce with the West and the illicit traffic in the drug organised by British merchants eager to make money at the trade ports. On the basis of free trade principles, Britain fought the emperor's attempt to ban its sale, resulting in the First Opium War and the Treaty of Nanking in 1842, which allowed the drug trade to continue and resulted in the British assuming control of Hong Kong.

The Taiping Rebellion of 1856 formed a violent background for the second Opium War, in which the French and British allied. The 1860 Peking Convention, which legalized the opium trade and compelled the transfer of further regions, led to the fall of the Qing empire in the early nineteenth century.

- *The 1848 Revolutions in Europe*

The 1848 Revolutions, also known as the *Springtime of the Nations*, were a series of political upheavals that occurred practically simultaneously throughout Europe and the rest of the world in 1848. The primary goal of these uprisings was to depose past monarchical power and create free nation governments.

In order to build a liberal government and gain independence from Austrian authority, nationalists in Italy launched revolutions in Sicily and the Italian peninsula republics. The *February Revolution* in France took place in Paris following the crackdown on the campagne des banquets, a violent insurrection against the monarchy that resulted in the overthrow of King Louis Philippe. Many other countries had revolutions against the Habsburg Monarchy, including Germany, Denmark, Hungary, Galicia, Sweden, and Switzerland.

- *Abolitionist movement*

The Atlantic slave trade was banned in the United States in 1808, and the

Slavery Abolition Act of 1833 prohibited slavery across the British Empire. Abolitionism triumphed throughout the nineteenth century. Abolitionism remained in the United States until the Civil War ended in 1865, resulting to the Thirteenth Amendment to the Constitution, which effectively abolished slavery.

- *The Women's Suffrage movement*

The campaign for comprehensive women's suffrage grew stronger and louder in the 1840s, with the Seneca Falls Convention in the United States and the National Women's Rights Convention in 1850. Margaret Fuller's seminal American feminist work *Woman in the Nineteenth Century* was published in 1839, while Sarah Grimké's *The Equality of the Sexes on the Condition of Women* was published in 1845.

Following the failure of suffragists to secure the right to vote in the early 1870s, a protracted and relentless effort was launched in each state in favour of a constitutional amendment on women's rights and suffrage. Wyoming was the first state to provide women the right to vote in 1869. Emmeline Pankhurst entered and helped lead the UK suffragette movement in 1880.

The edits and layout of this print version are Copyright © 2023+ by Bergenline Press

Printed in Great Britain
by Amazon

47513965R00179